D1476955

GARDEN AND GROVE

GARDEN AND GROVE

The Italian Renaissance Garden in
the English Imagination: 1600–1750

John Dixon Hunt

Princeton University Press
Princeton, New Jersey

Published by Princeton University Press, 41 William Street, Princeton, New Jersey 08540

First published 1986
© John Dixon Hunt 1986

This book is set in 10 on 12½pt VIP Plantin by
D. P. Media Limited, Hitchin, Hertfordshire
Printed in Great Britain by
Butler & Tanner Ltd, Frome

Library of Congress Cataloging-in-Publication Data

Hunt, John Dixon.
  Garden and grove.
  "The Franklin Jasper Walls lectures"—
  Includes index.
  1. Gardens, English—Italian influences. 2. Gardens, Italian—Influence. 3. Gardens, Renaissance—England.
4. Gardens, Renaissance—Italy—Influence. I. Title.
II. Title: Franklin Jasper Walls lectures.
SB457.6.H86 1986   712′.6′0942 86-5000
ISBN 0-691-04041-9

List of Contents

The Franklin Jasper Walls
Lectures

Franklin Jasper Walls, who died in 1963, bequeathed his residuary estate to The Pierpont Morgan Library to establish a lecture series in the fine arts, iconography, and archaeology, with the provision that the lectures be ultimately published in book form.

Throughout his life, Mr Walls was interested in the fine arts and in the study of art history. When the Association of Fellows of The Pierpont Morgan Library was organized in 1949, he became one of the founding members. He was particularly concerned with the Library's lecture programme, and served on the Association's Lecture Committee. Without ever revealing his testamentary plans, he followed with keen attention the design and construction of the Library's new Lecture Hall, completed a few months before his death.

Professor Hunt's lectures, here printed in revised and expanded form, are the ninth series of the Franklin Jasper Walls Lectures to be published.

For PHYLLIS
'The fairest garden in her looks
And in her mind the wisest books'

List of Illustrations

Photographs of Figures 17, 42, 51, 97 and 107 are from the Dumbarton Oaks (Trustees for Harvard University) Garden Library. Grateful thanks to Dr Peter Willis and Professor Jacques Carré for the loan of photographs of Figures 93 and 101 respectively.

Preface

This book consists of the much revised and somewhat expanded text of the Franklin Jasper Walls Lectures, delivered at the Pierpont Morgan Library in New York in November 1981. I am most grateful to Mr Charles Ryskamp, Director of the Morgan Library, and to the Library Trustees for extending the invitation to give those lectures and for the kindnesses shown to me during the period of their delivery. The opportunity to present in a series of lectures work that had been in progress for many years is rare, and I am conscious of the privilege afforded me just as I am grateful for the generosity of the Morgan Library in helping with the publication of the lectures in this form.

Garden and Grove is a study of the English fascination with Italian gardens during the seventeenth and early eighteenth centuries; first it looks at what visitors to Italy saw for themselves and recorded in their journals and publications; then it traces the history of the Italianization of the English garden. As such, *Garden and Grove* grew out of work for my earlier book, *The Figure in the Landscape: Poetry, Painting and Gardening during the Eighteenth Century* (1976), and the present volume may be taken as an extended prelude to the other book. However, it is only fair to say that it offers some revisions of the history of the English landscape garden that I narrated in 1976.

For a book that has been 'in progress' since the very early 1970s there are many debts to acknowledge. My research for it has, to start with, been most generously funded: first through a fellowship from the Leverhulme Trust, which allowed me to spend time in Italian gardens, libraries and archives, and a grant from the British Academy, which allowed me an extension of that time. Then a term at the Institute for Advanced Study, Princeton, gave me the chance to draft certain sections of the book and – above all – to discuss it with a group of colleagues, a source of endless stimulation and shared knowledge and ideas without which the book would be the poorer. Finally, a fellowship at Dumbarton Oaks (Trustees for Harvard University) enabled me to finish the final version away from other distractions and with the inestimable benefits of its Garden Library.

I have profited from working at a variety of libraries: I first discovered the wealth of Italian travel books in the library of the British School at Rome; the Hertziana in Rome and the German Art Institute in Florence were libraries and photograph collections where I could pursue the history of the gardens which English travellers had visited; the Pierpont Morgan Library, the Folger Library, the British Library, the Bodleian Library and the Johns Hopkins University Library have all given me assistance at various times.

The greatest help and stimulation for a book of this sort comes from the reactions of friends, colleagues and unknown members of lecture audiences who have responded to various of my earlier attempts to formulate its ideas with questions, comments and counter suggestions. To all of them, known and unknown, I am particularly grateful; special acknowledgements must go (alphabetically) to Michel Baridon, Douglas Chambers, David Coffin, Christopher Frommel, Richard Goldthwaite, Ron Inden, J. R. Jones, Irving Lavin, Michael Leslie, Elisabeth MacDougall, Dean Tolle Mace, Stephen Orgel and Lionello Puppi, who have commented upon early drafts of chapters, re-read my lecture scripts and generally tried to save me from my wilder errors. And finally I must thank my student assistant at the University of Leiden, Anneke Tjan-Bakker, whose cheerful and punctilious help with both library researches and typing saw this book into its home straight, and Robert Williams for his scrupulous proof-reading. Earlier sections of chapters 4, 6 and 11 (part iii) appeared in *Architectural Association Files 3*, *The Origins of Museums*, ed. Oliver Impey and Arthur MacGregor (1985), and *British and American Gardens in the Eighteenth Century*, ed. Robert P. Maccubbin and Peter Martin (1984).

This book is my wife's, not only because its life has been virtually coextensive with our marriage, but because her contributions to it – practical and intangible – are legion and because she came with me to almost all of the gardens.

Introduction

thence in the midst
Divided by a river, of whose banks
On each side an imperial city stood,
With towers and temples proudly elevate
On seven small hills, with palaces adorned,
Porches and theatres, baths, aqueducts,
Statues and trophies, and triumphant arcs,
Gardens and groves presented to his eyes . . .
  (John Milton)

This [Villa D'Este at Tivoli] shall by my patterne
for a Countrey seat.
  (John Raymond)

You show us, Rome was glorious, not profuse,
And pompous buildings once were things of Use.
  (Alexander Pope)

It should hardly be necessary to emphasize the importance to English arts and society of the Italian Renaissance. Yet in the matter of garden design patriotism has somewhat obscured the extent of that prime source of ideas and forms: for historians of the English landscape garden have seemed for the most part so eager to urge its originality that it might as well have sprung fully armed from the head of Shaftesbury, Addison or Pope. Few narratives of the English garden suggest anything at the start of the eighteenth century but a clean break between the earlier, foreign or what is (awkwardly) termed 'formal' and the 'informal' modes of design, the latter a pure English invention (like liberty) that swept its native land and then spread (like the Empire) to impose its natural and true taste upon the geometry of continental gardens. Alternative suggestions have, certainly, been aired in passing; but the map of garden history remains largely unchanged.[1]

This book proposes some alterations to that map, notably in arguing that the so-called English landscape garden before 'Capability' Brown owed much to a continuing emulation of Italian Renaissance models. This enduring enthusiasm for certain aspects of Italianate designs had a twofold origin: first, there was a long tradition of adapting Italian designs to English gardens dating back to the sixteenth century which did not simply collapse in face of French or Dutch taste at the end of the seventeenth but was maintained in innumerable estates around the country; second, there was much in the cultural, political and aesthetic climate of the early eighteenth century in England (whether labelled Palladianism or Augustanism or Whiggism) which looked to the Renaissance and its classical past, and it would seem odd if gardening was unique in ignoring that nostalgia.

There are two aspects of this long presence of the Italian Renaissance garden in the English imagination. The one concerns what English visitors to Italy saw upon the ground there. The other concerns what they made of those visits once they had returned home. Accordingly, this book will explore these two faces of Italian garden enthusiasm. In all that has been written about English travellers in Italy little if anything has been said about their visits to gardens;[2] this makes it extremely difficult to elaborate, even in the periods when an Italian garden influence is allowed, upon what exactly constituted an Italian taste in gardens. Therefore the first part of *Garden and Grove* has been devoted to what could be called an *identikit* of the seventeenth-century and early eighteenth-century Englishman's view of Italian gardening: beginning with some general considerations of the place of gardens in the grand tour, Part One then examines six aspects of the English interest in Italian gardens as that interest manifests itself in guidebooks and travel journals; a final section extends that synchronic examination into a consideration of changing attitudes between 1600 and 1750. Guidebooks and travel journals yield a surprising amount of information, hitherto virtually untapped, about what visitors saw and thought worth recording in their garden visits. The glut of evidence in these sections is essential to document the extent and the scope of English interest in Italian Renaissance garden art.

Part Two is a history and an analysis of how Italian garden ideas and forms were introduced and adapted in England during the same period. In this field of enquiry I have one recent predecessor, and I am very conscious of how my paths through some of this early material were smoothed by Sir Roy Strong's pioneering study of *The Renaissance Garden in England*, published in 1979. For the sake of offering a complete history I have often, in the first third of Part Two, covered some of the same territory; but my perspectives are in large measure different from Sir Roy's, and readers who know his book will discover that we sometimes differ on what is to be emphasized in any one particular garden. Furthermore, *The Renaissance Garden in England* stopped at the outbreak of the Civil War, whereas this book takes the story further. Italianate designs did not necessarily cease in 1640 nor succumb to the turmoils of the Interregnum; indeed, many gentry either went abroad (often to Italy) or retired to their estates and created, albeit in modest and often piecemeal fashion, images of what they remembered from earlier travels or their reading about Italy. This repertoire of Italian design even seems to have been preserved as something special and distinct in face of new foreign influences from France and the Low Countries. However hard it is for us to distinguish something Italianate as opposed to, say, French in an English garden of the late seventeenth century, it was clearly possible for knowledgeable enthusiasts like John Aubrey, John Evelyn or Timothy Nourse to see something worth labelling 'Italian'.[3] So a concern of this second part will be to probe the assumptions and preconceptions of contemporary thinking about gardens. This in its turn will lead to an examination of the topic which was in fact the original impulse behind this book: namely, to ask how English was the English landscape garden.

Interestingly, I discovered in the early stages of my work that one of the writers usually credited with inspiring the English landscape garden, Joseph Addison, had himself registered the importance of the Italian connection. In discussing Milton's description of the Garden of Eden in *Paradise Lost*, itself an eloquent example to many subsequent landscapists, Addison asked whether Milton could ever have penned his description without having seen the gardens of Italy.[4] That Addison left this insight unpublished in a *Spectator* manuscript suggests the power, even at that period, of the national myth of the Englishness of the new garden style. It was, moreover, true that the blind Milton did recall the gardens he had once seen in the city of Rome and figures them prominently in the vision of that eternal city in his *Paradise Regained*, quoted at the start of this Introduction: a phrase from that passage has been adapted – albeit neglecting the poet's irony – to serve as the title of this book.[5]

Part One

ITALY
THE GARDEN OF THE WORLD

1 THE GARDEN ON THE GRAND TOUR

'Such a rabble of English roam now in Italy.'[1] Yet when Sir Thomas Chaloner reported this to the Earl of Essex in 1596–7 there were relatively few visitors from England reaching Italy compared to the numbers that would be tempted by continental travel in the eighteenth century. Indeed, by the end of the period with which this book deals (1600–1750) tourism had increased to such an extent that we have sometimes invoked the phenomenon to name the 'Age of the Grand Tour'.[2] Yet many of the most interesting aspects of the Grand Tour can already be observed before the eighteenth century at which time travel became easier and more popular and when responses to Italian arts and customs were less fresh and sharp; by the eighteenth-century phase of the Grand Tour, moreover, gardens featured far less centrally in the repertoire of excitements than they had earlier. The actual phrase, the 'Grand Tour', appears to have been first used by Richard Lassels in the preface to a guidebook published posthumously in 1670.[3] For many years a professional tutor to travelling young noblemen, Lassels is typical of this earlier phase of Italian travel, not least for his lively attention to the subject which is the topic of this book, garden art.

The earliest travellers from England went to Rome as pilgrims or passed via Venice on their way to the Holy Land; others went as students to Italian universities. Not surprisingly, the earliest guidebooks are concerned either with practical matters of food, travel and lodging or with providing a conspectus of classical and Christian sites after the manner of *Mirabilia Urbis Romae*.[4] Later visitors, whose interests expanded to include art, architecture and society in the princely courts of Italy as well as its classical past, were correspondingly able to avail themselves of more and more sophisticated guidebooks; William Thomas's *Historie of Italie* (1549) was the first in English devoted to the whole country. Thereafter, especially during the seventeenth century, the literature about Italy flourished.

Books were generally of two sorts – personal narratives, like Lassels's *The Voyage of Italy*, or those directed at tourists' use, like Henry Cogan's *A Direction For Such As Shall Travell unto Rome*. But narratives based on much first-hand experience like Lassels's came to be used as guidebooks, praised as such in subsequent publications.[5] Lassels's published

Voyage of 1670 had begun life in two manuscript versions, both of which were commissioned in 1650 and 1654 for use by travellers as an *aide-memoire* and guidebook respectively.[6] As late as the 1740s the worldly Lovelace in Samuel Richardson's *Clarissa* undertakes to write down for the Harlowe family 'a good account of everything necessary for a young traveller to observe . . . [and] a description of the courts and countries he had visited, and what was most worthy of curiosity in them'.[7] The journals of many travellers were never published, though like John Evelyn's these were often written up in fair copy later. Some had their travel diaries written for them, like the Hon. Banister Maynard whose servant, Robert Moody, reports his humble determination

> to make the best improvement my Capacity would permit [i.e. his station in life] I perform'd in as compendious a Manner as I could by making a Diary, As Likewise particular Observations of all such Occurrences which I thought most Remarkable in your Honrs Progresse.[8]

And William Acton's *A New Journal of Italy* of 1691 was dedicated to Edward Harvey with the gloss that its author had waited upon him 'in your Travels to Rome . . . and from thence to Naples; where the Antiquities are not less curious than what you saw in Rome it self; which I here humbly present you with a review of in a piece of perspective . . . both Natural and Artificial Curiosities.' Some guidebooks issued for English readers were simply translations of works available on the ground in Italy itself; such is Edmund Warcupp's *Italy in Its Original Glory, Ruine and Revivall*, derived from the three-volume *Itinerarii Italiae rerumque* of François Schott, first published in 1600. And there were always local guides published expressly for foreign visitors in the major Italian tourist centres; Warcupp gives a reading list at the start of his section on Rome, while some years earlier John Raymond wrote that 'In a word, the Press is burdened with nothing more than descriptions of Rome. . . .'[9]

What is as important as the range of travel literature on Italy are the various motivations of the travellers themselves. Some visited Italy on professional business, like Sir Henry Wotton, the diplomat and three times ambassador at Venice; some, like the botanist, John Ray, went out of scientific curiosity. Many travellers sought to improve their political and classical education by visiting a country renowned (if not infamous) for its political interest and diversity as well as for being the site of classical Rome. Such travellers were invariably either nobility or gentry whose motives involved extending their schooling or preparing for some administrative career. Young noblemen at least would usually travel with tutors, so that a good number of interesting authors of Italian guidebooks had made the tour of Italy in the role of *cicerone* and teacher. By the eighteenth century travellers were tempted by the opportunities for extending their connoisseurship and for viewing what one modern commentator has called 'the most interesting museum in the world'.[10] Yet earlier travellers, as will be seen, were more interested in artistic and architectural matters than is usually allowed. A majority of tourists, of course, combined all these interests and, despite the rigours of the journey, went to Italy to satisfy their curiosity on a full range of topics – a range which Lassels's *The Voyage of Italy* deliberately stresses in its subtitle:

> *With the Characters Of The People, and the description of the chief Townes, Churches, Monasteries, Tombes, Libraries, Pallaces, Villas, Gardens, Pictures,*

4

Statues, Antiquities: As Also Of The Interest, Government, Riches, Force, &c. of all the Princes.

Finally, there were the eccentrics, like Thomas Coryate, who travelled throughout Europe on foot and upon his return dedicated his tattered shoes as a votive-offering in his father's church of Odcombe, Somerset.[11]

Of the many sights and sites throughout Italy to which the increasing number of guide books directed this variety of English tourists, gardens established themselves quickly as among the more interesting and unusual and with very widespread appeal. As early as Thomas's *Historie* the terraced gardens of the Doria family ('vi gardens one above an other') were noted as one of the remarkable features of Genoa, while throughout the country the traveller's and reader's attention was drawn to the novel fact that in 'the villages are many faire houses made onely for the owners passetime against the heate of the summer'.[12] So by 1549 the Italian habit and architecture of *villeggiatura* and the equally characteristic formation of ground into terraces are both noted. Otherwise Thomas pays no attention to garden or villa art, beyond recalling classical gardens on the Esquiline Hill in Rome and visiting the Belvedere Courtyard at the Vatican ('almoste another paradyse').[13] Yet at about the same time Sir Thomas Hoby, who would publish his fine translation of Castiglione's *Il Cortegiano* in 1561, was often noting gardens in his diary;[14] this suggests that although gardens may have been remarked upon by travellers they did not come to figure in their published guidebooks until later. Travellers like Fynes Moryson who was in Italy in the 1590s and Coryate who left England in 1608 were both attentive to garden art and recorded some impressions in their published works.[15] Nevertheless, such interests were obviously considered something of a luxury in comparison with political and religious matters. K. Palmer published an essay on profitable travelling in 1606, noting that '*Italy* moveth most of our Travilers to go and visit it, of any other state in the world'.[16] Among the main reasons he gives for this priority are 'the multiplex and different governments' (p. 44), whereas the least significant in his view

> is the speciall galleries of monuments and olde aged memorials of histories, records of persons and things to bee seene thorowout the Countrey. But this being a fantasticall attracter, and a glutton-feeder of the appetite, rather than of necessarie knowledge, I will mention no further thereof.

Yet if gardens did not seem a 'necessarie knowledge' to Palmer in 1606 (though he does suggest that travellers pay attention to fountains and palaces [pp. 86–7]), they would soon become both a profitable and a pleasurable study. By the 1650s James Howell and Henry Cogan were both listing gardens among their directions for the tourist: Howell urged him, as he travelled through Italy, to note 'the trace, forme and site of any famous *Structure*, the Platforms of *Gardens*, *Aqueducts*, *Grots*, *Sculptures*, and such particularities belonging to *accommodation* or *beauty* of dwelling'; Cogan, writing specifically about Rome, itemized 'Palaces, Churches, Gardens, Pyramids, Columns and other Fabricks' in his Preface as the highlights of the city.[17]

Gardens assumed importance on the Italian tour and thus in the travel literature for two, obviously connected, reasons. They were seen as intimately related to the new, classical-derived architecture of palace and villa, which the English were keen to understand and emulate. And they were also part of the strange and rare world of Italian curiosities, unlike anything (or almost anything) that could have been seen before leaving England. If the fine arts featured infrequently or not at all in the earlier Italian travel literature,[18] gardens were evidently an exception since they were either considered to be worth attention for practical reasons – on the lines of Lassels urging the visitor to Italy to learn there 'how to make a fine house'[19] – or seen as a further manifestation of the Italian love for collections of artificial and natural rarities.[20] Thus for practical or scientific reasons gardens began to attract attention in Italy even while appreciation of other fine arts lagged behind. Furthermore, those motives continued to sustain the English interest in Italian gardens; for John Raymond, travelling in 1646 and 1647, exclaimed 'This shall be my patterne for a Countrey seat' when he saw the Villa D'Este at Tivoli, thus registering his attention to its value as model, before going on to record his fascination with its elaborate hydraulic system of fountains.[21]

Yet the attraction of late Renaissance gardens for the English visitor to Italy would become far more complex than a simple interest in patterns for country seats or in collections of rarities. For reasons that those who were much interested in them never explicitly discussed, gardens seemed to offer illimitable interests. Often compared to the world itself in bringing together a conspectus of ideas as well as of plants, an Italian Renaissance garden focused – in ways that probably no other single feature of civilization ever did – a complete experience. Unlike other arts, a fine garden required its visitors to see, hear, smell, touch and (if its fruit were not forbidden) taste. A garden was both artificial *and* natural; in this it was also an exceptional art form. Moreover, it was an art that existed in four dimensions: time was needed to explore all the features of a garden, often from many perspectives; but time was also an essential element in the seasonal cycle of a garden, even when the fecundity of a southern climate made Englishmen, like Francis Mortoft, celebrate the 'perpetual spring' of the Villa Montalto in Rome.[22] Gardens were 'outside', yet also extensions both in form and use of 'inside'. They were sculpture galleries, museums, theatres, living botanical encyclopaedias, academies – models of the larger and less perfect world outside their grounds and therefore to be studied for the natural, moral and political lessons which could be incorporated into their design. Gardens functioned as solitudes for meditation and also as arenas for many kinds of social gathering. Finally, a garden acquired by association of ideas the status of earthly paradise (whether Eden or some classical equivalent) or that archetypal place of pleasure and content, the *locus amoenus*.[23]

Not all of such functions or concepts entered consciously into an Englishman's interest in Italian Renaissance gardens, and rarely did any one visitor suggest that gardens yielded him such a complete model of his mind. Yet behind the records of visits to individual gardens along the route of the *giro d'Italia* we shall constantly glimpse all of these wider concerns; and it is they which lent to the interest in gardens an importance which today we seem to have lost completely. Perhaps by looking briefly at two reactions to a few gardens we can recover something, not only of the surprises and excitement of seventeenth-century travel, but of the deeper structure of ideas and attitudes with which travellers explored gardens.

First, an anonymous visitor in Italy about 1610 wrote 'A true Description and Direction of what is most Worthy to be seen in all Italy', in which (among several gardens) he records one in Rome belonging to the Cardinal of Florence:

in the garden, a cage wherein are all kinds of birds making sweet harmony, divers rare water-works, and plentifully planted with cypress-trees, yielding a savour so admirable sweet, as the body therewith may be ravished. There are also mightly great vaults under ground, wherein they used to dine and sup in summer-time, by reason of the extraordinary heat, which are adorned with rare pictures, statues, and histories; the place in former time being a waste and ruined ground, and decayed wall, fallen from the temple of Peace, which stands just behind the same . . .[24]

It is a place where classical and modern meet in a newly created retreat, where grottoes shelter guests from the summer heat and provide a setting for *objets d'art*, a little world (notice the emphasis on *'all kinds* of birds') where the senses are pleasured and where 'harmony' reigns. And like the next garden, where the emphasis is more explicit, that Roman one was an admirable combination of art and nature.

An altogether more dedicated gardenist than that anonymous traveller, John Evelyn saw two fine gardens in his first Italian city, Genoa. The first was that of the 'Palas of Negros' and took the form which would soon be familiar throughout Italy of terraces ('hilly Garden', Evelyn calls it); it also comprised groves, in which lifelike sculptures of animals were set, and various water-works. But the garden which impressed Evelyn even more was at the Palazzo Doria: first he admired the furniture inside, elaborately decorated with all manner of precious stones, the 'Pictures and Statues innumerable', then he visited the 'three Gardens':

> the first whereoff is beautified with a tarrac supported by pillars of Marble: There is also a fountaine of Eagles, and one of Neptune with other Sea-Gods, all of the purest white marble that ever myne eyes beheld: These stand in a most ample basine of the same stone; and at the side of this Garden is such an Aviary as Sir Fra: Bacon describes in his Sermones fidelium or Essays, where in grow trees of more then 2 foote diameter, besides Cypresse, Myrtils, Lentiscs & other rare shrubs, which serve to nestle & pearch all sorts of birds, who have ayre, & place enough under their wyrie Canopy, supported with huge Iron Worke very stupendious to consider, both as to the fabrick, & the Charge. The other two Gardens are full of Orange-trees, Citrons & Pomegranads, Fountaines, Grotts & Statues; among which one of Jupiter of a Colossal magnitude, under which is the Sepulchre of a beloved dog . . . The Conserve of Water here is a most admirable piece for art, and so is likewise that incomparable grotto over against it.[25]

The extent of this fine garden, 'which reaches from the very Sea, to the Summit of the Mountaines' (figure 1), contributed to Evelyn's appreciation of its fullness – the listing of its impressive features, though doubtless an economy of diary style, was a typical tourist declaration of this completeness. The continuity of rarities from 'Onyxes, Cornelians, Lazulis, Pearle, Turquizes' on the furniture inside to the marble of the garden statuary seems one in Evelyn's mind with the collaboration of art and natural elements in the garden itself. Overall is his delight at an apparently miraculous world, peopled by representations of classical deities (figure 2), a realization of what before he had only read about in books.

Genoa was one of the usual starting points of the Italian tour, so its gardens – such a prominent feature of the city – may have alerted travellers to this particular Italian marvel. If English visitors did not first enter Italy at Genoa, they did so via Turin, where by the end

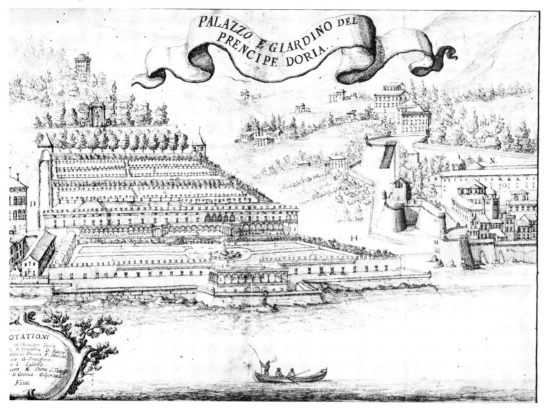

Figure 1 Johann Christoph Volkamer, Palace and gardens of the Principe Doria, late seventeenth century drawing.

of the seventeenth century there were equally rare gardens to be seen.[26] From either Genoa or Turin the traveller would follow a standard route which took him south to Lucca and Pisa, then probably inland to Florence; thence via Siena to Rome. Often a further southern excursion took him to Naples, then back to Rome where Christmas and Easter were festivals to fascinate a northerner (especially if he were Protestant). The *giro* concluded, often via Loreto, with a journey to Venice to witness the Ascensiontide ceremony of the Doge's marriage with the sea, and with travel westwards via Padua, Vicenza, and the Lakes to Milan; and so homewards across the Simplon. Especially after 1630, when Charles I and Philip IV signed a treaty of peace and friendship that included the latter's Italian vassals, English Protestants felt more secure in venturing south of the Veneto and Tuscany; many had done so none the less, though with caution and sometimes, as did Moryson, by passing himself off as a German.[27]

Along this standard route, made increasingly familiar as guidebooks proliferated and later travellers followed in their predecessors' tracks, were innumerable opportunities to see gardens. When Evelyn came to name the Italian gardens he proposed to consider in his vast undertaking, *Elysium Britannicum*, he first reviewed classical gardens and those in Rome, *'more moderne and at present'*, and then continued with a list which shows how gardens featured at almost every stage of his Italian itinerary:

Figure 2 Jan Massys, *Venus Cythera*, painting of 1561. Massys situates his mythical figure in the Doria gardens, glimpses of which are seen behind her.

> Ulmarini's at Vacenza, Count Giusti's at Verona, Mondragone, Frescati, D'este's at Tivoli. The gardens of the Palazzo de Pitti in Florence; Poggio, Imperiale, Pratoline, Hieronymo del Negro's pensile garden in Genoa, principe d'oria's garden, the Marquesi Devico's at Naples, the old gardens at Baiae, Fred. Duke of Urbino's garden, the gardens at Pisa, at Padoa, at Capraroula, at St Michael in Bosco, in Bolognia; the gardens about Lago di Como, Signior Sfondrati's, etc.[28]

Gardens were, of course, only one of many interests which travellers could satisfy during their tour of Italy, and they competed for tourists' attention with many other sights and monuments. Nevertheless, it is astonishing how many gardens were seen and how prominent in travellers' records was this particular enthusiasm. To many Englishmen Italy seemed one vast garden, 'a world of stately pallaces and gardens'.[29] To the author of *A Tour in France and Italy* of 1676 it seemed, 'in general, except the Appeninnes . . . a perfect garden',[30] while John Dennis, writing from Turin in 1688, referred to the tradition that 'Nature design'd [the Alps] only as a Mound to enclose her Garden Italy'.[31] The astonishing fecundity of the countryside, interspersed with beautiful gardens, gave extra force to the seventeenth-century cliché that Italy was 'the Garden of the World'.[32]

With hindsight we can see important and striking historical differences and regional variations in Italian gardens. Even within the territory of modern Tuscany, Medici villas and their gardens around Florence differ sharply from the dozens in the Duchy of Lucca, and both again from those in the hills near Siena.[33] Yet such distinctions were rarely, if at all, noted by English visitors, just as their enthusiasm for Italian Renaissance garden art seemed to take little account of date. For the ways in which modern art historians divide up the Renaissance, distinguishing for example between mannerist and baroque phases, were not of much consequence then. The English admiration for an Italian garden's 'variety', for example, was promoted alike in a simple sixteenth-century layout at Castello, near Florence, as in an elaborate seventeenth-century creation at Frascati.

This lack of regard for regional or historical differences in garden design means that the most profitable way in which to examine the seventeenth- and early eighteenth-century English interest in Italian gardens will not be geographical or chronological but thematic. For it would be the generality of their Italian garden experience that most visitors conveyed back to England rather than careful discriminations of individual gardens. An eloquent testimony to this general, though by no means therefore vague, attention to Italian gardens is Sir Henry Wotton's description in his *Elements of Architecture* of 1624:

> the first Accesse was a high walk like a *Tarrace*, from whence might be taken a generall view of the whole *Plot* below, but rather in a delightful confusion, then with any plain distinction of the pieces. From this the *Beholder* descending many steps, was afterwards conveyed again by several *mountings* and *valings*, to various entertainments of his *sent* and *sight*: which I shall not need to describe (for that were poetical) let me only note this, that every one of these diversities, was as if he had bin Magically transported into a new *Garden*.[34]

Wotton writes apparently of one particular garden – it was, he tells us, 'for the maner perchance incomparable'; but his account seems to convey a strongly generalized sense of many Italian gardens he must have seen throughout Italy. His description might be an epitome of the English experience: it is based, necessarily, upon the distinctive physical site of the garden, especially its terraces which entail descents and ascents; these in their turn and in conjunction with all the other features which Wotton goes on to note (fountains, grottoes, aviaries, waterworks) elicit from their visitor an active participation in the discovery of their 'various entertainments'. Finally, he conveys the impression of a total experience in which all the senses join, yet one which is equally suggestive of magic and of those extensions of our physical life for which poetry seems the only adequate language. It is to some of the constituent parts of that total experience that we must now turn in more detail.

2 CLASSICAL GROUND AND CLASSICAL GARDENS

Italy was, above all, classical ground. Whether its visitors were learned *virtuosi*, educated men (and so acquainted with Roman literature and history) or just simply curious, they could scarcely neglect the tangible evidence of ancient Rome. Most travellers, of course, sought out ruins or monuments of the classical past, which either their Latin reading or their guidebooks would complete and revive in their imaginations. It is precisely this approach which Warcupp enshrines in the English title of Schott's *Itinerarii* – he called it *Italy in Its Originall Glory, Ruine and Revivall*. In that way he acknowledged a perspective which (cliché though it may be) was central to the Renaissance: that the culture of classical Rome, now lost, fragmented, ruined or distant, was a glory capable of revival in the modern world. It was a conviction that applied equally to garden art.

Educated visitors to Italy were familiar from their Latin reading with the villas and gardens of the ancients. Some of them, like Addison, even prepared themselves for an Italian visit by reading relevant texts: 'before I entered on my Voyage I took care to refresh my Memory among the *Classic* Authors, and to make such Collections out of them as I might afterwards have Occasion for'.[1] Frequent allusions will be made to this range of literary documentation during the course of this book; but mention of some 'Collections' of the classical literature on gardens that English travellers would have known is in order here.[2]

The most extensive and therefore probably the most influential of all Latin texts were the two letters of the younger Pliny in which he described his villas in Tuscany and Laurentum, near Ostia. These were especially intriguing because they went into considerable detail; but the different ways in which the Plinian verbal accounts have been translated into visual reconstructions equally suggest that his words could be made to authorize a wide variety of actual designs. Each attempt to extrapolate designs from the Latin texts tells us as much about the translator as about the original disposition of the villas themselves. One such reconstruction was that of Robert Castell: *The Villas of the Ancients Illustrated* was published in 1728 and clearly reflects the concepts of garden design then current in the Burlington circle. Castell's consideration of the Pliny letters and other related Latin texts is careful and scholarly enough, but it reveals equally how difficult it was to avoid tendentious analysis.[3] So this enquiry is concerned precisely with this (maybe unconscious) tendency to read into classical garden literature what modern designers wanted to find rather than with any archaeological expertise that travellers may have shown.

The younger Pliny wrote his two influential letters between AD 100 and 105. They tell of the inter-relation of villa buildings and gardens; they emphasize the place of pleasant walks, arbours or colonnades in the design, and the supreme importance of vistas into the surrounding countryside. At the Laurentian villa these views took in seascape, mountains and rural landscape; in Tuscany the site was a 'vast amphitheatre such as could only be the work of nature' ('amphitheatrum aliquod immensum, et quale sola rerum natura possit effingere') and comprehended mountains, woods, fields, vineyards, meadows, cornfields. Streams, which had been lacking in Laurentum, were plentiful in this hillside villa and fed innumerable fountains and waterworks. Frescoes decorated an interior fountain room with *trompe l'oeil* images of birds resting on trees. There was a considerable display of topiary art, and some formal delight in alternating small obelisks of box with apparently naturally shaped fruit trees. At one point the elaborate art of the gardener was set off by a piece of rural landscape ('in opere urbanissimo subita velut illati ruris imitatio'). Pliny mentions terraces, insists upon a garden's variety of both design and social use, and focuses attention upon the perennial theme of the respective contributions of art and nature to a garden. There are elements such as temples and grottoes which we now associate with gardens that Pliny does not mention in these two letters; but otherwise his descriptions established in the minds of later readers the complete *idea* of a fine Roman villa garden.

These elements, individually and in conjunction, recur through Renaissance garden design and it is difficult to resist the view that the modern productions were deliberate attempts to re-create Pliny's descriptions. The account of his dining arrangements – water gushing out from under each seat and basins in which dishes are floated – surely supplies the inspiration for the stone table at Villa Lante with its central basin of water or the grotto at Pratolino, where water sprouted from seats set around a table. Pliny's Tuscan amphitheatre, as will be seen below, haunts Renaissance design, most obviously in re-creations like that behind the Pitti Palace. Raphael showed himself curiously faithful to an (imperfect) edition of Pliny's letters in creating a circular courtyard at the Villa Madama just outside Rome in emulation of Pliny's portico.[4] And what Pliny did not himself supply in these two accounts was derived from other sources. Thus Varro's famous description of the *ornithon* or aviary which provided him and his guests with a luxurious dining area at his own villa near Casinum – a revolving table brought the food and drink around and had spouts of hot and cold water – could obviously be creatively confused with Pliny's letters.[5] Other writers contributed further ingredients to this *identikit* of the Roman garden.

The urge to gather a composite picture of a Roman villa garden from what must have been frustratingly brief remarks may be illustrated with the example of Joseph Spence in the eighteenth century who transcribed an account of Horace's Sabine villa from the many passing references to it in his poetry.[6] From these he is quick to deduce that Horace 'had that taste for wild natural gardening which has obtained so much among us of late'. But such an assumption, while easy to understand, is probably unfounded. What Horace provides in his poetry are glimpses of a site with fine views, a variety of terrain where various parts of the estate were dedicated to different deities, a grotto and a spring of water (Spence jumps to the conclusion that this spring must have 'burst out of the side of the hill', whereas it could just as well have been shaped into some sort of architectural fountain). By no means can these hints authorize any specific plan or design; indeed, the attraction of Horace's garden glimpses, as with other poetic references to Roman villas, was just as much that they lent themselves to imaginative exploitation by Renaissance and later gardenists. Spence's friend, Alexander Pope, clearly accommodates Horace's Sabine villa to his Twickenham grounds in the poetry of his Horatian Imitations; it was presumably just as easy for him to think of his actual garden and grotto as if they had recovered something of the shapes and certainly much of the spirit of the Roman poet's country retreat.

A good deal of Latin literature was like Horace's in yielding only generalities on classical villa gardens. Martial's epigrams, for example, spoke of a grove, fountains, vines matted into arches, a conduit of refreshing water and meadows ('Hoc nemus, hi fontes, haec textilis umbra supini/palmitis, hoc riguae ductile flumen acquae,/prataque . . .') or groves of laurel, pine and plane trees with babbling streams on every side ('Daphnonas, platanonas et aerios pityonas . . . et pereuntis aquae fluctus ubique sonat').[7] But such resonant if vague gestures towards Roman garden arts could obviously be fleshed out with readers' deductions from longer passages like those of the younger Pliny. The elder Pliny's *Natural History* has references to imagery, especially sculptures, in gardens, to gazebos and summerhouses decorated with 'pumice [that hung] from the ceilings so as to create an artificial imitation of a cave'.[8] Juvenal, in his turn, attacks the verisimilitude of artificial grottoes.[9] In describing Nero's Domus Aurea Pliny emphasizes its decoration with the loot taken from others' properties, an observation that could readily be made of many Renaissance gardens. Statues are frequently mentioned in connection with classical gardens, and the aptness and propriety of their subjects in relation to different parts of the villa complex are discussed.[10]

It was a short step from such descriptions and from other accounts of gods, goddesses and nymphs, not necessarily in garden contexts, to the invocation of statues to preside over sections of a garden. Varro, for example, notes Venus as the presiding deity of gardens at the start of *De re rustica*, which is supported by Pliny's *Natural History* Book XIX and by Columella's *De re rustica* Book X: these authorized the prominence of Venus in garden statuary at least as late as William Kent's Vale of Venus at Rousham. But throughout Latin literature there were allusions to real or imagined spots sacred to nymphs or deities which those interested in gardens could readily appropriate. Claudian celebrates a Garden of Love as some 'enclosed country, ever bright with flowers' over which presides the 'goddess' many coloured palace' in the midst of which is a 'courtyard rich with flagrant flowers'.[11] Groves with temples were especially noted, including such a famous example as Pliny's account of the temple, spring and grove at Clitumnus:

> At the foot of a little hill, covered with venerable and shady cypress trees, the
> river . . . forms a broad pool so clear and glassy that you may count the shining
> pebbles and the little pieces of money which are thrown into it . . . The banks are
> thickly clad with ash and poplar trees, whose verdant reflections are as distinctly
> seen in the translucent stream as if they were actually sunk in it . . . Near it is a
> primitive and holy temple, wherein stands the river god Clitumnus clothed in a

purple-bordered robe . . . Several little chapels are scattered round, each containing the statue of a different god . . . there are several other lesser streams
which . . . lose themselves into the river . . . and villas, wherever the river is
most beautiful, are situated upon its banks'.[12]

Such passages endorsed innumerable garden scenes with temples, smaller buildings
graced with busts or statues, and the happy, almost preternatural congruence of grove,
water and villa. Pliny himself restored an ancient temple of Ceres that stood on his Tuscan
property, an augmentation of its *genius loci* that would find many imitators among English
landowners in the eighteenth century.[13]

The special resonances of the garden as sacred place or as a privileged location for
poetry, study, philosophical discourse or just simple, sensuous enjoyment were endorsed
by many classical writers. Varro tells how the playing of the lyre at a table in a clearing
brought beasts, as if to Orpheus, out of the surrounding woods.[14] Horace's *Carmine* are
especially rich in allusions to a garden's rare ambience.[15] Cicero's various works declared
gardens as places for and stimulants of dialogue, in this consciously emulating Hellenistic
precedents, while both Cicero and Horace associated the leisure of country retreat with
study, philosophy and poetic composition.[16] The particular aptness of a country villa for
reflection was endorsed by accounts of different parts of gardens being named or characterized in specific ways which consequently directed visitors' thinking: Hadrian's huge villa
complex at Tivoli was the best-known example of this, and a late Latin description tells
how 'parts of it [were given] the names of provinces and places of greatest renown, calling
them, for instance, Lyceum, Academia, Prytaneum, Canopus, Poecile and Tempe . . .
and even made a Hades'.[17] But other less grandiose villas, like that belonging to Cicero's
friend Atticus, also contained variously characterized parts within their total landscape
composition.[18]

So it is clear that travellers to Italy, who like Addison, compiled their own anthology
of garden, villa and landscape references in classical authors, decided that this literary
experience was confirmed and realized on classical ground. Depending on place or
topography, different texts could be recalled: Statius' ekphrastic descriptions of the villas
of Manilius Vopiscus and Pollius Felix, Columella's book on the garden in emulation of
Virgil's *Georgics*, combining practical advice ('hortorum cultus') with quasi-religious
attention to the deities that controlled the unfolding seasons, Ovid's nostalgia for his
Roman garden remembered in exile, or Seneca's eulogy of gardens, groves and streams on
the Bay of Baia[19] – all declared the Roman love of gardens, which travellers therefore
expected to discover in one form or another upon Italian soil.

On their travels they saw, or thought they saw, the remains of some famous examples:
Sir Thomas Hoby was an early tourist at Cicero's villa Formiana near Mola, 'full of
bewtifull gardines'; at Mola John Raymond, too, saw 'Ciceros Grote, in which he wrote
many of his familiar Epistles'.[20] But since the garden is the most fragile of art forms, no
tourist would actually have seen a classical garden, though he was doubtless encouraged to
think otherwise, if only by his guides. At most he would have seen the spaces where
Roman gardens had been, subsequently filled either by modern gardens or by wild flowers
and shrubs blooming among the fragments of building and sculpture. Even villa remains
were few and not systematically explored – Hadrian's Villa near Tivoli was an exception in
both its size and visibility.[21] But the visitor was prepared to fill these vacancies, to colonize

the ruins, from his readings in Cicero, Pliny, Varro, Ovid and others. Lassels mentions Nero's *Domus Aurea* or Golden House, which was certainly explored if not excavated during the Renaissance; he would have been able to imagine its extensive gardens by invoking his reading in Suetonius; Thomas Coryate saw Livy's House in Padua as well as plane trees for the first time having read about them in 'Vergil and other Authours'.[22] Indeed, it is clear that many travellers viewed classical remains simply in terms of what they had read, comparing 'the natural face of the country', in Joseph Addison's words, 'with the landskips that the Poets have given us of it'.[23] George Sandys invoked Virgil and Lucretius to describe and explain Mount Etna, while he concludes a long paragraph on a cistern seen in the Naples area with the remark that it was 'mentioned by Varro, Tacitus, and Pliny'; Fynes Moryson at Narni uses quotations from Cicero, Pliny and Virgil to evoke its natural scenery.[24] When travellers surveyed the seven hills of Rome they knew, as Ellis Veryard did on the Esquiline, that it had been 'famous for the Gardens of Mecanas [Maecenas]', so much celebrated by Horace.[25] At Tivoli or Frascati Englishmen knew from their reading that they were on territory 'much frequented by the ancient Romans, who had their Villa's'. At Frascati, surrounded by so many recent revivals of classical retreats (figure 3), Richard Lassels exclaimed that 'here Cato was born, here Lucullus delighted himself, and Cicero studied'.[26] From Frascati Veryard 'walk'd out to see the Ruins of the ancient *Tusculum*, lying on an Hill about two Miles from the Town, where we found nothing but a great heap of Rubbish, with some few old Walls; and an House almost entire, said to have been *Cicero's*, where he writ his *Tusculan Questions*', ruins which Raymond sketched and published in *Il Mercurio Italico*. The anonymous visitor of 1675 went to Mola where Cicero had another villa and found that 'several Grottoes with fountains in the sollid rock, divers Archt Vaults, with his place of Burial, are still remaining, the Garden close by the sea, and now full of tall Orange-trees'.[27] Some travellers, like the future Bishop Burnet visiting the Naples area in 1685–6, were sceptical of such remains: 'Cicero and Virgil's Houses, for which there is nothing but a dubious tradition'.[28]

Burnet must have had cause to be sceptical, if the popular guidebook by Giuseppe Mormile, *Descrittione della Città di Napoli*, is anything to go by: in a section on the well-known antiquities of Pozzuoli the same woodcut is used indifferently to illustrate chapters on two distinct villa and garden remains.[29] Mormile also cites many literary references to classical gardens. Other guidebooks to the Naples region, like Pompeo Sarnelli's *Guida de' Forestieri*, alerted visitors to the supposed sites of classical gardens and villas.[30] A considerably greater profusion of guidebooks to Rome all directed their readers' attention to the locations of classical gardens, sometimes by citing literary sources, sometimes by indexing classical gardens and sometimes by providing in a woodcut or engraving a reconstructed view.[31] The images of classical gardens in some of these guides suggest that antique garden art was visualized largely in terms of contemporary, Renaissance practice. The 1627 edition of *Ritratto di Roma antica*, produced by Pompilio Totti, purports to show two of Nero's famous gardens: that in the Campo Vaticano (figure 4) is envisaged as a simple, squared enclosure with central pavilion and corner belvederes, a layout available in innumerable small gardens in late-sixteenth-century Italy; while the more famous landscape of the *Domus Aurea* (figure 5) is represented in virtually the same form as that in which the modern Villa Lante was shown in contemporary woodcuts

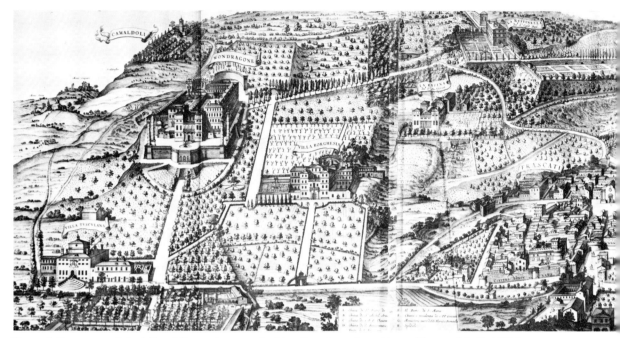

Figure 3 Panorama of the hills of Frascati, covered with villas, from Jean Blaeu, *Theatre d'Italie* (1704).

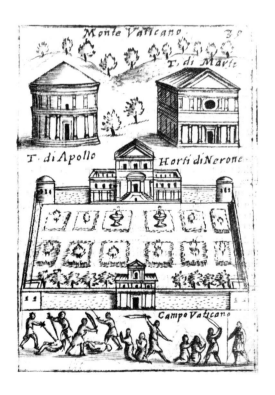

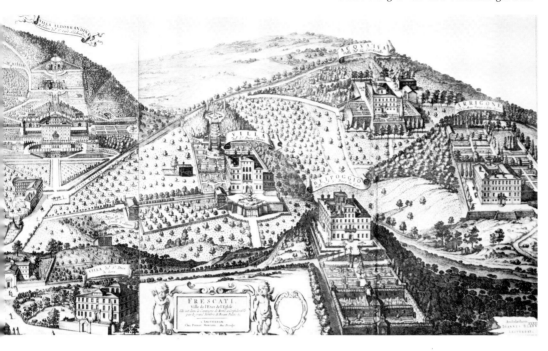

Figure 4 Reconstruction of Nero's gardens on Monte Vaticano, from P. Totti, *Ritratto di Roma antica* (1627 edition).

Figure 5 Reconstruction of the grounds of Nero's *Domus Aurea*, Golden House, from P. Totti, *Ritratto di Roma antica*.

Figure 6 Villa Lante, Bagnaia, from *Descrizione di Roma Moderna* (1697 edition).

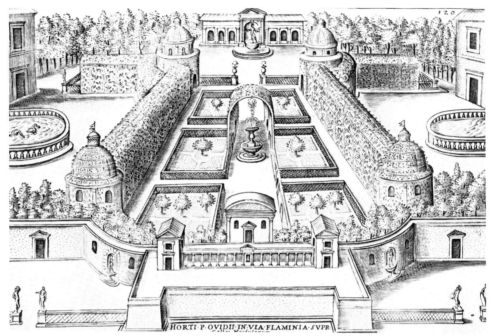

Figure 7 Reconstruction of the gardens of Ovid, from Giacomo Lauro, *Antiquae urbis splendor* (1612).

(figure 6), with fountains, a small exedra and pond in a grove. Without the benefit of systematic excavations, exceptionally difficult where gardens are concerned, the Renaissance simply envisaged literary descriptions in the light both of sundry architectural remains, not necessarily connected with gardens at all, and of contemporary garden architecture.

We should not underestimate the enormous importance which the English traveller attached either to what he thought were classical garden remains or to what, equally loosely, he considered modern reconstructions of them. Guidebooks were full of imaginary views of other famous Roman gardens, like those belonging to Ovid (figure 7) and to Sallust; reconstructions of the latter are substantially the same in books of 1627 and of 1750 (figure 8), so that visitors of different generations, buying guidebooks in which publishers merely repeated earlier cuts, were led to envisage classical gardens in terms which are more Renaissance than archaeological. Maps of the ancient city, like Alexandri Donati's *Roma Vetus ac Recens utriusque Aedificilis* of 1639, marked the famous garden areas such as the *Mons Hortorum*, as did Lauro's *Antiquae Urbis Vestigia* and Ligorio's elaborate reconstruction of the classical city (see figure 81). This Hill of Gardens was the modern Pincian, upon which Donati's and Lauro's readers could project the forms of antique gardens in the light of their experience of the modern layout of the Villa Medici (figure 9). This had been created in the full knowledge that it was established upon classical predecessors,[32] just as it was decorated with their spoils. Tourists frequently repeated the 'dubious traditions' of classical garden sites, as eager to know they walked above classical examples as to observe the new ones. Thus, John Raymond noted that the Villa Ludovisi in Rome 'stands on the same Soyle, where that renowned one of *Salust* anciently stood'; Philip Skippon at the

18

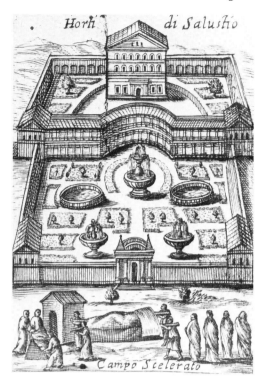

Figure 8 Reconstruction of the gardens of Sallust, from *Roma antica e moderna* (1750). In both its architectural details and the layout of the gardens this image exactly reproduces one from earlier volumes such as the *Ritratto di Roma antica* of 1627.

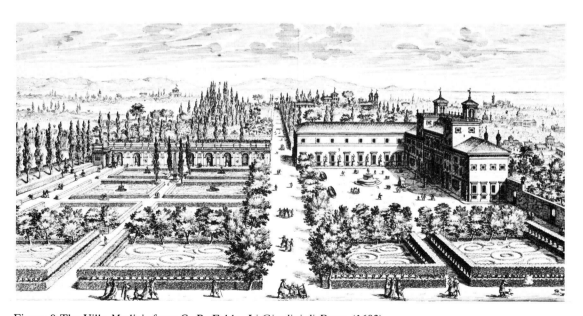

Figure 9 The Villa Medici, from G. B. Falda, *Li Giardini di Roma* (1683).

Figure 10 Virgil's tomb drawn by John Raymond and published in *Il Mercurio Italico* (1648).

Palazzo Colonna found 'in the gardens . . . considerable ruins of *Nero's Casa Aurea*, viz. many large rooms one above another, under the site of the hill'; in 'A Discourse of Rome' the author of *Horae Subsecivae* noted that the Borghese had built a palace 'in that place where Propertius the Poet lived'; while John Breval on Lake Como 'went . . . to have a view of what they call the Pliniano, about 7 miles off, from a receiv'd opinion (and not at all improbable) that it was the Villa belonging to the younger Pliny . . . and a fine country seat, that has been lately built upon the Fountain of the antient villa'.[33]

A traveller's consciousness of classical gardens was most alive at both Naples and Rome. The former was valued above all for its glimpses of classical villas in the surrounding countryside – the remains of Nero's villa, of Cicero's, of Servilius Vatia's, and the ruins of the palace of Lucullus 'amplified with Fabricks, Gardens and sumptuous Fishpools; the spaces of which Gardens appear to this day'.[34] Although the many examples of villa and garden at Pompeii and Herculaneum were not explored until the mid-eighteenth century, local traditions obviously perpetuated their memory – Lassels, discussing the destructions wrought by Vesuvius, notes that 'Here stood once a pleasant Villa beautifyed with *curious walks*, orange trees, fountains, and arbours, but Iam cinis est ubi Villa sunt'.[35] Whether this was an antique or a modern villa, he does not make clear. But that travellers equated them, seeing classical ruins transmogrified in Renaissance designs or just confusing them, is clear from various testimony.

One of the major classical attractions of Posilippo was the so-called tomb of Virgil and the tunnel cut through the hill supposedly by the 'art magick' of that poet.[36] Neither feature, whatever its origin, had been connected with gardens; yet as we shall see (p. 149), John Evelyn involved both in his design for the landscape at Albury without any sense of incongruity. That travellers would somehow register the tomb and tunnel as elements of a garden or landscape is clear from John Raymond's account of them: he writes of 'the famous Grotte, over which on the left hand, stands *Virgils* Tomb upon a high rock, so that it is scarce to be seen by those that passe below' (figure 10 & see figure 80). This sense of the tomb ('built in a *Rotunda*') as part of a landscape which invited the exploration of the visitor recalls Wotton's description of another magical garden experience (see above, p. 10). But Raymond also notes that to reach the tomb he passed through a garden – the classical ruin is thus explicitly associated with a modern garden setting.[37]

20

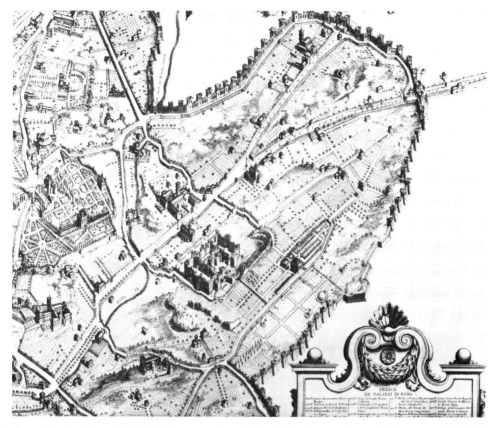

Figure 11 Detail from G. B. Falda's map of Rome (1676), showing gardens and *vigne* around classical ruins.

There were other experiences of gardens which reinforced this creative confusion of classical remains and modern gardens. Falda's 1676 map of Rome shows the richness of its contemporary gardens – for as Raymond insisted thirty years before, 'all Christendom affords [no gardens] so voluptuous, as those within the walls and Territory of *Rome*'.[38] Falda shows gardens filling not only the bastions of the city fortifications but the open spaces between ruins of classical baths and temples (figure 11). Everywhere that travellers looked in the Eternal City gardens, modern gardens, seemed part of a larger classical landscape: thus Veryard in the 1680s noted that the city was much 'taken up with wast Grounds, Gardens, Vineyards, and ruins of Ancient Rome'.[39] Many gardens were – deliberately as well as inevitably – created in the vicinity of ruins, the vaults of which provided a loggia or grotto effect, which the Renaissance garden made one of its own special features (figure 12). This was particularly remarked around Albano, where the Barberini had created a villa complex out of the remains of some antique buildings. In 1691 William Bromley visited 'pleasant gardens, large Caves in the Rocks, going a great way under ground; and by the Walls, on each side the Garden, are Ruines of ancient Baths, as is guessed from so much as remains'. The later response to the same mixture of modern garden and classical ruin by Wright reveals a more sophisticated understanding of the contribution of earlier remains to the forms of Renaissance gardens:

> the Villa Barberini . . . . was once the Villa of Pompey. Here were what they call'd *Horti Pensiles*, Gardens made upon Portico's, which were brought down in several Descents one below another, to the Lake on that side of the Hill. The like were on the other side, towards Albano, where the Porticoes do many of them now remain. There is one long and large Portico, which has some Remains of the old Painting now on its Vault, with ornaments of stucco.[40]

Figure 12 Remains of Roman baths with modern gardens, from A. Donati, *Roma vetus ac recens utriusque aedificiis illustrata* (1694).

Back in Rome the gardens of the Cardinal du Bellay are shown in Du Pérac's map of 1577 (figure 13) as well as in later plans of the city arranged *vis-à-vis* the remains of Diocletian's Baths, while the Colonna family possessed gardens on the slope of the Quirinal Hill where part of the Temple of Serapis provided 'a gigantic piece of garden sculpture'; the gardens themselves were laid out among the brick foundations of the huge double staircase that mounted the slope to the Temple.[41]

In the grounds of the Villa Medici until the later sixteenth century were still to be seen a hemicycle and flight of stairs leading to a nymphaeum, the remains of the Horti Aciliorum; these were eventually covered over to form the mound or 'Mount Parnassus' (see figure 9), so that the English visitors with whom this study is concerned would not have seen them. But both the name of the man-made hill and perhaps the contrivance of a grotto beneath it in what must have been the fabric of the nymphaeum served to make the

Figure 13 The Horti Bellaiani which utilized remains of the Baths of Diocletian, from Etienne du Pérac's map of Rome (1577).

Medici gardens also resonant with allusions to classical gardens. Moryson seems to be signalling this when he records that in the Medici grove was 'a most sweete Arbour, having foure roofes, and as it were chambers, one above the other. . . .'[42] Given the palimpsest of urban Rome, such juxtapositions and continuities were inevitable, and in one form or another must have impressed themselves upon visitors who were anyway eager to discover such connections. On sixteenth-century maps of Rome the Villa Lante on the Janiculum Hill was marked as occupying precisely the same spot as the gardens of Martial, as described in an epigram by that poet.[43]

The visitors with which this book is concerned, although well enough read in classical literature, were not professional archaeologists; rather, most of them were curious to see as much as possible of this unique city. It was in Rome above all that the continuities between classical and modern gardening were conspicuous; it is these continuities which are stressed – literally – in Evelyn's list of great Italian gardens sent to Sir Thomas Browne: first he mentions a series of classical ones, then those *more moderne and at present*. This second section of his list names examples which in one form or another were thought to perpetuate or to recover in even more splendid form the vanished glories of ancient Roman gardens:

23

Clement the 8th's garden; the Medicean, Mathaeo's garden, Cardinal Pio's; Farnesian, Lodovisian, Burghesean, Aldobrandino's, Barberini's, the Belvedere, Montalta's, Bossius's, Justiniane's, the Quirinal gardens, Cornelius's, Mazarini's, etc.[44]

Perhaps the most common and tangible form of connection between classical and modern gardens took the form of the decoration of villas with the spoils of ancient Rome. The earliest created in Rome, the Papal Belvedere Villa (figure 14), was used in part as a showpiece for Pope Julius II's collection of statues, and since in all travellers' accounts the Belvedere was usually discussed immediately after the classical and before the modern city, its antique sculpture garden became a clear instance of gardenist continuities. Most travellers would know from one classical text or other[45] of the fashion for decorating villas and gardens with appropriate statues; it mattered little that the antique examples in modern gardens may not originally have been garden decoration. John Raymond reported on the Belvedere:

> In the last garden in Niches, shut up are the best and most ancient statues of Rome, as that of Laocoon and his two sonnes, all of one Marble, the Cleopatra, the Niobe, the Romulus and Remus sucking the Wolfe; the Nilus; the Tybre, all famous pieces.[46]

In emulation of this Papal garden others sprang up in the sixteenth and seventeenth centuries: one of these, the Casa Galli, is well known through the sketch that Martin van Heemskerck made of its sculptural trophies, while Hendrick van Cleef III painted an eloquent picture of another created by Cardinal Cesi (figure 15). Cesi's antique sculpture garden was situated in the 'Borgo Vecchio' at the southern entrance to the Vatican; it no longer exists, having been partly removed to accommodate Bernini's colonnade in front of St Peter's. Van Cleef takes some liberties with the topography, but his representation captures strikingly the ambience of such a garden: visitors wander around with admiring gestures, artists are sketching the antique figures scattered throughout the various compartments of the garden, and other items are being excavated and carried away.[47]

Another famous garden was that at the Villa Carpi, where an anonymous English visitor about 1610 recorded his delight that, 'In the garden are many strange antiquities, most delightful to behold'.[48] Among its most famous features were the statue of the young shepherd – represented in the meditative pose of a hand supporting his head in a niche above the entrance to the grotto of the Sleeping Nymph – and that of the nymph herself, much admired and copied both in Italy and, as we shall see, in England.[49]

Neither the Cesi nor the Carpi garden survived beyond the first quarter of the seventeenth century, just as the Belvedere Courtyard was not seen in its original form after the late 1580s when it was built across at the halfway point. But other villa gardens maintained these traditions, whereby the classical past was realized afresh and Renaissance nostalgia was endorsed with what George Sandys called 'many excellent statues recovered from the decays of antiquitie'; it was above all sculpture's ability to recover or revive that 'decay' that made it so estimable – Raymond talked of 'marbles, which speak *Roman* history more palpably than any Author'.[50] A wealth of antique statues expressed the learning of its owner, as Warcupp's text declared of Rodolfo, Cardinal Pio da Carpe, whose collection was 'so well disposed that no Fancy could reach that Paradise, nor ocular

Figure 14 Henrick van Cleef III, *The Vatican Belvedere sculpture gardens*, painting of 1550.

Figure 15 Henrick van Cleef III, *Cardinal Cesi's Antique Sculpture Garden*, painting of 1584.

25

view scarce apprehend its glory, to say no more this garden was an Embleme of that Cardinal its Patron' and of his learning and knowledge of antiquity.[51] The Villa Ludovisi was another, even deriving some of its fine antiques from the Cesi and Carpi collections. Travellers appreciated these vestiges of classical Rome the more because at the Villa Ludovisi they were located beside 'the Ruins of Lucullus's Palace' (according to Bromley) or (as Evelyn records) where had been 'formerly the Viridarium of the Poet Sallust'.[52] In 1644 Evelyn recorded for his diary how the large 'Garden is in every quarter beset with antique statues, and Walkes planted with Cypresse, at the extreme of one, stands a Bassrelievo of white marble very antient & good'. Some fourteen years later Francis Mortoft expressed his pleasure with 'A Gallery, as they call it, which is like a Laborinth running out of one round into another and cut soe prettily that one shall hardly see any other garden in such a fashion, and at least 100 Roman statues about these Cutts' (figure 16)[53].

Other villas incorporated their treasure trove of classical artifacts. Philip Skippon in the 1660s admired the 'fair ancient sepulchre, having the muses and Apollo in relievo

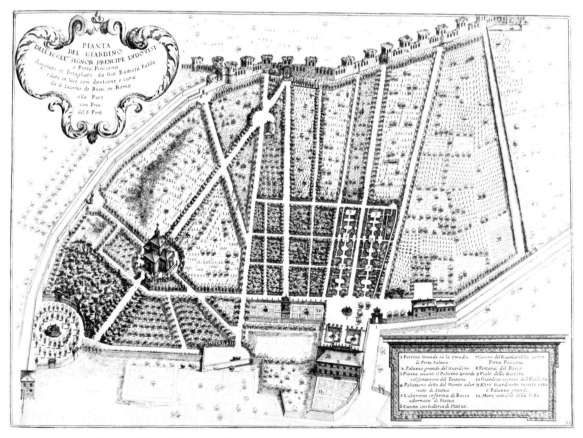

Figure 16 The Villa Ludovisi, from Falda, *Li Giardini di Roma*. The section of the gardens adorned with sculpture is marked '5' on the engraving: it is represented by opening and closing spaces in a dense grove to the right of centre.

26

Figure 17 The Villa Mattei, from Falda, *Li Giardini di Roma*.

about it' at the Villa Mattei (figure 17) and listed many antiquities at the Villa Montalto.[54] Villa Borghese was, for Evelyn, encrusted with 'history', while Raymond, from whom Evelyn borrowed in writing up his journal, had elaborated upon its 'foure Frontispieces of ancient sculptures, in Basso Relievo'.[55] At the Villa Medici, where a magnificent collection of reliefs and sculpture was installed on the garden façade and along the gallery to the south of the main parterre in the late sixteenth century, Mortoft was confronted with 'multitudes of ancient statues', just as in the late 1590s Moryson had discovered 'many Images of White Marble, of Pegasus, of the Muses' and so on.[56] Sometimes these collections were intriguing to English visitors because they had already been copied back home – thus the visitor of 1675 noted that the statue of the Gladiator at the Villa Borghese was the 'Original of that in St James's Park'.[57] But there were other visitors who were quickly surfeited by the classical debris. One thought that the Palazzo Giustiniani, where Evelyn had been delighted with 'Gardens . . . exceedingly full of statues & Antiquities, especially Urnes', was simply so 'well stor'd with Statues . . . that it seemed a Ware-house of them'.[58] A few years later Veryard confessed that, 'If antient *Rome* had Thirty thousand Gods, as *Varro* assures us it had, I am confident one might find a Limb of each in some part or other of this Palace [Giustiniani]'.[59] Certainly by the end of the seventeenth and the beginning of the eighteenth century it would have been abundantly clear to Englishmen that, as John Worlidge put it,

> 'the ancient *Romans* were excessively prodigal, sparing of no cost, to adorn their avenues with curious figures [i.e. statues] . . . . Which vanity (although one of the most excusable) is descended on the *Italians*, whose Gardens are the mirrors of the World, as well for those ornaments as for their excellency of the Plants that are propogated in them'.[60]

27

And by 1722 the Richardsons' *Account of Some of the Statues, Bas-reliefs, Drawings and Pictures in Italy* frequently notes the location or discovery of antique art in gardens.[61]

The whole classical ambience of modern Roman gardens was perhaps summed up most vividly for tourists in the much visited and admired Farnese gardens on the Palatine Hill, 'where are pretty gardens, and on the top an aviary; many old ruins and grotte about the garden'.[62] Skippon refers there to Vignola's creation of the Palatine gardens for Cardinal Farnese, dating from the second half of the sixteenth century. Each of his emphases is supported in some of the visual representations of the Orti Farnesiani: a woodcut in Bartolomeo Marliani's *Urbis Romae Topographis* (1588 edition) seems to emphasize their connection with classical ruins, showing what an English visitor later called 'ruins, and a multitude of subterrean vaults' (figure 18)[63]; whereas Falda's view in the seventeenth century displays the wide spread of the gardens themselves (figure 19). Both emphases are justified, as Mortoft implies with his description of the Palatine Hill as 'onely a garden and ruins'.[64] The Orti Farnesiani were created (and what remains of them still exist) above an intricate labyrinth of old Roman buildings, and this final horticultural layer on the urban palimpsest became a famous botanical collection with its own catalogue.[65] In addition, the gardens' magnificent situation allowed views – what Maximilian Misson called a 'fine prospect' over the Forum to the northeast and the Circus Maximus to the southwest. Vignola's entrance to the gardens was a suitably classical archway (now removed to a different side of the hill), through which the visitor mounted via a series of ramps, stairways and terraces, visible at the left of figure 19; these Lassels remembered as 'some pretty waterworks & grottoes at the entrance, and fine high walks above'.[66] The interior rooms as well as the exterior spaces were filled with statuary recovered from adjacent land, though the gardens themselves must have offered a rich source of such classical spoils; Edward Wright in the 1720s saw men digging for antique sculpture in some waste parts of the Orti Farnesiani.[67] When George Turnbull comes to publish *A Curious Collection of Ancient Paintings* . . . in 1741, he often notes that items were discovered in Roman gardens: thus a mosaic of a siren was 'dug up in the *Farnese Gardens* at Rome, in the year 1737', and a painting of Augustus was found while 'searching the Ruins in Monte Palatino, now called Orti Farnesiani'.[68]

The Farnese gardens, then, finely epitomized the English experience of modern Italian gardens created in and out of classical predecessors. The creative confusions of old and new would have important consequences for English garden design. If the frequent juxtaposition of Roman remains with gardens could have led even such an antiquarian as Andrea Palladio to assume (mistakenly) that the Temple of the Sun had been a classical garden building,[69] there can be no doubt that others, less qualified, frequently made the same mistake. Travellers would have seen and perhaps bought engravings of similarly happy conjunctions of architectural remains and new gardens, and their souvenirs would in turn authorize a role for temples in gardens that classical Rome in practice may not have intended. The English landscape garden's use of temples and its love of ruins derive as much from a recollection of the happenstance of the Roman scene as from careful observation of modern Italian garden design. Even the profusion of antique sculpture, with a limb of every Roman divinity, according to Veryard, seemingly salvaged for garden use, would be responsible for a curious but nonetheless important episode in English landscape history (see pp. 220–1).

Two further aspects of classical gardening and their effects upon modern recreations deserve separate consideration. Both fulfill something of the patterns which have been examined already – that is to say, the reading of Latin literary texts for insights into Roman garden designs and ideas, and the extrapolation of these literary sources into the forms of Renaissance and later English architecture and layout.

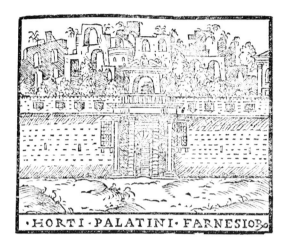

Figure 18 The Orti Farnesiani on the Palatine Hill, from B. Marliani, *Urbis Romae Topographia* (1588 edition).

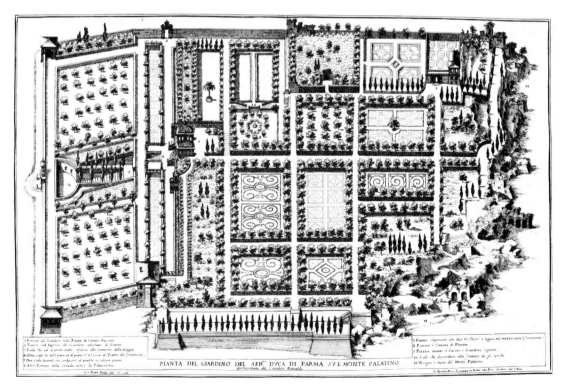

Figure 19 The Duke of Parma's gardens (formerly the Orti Farnesiani) on the Palatine Hill, from Falda, *Li Giardini di Roma*.

3 *VILLA* AND *VIGNA*

The earliest application of the term *villa* to an English country estate that is recorded by the *OED* occurs in Shaftesbury's *Characteristics* of 1711.[1] But it was current much earlier. Writing from Padua in 1646, Lord Arundel told John Evelyn that he would 'have sold any Estate he had in *England*, (*Arundel* excepted), before he would have parted with this Darling *Villa*' at Albury, in Surrey.[2] Some twenty years later John Aubrey would inscribe the word VILLA in the titlepage cartouche of the manuscript plans for his house and grounds at Easton Piercy in Wiltshire.[3] The term *villa* clearly had Roman and Italian connotations as well as etymology, for Aubrey surrounds the word with quotations from the classics; his fondness for tracing the progress of Italianate gardening in England makes his use of *villa* for his own hortulan projections a signal of a conscious participation in that progress.

Yet the word was a recent introduction into English, instinct with strangeness as well as modishness. The essay 'Of a Country Life' in *Horae Subsecivae* (1620) notes that in other countries than England people go in summer to their '*Villaes*, as they terme them'.[4] The frequent drawing of a reader's attention to the foreign term suggests its relative usefulness as well as newness. Raymond's *Il Mercurio Italico* describes 'a multitude of *Villa's*, or Countrey houses' on both sides of the Brenta canal.[5] George Sandys shows his familiarity with the classical term when in the vicinity of Naples he observes '*Ciceroes* Villa, even at this day so called'; however, not so long afterwards he takes an English term to describe 'the Manor House of Servilius Vatia . . . with her ruines'.[6] Lassels viewed the Tuscan countryside from the Duomo at Florence and estimated that he could see '*two thousand Villas* or country houses'.[7] Such parenthetical glosses on this new, foreign word continue long after we might suppose that 'villa' had been assimilated into English. When John Ray reaches Rome he immediately records 'The *ville* (as they now call them) of the Princes and prime Nobility of Rome, for gardens of flowers, groves and thickets of trees, cut hedges . . . , close and open walks of great length, orchards of fruit-trees, Labyrinths, fountains and ingenious water-works, Bird-cages, statues and other ornaments . . . excel the orchards, gardens and walks of any Prince in Christendom that I have seen.'[8] Veryard, arriving at Turin in 1682, notes that 'The Duke and Dutchess have several Villa's, or

Country-Houses, near the City . . .'; later, in Rome, he writes of the '*Villa's*, or Gardens, where the Noble *Romans* divert themselves in Summer time'.[9] In the 1750s a traveller like John Northall is still intent upon this particular feature of Italian life: the climate, he writes,

> necessarily renders the inhabitants fond of villas and gardens, where they may retire in summer for the benefit of fresh air. In England the nobility generally make their country seats the most magnificent, and content themselves with little more than mere conveniences in town, but in Italy it is quite the reverse; the city house is much larger, and generally more splendid, than the villa, which is only intended for a short retreat in the hot season. Therefore, the gardens of these villas have great numbers of tall trees and high hedges, with many fountains and waterworks.[10]

The general fascination with Italian Renaissance architecture displayed by early English travellers obviously went hand in hand with the need to acquire an apt terminology with which to discuss this new experience. When the mid-sixteenth-century writer, William Thomas, absorbed a fresh term he glossed it for his readers: over the choir of the Duomo at Florence 'is a whole vault called Cupola, fashioned like the half of an egg'.[11] And it was his *Historie of Italie* (1549) that first introduced English readers, as we have seen (above p. 5), to the idea of *villeggiatura* and to the excitements of terraced gardens, just as his enthusiasm for the advantages of the climate made him exclaim at the impression of continuous springtime in the Neopolitan countryside.[12] The strangeness of Italian gardens for early travellers is most clearly seen in Fynes Moryson's explanation of one of the main features of the Medici gardens at Pratolino:

> There is a Fountaine which hath the name of a Laberinth close by it. And a Fountaine of Jupiter & Iris distilling water; the Fountaine of the Beare; the Fountaine of Æsculapius; and the Fountaine of Bersia. I call these by the name of Fountaines, vulgarly called Fontana, which are buildings of stone, adorned with many carved Images distilling water, and such are placed in most parts of Italy in the marketplaces, open and uncovered: but in this and like Gardens, these Fountaines are wrought within little houses, which house is vulgarly called grotta, that is, Cave (or Den), yet are they not built under the earth but above in the manner of a Cave.[13]

Moryson's rather fuzzy definition suggests the strangeness of these garden elements to a northern eye.

Yet more than *cupola* or *grotto* the term *villa* seemed to embrace a variety of ideas and to be in special need of explanation. Sandys considered 'manor house' an apt translation; this probably had more justification if he were thinking of its classical rather than its modern Italian application; Italian villas were rarely the residential base of gentry or patrician classes as they were in contemporary England and as they may have appeared to be in Roman times. *Villa*, besides seeming the equivalent of manor house, also signified 'country house' for Raymond and Veryard, presumably with the same blur of social usage and significance; Veryard glossed it equally as 'garden', while Ray seemed to include in its scope the whole richness and variety of Italian patrician garden art. But other equivalents were invoked by travellers, the most interesting of which was certainly *vineyards*.

Veryard, again, describing the garden-like appearance of late seventeenth-century Rome noted that it was originally 'thirty (some say fifty) Miles in compass, [but] is at present brought within the circuit of thirteen, and a good part of the inclosure is taken up with waste Grounds, Gardens, Vineyards, and Ruins. . . .'[14] Of the Orti Farnesiani on the Palatine, which we have already seen as something of an epitome of modern gardens arising from the ruins of the classical city (above, p. 28), Warcupp wrote that it was nothing but ruins and 'a vineyard of Cardinal Farnese'. In the section of his book that brings the traveller towards Rome he also notes at Brisighella the palace of Signior Spadi 'which hath all the commodities of Church, Fishponds, Fountains, Gardens, Vineyards . . .',[15] Philip Skippon, travelling with the botanist Ray during the early 1660s, visited the gardens of the Villa Ludovisi in Rome and remarked upon the large gardens, the 'long walks and pretty groves', and 'Fair vineyards and fountains'; while near Santa Croce he found 'a garden enclosed by the city walls, and the ruins of *Amphitheatrum Castreuse*. In the vineyard are the remains of the temple of *Venus* and *Cupid*. An old arch near it made like a grotto'.[16] In the 1720s Edward Wright, proceeding down the Via Flaminia, recorded his impression of 'good Buildings, pleasant Villas and Vineyards on each hand'.[17]

In 1558 that same Via Flaminia had ninety owners of *vigne* or vineyards between the Porta del Popolo and the Ponte Milvio; by 1570 the number was 118.[18] What Wright saw over a hundred and fifty years later was the same landscape of vineyards, but decorated with more imposing buildings, including villas. Doubtless the similarity of the words *villa* and *vigna* caused some confusion to English visitors; but it is far more likely that the Italian habit of establishing a villa where vines or other farming land already existed or of surrounding a country house with vineyards added a visual to a verbal confusion. The coinage of *villatic* by John Milton in *Samson Agonistes* (line 1695) with the meaning of farmyard suggests indeed that the associations of the two words overlapped; and Milton had travelled to Rome in the 1640s and would have seen for himself a landscape that promoted such meanings. Maps of both sixteenth and seventeenth centuries showed Rome as an intricate mixture of gardens and cultivated land (see figure 11), and David Coffin has argued that the Italian habit of retreat to the countryside in summer – *villeggiatura* – 'was basically an aspect of an agricultural society'.[19] He has noted the incidence of *vigne* in and immediately outside Rome: some were simply cultivated land, some augmented with modest farmhouses which survived into the eighteenth century and were well known through painted views of the Roman Campagna.[20] Some of these farms were augmented with casinos, usually with loggias, in which families from the city could spend an afternoon or evening on their country property. In their turn grander villas were constructed: the park of the Villa Giulia (built in the mid-sixteenth century) still retains its older farm building, the so-called Casa del Curato.

The English traveller, then, invoking both villa, vigna and garden to describe his experience of the Italian countryside, was acknowledging the physical interconnection of those elements. But his sight and his etymology were sustained also by his classical reading. If *villeggiatura* was basically an aspect of an agricultural society, it came to be a rural way of life seen increasingly through the mythopoeic spectacles of the urban dweller who knew his classical literature of rural retreat. The creative confusion of gardens, villas and vineyards with other farm lands was prompted by the writings of Pliny, Varro, Horace, Virgil and other classical writers.

Pliny had written memorably of the involvements of villa, vigna, farm and garden at Laurentum: in one direction he saw 'many flocks of sheep and herds of horses and cattle' from which 'all inland produce . . . especially milk' was provided for the household, while to the west was the sea which yielded 'excellent soles and prawns'.[21] Horace, too, gave an impression of modest self-sufficiency on the Sabine Farm, which Pope mimicked in his imitations.[22] Virgil had written his poem, *The Georgics*, as a guide to farming practice, but had deliberately omitted to treat the garden; Columella took up what the older poet had left out and wrote poetically of garden cultivation. Varro's Book III had treated of villa husbandry. Primed by such literary expectations, English travellers responded enthusiastically to the agricultural richnesses of the Italian countryside. Addison, who had gone to Italy with the specific purpose of comparing the countryside to descriptions of it in Latin poetry, found that his 'greatest pleasure' on the journey between Rome and Naples came from 'seeing the fields, towns and rivers that have been described by so many classic authors'; in the countryside around Pozzuoli the picturesque prospect of 'Oranges, Almonds, Olives, Myrtles, and fields of Corn' particularly delighted him.[23] Other travellers invoked the classics to gloss their experiences: De Blainville's travels, translated into English in 1743, described the landscape around Foligno, remarked upon by others, and added that it was this kind of landscape that Virgil must have had in mind when composing the second book of his *Georgics*.[24] Lassels thought the 'country itself . . . [was] Nature's darling' and he dedicates the four opening pages of *The Voyage of Italy* to the profusion of Italian crops.

There is much independent visual evidence to support travellers' views of the interpenetration of garden and farm. Paul Brill's drawings of the months in the Louvre present an elaborate villa (reminiscent of the Villa Medici in Rome) rising above gardens and a lakeside where elegant ladies and gentlemen promenade. Its summerhouse in one drawing is seen in a second from another viewpoint where the garden architecture projects into and over a scene of agricultural activity, and Brill clearly demonstrates the contiguous, interpenetrating areas of garden and field (figures 20 & 21). The series of lunettes of Medici villas painted by Gustave Utens in 1599 likewise declare this juxtaposition of *villa* and *vigna*.[25] Some of the more modest of these, such as La Peggio or Colli Salvetti, are simple buildings that seem to have grown out of the agricultural terrain; others, however, are grander and have been provided with more or less elaborate gardens, like Castello on the hills north of Florence (figure 22) with its pergolas, ponds, fountains and private gardens (*giardini segreti*), or La Petraia, half a mile to the east, with its circular pergolas and groves, descending terraces and fruit trees set out in terracotta pots. But most of these Medici villas are seen to retain their connections with the worked land on which they were established and elaborated. Poggio a Caiano (figure 23), to the west of Florence, is an elegant building raised upon loggias inside a square, walled garden decorated with many rectangular flower beds; but immediately beyond that and clearly visible from the house are orchards and vineyards, with farm buildings at the edge of Utens's scene. That was what Sir John Reresby saw in the late 1650s, noticing the hillsides covered with vines and olive trees, the Duke's paddock and a large park for hunting.[26]

A recent interest in Italian *paesaggismo* has yielded many documents which attest to the cultivated forms of the Italian countryside; this means, too, that the visual habits of painters and artists employed, like Utens, to celebrate patrons' country properties can be clarified and supported from other kinds of material. An exhibition in Bologna in 1983 brought together 'poetic', idealized landscapes of the surrounding countryside as well as

Figure 20 Paul Brill, *The month of May: walking on the terrace*, drawing of 1598.

Figure 21 Paul Brill, *The month of May: work in the vineyard*, drawing of 1598. The handsome villa shown in Figure 20 seems to appear again in the back left of this view.

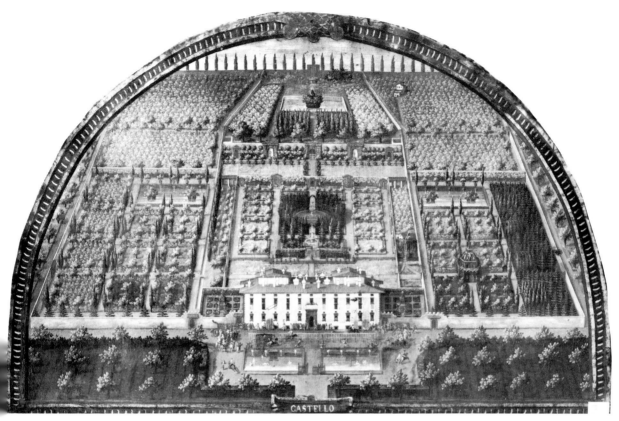

Figure 22 Gustave Utens, *The Medici Villa of Castello*, painted lunette of 1599.

maps and plans from legal archives, notably plans of properties sold or inherited and from civic schemes, such as details of waterworks and rivers; in all it established a clear picture of an extensive rural landscape dotted with villas, each set according to its status in a specific garden area and then surrounded in turn by carefully maintained and cultivated land.[27] Such visual evidence amply endorses English travellers who viewed parts especially of northern Italy as a veritable and extended garden. The Earl of Cork and Orrery was travelling in this area in the mid-1750s and was appreciative of the vineyards planted on each side of this road ('The vines have a beautiful effect, by hanging in festoons from one tree to another') and of the ploughed land, though he was puzzled by the total absence of people.[28] So, too, Francis Mortoft, riding to Bologna from the Veneto, recorded that the roads 'were as even as if they had been walks in a garden'[29]. Coming in the same direction, Maximilian Misson noted that 'the Country is Even and Fruitful, watered with several Rivers, and well cultivated. It is every where full of Meadows, Groves, Vineyards and well-till'd Spots of Ground.'[30]

The Veneto was particularly noted for its garden-like appearance. Travelling slowly by barge along the Brenta travellers like Raymond had the leisure to observe 'on both sides . . . a garden-like country, and a multitude of *villa's*, or Country Houses, with Gardens of Orange trees, and other greens after the Italian way'.[31] Warcupp's *Italy* depicted a scene

Figure 23 Gustave Utens, *The Medici Villa of Poggio a Caiano*, painted lunette of 1599.

that many English who searched out the work of Palladio would have seen for themselves: from the Villa Rotunda outside Vicenza there were views in all directions – 'from one [side] an *immense campagna*, another the large Theatre and Town, the third mountains over Mountains, the Fourth land intermixt with Waters, so that the Eye rests marvelously contented'.[32] It reads in part like a modern version of Pliny's Tuscan scenery in which a profitable rural landscape also featured prominently. Near Virgil's birthplace Edward Browne saw many gardens along this road, but also 'La Virgiliana . . . another pleasant Country House with a Farm adjoyning to it'.[33] Palladio's villas in this area of Italy were usually erected on profitably arable land and combined the offices of a farm with the accommodations of a country residence.[34] Of his route between Vicenza and Padua in 1685 Burnet thought the eighteen miles were 'all like a garden'.[35]

Tuscany, too, received its tributes from visitors, enraptured with its realization of their visions of Italian countryside, which in turn promoted the idea of villas and gardens as necessarily belonging in a rich agricultural scenery. John Breval in the second quarter of the eighteenth century saw the territory around Lucca as 'one continued Garden', full of an intermixture of villa and fields which some years earlier Addison had found 'cultivated to the best advantage, so that one cannot find the least spot of ground, that is not made to contribute its utmost to the owner'.[36] The countryside around Florence seemed another

36

city, 'so full are the Fields speckled with Country Seats'.[37] After rehearsing the usual cliché about Italy being one whole and perfect garden, the anonymous writer of 1675 discusses the plain in which Florence stands, a plain 'enclos'd with Hills; in which are an infinite number of Villas, and some of them very fine'. One of these is Poggio Imperiale, where he notices its 'quantity of Meadow-ground well Wooded, with a Farm House upon it, where the G. Duke keeps his Dairy, and in the Summer is very pleasant'.[38] By the mid-eighteenth century when love of prospect had acquired a far wider appeal John Northall first describes the same Poggio Imperiale and then the whole Arno's 'fertile vale, and fine large mountains, some covered with vines and olives, interspersed with great numbers of delightful villas, adorned with beautiful gardens, laid out in the most elegant manner, and surrounded with corn-fields, vineyards and olive trees intermixed, forming on the whole one of the most agreeable prospects imaginable'.[39]

These viewpoints, a mixture of real observation as well as of idealizing perspectives, were inevitably extended as landscape became more fashionable. Giuseppe Zocchi's volume of *Vedute delle ville e d'altri luoghi della Toscana*, issued in 1744 and again in 1754, observes country houses set in a rural landscape which is often 'poetized' with arcadian figures resting on tombs but also actively managed by farm workers and serviced by commercial wagons and riverboats.[40] Another set of Tuscan landscapes, drawn by an early nineteenth-century artist and held in the Municipal Library, Siena, show sixteenth- and seventeenth-century villas with their old terraces and smallish gardens settled into a landscape of larger agricultural concerns that was virtually unchanged for two hundred years (figure 24).[41] The anonymous visitor to this part of the country in 1610 was particularly struck by the fact that 'the whole way [from Siena to Pisa was] a most pleasant and delightful garden'.[42]

Figure 24 Ettore Romagnoli, drawing of the Villa Celsa, near Siena, dated 1863.

The testimony of travellers to a marvellous mixture of garden and rural landscapes at some of the favoured spots on the Grand Tour would have a considerable impact on English garden design. Not only did it authorize what Pope would term 'call[ing] in the country' during the landscape movement but it equally left its mark upon earlier designs. For the typical Renaissance villa, built as Alberti recommended where it would enjoy fine prospects,[43] necessarily looked out over a countryside attuned to man's agricultural needs. Misson described the marvellous vista from the Villa Madama, which Richard Wilson would paint sixty-five years later: it enjoyed 'a Prospect of Rome, with several Gardens, and many pleasant Seats; and on the other the Eye is ravish'd with a beautiful Landskip of little and well cultivated Hills: over-against it the Tiber creeps thro' the Fields and Meadows . . .'.[44] Such vistas confirmed travellers in their anticipated hopes of a fecund Italy. Early tourists especially seem to have been prepared for surpassing georgic richness: Robert Dallington in 1596 exclaimed that 'their valleys . . . indeed . . . are like Gardens'.[45] Coryate in his turn, not without some geographical confusions, waxed even more enthusiastic: 'For as Italy is the garden of the world, so is Lombardy the garden of Italy, and Venice the garden of Lombardy. It is wholly plaine and beautified with such abundance of goodly rivers, pleasant meadowes, fruitfull vineyardes, fat pastures, delectable gardens . . . that the first view thereof did even refocillate my spirits, and tickle my senses with inward joy.'[46]

Perhaps on no topic does the mythopoeic vision of a preternaturally fecund landscape become more palpable than the cultivation of oranges. Coryate himself at the Valmarana Gardens in Vicenza transcribed the inscriptions which beckoned visitors into a world of Vertumnus and Pomona and then was delighted by the profusion of citrus fruits.[47] The orange was relatively unknown to English tourists except in specially maintained conservatories in England and its availability everywhere in Italy readily contributed to a mythic vision of Italian gardens: for it was the Hesperian Apple, as Raymond put it, 'of a most ravishing beauty perpetually Verdant'.[48] The story of Hercules stealing the golden apples from the Garden of the Hesperides was linked to their successful cultivation in Italy; innumerable publications offered this mythic gloss upon orange growing, claiming in text and title, like Ferrari's *Hesperides sive de Malorum Auvreorum*, that the fabled garden of the Hesperides had been realized again throughout Italy.[49]

English travellers returning home, then, could take with them visions of Italian villa gardens set in rich agricultural land, apparently instinct with mythical colour and eloquent of what classical writers had reported of Roman villas and *vigne*. When tourists had seen within a Roman vineyard the remains of rooms which they were ready to believe 'were Claudius's Nymphaeum, or Water-House',[50] the connections between villa and *vigna* were consolidated for them. When Joseph Spence came to explain Philip Southcote's so-called *ferme ornée* at Woburn in the mid-eighteenth century he traced its inspiration precisely to memories of the Italian countryside – 'fields', as he put it, 'going from Rome to Naples'.[51] Spence's own letters written on the grand tour are constantly alert to this congruence of villas and fields: the Cascine Park outside the Porta al Prato of Florence had 'a long run of groves and pretty artificial islands full of arbours, and on the right lie the vineyards and cornfields interspersed'; in Rome, too, he was struck by 'this mixture of city, country and gardens'.[52]

But Spence's reactions were not just a result of a much increased taste for the 'natural' disposition of ground. The English fascination with the Italian landscape, especially its 'mixture of . . . country and gardens', had existed throughout the seventeenth century; it had attracted, too, the same kinds of mythopoeic attention. Inigo Jones recalls the symbolic colour of a rich georgic landscape in one of his masque designs (figure 25). John Evelyn, with his Italian tour some ten years behind him, chose to copy a Titian scene of rural prospect, with farm buildings and a nymph poised to bathe in a stream (figure 26); Aubrey made a point of considering the views from his 'villa' at Easton Pierse; the frontispiece to Timothy Nourse's *Campania Foelix* of 1700, a book in which the author singles out Italian villas for praise, situates its country house and garden in juxtaposition to worked, arable farmland.[53] And it is these traditions of looking at the country with classical-italianate eyes that were absorbed into the so-called English landscape movement. When an anonymous designer prepared a plan and elevation of a belvedere (perhaps for Castle Howard in Yorkshire) in 1723 he annotated his work boldly with the legend 'After ye Antique. Vid [i.e. *vide*, see] Herodotus, Pliny, and M Varo' (figure 27). He was merely responding to his task of creating some temple for a landscape by reminding his patron of the strong classical precedents for such a belvedere from where that patron's own and presumably prosperous landscape could be viewed. The English gentleman's Italian experience jibed with his habit of residing on the land in the English shires.

The literary tincture of such customs of rural residence is clear, as will be seen in more detail in the second part, from the writings of Stephen Switzer and Alexander Pope in the

Figure 25 Inigo Jones, *A Peaceful Country*, masque design of 1640.

early years of the eighteenth century. A *Guardian* essay by the latter in 1713 urged the example of Alcinous' garden from Homer's *Odyssey* and added that Sir William Temple, too, had 'remark'd that this Description contains all the justest Rules and Provisions which can go towards composing the best Gardens'. What is striking about the passage in Pope's translation is the relative absence of specific design hints but the strong emphasis on cultivation, vines and 'all th'United Labours of the Year'.[54] Switzer invoked the example of Virgil in *Ichnographia Rustica* and generally emphasized the Roman contribution to the style of 'rural and extensive Gardening'; part of what is involved in that 'extent' is the chance to view, very much after Pliny's fashion, 'goodly Hills and Theatres of Wood and Corn that are about us, and present themselves every where to our View . . .'[55]

Figure 26 John Evelyn, drawing of Italian countryside after Titian, dated 1656.

40

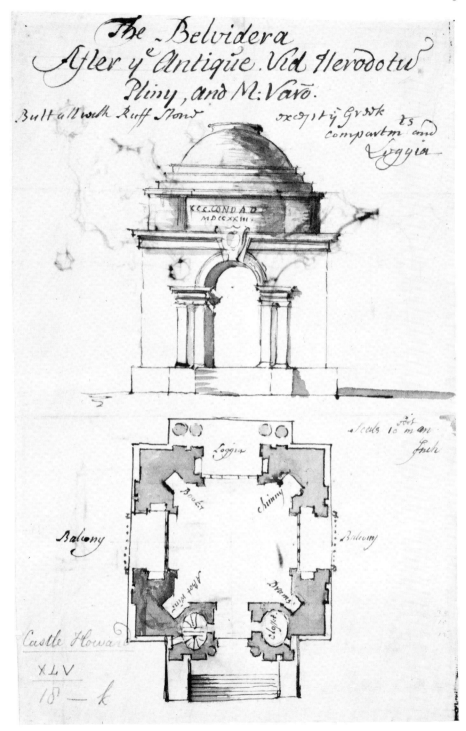

Figure 27 Anonymous design for a 'Belvidera After yᵉ Antique . . .', dated 1723 on the proposed building.

4 OVID IN THE GARDEN

Ovid's *Metamorphoses* was extensively invoked, not to say pillaged, by Renaissance writers and visual artists. It is therefore unsurprising that the poem should also have featured prominently in garden art, both as a source of motifs and stories for architects and designers and as a significant focus of ideas and responses in visitors. It is doubtful whether any garden of the sixteenth and seventeenth centuries avoided some appeal, specific or general, to Ovid's poetic world. Sir Henry Wotton appears to imply the metamorphic experience of one 'incomparable' garden when his description of it (a passage already quoted on p. 10) makes explicit mention of visitors' being translated magically from one part of a garden to another and, further, appeals to 'delightful confusion' and 'various entertainments' of the senses. He could just as well have been describing our experience of reading the *Metamorphoses*.

The relevance of Ovid's poem to garden art is not hard to seek. Landscape, according to one commentator[1], is among its main subjects, especially in Books I–IV, XIII and XIV. Its *dramatis personae* inhabit a world where natural features are prominent and the narratives frequently relate characters' actions and transformations to that habitat. Equally, features of the physical landscape are explained in terms of its presiding deities, whose stories are often told to validate some particular *numen* of a territory: a fountain has enervating properties because in it the nymph Salmacis overpowered Hermaphroditus; the Aventine Hill commemorates the hero who lies buried beneath it.[2] Springs may have been nymphs in previous incarnations, or simply the bathing-places of Diana; groves may be haunted by those whom Circe has transformed or be the more propitious habitation of Father Tiber.[3] Animals, birds, fish, flowers, trees and stones are all at some point in the poem explained as having a mythic origin. Ovid's descriptions declare an art that belies their supposedly natural forms; how easy then to translate, transform, the scenery of his poem into garden art.

The constituent parts of a Renaissance garden are relatively few: fountains, statues, pergolas, arbours, grottoes, groves (that is to say, trees arranged in some formal pattern, including a pattern that appeared to deny any order), and flowers. The *Metamorphoses* provides examples, in some cases many, of each of these features. In Book III we are told that there 'was an ancient forest which no axe had ever touched, and in the heart of it a cave, overgrown with branches and osiers, forming a low arch with its rocky walls, rich in bubbling springs'. That 'forming' (the Latin *efficiens*) ascribes to nature the same properties as those derived from an architect; such effects were readily achieved in gardens, too. A little later in the third book Ovid explicitly claims an artistry for nature (his own poetry, of course, being analogous to that art in its presentation of scenery). We are told of a sacred valley, 'thickly overgrown', far in the depths of which 'lay a woodland cave, which no hand of man had wrought: but nature by her own devices had imitated art. She had carved a natural arch from the living stone and the soft tufa rocks'.[4] Vines are described as tapestry, and pools of water are preternaturally clear.[5] Even where the description is explicitly of a natural scene, Ovid's palpable effect is artificial. Setting the scene in Book V for the narrative of the rape of Proserpine, the poet first alludes to the 'music' of swans on the lake of Pergus and then describes how a 'ring of trees encircles the pool, clothing [*sic*] the lakeside all around'; their 'boughs afford cool shade, and the lush meadow is bright with flowers'.[6]

Just as sixteenth- and seventeenth-century readers of Ovid's *Metamorphoses* could appreciate this art in his descriptions or in the natural things he describes, so visitors to Renaissance gardens could see their mixture of art and nature. As we shall examine later, this mixture was susceptible to various interpretations, some seeing nature brought out by art, some seeing art as mimicking nature. Man's own arts, in another formulation, were applied to the fallen natural world in order to recover his lost Eden; or, if gardens were thought of in classical not Christian terms, then Ovid had told of how the rare landscape of Arcady, too, had been re-created by Jupiter's art after being destroyed by Phaethon's rash act: the god 'restored its springs and the rivers . . . he clothed the earth with grass, the trees with leaves, and commanded the blasted forests to grow green again'.[7] What was achieved by divine or human art could none the less be viewed as if it were natural: Fynes Moryson, as we have already seen (above p. 31), described the grottoes at Pratolino as 'caves'. Garden art feigned a nature, and as Shakespeare's Touchstone put it 'The truest poetry is the most feigning'.[8]

Gardens encouraged visitors to think of Ovid: sometimes by an iconography which drew explicitly upon the *Metamorphoses*, sometimes by less deliberate but nonetheless palpable references, which in their turn recalled a poem which itself invoked gardens and garden art. Ovid glances at gardens when he likens the creation of the hermaphrodite to a gardener's grafting or lets Polyphemus sing of Galatea as 'fairer than a well-watered garden'.[9] There are other occasions when Ovid actually uses gardens as settings – most obviously when he narrates the story of such quintessentially hortulan characters as Pomona and Vertumnus in Book XIV. Moreover, some of his modern illustrators drew garden backgrounds when the text gave no warrant; such images were largely of Italianate gardens.[9]

One particular example of a garden's deliberate invocation of the Latin poem was at the Villa D'Este. Here in 1645 John Evelyn found 'a long & spacious Walk, full of Fountaines, under which is historiz'd the whole *Ovidian* Metamorphosis in *mezzo relievo* rarely sculptur'd'.[10] These terracotta plaques along the Walk of the Hundred Fountains are illustrated in various contemporary engravings (figure 28), although without any precision of subject. Today these plaques are obliterated with moss and maidenfern.

Figure 28 Walk of the Hundred Fountains with the bas-reliefs from Ovid's *Metamorphoses*, from Falda, *La Fontane . . . di Roma* (1675–1691), Part IV.

Maybe their condition pleases our latterday sense of the picturesque, but we thereby lose an essential aspect of the seventeenth-century experience of Italian Renaissance gardens. And around this specific allusion to Ovid the whole garden deploys scenery, images and designs which are ineluctably metamorphic. One anonymous traveller of 1610 certainly recorded his experience there in terms which rehearse characteristic elements of the poem:

> Then you may go down from the palace into the garden, where you shall be led into a vault, or grotto, where you shall see a terrible downfall of water, from whence all the other artificial water-works have their motions. . . . Go a little further, and you shall see a dragon with four heads, spouting water the height of six men, with so great a noise . . . the water being of so black a colour, that it resembleth an ugly smoke, fearful to behold. Then you shall see the Grotto, named Sybilla, full of admirable antiquities and statues. The grotto, both above on the ceiling, and all over on the sides, is richly adorned with oriental coral and mother of pearl. A little further you shall see the temples of the Seven Planets, naturally resembling those which formerly stood in Rome . . . Not far from thence is an artificial water-work, which being let go, the birds do sing, sitting upon twigs so naturally, as one would verily think they were all quick and living birds . . . and, when they are in the midst of their best singing, then comes an owl flying, and the birds suddenly, all at once, are still. Then go a little further, and you shall see twenty-four square stones, like chests, having on each side spouts, spiriting water one against another; and, when the sun doth shine thereinto, the spouts and water do give a natural rainbow, notwithstanding the weather be clear; which is a very great wonder, and, those who see it, would swear it were a natural rainbow indeed.[11]

44

The Villa Aldobrandini at Frascati has a garden which takes its theme of metamorphosis from a group of landscape paintings with Ovidian subjects originally displayed in the Hall of Apollo (figure 29) situated at one end of its water theatre (they are now in the National Gallery, London) (figure 30). Images of transformation, some of them wittily presented in *trompe l'oeil*, seemed an apt decoration for a Hall of Apollo, especially when at one end of it was

> fashioned a hill, Parnassus whereon set the nine Muses with severall winde Instruments that sound by art. Underneath this hill are Organs, which plaid divers tunes so distinctly, that wee conceiv'd some Master was playing on them, but looking we saw they went of themselves, the cause of all this wee afterwards saw; In the midst of the roome, there being a Hole out of which winde issueth, so violently, that for halfe a quarter of an houre it beares up a Ball.[12]

The imagery of this Hall of Apollo was echoed in the surrounding gardens, most immediately in the waterworks and their subjects: an Atlas with his globe spouting jets, the Centaur 'with a hunters horn at his mouth, who windeth it duly, and in perfect measure', the figure sounding its syrinx, 'whilst the Lyon and the Leopard fighting together spit angrily in one anothers faces, though all pass in cold blood, because in cold water'.[13] But the baroque handling of the architecture of this water theatre itself (figure 31) continues the motif of changefulness and surprise as well as incorporating more representations of Ovidian characters. Ionic capitals break out in wreaths or cornucopias; the rhythm of the columns around the theatre alternates flat ones which break through the line of the lower entablature with shorter round ones flanking the niches; while the columns that flank the three large alcoves are composed of caryatids or atlantes surmounted with urns overbrimming with fruit. Inside these larger alcoves tufa and pumice stone simulate natural rockwork, while in the two smaller ones pebbles and coloured stones are arranged more artificially. When the water was set in motion its facsimile storm 'imitated Rain, Hail, Snow and Thunder, which may be heard for miles'.[14]

Above the water theatre the gardens maintain the metamorphic play with the elements of art and nature. Evelyn's account, which draws and elaborates upon earlier descriptions, notes how the gardens have been transformed out of 'an high hill or mountaine all over clad with tall wood, and so form'd by nature, as if it had been cut out by Art'. Down this steep site, writes Evelyn,

> falls a horrid Cascade seeming rather a greate River than a streame, precipitating into a large Theater of Water representing a exact & perfect Raine-bow when the sun shines out: Under this is made an artificiall Grott, where in are curious rocks, hydraulic Organs & all sorts of singing birds moving & chirping by force of the water, with several other pageants and surprizing inventions . . .

The formal ingenuity of the water in the cascade was especially striking to the anonymous visitor of 1675: he saw the 'River' fall over in 'Cascata's, and other infinit forms seaven several times'.[15] But above the cascade, visible best from the *piano nobile* of the villa, the water was put through even more transformations, flowing down spiral troughs on two pillars. As the visitor ascended the hillside along the banks of Evelyn's 'seeming . . . River' he discovered that the water emerged from increasingly rustic fountains (see figure 112) – a witty surrender by art to a natural domain which it had nonetheless

Figure 29 The Hall of Apollo, Villa Aldobrandini, Frascati, from Falda, *La Fontane*, Part III.
Mount Parnassis is represented at the end, and on the walls are the rectangles where the paintings of
Ovidian subjects (see next Figure) hung.

Figure 30 Domenichino and assistants, *Apollo and Daphne*, fresco originally in the Hall of Apollo, Villa Aldobrandini, Frascati, 1605–6.

Figure 31 The Water Theatre, Villa Aldobrandini, Frascati, from Falda, *Le Fontane*, Part III.

created.[16] One further effect strikes the visitor who climbs the hill into these 'rustick' groves, for it is only from this elevation that he appreciates the formal significance of those two pillars ringed with water: for they exactly frame the strangely shaped central section of the villa, the gap between them echoing the vertical block of the house when seen from this 'natural' perspective.

An Ovidian response to gardens was doubtless inevitable when their designers and visitors alike were so alert to the aptness of his poem. Indeed, Joseph Addison in *Spectator* 523 denigrated 'Many of our Modern Authors, whose learning very often extends no further than Ovid's *Metamorphoses*'. But in another *Spectator* (no 417) he also – more tolerantly – equated Ovid with enchanted ground. So beyond or in addition to the Latin poet's contribution of metamorphic themes and mythical personages to garden iconography he signalled a territory where the natural and the rational were displaced by preternatural magic.[17] The more sophisticated or 'Mannerist' Italian gardens became, the more likely was the incidence of such enchanted ground.

In the Boboli Gardens in Florence Bernardo Buontalenti created a triple grotto which not only seems to play with formal metamorphoses but takes its narrative from Ovid's poem.[18] Even as we approach the façade of the grotto from the side of the Pitti Palace its architecture seems to yield to 'natural' rock which decorates the ridge of the building and descends around the arched entrance. By the time we reach the entrance and see inside, our experience is of a transformation of architecture into its natural materials; or, such is the ambiguity, of an opposite metamorphosis – rock and stone gradually shaping themselves into artifact. Inside the first room this ambiguous world is heightened by a scenery of men and animals who are either emerging out of or changing into stone (figure 32). The realism of the illusion is heightened by the frescoes of Bernardino Poccetti which depict a bizarre countryside glimpsed through imaginary cracks in the vault.

On the one hand, the 'cave' offers a scenario of impending disaster, with copies of Michelangelo's slaves (the originals were removed to the Accademia in 1908) struggling in the four corners to evade the disaster; alternatively, just as Michelangelo's slaves struggle to emerge from their own stone and from the rocky walls of the cavern, so do the shepherds, sheep and other animals appear to be growing from the porous and fretted rockwork, the same *spunge* (a Tuscan limestone) we first saw on the façade of the grotto. Such visual ambiguity derives from the grotto's rendition of a literary narrative in Ovid's Book I: first the destruction of the world by gods angered at mankind's impiety, then its regeneration by the two survivors, Deucalion and Pyrrha, who threw stones behind them which changed into men and women. Of course, what we read in temporal sequence in the poem has to be offered simultaneously in the grotto; but this increases what has been called the 'unexpected harmony' of the various media and their imagery.[19]

Figure 32 The first room of Buontalenti's grotto, Boboli Gardens, Florence.

The Ovidian resonance of this corner of the Boboli Gardens is augmented, in the same fashion as we have seen at Tivoli and Frascati, by statues which depict classical characters, some of whom might have been encountered first in the pages of the Roman poet. Outside the grotto are a Ceres and Apollo in niches; within the second chamber Paris abducting Helen; within the third, Venus emerging from her bath. Statues would recall characters from the *Metamorphoses*, especially if they had been transformed into stone;[20] but the decoration of special places in gardens with sculpture of mythical beings gave to pools, waterfalls, grottoes and groves the anthropomorphic presence that Ovid had set out to narrate; temples or other buildings and inscriptions equally recalled similar devices in Ovid whereby the meaning of some particular spot was made palpable.[21]

So when Raymond praised the villas of Frascati as 'fitter for the Gods to inhabit than men',[22] he was not speaking entire hyperbole: for gods and mythical creatures *did* inhabit the gardens in the form of their sculptural representations (see figure 2). In the 'Duke of Toledo's orchard' at Naples George Sandys discovered 'a place of surpassing delight; in which are many excellent Statues . . . and everywhere fountains of fresh water adorned with Nymphs & Satyres'.[23] Now Sandys was the translator of Ovid's *Metamorphoses* and could be expected to recognize readily the Ovidian resonance of Italian gardens. *Dramatis personae* from Ovid's poetry were certainly ubiquitous. What Lassels at the Villa Borghese in Rome called a 'world of such like fables'[24] included the rape of Europa; and at the Villa Giustiniani at the end of the seventeenth century the Frenchman, Bernard de Mont-faucon, whose book *The Antiquities of Italy* was translated twice into English during the early years of the eighteenth century, reported that he had seen a stone inscribed with Ovid's lines about Egeria, who was (he noted) 'formerly famous for that fictitious and receiv'd familiarity with Numa Pompilius'. Montfaucon was probably wrong to attribute the lines he read to Ovid;[25] but what concerns us is that a man who made a point of studying inscriptions should use one of them in conjunction with his knowledge of Ovid to identify the 'Grove of Egeria, and the Muses' in the Giustiniani gardens.

Evelyn encountered the statue of Ovid – along with those of Virgil, Petrarch and Dante – as he ascended to the Villa Poggio Imperiale from the Porta Romana of Florence 'by a stately Gallery as it were of talle & overgrown Cypresse trees for neere halfe a mile'.[26] That Ovid should be associated with an avenue that seemed an interior gallery is apt. Many were the transformations of form and material that other villas and gardens authorized directly or by implication in his name. Similar metamorphoses of trees into galleries were noted elsewhere.[27] At the Villa Lante even arcs of water formed a long tunnel through which 'a man may passe drye under the element of water'.[28] The formal ambiguities of inside/outside were specifically appreciated in loggias (figure 33), indeterminate areas between house and garden which must have seemed strange sights to early English visitors. Fynes Moryson at the Villa Medici in Rome in 1593 spoke wonderingly of 'a Gallery open on the sides towards the Garden'; indeed he saw the whole garden as somehow a *mélange* of inside and out – its walks were like corridors, its arbours 'as it were chambers' and the ascent to the mount made by 'stairs paved with carved Marble'.[29] That the 'Gallery' was also 'full of beautiful Images' was appropriate, too, since other loggias were famous for their Ovidian motifs. At the Farnesina Evelyn noticed a fresco 'on the Volto of the Portico towards the Garden, the story is the Amours of Cupid & Psyche'; so impressed was he that he returned to the Farnesina during his second visit to Rome in

Figure 33 Gerrit Houckgeest, Loggia of a Renaissance Palance, painting of mid-seventeenth century.

order to admire 'the Terrace where is that admirable paynting of Raphael being a Cupid playing with a Dolphin'.[30] If he refers, as presumably he must, to the Galatea, he would probably have come across her story first in his Ovid.

The impression that loggias were a marvellously indeterminate world of both inside and outside was cultivated to a fine pitch at the Villa Giulia in Rome.[31] The loggias stretching out from the main building were decorated by Taddeo Zuccaro or his assistants to give the illusion of a pergola bearing roses, vines and jasmine on which birds and *putti* are perched. When the visitor reached the sunken nymphaeum itself (figure 34) the complexities of inside and outside were further intensified by the excitements of its different levels. This exquisite sunken garden room, like other less handsome nymphaeums, was fully Ovidian in its recall of the poet's many descriptions of nymphs and springs. The English visitor of 1610 was delighted by 'excellent artificial water-works . . . rare antiquities and statues'.[32] The nymphs at Villa Giulia are transformed into the pillars above the pool, while on a higher level river gods and inscriptions which draw attention to the history of the villa and to the pleasures afforded by its flowers, trees, fountains, statues and paintings all contribute to the visitor's recognition of this garden's particular

51

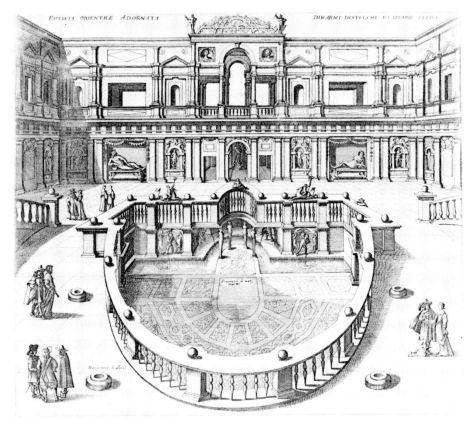

Figure 34 The nymphaeum and its courtyard in the Villa Giulia, Rome, from Falda, *Le Fontane*, Part III.

resonance. Even where inscriptions were not available to direct the mind's attention, visual clues were sufficient: we have already seen how Evelyn responded to the statues of Neptune and Jupiter, prime actors in Ovid's dramas, when he encountered them on the Doria terraces at Genoa.

Even before Richard Lassels reached Italy he was remarking upon the metamorphic effects of Italianate waterworks at some house on the road from Paris to Lyon: a stream was directed into 'little open channells of free stone built like knots of flowers; all which it fills brimfull, and makes even flowers of water'.[33] The transforming powers of water, to which Ovid's poem makes frequent reference, were called upon to perform many of a garden's wonders. It worked the 'false birds chirping upon true trees' at Tivoli as well as the hydraulic organs that made the beautiful music there and at the Palace on the Quirinal, 'without any fingers to touch it'. It made artificial rain at the Villa Borghese and at the Villa D'Este.[34] And it activated the *giocchi d'acqua* – water jokes or wetting places – which by the quick turn of a concealed stopcock trapped unwary visitors in watery ambushes (the wise, apparently, carried a change of clothing). These water jokes elicit rather stern disapproval from modern commentators, like A. H. S. Yeames who talks of an Englishman's 'naive delight in the waterworks at the villas, a delight shared even by men like

Montaigne'.[35] Perhaps the mention of Montaigne, who indeed much enjoyed these devices as did Mortoft in the 1650s and Bromley in the 1690s,[36] should alert us to their true significance which was, surely, less their childish practical joking than their contribution to a garden's larger world of change and wonder.

At Villa Lante – which Lassels reports as a 'Garden of waterworks and Fountains, worth seeing' – water was manipulated into various ingenious forms besides the tunnel already noticed. First, in the *catena d'acqua* (figure 35), where the outside of the stone trough is sculpted to look like waves, the water flows so fast over roughly worked stone that it assumes itself the appearance of stone. It is next transformed into balustrades on the staircases, a device ('out of every Rail . . . runs a thread of Water') also invoked at Frascati and Tivoli (see figure 44). Then after providing pools for two river gods it transforms the top of a stone table into a wine cooler, and finally it simulates cannon shot from the boats in the miniature *naumachia* on the parterre.[37] At Frascati visitors noticed water used not only as stair rails but as 'an open staircase of water'; when it was not involved in such formal conceits – falling in 'divers figures', as Warcupp reported of the Villa D'Este – it was admired for its perfect stillness and its resemblance to 'Looking Glasses'.[38]

But above all water manipulated the automata in grottoes, and since the motifs of most of these devices were or could be associated with Ovidian characters the changeful element of water became an integral part of the Latin poet's gardenist contribution. In the Boboli Gardens Francis Mortoft found, among the 'invention(s) and rare Art of man', 'a

Figure 35 The *catena d'acqua* at the Villa Lante, Bagnaia, with beyond it the table with water trough and the water parterre.

great Pillar of Marble with a very great Basin of Marble on the top of it, and in it the statue of Neptune, and many other Images about him out of which the water flows'.[39] And when Raymond lists the fountains among the groves of the Villa D'Este, it is the Ovidian *dramatis personae* he names as their centrepieces: Tethys, Arethusa, Pomona and Flora. Even when such mythical characters were not originally associated with water, as Neptune and Tethys always were, it is nevertheless by water that they were presented to visitors: so Mortoft at the Villa Mattei in Rome found Hercules slaying the Hydra in an arbour where waterworks were installed to wet spectators. By far the most famous and prolific series of such hydraulic wonders, seemingly able to animate their legendary figures, was to be found at the Medici villa of Pratolino, north of Florence (figure 36).

There are many descriptions of the Ovidian marvels of Pratolino from Fynes Moryson to William Kent. The most concise and useful for present purposes is that in Lassels's *The Voyage of Italy*. Having first stressed the sloping site down which the 'Excellent Grotts, Fountains [and] waterworks' were distributed, he then details some of the 'action' presented in them:

> that of Pan striking up a melodious tune upon his mouthorgan at the sight of his Mistress, appearing over against him: that where the Angel carries a trumpet to his Mouth, and soundeth it; and where the Country Clown offers a Dish of Water to a Serpent, who drinks it, and lifteth up his head when he hath drunk: that of the Mill which seems to break and grind Olives: the Paper Mill: the Man with the Grinding Stones: the Sarazens head gaping and spewing out Water; the Grotte of Galatea who comes out of a Dore in a Sea Chariot with two Nymphs, and saileth a while upon the Water, and so returns again in at the same Dore; the curious round table capable of twelve or fifteen men, with a curious fountain playing constantly in the midst of it, and places between every trencher, or person, for every man to set his bottle of wine in cold water: the Samaritan Woman coming out of her house with her buckets to fetch water at the fountain, and having filled her buckets, returns back again the same way: in the mean time you see Smiths thumping, Birds chirping in trees, Mills grinding: and all this done by Water, which sets these little inventions awork, and makes them move as it were of themselves . . .

Obviously the range of a garden's reference was always wider than one single poem, the *Metamorphoses*; but its central and most prized events of this kind seem to have been Ovidian. Literary descriptions are perhaps somewhat more successful at communicating these moving contraptions than static visual images; but the Modenese artist Giovanni Guerra, who sketched at Pratolino in the late sixteenth century, did manage with the aid of annotations to capture some impression of these automata at Pratolino in motion (see figure 37).[40] As Guerra's drawings testify, it is the sheer mechanical virtuosity of these images as much as their iconographical meaning that impressed visitors. And despite a growing familiarity with the technical explanations of these marvels – derived either from handbooks of hydraulic science[41] or from visits behind the scenes to see how things worked – it is the illusion of reality that continued to delight visitors. Fifty years after Moryson admired the cave 'by Art so made, as you would feare to enter it, least great stones should fall upon your head', John Evelyn considered the 'Laundresse [fountain] wringing Water out of a piece of linnen' done 'very naturally'; more than fifty years later still William Kent seems to have been enchanted by 'Galatea coming out of her Grotto drawn by Dolfini' (figure 37).[42]

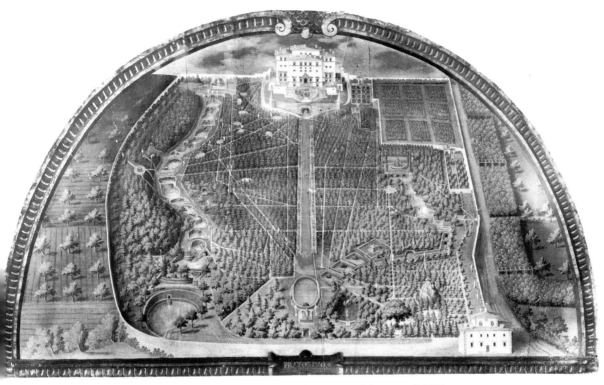

Figure 36 Gustave Utens, *The Medici Villa of Pratolino*, painted lunette of 1599.

The mythical narratives which Pratolino enacted – Pan, Hercules, Galatea, Pegasus and the Helicon spring on Mount Parnassus, Vulcan and Jupiter, among others – all have their literary counterparts if not their sources in Ovid's *Metamorphoses*. The largest item in the gardens, Giambologna's figure of the Apennines, not only recalled various specific moments in the poem but (it has been suggested) seems even to derive from illustrated editions of Ovid.[43] In Book IV we read that 'Atlas was changed into a mountain as huge as the giant he had been', and certainly the figure at Pratolino seems to enact that very transformation (figure 38). But the flexibility of response which such garden imagery allowed, since nothing specifically directs the visitor's attention to a particular passage in Ovid, also authorized the colossal figure's being interpreted in ways that referred to other incidents. Various visitors thought the figures was bending down to pick up a stone to hurl at them, thus perhaps recalling two occasions in Books XIII and XIV when the Cyclops tore up earth and boulders to throw at his enemies.[44]

What the Apennines statue also declares is a fascination with representing or registering movement which the garden's metamorphic ambience promoted. Hydraulic machinery was used extensively to make mute stones both sing and move; but even non-hydraulic objects in gardens were observed as if they were moving. Lassels saw the huge figure at Pratolino '*stooping* to catch at a rock, to throw' and another statue in the Vatican Belvedere he recorded as 'Venus *coming out* of a bath'.[45] The Grotto of the Unicorn at Castello

55

Figure 37 Giovanni Guerra, hydraulic show in a grotto at Pratolino, drawing of 1600. The drawing is inscribed with the words, 'When the Triton sounds his horn, Galatea comes forth'.

contained no hydraulic equipment, yet the lifelike attitudes of the animals – cunningly created with real horn and tusks and lifelike colouring – often convinced visitors that the creatures were about to move; indeed, the part they have been shown to play in the villa's iconographical programme specifically involved the illusion of movement, as the unicorn has supposedly just arrived in order to dip his horn into the poisoned waters so that the other animals could drink.[46]

The fascination with illusionary motion in sculpture was, of course, not restricted to gardens. In the verses which Evelyn composed to summarize his experiences in the Eternal City he singles out the metamorphic qualities of sculpture that seemed to move:

> The furious *Bull*, calv'd from a rock, like this
> There never was a *Metamorphosis*:
> The *Gladiator* who still seems to fight,
> And the hard-soft, bed-rid *Hermaphrodite*:
> Chast *Daphne's* limbs into the Laurel shoote,
> Whilst her swift feete the amorous Center roote;
> How the rude bark invades her virgin Snow,
> And dos to that well timber'd body grow!

He refers there to both the Farnese Bull and to two of Bernini's statues inside the Villa Borghese, which seemed entirely consonant with the marvels outside in the gardens. Other visitors commented upon the *Apollo and Daphne* and the *Hermaphrodite* 'that turns in her sleep to a man, lying upon a quilt', of which Evelyn in fact bought an ivory copy.

56

Figure 38 Giambologna, statue of the Apennines, Pratolino.

When in 1726 Breval comes to discuss this particular piece of sculpture in *Remarks on Several Parts of Europe* he actually quotes the relevant lines from Ovid's Book IV.[47]

The theme of Ovid in the garden obviously touches upon many other aspects of late sixteenth- and seventeenth-century culture which it is not possible or necessary to expound here. For example, the delight in a garden's changeful forms is of a piece with the fascination with anamorphic landscapes or the paintings of Giuseppe Arcimboldo, and all three are elements of the contemporary absorption in perspective and other forms of illusion and wit.[48] Jean Dubreuil in his *Perspective practique* offers suggestions for large-scale perspectives and *trompe l'oeil* vistas for gardens, and many of the latter were constructed. But the direct and the implied references to Ovid's poem by both designers and visitors give the Latin poet a prime role in the garden and its history. He authorized marvels and enchantments: it seemed perfectly apt that the Dragon from the Hesperidean Garden should be found on guard in the Villa D'Este (figure 48); it was one of those 'stupendous things' which Taegio's dialogue on the villa acknowledged in Scipione Simonetta's garden in Milan.[49]

Ovid's poem encouraged habits of mind which could find references to his work in landscape otherwise innocent of it, as when Raymond, after leaving the villas of Frascati that he had thought a territory fit for the gods, says that he passed 'Diana's Lake, and the wood famous for the fiction of Acteon'.[50] Equally, the play with forms which was so essential to the later Italian Renaissance garden did not derive solely if at all from Ovid; but it gained from the *Metamorphoses* a suitable literary authority. The anonymous traveller who was in Italy in 1675 could be impressed variously with the curves of a wall in the gardens of La Veneria outside Turin, the various shapes of trees ('great round tops, and streight Stocks') in a garden at Veletri, a turning picture and a landscape in mosaic at the Villa Montalto in Rome, and at the Vatican with a fountain 'like a River out of rude Rock cover'd with Greens'. They all reveal his delight in a range of experiences which I have called Ovidian.[51]

One visitor to the Valmarana Gardens at Vicenza gave as the 'substance' of an inscription he had read on one of its gates

> Stop, dear Traveller, then, who searchest for rare things, and enchanted places,
> for here thou may'st find satisfaction . . .

There were, in fact, three inscriptions, which Thomas Coryate carefully noted in 1608, and they all speak of a garden world of mythical proportions – Vertumnus and Pomona are the sacred genii of the place, all things obnoxious are banished from it, and it announces itself as a *locus amoenus*, the traditionally pleasant or lovely place, using a phrase which carries the full *imprimatur* of the classic poets.[52] Exclamations that some Italian garden is 'a terrestriall Paradise', 'the very Elysian Fields', or 'a Heaven on Earth' are commonplace.[53] But it is the specific edge that Ovidian reference gives to such clichés that is crucial. His presence will also be felt in later discussions of variety in a garden, of its dialogues between art and nature, and in the topic to which we must now turn, the relationship of garden to theatre.

5 Garden and Theatre

The organization of garden space to accommodate and present visitors with the Ovidian narratives discussed in the previous section clearly recalls contemporary theatrical experience in ballets, *intermezzi*, *drame per musica*, operas or masques. Especially when the Ovidian incidents were animated by hydraulic machinery (figure 39) and thus moved in front of spectators, often to the accompaniment of music as at Pratolino, the equivalence of garden and theatre was palpable. Indeed, the relationship of theatre and garden in the late Italian Renaissance was particularly close and indelibly marked the English reaction to the latter.[1]

The progress of that relationship need not concern us in detail. It is necessary simply to rehearse what is by now established in theatre history, namely that Renaissance gardens came to play a significant part in the search for an appropriate theatrical space, a *lieu théâtral* or *luogo teatrale*. In medieval times dramatic presentations had been given on carts or specially erected platforms in public spaces of the city. Renaissance princes took over this *ad hoc* staging and carried their stately rituals, entries and ceremonies to a fine and elaborate perfection.[2] They presented their festivals and celebrations in various specially constructed spaces, sometimes indoors, sometimes outside in cities or – since these were also a recent example of princely status – in the gardens of their palaces. One English visitor to Florence was pleased by festivities which included 'a Horse dance . . . in a Garden behind the Great Dukes Pallace'.[3] Such presentations usually necessitated extravagant but ephemeral structures and special effects. Gradually, however, buildings and gardens came to include areas which would serve permanently as arenas, to be decorated and augmented with scenery on given occasions. We know, for example, that the lowest level of Bramante's Belvedere Courtyard at the Vatican was in part designed to accommodate the rituals of state entries as well as entertainments: in 1565 it was used for a tournament during carnival time.[4]

Theatres were often as sophisticated and rare a sight for the early tourists as gardens, and responses to their Italian experience were often coloured by this: thus Sir Thomas Hoby in the mid-sixteenth century noted that the piazza at Siena was 'made after the maner of a theatre'; Raymond made the same observation a hundred years later about the

Figure 39 Grotto, from Salomon de Caus, *Les Raisons des Forces Mouvantes* (1615). De Caus shows Galatea and Polyphemus, and the machinery that animated them.

port of Genoa.[5] This interest in theatrical space and architecture was shown – and with more justification – in their reactions to gardens. Philip Skippon described the Boboli Gardens as 'a large green spot of ground built about with seats of stone, like a theatre . . .'; and William Acton found a church garden in Rome that 'was heretofore a Theatre'.[6] At Parma Richard Lassels saw the Duke's palace 'with the Gardens, Fountains . . . & admirable Theatre to exhibit opera's in', and Edward Browne records that the Marchese Obizzi's country house near Padua had a 'Theatre for Comedies'.[7] The courtyard of the Pitti Palace in Florence and the amphitheatre of the Boboli Gardens behind it were used for Medici spectacles, and Veryard admired the ranges of seats 'on which people sit and see the sports that are here exhibited'.[8] Several engravings of festivities in this amphitheatre survive,[9] and it is by means of such permanent records of ephemeral occasions that Englishmen would become acquainted with theatrical events with which their visits did not coincide.

Gardens, of course, offered ideal locations for patrician festivals in a hot climate, and gradually, from simply including in their spaces areas adaptable for dramatic performances, they came to possess actual theatres. By the second half of the seventeenth century the Villa Marlia, near Lucca, had a green theatre, with a stage and stepped semicircular 'auditorium', in addition to other areas shaped with the same theatrical effect (figure 40). Nearby the Villa Garzoni at Collodi included another small theatre, but the whole garden was itself designed in theatrical format.

Figure 40 The gardens of the Villa Marlia, near Lucca, in a late seventeenth-century engraving. The theatre is to the extreme right, but other 'theatrical' areas can also be seen.

Such 'theatrically' shaped space in Italian gardens had complex origins. It derived from a study of classical architecture and from an adaptation to new purposes of old structures not necessarily used or known to be used as theatres. At the highest point of the Temple of Fortune at Palestrina (see figure 83) performances were probably given in Roman times,[10] but it is unlikely that Bramante knew this when he adapted its exedra for the Vatican Belvedere courtyard (figure 41). This striking feature – a descending concave set of steps leading to a circular platform from which an answering set of convex steps descended further – became a distinctive garden form. Doubtless this was because the Temple at Palestrina was explored by influential architects and garden designers like Ligorio and Palladio and because the Vatican adaptation of its stairs was codified and illustrated by Serlio.[11] But the attraction of these steps for their own sake, their ability to negotiate a hillside while allowing the spectator to pause and view above and below, must have urged their use as well. One finds them everywhere, miniaturized echoes of the Serlio/Bramante original or full-scale adaptations like that on the Isola Bella in Lake Maggiore (figure 42). Burnet wrote about this in a letter from Milan, describing 'a great Mount':

> that face of it that looks to the Parterre is made like a Theatre, all full of Fountains and Statues, the height rising up in five several Rows, it being about 50 foot high, and about fourscore foot in front; and round this Mount, answering to the five rows into which the Theatre is divided, there goes as many Terraces of noble walks . . .[12]

Figure 41 Exedra in the Vatican Belvedere, from Serlio, *Tutto l'opere d'architettura*, Book III (1619).

Figure 42 Theatre in the gardens of the Isola Bella, Lake Maggiore, from M. A. Dal Re, *Ville di Delizia* (1726).

The survival of an identical structure, in grass rather than in stone, in Bridgeman's Claremont gardens in the 1720s (see figure 95) suggests the persistence of both Italian gardens and their theatrical dimension in the English landscape movement.

But those steps were not the only classically derived shape which lent theatrical colour to garden design. From a study of extant ruins – exedras, nymphaeums, actual theatres and amphitheatres, but also baths, temples and libraries which had apsidal features – and from classical texts which discussed ancient architecture (above all, but not exclusively, Vitruvius) the architects of Renaissance gardens freely adapted features which gave some 'theatrical' potential to their design. Roman arenas were generally known and were imitated in large spaces like the Boboli Gardens and in the smaller openings among the groves of such parks as the Villa Doria Pamphili. Especially nymphaeums were seen to have considerable theatrical possibilities (see figures 2 and 43):[13] originally natural caves, with sacred springs haunted by water nymphs, they were developed by the Romans into architectural structures, which in their turn were imitated widely in the Renaissance – the Villa Giulia in Rome has a particularly beautiful one; Palladio's at Maser is strikingly apsidal in shape. Other more cave-like nymphaeums (see figure 37) readily presented themselves as models for 'scenes' which new statuary or automata would confirm. Even etymological confusions yielded their contribution: the apparent confusion of *cava* (cave or grotto) and *cavea* (the tiers of seats in a theatre) occasioned a particularly notable feature at the Villa Lante – semicircular tiers, convex not concave, with water jets at regular intervals, from which a view of the 'naumachia' below could be taken.[14] Fountains, as there at the Villa Lante, could recreate another form of antique spectacle, the sea-battle; or courtyards, as at the Pitti Palace, could be flooded on occasions to hold naumachias in a more authentically classical manner.[15]

Pliny's celebrated description of 'some immense amphitheatre' at his Tuscan villa was echoed, as we have seen, by many Renaissance architects eager for classical authority to back their own productions. Palladio in particular continued the classical tradition by suggesting that the ground immediately surrounding a villa should be given the 'aspetto di grande teatro'.[16] Such organization of space outside the immediate garden was obviously not the same thing as creating actual theatres or theatrically shaped spaces inside: but it contributed to the overall connection of gardens and theatres and by its attention to land outside the garden ensured that such connections continued to be of significance during the English landscape movement.

Just to glance at an engraving of the Villa D'Este (figure 43) is to be struck by the number of spaces which deploy versions of various antique structures in order to present statues and waterworks as if they were an entertainment – 'the great Father Oceanus placed in a semicircle like a Theatre'[17] – while spaces were terminated by façades of grottoes (figure 44) which invited visitors to their 'theatres' within. Alternatively, the view over the Campagna towards Rome gave the Este gardens the air – à la Pliny – of a viewing-stand for the amphitheatre of the plain. That these and other gardens, grottoes and vistas were indeed seen as theatres is clear from various testimony: Maximilian Misson was at Genoa in the late 1680s and rather deprecated the calculated scenographic effects of the city's famous gardens and grottoes by likening them to the 'Machins of an Opera'.[18] But in Rome in the 1720s Edward Wright described the 'Grotto finta' at the Villa Altieri with its rocky hermitage as 'disposed in a scene-like manner, romantick enough'.[19] It is not surprising, therefore, that Warcupp's English translation of Schott invokes the language of a masque's stage directions to describe the visitor's experiences at Tivoli: 'In the descent into the first garden, shews itself the Colossus of Pegasus', or 'riseth an Island cut in the shape of a ship'.[20] And Fynes Moryson's account of Pratolino, another garden much disposed in theatrical forms, uses the language of the dumb show:

> Syrinx beckening to Pan, to play upon the pipe, Pan puts away his stoole with one hand, then standing on foot, plaies upon his pipe, and this done, lookes upon his mistresse, as if he desired thanks or a kisse for his paines: and then takes his stoole againe, and sits down with a sad countenance.[21]

The organization of the grotto of Fame and Pan at Pratolino clearly promoted and enhanced a visitor's expectations of 'dramas'. Once entered he looked to left or right

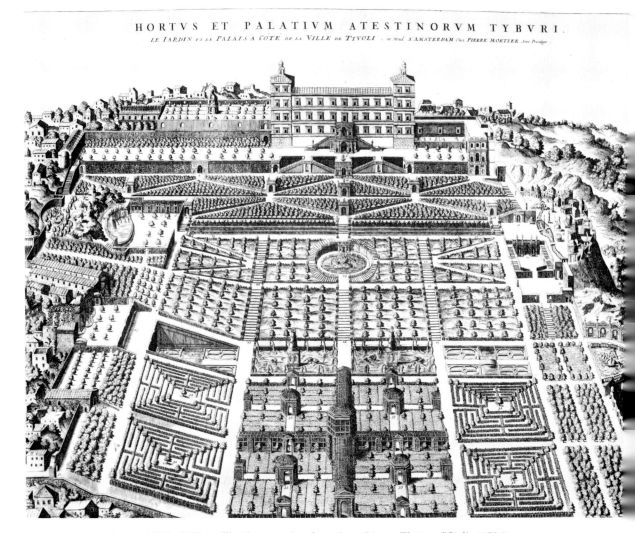

HORTVS ET PALATIVM ATESTINORVM TYBVRI.
LE IARDIN ET LE PALAIS A COTE DE LA VILLE DE TIVOLI . se vend A AMSTERDAM Chez PIERRE MORTIER Avec Privilege .

Figure 43 Villa D'Este, Tivoli, engraving from Jean Bleau, *Théâtre d'Italie* (1704).

Figure 44 Fountain of the Dragons, Villa D'Este, Tivoli, from Falda, *Le Fontane di Roma*. Notice the 'balustrades' of the double staircase which are in fact streams of water.

(figure 45) where the hydraulic figures were set at the ends of the arcade as if in two proscenium arches. In other parts of these gardens alternative theatrical forms were used, such as the simple horseshoe bench opposite the Parnassus from which visitors could watch the Muses' concert (figure 46). Later, more baroque garden designs, like that of the Aldobrandini water theatre, were far more emphatic in name as well as form.[22] At Aldobrandini the concave semicircle, associated with Roman baths or the auditoria of antique theatres, becomes a stage to be watched from the central loggia and windows of the villa; a visitor like Raymond specifically writes of those watching the centaur, the faun and Atlas in this arena as 'spectators'.[23] In Rome at the Villa Borghese Wright thought that its grounds were 'a perfect countrey, cut out into various scenes . . .'[24]

A revealing testimony of the English visitor's linking of garden and theatre was left by John Evelyn. Of a visit to the Villa Mondragone at Frascati his diary records its 'Theater for Pastimes'.[25] The phrase is interesting, not least because he neglected the expression ('Ampio theatro') available to him in one of his sources in favour of his own. To what extent Evelyn intended to load his expression with significance is unclear, but some of its possible connotations are worth elucidating.

In the first place Evelyn was obviously referring to the Mondragone water theatre (figure 47), so-called because of its shape and its provision of hydraulic entertainments. Like its larger neighbour, Aldobrandini, Mondragone had a curving, apsidal wall broken by seven niches filled with statues, these niches echoing the seven entrances in Alberti's antique theatre. This exedra, furthermore, is set upon a platform which gives it an even

65

Figure 45 The Grotta del Mugnone, Pratolino, engraving by Stephano della Bella. The Mugnone rivergod faced the visitor upon entering, at which point there was a scene at either end of the grotto, which is what is shown here.

Figure 46 Giovanni Guerra, Parnassus, Pratolino, and the 'theatre' for viewing it, drawing of 1600.

66

Figure 47 Water theatre, Villa Mondragone, Frascati, from Falda, *La Fontane di Roma*.

greater appearance of a stage. On this was a sunken nymphaeum where additional
waterworks presented what the President de Brosses in 1739 called 'polypriapic' entertainments:[26] these were presumably among Evelyn's 'pastimes'. But the variety and extent
of such waterworks in these Frascati villas also struck visitors with such an impression of
fullness that these were theatres in the sense of compendia or collections (as in Jean Blaeu's
Théâtre d'Italie, a three-volume compilation of all the noteworthy sights, or John Parkinson's *Theatrum Botanicum. The Theatre of Plants, or an Universall and Compleate Herball*).
Significantly perhaps, another word much in vogue to signal such a compendium was
garden, as when Peacham described his *Minerva Britanna* as 'a Garden of Heroicall
Devises, furnished, and adorned with *Emblemes* and *Impresa's*'.[27] This coincidence of
usage between theatre and garden is not therefore entirely fortuitous. Evelyn's 'Theater
for Pastimes' implies both a collection or conspectus of amusements and a stage or arena on
which they were presented.

Italian gardens were much admired, as will be seen, for their fullness and variety; they
offered miniature worlds, in the same way that an Elizabethan theatre like the Globe had
done. Sir Henry Wotton thought that a man's house was the theatre of his self-fruition
both because it was a stage for his self-knowledge and because 'to the possessors thereof [it
was] an Epitome of the whole world'.[28] So gardens could participate in this theme of
theatrum mundi, representing along with the house an epitome of the world envisaged like a
theatre. This was a popular perspective, which saw that, just as a theatre stage could
represent the world, the globe, in miniature, so could all the world be a stage (to use
Shakespeare's famous formulation of this commonplace). As one commentator puts it, all

67

the world's 'events, or plot, and its inhabitants, or *dramatis personae*, are depicted as taking place and acting within its confines and within its particular terms as a medium of representation'.[29] And in this view of the garden, as in the more complex versions of *theatrum mundi*, man was both spectator and actor. At Mondragone, therefore, the platform with its apsidal 'set' could be viewed as the stage from the courtyard below; but once upon the stage and a part of its dramas a visitor was also able to turn his attention to the garden court below, in which case the curved wall now behind him on the platform recalled the curved auditorium of the Vitruvian theatre and so became the *cavea* from which he viewed the lower garden and its visitors.

If a garden recalled the world, then its imagery functioned as a device to remind visitors of that plenitude beyond its grounds. The iconographical programmes of Villa D'Este, Castello or Villa Lante were designed to trigger certain responses in visitors, release specific ideas and themes stored previously in their memory. These habits of shaping responses to a Renaissance garden recall the classical art of training the memory as formulated in Cicero's *De oratore* and Quintilian's *Institutio oratoria*. The art of systematizing memory was devised to assist orators in the delivery of long speeches before the days of paper and pencil; they organized their ideas beforehand in a proper sequence, storing these *imagines* in a series of *loci* in some building. Quntilian says it must be a varied building and that the orator should use all its rooms, ornaments and statues as his *aides-mémoires*. We then have to think of the orator as he delivered his speech moving in imagination through the sequence of these *topoi*, *sedes* or common *places* and retrieving his ideas from the locations where he had stored them. Later commentators on the technique insisted that buildings should be real ones, well-known to the orator and, for obvious reasons, memorable 'aut natura aut manu'. The relevance of this rhetorical method to the art of constructing and reading gardens is as obvious as it is exciting. Frances Yates's book *The Art of Memory* continuously provides material which – though she is not concerned to make the connections – is analogous to garden experience. For example, Cicero's five rules for choosing memory places could well be prescriptions for Italianate garden design: quiet spots to avoid having one's concentration disturbed, various so that the memory would not be confused with too much repetition, neither too large nor too small, neither too dark nor too well-lighted, with intervals between them of about 30 feet – just as a garden spaces out its imagery, grottoes, statues and inscriptions.[30]

The art of memory shares with garden art an essential overlap between inner and outer images – sight and insight working together. It is therefore no wonder that Yates suggests the presence of memory systems behind Colonna's *Hypnerotomachia*, where in his dream Polifilus wanders through a sequence of marvellous landscapes and garden scenes in each of which he learns or remembers.[31] Both Tasso and Ariosto, also, whose works drew upon and in their turn lent themselves to garden imagery, acknowledged the work of one of the most strenuous proponents during the Renaissance of the art of memory – Giulio Camillo.[32] He actually created and built a wooden memory theatre, with images and inscriptions hung up inside or in drawers underneath the relevant images; it was intended as a complete conspectus of knowledge, quite literally and in a double sense a *theatrum mundi*. Its design was probably based on that of the Vitruvian theatre, which reflected the proportions of the world. Camillo himself actually compared his theatre to a large landscape prospect, and we know of one villa near Milan in the mid-sixteenth century where, apparently, a model of Camillo's theatre was incorporated into the estate of Pomponio Cotta; a local guidebook reports that 'amongst the marvellous pictures which are there, may be seen the lofty and incomparable fabric of the marvellous Theatre of the excellent Giulio Camillo'. Above all, Camillo reverses the 'normal function of the theatre', as Yates points out: 'There is no audience sitting in the seats watching a play on the stage. The solitary "spectator" of the Theatre stands where the stage would be and looks toward the auditorium, gazing at the images on the seven times seven gates on the seven rising grades.'[33] In other words, the same reversal of functions and forms that we have noticed in the theatre-garden of Mondragone.

Camillo's determination to establish a 'total world-reflecting system' was vastly more ambitious than some of the programmes invented for Renaissance gardens like the Villa D'Este and the Medici villa at Castello, yet the reactions expected of spectators in each were very similar. Edward Wright in the 1720s responded to Italian gardens as if his memory was being tapped for what it had previously stored: visiting Naples and finding himself at Scipio Africanus's villa he recalled a story from Valerius Maximus because (as he put it) 'I happen to be now at that Place of Retirement which was the *scene* of it'; more generally, he numbered among the entertainments of Italy the opportunities in face of antique imagery to cast his mind 'almost two thousand years backwards, and mix (. . .) the past ages with the present'.[34] What is particularly interesting about the parallels between the theatre of memory and the garden is that when a garden did not in fact complete the installation of all the objects necessary for its programme, guidebooks would nevertheless enlarge upon the items that were there, using those hints to trigger off a range of further memories that would indeed complete the 'scene' for the visitor. At Tivoli, for example, of a series of statues representing Leda and her children by the swan (Castor and Pollux, Helen of Troy) only Leda's was installed: yet Warcupp's account presents this part of the garden as if *all* the pieces were there.[35]

All this is heavy freightage to load upon John Evelyn's phrase, 'Theater for Pastimes'. Obviously, he himself did not intend to articulate all those connotations. Yet it has already been argued (above p. 6) that English visitors responded to gardens with a whole range of assumptions and ideas that were not necessarily available together or at a conscious level but nevertheless seemed to be implied in their reactions. So in the casual remarks of English visitors on gardens and theatres it is possible to see hints of larger structures of response not always available at the surface of the mind. It seems clear to me that these habits of registering gardens as theatrical spaces, as anthologies of the fuller world beyond their walls or ha-has and as commonplaces to initiate sometimes quite complicated trains of thought were invoked at least unconsciously, but sometimes deliberately, throughout the seventeenth century and would continue to be of consequence to the early landscape garden.[36]

The theatrical possibilities of gardens were complemented and confirmed by the incidence of gardens in theatre settings. Travellers seem to have made the connection themselves. When John Raymond's introduction to *Il Mercurio Italico* reviews the opportunities of Italy, he passes directly from its garden art to its theatre or 'sceanes', where he instances Venetian opera and the entertainments for the Duke of Florence's marriage. While he was in Siena he saw an opera 'with severall changes of Scenes, as a Garden, Sea, Pallace, and other Machines, at which Italians are spoke to be excellent'.[37] Other visitors noticed changing scenery, something of a rarity in the public theatres of England before the Restoration: Skippon mentioned it in connection with the Venetian theatre, and Lassels reported how among the 'Shows of Rome' was 'the curious Opere, or musical Drammata . . . set forth with such wonderful changes of *scenes*, that nothing could be more surprizing'.[38] English visitors with memories of Stuart masques or with experience of reading their published texts should have been less surprised.

Gardens were prominent among such theatrical settings: Lassels singled out 'Temples and Boscos' (i.e. groves). Some part of the explanation for their prominence was the authority that Serlio's satyric scene (figure 48) may have lent to representations of woodland groves.[39] Further, many operas and musical dramas had pastoral subjects, in which gardens and groves inevitably featured; or their dramatic actions involved Ovidian worlds of transformation and mythical personages, with which gardens had also been associated. But another probable reason was that, since dramatic entertainments had been presented in gardens during the Renaissance, seventeenth-century stage-designers saw garden scenery as intrinsic to a dramatic experience; to have garden scenes within a theatre, the reverse of having theatre outside in a garden, was a metamorphic interchange made all the more

Figure 48 The satyric scene, from Serlio, *Tutto l'opere dell'architettura*, Book II.

70

Figure 49 Fountain theatre in the gardens of the Villa Doria Pamphili, Rome, from Falda, *Le Fontane di Roma*.

inevitable since artists and technicians designed for both gardens and theatres. Bernardo Buontalenti, for example, worked on the villa and probably on the grotto entertainments at Pratolino, and was also employed to design *intermezzi* for Medici. But stage-designers like the Venetian Giacomo Torelli (1608–78) produced many stage sets of gardens which obviously re-created inside theatres recognizable, if sophisticated, versions of what the audience could see during visits to neighbouring villas.[40] Axial vistas in gardens, for one thing, were ideal for translation into sets on a perspectival stage; grotto façades or nymphaeum exedras (figure 49) had already served as what we would now call 'backdrops' for garden clearings and could have the same effect on stages. That this exchange of imagery between garden and theatre design was often deliberate as well as subtle at least two instances, one Italian, one Hispano-Italian, testify. An opera performed inside the Barberini Palace in 1656 had one painted set of a garden, while across the proscenium opening ran a row of fountains for which real water was piped from the gardens where on other occasions entertainments had been presented.[41] A theatre constructed somewhat earlier at the Buen Retiro Palace at Madrid, where Italian technicians were employed for both the garden hydraulics and the theatre, had a rear wall which somehow opened to show, beyond the illusionistic garden scenery of the stage, the real scenes outside.[42]

These exchanges between garden and theatre are fascinating and endless. But for the purposes of our exploration of the Italian debts of English garden history between 1600 and 1750 four elements are especially vital. First, the organization of garden space either to cater for theatrical representations (figure 50) or to suggest that they might take place:

Figure 50 G. F. Barbiere, theatrical performance with audience in a garden, drawing of the mid-seventeenth century.

these could be relatively simple, like the four niches ranged in a hemicircle in the higher woodland garden of the Villa Farnese at Caprarola, or heavily elaborate, as revealed in the engravings of Savoy gardens in *Theatrum Statuum Regiae Celsitudinis Sabaudiae Ducis* (Amsterdam, 1682), which seems to organize all the villa and garden space into theatrical forms.[43] Second, the contrivance within gardens of grottoes, pools or other features which seemed to be like scenes in the theatre. Third, the way in which this theatrical ambience of a garden affected the spectator-visitor, making him believe he was also an actor in the garden's dramas; this theme undergoes interesting transformations in the social theatre of the English eighteenth-century country house. Fourth, the exchange of imagery between theatre designs and garden scenery sustained the connections, not always overt, between them: early in the period with which we are concerned Inigo Jones invoked an audience's experiences of moving through a garden for his masque transformations; the expectation of similar entertainments, changing scenes and mythological personages seem, if the language of visits is reliable, to have been carried back into gardens. Later in the period, when gardens became a familiar setting in the English theatre, an interchange of response and behaviour between stage and country house again seems to have been possible: that it has not been much noticed in connection with the beginnings of the English landscape movement is due perhaps to the neglect of the Italian context.[44]

6 Cabinets of Curiosity

Many visitors to Italy, especially in the first half of the period with which this book deals, were led to comment enthusiastically on the 'curiosities' they saw. Thomas Coryate thought that the Giusti gardens at Verona were 'contrived with as admirable curiosity as ever I saw'. Some years later John Raymond commented upon 'two Cabinets or Galeries of rare curiosities' at a palace in Monaco, these being themselves beautified with 'Marbles and waterworks'; the introduction to his book of Italian travel shows him fascinated by the 'curiosities' of that country (among which are included both poisons and operas!). John Ray, for reasons we shall soon see, was particularly attentive to curiosities, which he says he would have described in his *Observations* if Lassels had not already done it so thoroughly. Lassels indeed gives much emphasis to both 'curiosities' themselves and to other matters 'no less curious'.[1]

In the seventeenth century the word *curious* had a meaning of careful or scrupulous; so that a curious traveller would be one who was attentive and industrious in seeing the sights, and curiosities were things which rewarded especially scrupulous attention, or presented themselves as items upon which care and pains had been bestowed. And further it signalled things strange, odd, unusual and ingenious (like operas or poisons). Whatever attracted the attention of the curious could be called curiosities: thus, at least for the earlier travellers from England, Renaissance gardens presented such an unusual and delightful aspect that they were among the prime curiosities of an Italian visit and listed as such by the guidebooks (see above pp. 5–10). Since they were unlike anything that could be seen at home, they repaid – indeed, some like the Villa D'Este required – careful exploration.

But the term 'curiosities' had also a more precise reference to actual collections of rare, strange, 'curious' objects, both natural and man-made, that were the precursors of modern museums.[2] Like theatres for dramatic performance, just discussed, these early museums or 'cabinets of curiosity' were situated and displayed in various forms and places: because gardens were one of these locations it is of interest here. Already in sixteenth-century English the word cabinet had signified a 'summer-house or bower in a garden', and it continued to be so used at least until Miller's *Gardeners dictionary* of 1737.[3]

But new developments in gardens, specifically their display of sculpture or botanical specimens as well as their being 'theatres' or conspectuses of natural and artificial wonders, augmented the scope and idea of both cabinets and gardens. Such a new attitude is clearly suggested by John Evelyn's diary which, recording a visit to Sir Thomas Browne in October 1671, notes that Browne's 'whole house and garden' was 'a paradise and cabinet of rarities, and that of the best collection, especially medals, books, plants, and natural things'.[4]

While he was in Italy thirty years before, Evelyn had ample opportunity to visit many such gardens and cabinets. The Italian Renaissance garden had been annexed in its earliest stages for the display of 'curious' collections: the Vatican Belvedere was organized in order to present the papal collection of antique sculpture (see figure 14), and English visitors to it clearly registered this interpenetration of garden and 'museum' when they recorded 'many brave fountaines, faire and antient statues, gardaines and many long galleries'.[5] Indications that gardens and cabinets were both part of a larger enterprise are given by other travellers and are substantiated by what we know of the gardens themselves. Many came to be dedicated to the display of objects which could also be found elsewhere, and garden designers accordingly made provision for the display of collections in galleries, loggias (see figure 33), special pavilions and grottoes. In the Orti Oricellari at Florence classical sculpture was displayed alongside every plant mentioned in classical literature.[6] At Mantua Isabella D'Este created in the Corte Vecchia of the Ducal Palace a small complex of spaces for the display of sculpture, paintings and precious stones which included a *studiolo*, a room known as the *grotta*, as well as a *giardino segreto*.[7] And of course botanical gardens – by the very nature of their existence as study and teaching collections – usually incorporated buildings where natural rarities and curiosities were also displayed. Such was the case with the earliest botanical garden, founded at Pisa in 1543.

At Pisa in the 1640s Evelyn remarked that the garden 'joynes a Gallery . . . furnish'd with natural rarities, stones, minerals, shells, dryed Animals . . . etc'.[8] The inventories of that Gallery show that by the time of his visit the collections included not only natural objects, what Aldrovandi, the Bolognese naturalist, called 'le cose sotterranee et le altre sopraterranee' (subterranean things and others above the earth), but pictures, engravings and drawings.[9] Some of these last, still surviving at Pisa, are beautiful representations of flowers, animals and birds; but the collections included religious pictures, landscapes and portraits of European botanists, including Clusius. Later travellers continued to be attracted to this garden and 'museum'. Raymond thought that the garden was 'more for use than delight, although there be good walks, & water-works that well washt us, yet for the most 'tis cover'd with simples, outlandish Plants and the like. Joyning to it a gallery very commodious for Medecinall things, it abounding with all curiosities of Nature, as foreign creatures, Stones, Mineralls . . .'. Half a century later William Acton 'saw the physick-garden of the Great Duke of Florence [at Pisa], in which there is a Gallery furnished with abundance of Curiosities . . .'[10]

Some botanical gardens, like Florence, had a simple layout of their plant beds, as readily accessible to the mind's categorizing and understanding as to the gardener's hands and care. But others, Pisa and Mantua for example, had far more elaborate designs, borrowed from shapes and decorations which artists and architects had devised for other projects.[11] These alert us to a familiar Renaissance theme, the debates of art and nature, which also made common ground between cabinet and garden in the Renaissance. Despite the objections of Giovan Battista Ferrari, the Sienese writer, who considered elaborately shaped beds 'quite unsuitable both for sowing seeds and for growing them', it became fashionable to arrange plants in what Agostino del Riccio called 'beautiful patterns in the forms, variously, of pyramids, maps, dragons, stars, and other *fantasie*'.[12] It is this kind of artifice which helped to register the affinities between garden and cabinet.

Evelyn's experience of gardens and cabinets and his sense of their congruence are everywhere apparent in his Italian diary. From his first entry into Italy, at Genoa, he was impressed by the palaces and their gardens: his mind seems to make immediate connections between them and their collections or cabinets. At the Palazzo Doria he passes from the 'Achates, Onyxes, Cornelians, Lazulis, Pearle, Turquizes, & other precious stones' of the house into the three-tiered gardens where the 'rare shrubs' and fine marbles seem an extension of the rich interior. At the 'Palas of Negros' it was the terraced garden and its grottoes, similarly juxtaposed to 'rarest pictures, & other collections', which he records. But he was also struck by the imitations of animals in stone, part of an elaborate metamorphic display of plants and flowers rendered in shells, stones and other precious materials. Just the same fascination with materials and their presentation was shown by Furttenbach in his *Newes Itinerarium Italiae* of 1627 (figure 51); but the ease and sophistication of Furttenbach's handling of these topics throws into relief Evelyn's relative inexperience of such wonders – in this he is typical of most English visitors before mid-century.[13]

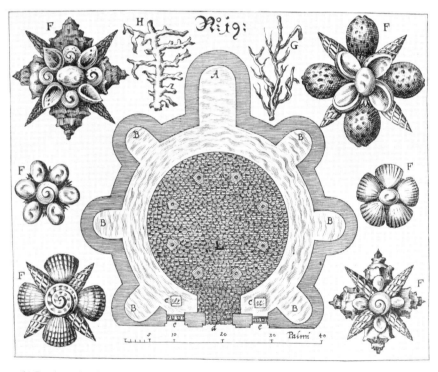

Figure 51 Rockwork within a grotto and grotto plan, from Joseph Furttenbach, *Newes Irinerarium Italiae* (1627).

75

However, by the time Evelyn had almost concluded his Italian itinerary and was in Rome for his second visit his knowledge and assessment of these intricate relations between garden and cabinet were more assured. In some doggerel verses he tells the Eternal City that she 'Justly [is] term'd the *Worlds sole Cabinet*'.[14] That Rome should seem the epitome of cabinets is not surprising, and Evelyn's verses rehearse the wealth of its collections, the 'thousand wonders' of its buildings and its '*Villas's*, *Fountaines*, & *Luxurious Fields*'. During his two stays in the city Evelyn had visited at least seven collections or cabinets and twice as many gardens. Some cabinets were unconnected with gardens: that belonging to Francesco Angeloni – 'divers good Pictures, many outlandish & Indian Curiosities & things of nature' was what Evelyn recorded; that of Cassiano dal Pozzo, who owned a 'choice Library', drawings, medals and a 'rare collection of Antique Bassirelievos'; and the medal collection and antiquities of the brothers Gottifredi.[15]

Other cabinets, like those of the Vatican, were closely linked to gardens, where some of the collections were displayed. Even when Evelyn does not go into detail the diary entries seem to imply a connection between cabinets and gardens; that this is not simply an accident of a journal's abbreviated structure is clear from Evelyn's more detailed visits. At the Vatican he proceeded from the Palatine Library, noting the frescoes by Domenico Fontana which recorded the raising of the obelisk, to the Armoury – a 'Library of Mars' – and out into the Belvedere courtyard, where the many famous statues were protected in shuttered alcoves, and finally to the Gardens, where it is the ingenuity of the waterworks, 'divers other pleasant inventions' and its fruit trees that he notices.[16] All items in the Vatican collection elicited from him an equal attention, and the passage from inside to outside appears as inevitable as it does in his other visits. At the Villa Aldobrandini, for instance, he proceeded from the gardens, which he recorded in detail and with special attention to the range of effects 'so form'd by nature, as if [they] had been cut out by Art', into the 'Palace' which he considered was 'indeede built more like a Cabinet': its central hallway was 'furnished with excellent Marbles, & rare Pictures . . .'[17] Similarly at the Villa Ludovisi in Rome the kind and degree of his attention are the same: whether he is outside in the garden where 'every quarter [is] beset with antique statues, and Walkes planted with Cypresse'; in its Casino dell'Aurora – a pavilion in the gardens decorated with paintings and displaying a clock 'full of rare & extraordinary motions', 'many precious Marbles – – – and other rare materials' as well as 'a mans body flesh & all Petrified, and even converted to marble'; or inside the villa with its huge and diverse collections, some of them contained within what Evelyn specifically terms the 'Cabinet'.[18]

But gardens were used not simply as spill-overs for extensive collections, but as an integral part of the display. The presentation of the Papal collection of sculpture in the Belvedere, inspired by antique models, had set a pattern which was imitated throughout the sixteenth and seventeenth centuries. We have already noticed the museum-like garden of Cardinal Cesi which van Cleef painted (see figure 15): travellers of Evelyn's generation would not have seen it, but the Villa Ludovisi not only maintained the same combination of garden and cabinet but also displayed items originally in the Cesi sculpture garden (see figure 16), famous for its fountains and for its *Antiquario* with adjacent supper room and covered loggia.[19]

Loggias, especially, were used to display collections – useful because they offered protection while being still outside; and they were, too, an intriguing architectural feature, because so unfamiliar, to English visitors.[20] Besides loggias, gardens like those of the Villa Medici were provided with open galleries for the display of their collections: Evelyn recorded 'a Portico with Columns towards the Gardens' or 'the Arcado'. At both the Villa Medici and the Villa Borghese he was taken with the device of embedding antiquities, notably bas-reliefs, in the walls of both the galleries in the garden and the façades of the house – the garden 'facciata [of the Medici Villa] is incrusted with antique & rare Basse-relievis & statues', whereas 'the enterance of the [Borghese] Garden, presents us with a . . . dore-Case adorned with divers excellent marble statues'.[21]

Cabinets of curiosity included items that were natural as well as man-made – *naturalia* and *artificialia*; indeed, it was precisely their juxtaposition which was the focus of curiosity, since human ingenuity was seen to be rivalled by nature's inventions and nature, 'outnatured' by art.[22] Gardens were therefore apt locations for curiosity and curiosities. Their botanical and horticultural riches being nature's contribution – albeit aided by human gardening skill – to the ensemble of antique sculptures, bas-reliefs and other precious artifacts. One of the disappointments, however, of the travel literature on Italy is the relative lack of detailed commentary on the *naturalia* of garden cabinets. Evelyn, whom we would expect to be alert to such matters, is generally silent: this may in part be explained by the fact that the printed sources he was using to refresh his memory when he wrote up his Italian journal years afterwards did not concern themselves with the botanical aspect of gardens except in the most general terms. Yet his occasional notes on what he saw growing in Italian gardens are of a piece with his experience of them as cabinets of both natural and artificial rarities. In the 'spacious Parke full of Fountaines' at the Villa Montalto he noted fish ponds, statues, inscriptions, ancient marbles and ('that which much surpris'd me') 'monstrous Citron-Trees'. At the Villa Aldobrandini he was impressed by the 'Citron-Trees . . . rarely spread [which] invest the stone worke intirely' as much as by the collections 'all for antiquity and curiosity'.

The garden of the Villa Borghese, he wrote, 'abounded with all sorts of the most delicious fruit, and Exotique simples'; he continues with notes on 'Fountaines of sundry inventions' and the miniature zoo ('divers strange Beasts').[23] It is clear from certain visual records of the Borghese gardens that its flower beds were obviously designed to display such floral collections. Further north in Florence, where the Medici also took a lively interest in flower-collecting, similar layouts can be seen in the series of lunettes of Medici villas which Gustave Utens painted in 1599 (see figures 22, 23).[24] Unfortunately, those images are scarcely explicit about the planting; indeed we are grievously short of adequate documentation on late sixteenth and early seventeenth-century plants and planting. As Utens and other evidence suggest, it was largely in the *giardini segreti*, private spaces to the sides of villas, where the visitors would not usually be admitted, that were to be found the plant collections to rival the antiquities, medals, precious stones and so on. Francis Mortoft is exceptional in his record of 'the little flowered garden' at the Villa Montalto in Rome; Evelyn writes only of its 'spacious park'.[20] What records we do have of these small, private flower gardens confirm their contribution to the overall cabinet of a villa. Georgina Masson's pioneering article on Italian flower collectors' gardens gives ample testimony of owners' pride in displaying floral specimens, often new importations, which were prized as much as antiquities. Catalogues, published and in manuscript, further testify to the pride taken in such botanical collections.[25]

If the dozens of English visitors to Italy are not precise about the cultivated materials in gardens, they are nonetheless alert to the gardens as cabinets of rare *naturalia*; this was notably true when they were faced with oranges and lemons, by no means unknown in England in the seventeenth century, but when encountered everywhere and in profusion seemed to travellers to be revivals of the mythic Hesperides.[26] Thus the manuscript journal of Banister Maynard records outside Turin 'a most pleasant garden with Leamonds, Oranges, Pomegranads and many other sorts of Rich fruite'.[27] Maynard was travelling in the 1660s; earlier travellers were more enthusiastic because more surprised – Fynes Moryson saw the gardens near Naples as rivalling the Hesperides.[28]

Necessarily, it was botanical gardens where visitors were specifically attentive to plant collections. Pury Cust, at Pisa when he was aged 21, is among the most explicit when he records

> The Phisicke garden very fine and adorned with many simples, many fine smelling herbs, all manner of rare flowers, and aboundinge in all kinds of most rare oranges and limons . . . palm trees . . . pepper trees . . . Spanish allowes . . .[29]

As one would expect of a member of the Royal Society, John Ray is more attentive than most visitors to the botanical elements in these gardens/cabinets, though at least in the published *Observations, Topographical, Moral & Physiological* of 1673 these tend to be fairly general: 'goodly flowers and choice plants' in the Boboli Gardens, and in the villas of Roman nobility 'gardens of flowers, groves and thickets, cut hedges of Cypress, Alaternus, Laurel, Bay, Phillyrea, Laurus tinus and other semper-virent plants'.[30] Ray has some lively accounts of cabinets as well as gardens, and many of them are marked in the margins of Evelyn's own copy of *Observations*.[31]

Both Ray and Evelyn are prime spokesmen for the congruities of cabinet and garden that were perceived to exist in Italy. But they are by no means the only commentators on this phenomenon. As late as the 1780s Hester Lynch Piozzi cast a quizzical eye upon 'all the curiosities belonging to this wealthy and illustrious family' of the Borghese:

> But the vases in this Borghese villa! the tables! the walls! the cameos stuck in the walls! the frames of the doors, all agate, porphyry, onyx, or verd antique! the enormous riches contained in every chamber, actually takes away my breath and leaves me stunned. Nor are the gardens unbecoming or inadequate to the house . . .

Ninety years before, William Acton had written of the Palace of 'Cardinal Ghisi, where there is a very pretty Armory, and many natural Curiosities, amongst the rest the Cockatrices were worth remark: His fine Garden, and those many Artifices by water, from which it is almost impossible to avoid being wet, unless the Gardiner be your Friend . . .'[32] As Acton implies, a crucial element of an Italian garden's curiosities was its various hydraulic effects; to these can be added the grottoes where such aquatic shows were often presented. The elaborate machinery which set in motion the various events in the grottoes at Pratolino or in the Hall of Parnassus at the Villa Aldobrandini elicited the same interest as did the actual formation and decoration of the grottoes themselves: both were curious instances of collaboration between art and nature. Just as John Ray could be fascinated by the geological mutations on display in a Milanese cabinet, so Sir John Reresby could praise the walls of some Medici grotto ('enamelled with stones of all colours and shells of fish') as well as its aquatic effects ('springs forth water in several places, as also from the top and bottom').[33] At Verona, Reresby also recorded that

> The palace are many; the garden extraordinary . . . for not only great variety of plants, flowers, and greens, but for volories of birds, grottoes, fountaines, from whence water throws itself by the turning of keys, in the shape of birds and beasts.[34]

It is not only the variety of *naturalia* but the witty ingenuity of *artificialia* in imitating that variety that strikes him. A grotto allowed the presentation in one room or cabinet of a collection of rocks, shells, even real horns and tusks (in the Castello grotto), together with examples of human contrivances or 'conceits', as Coryate put it.'[35] The Villa Aldobrandini at Frascati, as we have already seen, achieved a rich anthology of such effects from the art collection inside the house to the natural materials fashioned into the niches of the water theatre and to the aquatic display inside the Hall of Parnassus: these produced rain, rainbows, music, birdsong, an ingenious metal ball bounced on a jet of air, besides (as Evelyn put it) 'other pageants and surprising inventions'.[36]

Many of the Aldobrandini conceits were imitated in English grottoes, notably that of Thomas Bushell at Enstone.[37] Such imitations by no means implied direct knowledge of Italian gardens, since these devices had been widely popularized and their workings described and illustrated in works like Salomon de Caus's *Les Raisons des forces mouvantes* (1615). But whether at first hand or via printed accounts Italy authorized English connections between garden art and other central, especially scientific, concerns of the period. And it is because gardens reflected some of these scientific attitudes and interests and because gardeners like Evelyn were also involved with the Royal Society that changes in garden design and aesthetics must be seen in this larger context of scientific developments during the seventeenth century.[33]

The interest in the contents of cabinets and gardens which has been explored in this section was typical of the *virtuoso*, the amateur fascinated by a wide range of the world's art and nature.[39] An early example for our purposes would be Fynes Moryson visiting the 'rarities' of Pratolino in the 1590s and recounting them with awe and a relative lack of discrimination – 'I know not that any place in the World affords such rare sights in this kind'.[40] Later travellers like Lassels are even more attentive to 'curiosities' – indeed, the word is endlessly invoked throughout *The Voyage of Italy*. Another typical virtuoso in his modest way was John Bargrave, a canon of Canterbury, and a frequent visitor to Italy: on one occasion he travelled with his nephew, John Raymond, the author of *Il Mercurio Italico*. The remnants of his collection, including three wooden cabinets with medals, coins, statuettes, lamps, fragments of stone and mosaic, and notes on his Italian purchases, can still be seen in Canterbury Cathedral Library.[41] In a little notebook kept during 1670 he notes a visit to the Villa Ludovisi ('formerly Salusts garden') and observes an obelisk which 'layeth all along full of Hyerogliphics'. Earlier he had bought, according to a memorandum of 28 April 1658, 'Cutts [i.e. engravings] of the fountaines, Baserielivos, statues, Pallaces, etc of Rome', and these are recorded in his bequest to the cathedral library of 'His larger and lesser mapps of Italy, old Rome and new, in sheete at large. very ffair, together with all the cutts in his trunks of all the ancient ruins, the pallaces, statues, fountaines . . .'. The mentality of a virtuoso like Bargrave, his delighted fascination with bits and pieces of the antique and modern Italian worlds, comes across vividly in the scraps of notes that record his acquisitions: a metamorphic obsession is there in the purchase of a large octagonal marble table, inlaid with scenes from Ovid, and other oddities ('several serpents teeth turned in to stone'), as well as a keen interest in optical illusions, for he writes of an optic glass which presented him with a picture, among others, of 'a fayre garden with Oranges and Lemon trees, and fountaynes and walkes'; he displays the usual Protestant scepticism mixed with unabashed absorption in Catholic practices ('For Curiosity – because sould in Shoppe at Roome, so that for 2s-6[d] I had these 34 (pretended) reliques of Saincts bones'); his antiquarian bent shows itself in purchases of many Roman gems, of a red stone River God ('The River of Tyber, carved on a piece of coral; ancient') and a bronze plaque labelled 'Frō Hercules temple under the Aventin Hill at Rome where he killed Cacus where now stands St Stevens Church caled Sto Stefano del Cacco' – this last being another, small insight into the kinds of ways in which private memory systems worked. And his quasi-scientific bent is shown in Bargrave's collection of 'ye floor of brimstone frō puzzuolo' and other geological examples.

But very slowly this enthusiastic and rather indiscriminate regard surrendered to what we would, with hindsight, call specialization and to an increasingly pragmatic scientific spirit. Philip Skippon, travelling with Ray, inspected a botanical garden in Messina, but one cannot imagine them much satisfied with its unscientific division into twelve plots named after the apostles.[42] In 1691 William Bromley saw the cabinet of the famous Bolognese, Aldrovandi, but his note of 'more Curiosities, some natural, others artificial' implies a rather patronizing attitude towards the oddities and quirks of nature (indeed, the word *curiosities* is beginning to acquire something of its more dismissive modern meaning).[43]

Similar changes in garden taste may be traced. The growing scepticism with what seemed a merely self-indulgent taste for collecting curiosities or rarities was paralleled by less tolerance of what Coryate had called the 'conceits' of an Italian garden, notably its grottoes and hydraulic entertainments. Or, if these continued to be admired, the earlier wonder was converted into a keener interest in their mechanical workings. The imitation of Italian waterworks and grottoes would be a conspicuous feature of early seventeenth-century English gardens; but their world of theatrical delight gradually, if by no means wholly, surrendered to a more pragmatic attitude towards hydraulics and the geological specimens from which grottoes were constructed. Gardens still accommodate such devices, but increasingly in the spirit of scientific enquiry: the garden as laboratory was the true descendant of the garden as cabinet of curiosities.[44]

The long career of John Evelyn, as will be seen in Part Two, reflects these declensions in garden ideas. In his early Italian travels he displayed the omnivorous curiosity of the true *virtuoso*; by his death in 1706 at the age of 86 his interests had become more specialized. In the 1640s his Italian journeys led him to admire not only individual gardens and cabinets but to hail Rome, the epitome of Italy, as the 'Worlds sole Cabinet'. Beyond the claim that it was the biggest and best, such a phrase signals that in its various collections all the world was represented. Moreover, it was all the *pre-lapsarian* world's fullness: man's modern ingenuity and care ('curiosity'), it was claimed, could recover the complete Edenic world lost by Adam at the Fall. The point was made explicitly in the verses prefixed to the catalogue of the garden and cabinet owned by the Tradescants in Lambeth:

> Nor court, nor shop-crafts were thine ARTES, but those
> Which *Adam* studied ere he did transgresse,
> The Wonders of the Creatures, and to dresse
> The worlds great Garden.[45]

Evelyn implies the same ambition when he assigns to the garden the task to 'comprehend the principall and most useful plants, and to be as a rich and noble Compendium of what the whole Globe of the Earth has flourishing upon her boosome'.[46] Similarly, the sculpture collection of the Earl of Arundel, housed after the Italian model in galleries and garden courtyards beside the Thames, struck at least one visitor with its success in redeeming the losses and dispersals of history: Christopher Arnold, afterwards Professor of History at Nuremberg, noted in 1651 his impressions of 'certain gardens on the Thames, where there are rare Greek and Roman inscriptions, stones, marbles: the reading of which is actually like viewing Greece and Italy at once within the bounds of Great Britain'.[47]

Arundel's collection fell into decay during the Commonwealth. But it is not simply (if at all) the accidents of Civil War that are interesting, but a whole congeries of new attitudes and developments in collecting and presenting what gardens and cabinets had hitherto managed to contain. Evelyn rescued many of Arundel's items for Oxford University, but only a few inscriptions were set up (at his suggestion) in a garden – the holly hedge around the Sheldonian. The remainder became part of Ashmole's museum, while other items came to decorate country houses like Easton Neston in Northamptonshire or public pleasure gardens like Cuper's or Cupid's on the Thames: here later antiquaries like Stukeley found and sketched them. What has vanished along with Arundel's collection and garden is any ambition to present a conspectus of classical civilization; the garden uses of statuary may continue to provoke memories of the past, but they are above all discrete; the aesthetic pleasure in individual pieces predominates.

The same kinds of change are also apparent in the botanical and natural history side of gardens. The Tradescants' garden in Lambeth was remarkable for its wide range (for that time) of English wild flowers as well as of ever-increasing numbers of importations. A catalogue of some 750 species and varieties was issued in 1634, and this had more than doubled by 1656. As greater quantities of species became available to gardeners, any ambition to re-create the fullness of the Garden of Eden was less and less practicable.[48] This seems to have been clear to Peter Mundy as early as 1634; when he called on the Tradescants he found a 'little garden with divers outlandish herbes and flowers' and he was *'almost perswaded* a Man might in one day behold and collecte into one place more Curiosities than hee should see if he spent all his life in Travell'.[49] It is clear that the extent of the collector's task was defeated by the spaces and methods then available to him as well as by the hugeness of the world's cabinet. Similarly, I think, the equally famous museum of curiosities, probably housed in a purpose-built gallery in the Tradescants' garden, must have been strained to absorb the many 'rarities of . . . shells' (among other trophies) which the younger Tradescant brought back from his visits to America. The son sought to gather more plants and natural objects to augment the family's and others' collections; yet although their 'Ark', both garden and museum, emulated the inclusiveness of Noah's divinely inspired salvage operation, it barely survived the death of the younger Tradescant in 1662. The inscription on their tomb in Lambeth celebrated the father's and son's travels through Art and Nature as witnessed by 'A world of wonders in one closet shut'. That one closet already seemed inadequate to some contemporaries, the Tradescants' labours mere 'minims of art and nature'. The poet Cleveland registered that even 'Nature's whimsey . . . outvies/Tradescent and his ark of novelties'.[50] It would take the more ample spaces which Ashmole could supply as well as the more specialized skills that were starting to emerge – garden architect, garden plantsman, conchologist and so on – to attend adequately to the full range of the Tradescants' concerns. And, furthermore, more scientific attitudes developed: Sprat in the *History of the Royal Society*, though doubtless making some tactical capital on the Society's behalf, wrote that 'In every one of these *Transplantations* [of vegetables and living creatures], the chief Progress that has hitherto been made, has been rather for the Collection of *Curiosities* to adorne *Cabinets* and *Gardens*, than for the Solidity of *Philosophical Discoveries*'.[51]

7 VARIETY

'Aside from the principle of decorum, there was probably no aesthetic principle which critical writers, creative writers, and artists of the sixteenth and seventeenth centuries regarded as more important than the associated principles of variety and contrast.'[1] The principle of variety was founded upon the mutually supporting traditions of the human mind's delight in change, which is urged in Aristotle's *Rhetoric*, and of God's essential goodness and optimism which fathered 'unoutspeakable riches'. These two traditions can be seen converging and sustaining each other in the gardens and cabinets which the last section considered. Often praise of variety carried with it no explicit reason for that enthusiasm: it became a self-explicating quality in the best of God's and man's works. Tasso argues for the delightfulness of *varietà*, Shakespeare gives to Enobarbus the iconic description of Cleopatra's 'infinite variety', Francis Bacon praises poetry for its 'more absolute variety' of mimesis, Serlio loves an architect who is 'abundant in inventions' and Henry Peacham's *The Compleat Gentleman* rehearses the idea of variety and is among the first in England to apply it to landscape and landscape painting. Not surprisingly, therefore, it was a quality sought for and celebrated in gardens, especially those which we might now characterize as mannerist.

In their visits to Italian gardens Englishmen were quick to register their appreciation of variety, which then rapidly established itself as a *sine qua non* of a fine garden, at times without any reference whatsoever to larger theories of the universe in which variety figured. Veryard is quite specific that the Villa D'Este gardens at Tivoli are superior to any either in Italy or the whole world by reason of their 'greater Variety of Rarities . . .'[2] And it is the variousness of the waterworks there and in the villas at Frascati, especially Villa Aldobrandini, that presents itself as the most conspicuous reason for almost every visitor's admiration.[3] Sir Henry Wotton's praise has already been quoted (above p. 10) as typical: of some 'incomparable' Italian garden he twice mentions its variety: first, its 'various entertainments' of the senses; then the visitor's magical transportation from each of the garden's 'diversities' to the next. Such emphases would become frequent. Warcupp's *Italy in its Glory, Ruine and Revivall* praised the Este gardens on Monte Cavallo for their 'Variety' and 'diversity'; at the Villa Mattei, also in Rome, a series of visitors applauded its 'diversity'.[4] Along the Brenta Canal the future Bishop Burnet commented especially upon the 'diversity in the laying out' of gardens.[5]

The English relish for this variety was a response to several or (as they would have it) *divers* effects. To start with, it was an enthusiasm for the multiplicity of things to be noticed, especially in comparison with the more simple English gardens that were common in the early years of the seventeenth century. Yet as late as the 1690s at the Villa Borghese, for example, Throckmorton enumerated the 'Grotto's, Thickets, and pleasant Park of Deer . . . with the Fish Ponds, and other Advantages' which altogether made it 'the most pleasant Country Seat that can be wished for'.[6] At the Villa D'Este (see figure 43), always a particularly rich experience for visitors, Veryard found 'such variety that I think it impossible to describe all the particulars' of 'pleasant Walks, Labarinths, Grotto's, Fountains, Statues, and the like'.[7] Besides the experience of veritable collections ('theatres') of statues, mythical and legendary stories and mechanical devices, a sense of variety was also created by the need to negotiate the divisions or compartments of a garden. English visitors at Tivoli, for instance, noticed that the Este gardens comprised 'four partitions'; at the Vatican another tourist counted five; on his first encounter with Italian gardens at Genoa, Evelyn was struck by the division into three separate sections of the Doria gardens.[8] Each of these was treated differently in terms both of style and content, just as the layout of the Villa D'Este incorporated various design elements such as labyrinths, long terrace walks, exedras, fountains with viewing areas in front of them and 'secret gardens' at the side of the house.[9]

Those gardens were all fairly complex designs, where mannerist and baroque variety could be expected. But in smaller, less obviously diversified layouts visitors could nevertheless experience the same call to explore a garden section by section: Fynes Moryson said that the Medici garden at Castello (see figure 22) was 'full of pleasant hills', and Sir John Reresby was delighted by the 'great variety' of plants and design elements at the Giusti in Verona.[10] This experience was always augmented whenever a garden was sited on a hillside, the negotiation of which by ramps or stairs was an important contribution to its variety. Wotton gave eloquent testimony to this aspect, too, noticing how a general view of the whole garden 'in a delightful confusion' was succeeded by the visitor's discovery and movement by ascent and descent through each distinct 'piece'. His interest was echoed by other visitors. Skippon recorded 'a descent from the house' at Boschetto near Città Nobile 'into long and large gardens', while of the Boboli Gardens he noted that it 'is about 1½ miles in compass, and is uneven, being up-hill and down-hill'.[11] Lassels specifically draws attention to the fact that another Medici estate, Pratolino, is situated upon a hillside.[12] An anonymous traveller of 1648 who left a 'breife description of my traveils' in manuscript was fascinated by the stairs at Tivoli and Frascati, especially when they were also waterways.[13] Wright in the 1720s was still commenting upon '2 or 3 ascents of Gardens' at the Palazzo Colonna in Rome.[14]

It is generally agreed that Bramante's design for the Belvedere Courtyard in the Vatican was the inspiration for what became a characteristic Italian structure, the criss-cross ramps and stairs.[15] Bramante himself had taken the idea from the ruined structure of the Temple of Fortune at Palestrina, the classical Praeneste (see figure 83). There they were an admirable solution to the problem of building an extensive complex on sloping ground, which is where many Italian buildings sought to become established in order to take advantage of healthy breezes during the hot summers. Englishmen seemed always to be particularly impressed by such terraces: at the Palace of Negro in Genoa Evelyn found that 'nothing . . . more delighted me then the terrace, or hilly Garden'. The visitor of 1675 similarly expressed his pleasure with the garden of the Marchesa di Vico at Naples, which 'being on the side of a hill, is so prettily contrived, that there are Gardens like Rooms, one over another, for 3 or 4 storeies'.[16] Such an experience of a garden's variety readily elicited a sense of its invitations to discovery, its leading on of the visitor. Lassels writes of being 'led about' the gardens at Pratolino, while Warcupp discusses those who 'go walking from one part to another' in the context of the diversity of the Villa D'Este and the 'passage' through 'divers walks'.[17] As a consequence of having to negotiate such steep sites by zig-zag ramps and/or stairs, visitors, ascending or descending, were obliged to choose between the forking paths; whichever way they opted to proceed necessitated turning their backs upon items or views, even whole sectors of a garden, which only further explorations would allow them to see. At the Villa D'Este this frequent need to make decisions on which routes to follow up and down the hillside was very cleverly incorporated into the garden's iconography of the Choice of Hercules. David Coffin has demonstrated that the garden visitor was obliged at one stage to decide between 'two diverging paths', one of which would lead to the Grotto of Venus or Voluptas, the other to the Grotto of Diana or Chastity; so that the aspect of a garden's variety actively worked to involve the visitor not just in discovering the full extent, all the compartments, of a garden's territory but in learning its themes as well.[18]

If earlier travellers generally remarked upon the variety of an Italian garden, later ones who grew used to, even bored by, such experiences nevertheless found that two particular aspects of this garden diversity did maintain their interest. The first was the frequent division of ground into what was usually called garden and grove, a distinctive feature of Italian experience that, especially, eighteenth-century travellers like Addison and Spence record everywhere, even on the island of Capri.[19] Secondly, there was the fashion in which views out into the countryside from (especially hillside) gardens augmented the scenery inside them.

From the fifteenth century there were traditions of *boschetti* in Italian gardens, as Elisabeth MacDougall has shown: wooded areas with winding paths, less formal buildings and somewhat naturalistic planting, all of which contrasted with the regular garden spaces around the house.[20] When Joseph Furttenbach designed an ideal villa garden for his *Architectura Civilis* of 1628, it contained both what we would today call a 'formal' part, geometrical and with elaborate artifice, and a 'natural', landscaped section beyond (figure 52); indeed, the variety of garden imagery and effects Furttenbach has crowded into this project confirms the sense of an Italian garden's essential diversity. During his travels in Italy he must have seen many such juxtapositions of elaborate, artificial layouts with parkland: the garden and groves of the Villa Lante at Bagnaia (see figure 6) is a particularly striking instance. English travellers, too, remarked upon this: at the Villa Borghese (figures 53 & 54) Skippon recorded its 'noble and large gardens, with curious shady walks, and pleasant groves', while Lassels said that 'you have store of walks, both open and close, fish ponds, vast cages of birds, thickets of trees, store of fountains, a park of deer, a world of fruit trees . . .'[21] Burnet was reminded of an English park by these same Borghese grounds, and Mortoft describes how his party walked 'along the garden

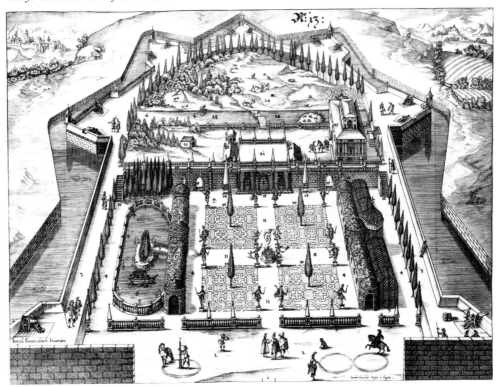

Figure 52 Imaginary garden, from Furttenbach, *Architectura civilis* (1628).

. . . into the Park adjoyning to it'.[22] The siting of Roman villas in vigne or farmland, already discussed, obviously contributed to this impression of a mixed design of regular and less contrived areas (see figure 16). Mortoft found a 'little flowered garden' at the Villa Montalto which led him into a 'large Paradise', what Evelyn called a 'spacious park'.[23] The layout of the Villa Doria Pamphili (figure 55) seemed to make a special feature of this double scheme, the two distinct parts of the garden being linked by the avenue of trees along the water course which stretched out to the basin or pool set in the 'fields'; one traveller distinguished specifically between its gardens and 'many large walks in and about the Park'.[24] Equally, a considerable number of travellers spoke of visiting Caprarola, where the Villa Farnese possessed, besides its two rectangular gardens immediately adjacent to the fortress-like house, a beautiful casino retreat reached by climbing through the meadows behind: Lassels called it 'the Garden upon the Hill-side with the great variety of waterworks . . .'[25] Later travellers accustomed to more informality in garden design, like John Northall who was in Italy in 1752, appreciated how gardens there were 'in some measure counterbalanced by leaving some spots free from artificial improvements, where nature displays its beauties'.[26]

Views out from a country house, like the mixture of 'natural' and regular designs within a garden, had received the crucial *imprimatur* of the younger Pliny, as well as codification by treatises such as Alberti's and the authority of much practice (figure 56).[27] The prospects that Italian gardens afforded are a leitmotif throughout the travel literature

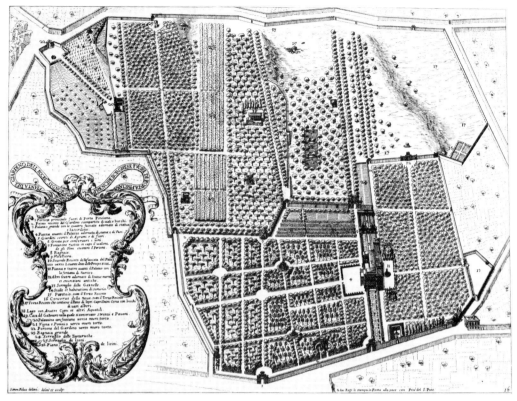

Figure 53 Plan of the Villa Borghese, Rome, from Falda, *Li Giardini di Roma*.

Figure 54 View of the grounds of the Villa Borghese, Roma, from Falda, *Li Giardini di Roma*.

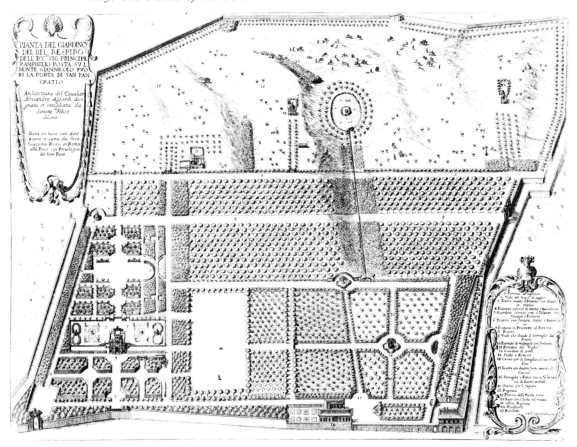

Figure 55 Plan of the grounds of the Villa Doria Pamphili, from Falda, *Li Giardini di Roma*. The long water course that stretches to the pool in the meadows can be seen in perspective in Figure 98 below.

between 1600 and the mid-eighteenth century. And as tastes grew more and more disposed towards the natural – a topic that will be taken up in the next section – the opportunities to see out of the ordered garden into a larger landscape were eagerly seized. Early travellers, however, appreciated 'a faire prospect'[28] just as much as Addison, Wright or Joseph Spence. Thomas Hoby was delighted by the 'helthsom prospects' from the gardens on the Bay of Baia; Philip Skippon was pleased with the view from the summit of the Giusti Gardens in Verona, and was virtually unique among Englishmen for singling out a Venetian city garden with a view.[29] Certain villas provided prospects that were always commended: those from the Doria gardens in Genoa; those from Palladio's Rotunda outside Vicenza were praised both by Warcupp (see above p. 36) and in William Acton's *A New Journal of Italy*.[30] The topography of Rome with its seven hills gave frequent opportunity for prospects to become an established part of a villa's pleasures: the anonymous traveller of 1675 is particularly eager to point them out at the Villa Borghese ('incomparable prospect'), the Villa Doria Pamphili and the Villa Mattei.[31] Not surprisingly once he reaches Frascati and Tivoli his reiteration of the variety of prospects enjoyed from the villas there is marked. The Villa Aldobrandini was also known as the Belvedere to emphasize its unique position with panoramas over the Campagna: Lassels was just one of many tourists who singled out its view.[32] Eighteenth-century travellers, obviously much more attuned to at least the pleasures of landscape paintings, are more eloquent: Spence was struck by the views from the Medici villa at Poggio a Caiano, Wright by those from the summer-house ('in the middle of a Wilderness or Maze') of the Papafava family in Padua.[33] A garden's prospects, what Alexander Pope would term 'call[ing] in the country',[34] together with the sense that an ideal garden variety involved both regular and irregular dispositions of ground would both prove of enormous consequence to the landscape movement.

Figure 56 The Villa Medici, Fiesole. This is a typical use of a hillside on which to build a villa, with the consequent need to negotiate several levels with terraces, arcades or loggias or a combination of all three.

8 ART AND NATURE

The garden is *par excellence* territory where we register the work of both art and nature. Indeed, one without the other would simply not make sense: as Anthony Hecht puts it in his poem on 'The Gardens of the Villa D'Este'

> For thus it was designed:
> Controlled disorder at the heart
> Of everything, the paradox, the old
> Oxymoronic itch to set the formal strictures
> Within a natural context, where the tension lectures
> Us on our mortal state, and by controlled
> Disorder, labors to keep art
> From being too refined.

No garden (since the Fall) comes into being without human intervention; none exists without natural and living materials. The design, layout and care of gardens are man's contributions, but nature provides the essential ingredients with which he works. Art, it is claimed, transcends time; yet garden art, supremely vulnerable to the depredations of time, must actually invoke time in its most successful creations – time in which plants, shrubs and trees may grow, seasonal change which alters the whole appearance of a garden four times each year, and even the length of time during which the full extent of a garden's riches is discovered by its visitor. This composite endeavour of gardening, then, unlike any other art form, relates art and nature; but if it alerts us to their collaboration, it may equally strike us that they engage in some contest, what the Renaissance called a *paragone*.[1] However this alliance, rivalry or even animosity is seen, the garden has offered a prime location for aesthetic adventure and debate, and never more so than during the period dealt with in this book.

Broadly speaking, the early visitors to Italian gardens recognized and gave a privileged place to art, while later ones rather sought the effects of nature. Yet these changes in taste did not proceed with that unfaltering momentum which historians sometimes seem to impute to them; indeed it is relatively easy to find evidence that contradicts the apparently pleasing story of the advance of nature at the expense of art.

90

William Kent, who (according to Horace Walpole) 'leaped the fence, and saw that all nature was a garden', singles out the grottoes and hydraulic effects at Pratolino for special mention in his diary of an Italian tour in 1714; conversely, Raymond's visit to the Villa D'Este in 1646–7 ends with him quitting the gardens ('Tyr'd with these masterpieces of Art') and going in search of the 'Natural Cascata' of the Aniene nearby.[2] While it would be foolish to try and argue that by 1750 there was not a more widespread taste for either actual landscape or for landscape contrived to look natural than there had been in 1600, we must not let ourselves be seduced by the lures of a Whiggish garden history which sees English connoisseurs moving surely from the lures of art to the liberties of nature. It is far more useful to chart the different kinds of relationships that were held to be possible between art and nature in Italian gardens during this period; while these may readily be located along a graph of an accelerating tolerance of natural over artificial effects, their significance lies less in that teleology than in the sheer range of aesthetic attitudes that were available to garden visitors during the seventeenth and early eighteenth centuries.

English travellers in Italy were themselves by no means certain how to adjudicate between art and nature, teasing matters which the Italian garden seemed often to complicate rather than elucidate. The Villa Lante at Bagnaia has been shown to maintain a 'perfect balance' between art and nature and allegorized that interaction in its iconological programme. Whether much of its elaborate 'message' got through to later visitors is doubtful: iconography is more about encoding than decoding.[3] But given the garden's privileged location as a place where the joint contributions of art and nature to human civilization may be judged it would not be surprising that some glimpses of Lante's programme were taken by visitors. Of its tunnel of water through which a 'man may pass drye under the Element of water' Raymond thought it was a 'trick [which] might raise a Question in the Schooles'. While Blainville's *Travels*, after quoting a predecessor to the effect that everything at the Villa Aldobrandini was 'natural', adds 'which by the way is false, for the Water-works are artificial'.[4] And it must be already evident from the previous discussion of cabinets of curiosity and of variety in gardens that clear discriminations between artifice and nature were not always what English visitors in Italy were apt or eager to make. Evelyn's delight with the 'Palas of Negros' in Genoa is precisely that it offered him an experience where both elements were present with equal force ('a grove of stately trees, furnish'd with *artificial* Sheepe, Shepheards, & Wild Beasts, so *naturaly* cut in a greystone'[5]). However, it will help some of the discussions in Part Two if we try and disentangle these involvements of art and nature in Italian garden achievements.

Some distinct relationships may be isolated, though in practice they are often blurred. There is, first, the simple surrender to the utmost of art – 'as artificial, as is possible to be made' – at Ferrara, for instance, where the Duke's garden was 'garnished' with fountains or at Bagnaia, where the Villa Lante was 'adorned with wonderful rare waterworks'. For this same traveller evidence of art is exactly what he seems to expect of Italian luxury, where 'rich' and 'costly' shows always mean elaborate contrivances. Yet at the Villa D'Este even he saluted the 'artificial water-work, which being let go, the birds do sing, sitting upon twigs, so naturally, as one would verily think they were all quick and living birds, which is occasioned by the water'.[6] That final clause, however, pulls him back from the brink of committing himself wholly to the delights of verisimilitude.

Then there is an art that imitates nature and deceives the eye into thinking that there is no artifice involved: Robert Moody recorded for his master, Banister Maynard, that in Turin the Cappucins had 'A very pleasant Garden, and that in it many pretty devises as Rocks, shells and watter sprut-ing out as if they were things naturall'.[7] Equally George Sandys in a Neapolitan garden thought the 'artificial rocks, shells, mosse and tophas' of the fountains 'seem to excell even that which they imitate'.[8] His remark, however, is somewhat ambiguous: do the fountains *deceive* him into thinking them natural or *draw attention* to their deceit? Indeed, is it deceit that Sandys applauds or art's bringing nature to perfection?

This suggests another relationship in which a recognition of art's mimicry of natural things becomes part of the pleasure. Moryson found at the Quirinal Palace gardens a 'Rocke artificially distilling water' and at Pratolino 'a cave strongly built, yet by art so made, as you feare to enter it, lest great stones should fall upon your head'.[9] Clearly, though his appreciation of art's mimetic success, its verisimilitude, was keen, he still realized that he was dealing with a feigned nature. Such double recognition would become part of contemporary aesthetics: here in 1664 is Daniello Bartoli writing of inlay or mosaic work –

> one wishes to make it appear as if nature had imitated art, contriving in such a way that art may not be distinguished from nature. Is not the source of wonder, and therefore of delight in such works, the fact that one sees one thing used to express another? the deception being all the more innocent in that in the whole composition of a false thing there is yet no element which is not true[10]

Such sophistication was rapidly acquired by English visitors to Italy, but it is worth remembering that it was their Italian experiences which would in large part teach it to them. We have noticed already (above, p. 75) how Furttenbach's response to Genoese grottoes seemed far more assured than Evelyn's upon his arrival. The servant Moody's reaction to the natural fountains in the Capuchins' garden in Turin is somewhat naive for the year 1660, yet if he had little experience of such garden art before he reached Italy with his master it is clearly explicable. Indeed, one of the indeterminates in adjudicating how various travellers saw the relations between art and nature is the experience and taste of the individual.[11] However, there were many travellers who either came expecting or quickly learnt to appreciate the utmost of art and ingenuity in gardens: for them, as for Howell, Italy was not for nothing 'that great limbique of working brains'.[12]

Part of art's beguiling yet noticeable imitation of nature was its concern with representation: natural things were re-presented, presented over again, in art. Depending upon the attitude of the observer, gardens could either strike visitors with their lifelike imagery or with the mechanics of such imitations. Moryson at Pratolino seems a good example of the first: in the grottoes and the lower gardens he relishes the creation of events whose lifelikeness he recorded ('Images of Duckes dabble in the water'); the animated hydraulic dramas, too, were convincing representations ('Pan . . . lookes upon his mistresse, as if he desired thanks or a kisse for his paines').[13] Yet within a few years of Moryson another visitor, Robert Dallington, derived a rather different experience; it is the means, the how, rather than the effects, the what, of the imagery which he notices:

> The house . . . is seated between two high Hilles, upon a third lower than they,
> fro which hilles ye descend some quarter of a mile, by the way set with quick-set

& kept after our English fashion, yee mount up to the *Terreno* of the Front by twelve staires, very faire of stone, directly whereupon, at the head of a Garden set round with statues of the Muses in a ground sensibly ascending, is seen a huge Giant cut out of the maine Rock, with al his parts, as armes, hands, legges, and feet, symmetricall to his head, wherein may stand a dozen men: in it are kept Pigeons; the loovers whereat they come in and out, are his eares; the windows which give light to the roome, are his eyes. Out of his mouth falleth into a very faire poole, al the water that serves the worke on the other side of the Pallace, among which are many sights yeelding very great content, as Noes Arke with all kinds of beasts, *Hercules* fighting with a Dragon, Birds artificially singing, Organs musically playing, showres of raine plentifully downe powring, and infinite sort of such devise, more delightsome to be seene, than pleasant to be discoursed off. . . .[14]

Dallington even seems aware that to describe Pratolino will involve him in focusing upon the mechanics of what, on the spot, merely delighted him. Again, it is salutary to remember that the crucial difference between experiencing representation in a grotto and recounting it later necessarily shifts the emphasis from art's verisimilitude to art's methods and devices.

We see such distinctions registered by mid-seventeenth-century travellers at the Villa D'Este or the various villas in Frascati. At Aldobrandini Raymond saw the 'Fountaine, in which is represented Atlas throwing up water, which forceth artificiall Thunder, and a perfect Rainbow'. What his prose implies (a mixture of recognizing the act of representation plus the 'astonishment' of being convinced) his actions clearly reveal a little later in the Hall of Apollo (see figure 29): the Muses are shown

with severall winde Instruments that sound by art. Underneath this hill are Organs, which plaid divers tunes so distinctly, that wee conceived some Master was playing on them, but looking wee saw they went of themselves, the cause of all this wee afterwards saw. . . .[15]

First, the striking representation; then learning the 'cause'. Raymond is fond of noticing such marvels of ingenuity, and of Italian operas remarks in his introduction that 'In this they but imitate Nature, marke how they subdue her . . .' It is art's infinite capacity to outdo natural things, while still being seen to imitate them, that is striking. Hence Raymond's and other garden visitor's admiration for mixed effects – 'amongst the Branches of [real] Trees, Artificiall Birds move their Wings and sing sweetly'.[16]

Gardens used their combined resources of nature and art (including architecture, sculpture and hydraulics) to represent many things. Reresby at the Giusti gardens in Verona saw 'water throw itself . . . in the shape of birds and beasts'. Hadrian's Villa represented, says Warcupp, other famous places –

his Villa caused draughts or as we may better say the similitudes of the most celebrious places of the world to be made, causing them afterwards to be called after the proper names of the imitated places . . . . Fabricks made and nominated in imitation of the True . . . . [even] the place or representation of hell . . .

And doubtless in emulation of that antique site the nearby Villa D'Este represented ancient Rome in a model at the end of the Walk of a Hundred Fountains (see figure 109) 'having a channel imitating the Tyber'. A fountain, for Skippon, 'represents' a rock, or a Roman arch has been 'made like a grotto'. For the anonymous traveller of 1675 the water theatre at Aldobrandini 'imitated Rain, Hail, Snow and Thunder'.[17] These and many more notices of representations make it clear that English visitors expected gardens to draw upon their own particular resources to imitate various aspects of the 'real' world in exactly the same way as they would expect it of a theatrical performance, a painting or a statue. And though such expectations were less conspicuous by the eighteenth century the tradition of reading garden scenery as forms of representation would still exercise a powerful hold upon the early landscape garden.

From the second half of the seventeenth century there seems to have been as much attention paid to the *paragone*, the comparisons and rivalries between art and nature, as to the various fashions in which they collaborated. Raymond, already quoted, recorded how in Italian operas art subdued nature, while Warcupp (translating, of course, an earlier Italian guidebook) reported that some pictures at Milan were so lifelike that 'Art here hath overcome Nature'.[18] But Warcupp can also note that art adds to nature in the Papafava garden in Padua. This traditional notion, whereby nature's best is brought out and heightened and its potential redeemed from accidental blemishes by art, is obviously of particular relevance where gardens are concerned. For Raymond art 'enriches' the gardens at Genoa; planting – the *art* of the horticulturist and arboriculturist – joins with that of the fountain-engineer to make the same gardens 'more pleasant' for the anonymous visitor of 1675; Francis Mortoft in 1658 considered that the birds in the aviary of the Doria Palace gardens at Genoa, owing partly to its size and partly to the many trees growing inside it, 'live, not as in a Cage, but as it were in a field'.[19] His 'as it were' alerts one to his recognition that art is able to present or represent natural events like fields more purely than they ever could be in an unmediated form. But, equally, he is not deceived; he could tell an actual field from one represented in a garden.

The apprehension of art did not in itself make a garden either good or bad nor mean that its representations of nature could not also be acknowledged and admired. Veryard displays an evenly balanced response to both art ('artificial water-works') and nature ('fountains fall[ing] on a Rocke in manner of a Cascade'); his account of the Villa D'Este gives equal value to both aspects, while in the gardens of the Villa Doria Pamphili – I suspect as he faced down the vista engraved in figure 98 – he is afforded 'a natural and most agreeable Perspective', in other words, an artificially organized prospect that still seemed 'natural'.[20] When both art and nature may be praised in the same garden scene, as Burnet does on the Isola Bella and Misson at the Villa Pamphili,[21] what becomes of consequence is the quality and the kind of artistic management of the ground. Burnet is reproached by Blainville for failing to judge Italian waterworks by French standards, just as Misson and Blainville are supremely condescending towards the Villa Aldobrandini – not because it is artificial but because the art, especially of grottoes and waterworks, is childish: 'petty Toys' are what Misson calls Italian gardens and waterworks; a 'puppet-show', Blainville the model of ancient Rome in the Villa D'Este. Yet Blainville liked the Dragon Fountain there and in face of what he finds at Tivoli even seems to be willing to withdraw his criticism of those who over-praise Italian garden art ('Froth of Hyperbolism').[22]

We must assume that he considered the Dragon Fountain was managed in an agreeable enough manner to accommodate its potential childishness, the *merely* fabulous, in a striking verisimilitude. In a similar fashion Joseph Spence's judgement of the huge statue of the Apennines (see figure 38) at Pratolino was based upon its being 'ill contrived' for frontal viewing; but sideways 'it shows a *grand* idea', though even here Spence would have liked the figure to have been supplemented with a suitable landscape setting, 'a vast rock under him and several streams rolling down rude rough channels, as they do really in the Apennines'. Such attention to the *decorum* of representation would have made it 'much nobler'.[23] What is interesting is that Spence accepts the allegorical image but wants it situated in suitably expressive scenery: the balance between art and nature has shifted, but both are still required.

That same dual perspective operates in various remarks on the Italian countryside from later travellers like Spence. Blainville, who praises Versailles, also expresses his pleasure in natural scenery; but it is a pleasure clearly mediated by art. His acclaim both of Foligno and the falls near Terni are linked to his reading in classical literature: Virgil's second *Georgic* must have had such a landscape as the first in mind, Virgil's *Aeneid* VII, the second.[24] In other words, he views the Italian countryside as somehow already invested with literary art. This was exactly Addison's perspective: he departs for Italy prepared to compare the 'natural face of the country with the landskips that the Poets have given us of it'.[25] What transpires, at least in his *Remarks* and presumably in his actual experience of the Italian countryside, is that scenery is matched with a passage from a Latin poet like Claudian or Lucan and found to be similar; literary art, itself read routinely after the contemporary fashion in terms of paintings (a *Landskip* being the Dutch word for a painted landscape), shaped Addison's responses so that what he sees is determined by what he reads plus a trick of *ut pictura poesis*. The simple application of art terms to natural scenery 'colonizes' it for art, makes it seem to be shaped by the human imagination even when it is in fact untouched: thus Addison also views the Roman campagna as if it were a theatre set (cf. figure 25) – 'a more broken and interrupted Scene, made up of an infinite variety of inequalities and shadowings, that naturally arise from an agreeable mixture of hills, groves and vallies'.[26] That such an artificial *scene* arises *naturally* from the configurations of the ground is of a piece with those many puzzling claims by English seventeenth-century writers that nature was herself an artist: so Cowley can assert that 'My Garden painted o're / With Natures hand, not Arts', or Hanmer in his *Garden Book* that 'Nature seems to sport, imitating in its flowers the shapes of severall creatures, as beasts, birds, flyes, and even Man himselfe too, and from their resemblances the severall sorts are denominated'.[27] Both remarks declare the mental processes of their speakers rather than any descriptive ambition: natural objects may look artful to those who know their art. So Addison, viewing the mosaic pavement at the Temple of Fortune at Palestrina (the classical Praeneste), admired 'little landskips which look very lively and well painted, though they are made of the natural colours and shadows of the marbel'.[28] For a writer who is often claimed as a spokesman for 'natural' taste in landscape and landscape gardens, this is a remarkable sentence: not only in its choice of topic (mosaic), but in its intricate linguistic control of the art/nature tension – *landskips* look lively (i.e. real) *and* well painted; 'though' is about to undo what 'painted' contributed only to be undercut itself by 'made of' and then sustained by the emphasis on 'natural colours and shadows' of the stone.

The range, versatility and even confusion[29] of English adjudications of art and nature by the end of the seventeenth century should make us wary of assumptions about the spread of 'natural taste' in garden design. Shaftesbury, like Addison, is often claimed as a spokesman for this 'new' aesthetics and much has been made of his declaration, 'I shall no longer resist the passion growing in me for things of a natural kind'.[30] It has however, been something of an embarrassment to garden historians that Shaftesbury's preference for 'untamed nature' did not jibe with his own garden nor, when it was written in 1705, could it be matched with any known examples of such garden design. But it transpires that we have all along misunderstood him, and that his plea for nature was in fact a plea for the idea of pure nature, which since it rarely discloses itself to the naked eye must be studied in the 'perfected forms' which art provides. Art in gardens is dedicated, then, to bringing out the intrinsic character of natural items.[31] What Shaftesbury's theory did require of gardens was a gradated sequence of design whereby regulated nature near the house gradually gave way to the untouched forms of nature on the horizon, this scale of diminishing artifice being observed along avenues or walks which gave a unified perspective to the variety of natural forms in view; what art organized near to the beholder taught him to understand the potential in untouched forms further off.

The same determination to discuss the relations of art and nature in gardens as a matter of perspective and within a context of the contemporary concepts of variety and contrast characterizes Addison. On his way to Italy in 1699 he wrote to Congreve about his impressions of French gardens:

> I dont believe, as good a poet as you are, that you can make finer landskips than those about the Kings houses or with all your descriptions build a more magnificent palace than Versailles. I am however so singular as to prefer Fontaine-bleau to all the rest. It is situated among rocks and woods that give you a fine varietie of Savage prospects. The King has Humoured the Genius of the place and only made use of so much Art as is necessary to Help and regulate Nature without reforming her too much. The Cascades seem to break through the Clefts and cracks of Rocks that are cover'd over with Moss and look as if they were pil'd upon one another by Accident. There is an Artificial Wildness in the Meadows Walks and Canals and the Garden instead of a Wall is Fenc'd on the Lower End by a Natural mound of Rock-work that strikes the Eye very Agree-ably. For my part I think there is something more charming in these rude heaps of Stone than in so many Statues and woud as soon see a River winding through Woods and Meadows as it dos near Fontain-bleau than as when it is toss'd up in such a Variety of figures at Versailles.[32]

Nature has been 'reformed' sufficiently by art to bring out her potential, but this apprehension depends upon Addison's registering the gardens at Fontainebleau on a scale or in some perspective (albeit a mental one) that allows him to compare their ratio of art:nature not only with Versailles but with, say, the Alps still ahead of him. And such perspectives also take the variety and contrasts of nature into account as well as the variety and contrasts that a fine artifice will bring to them. Once in Italy, as both his prose *Remarks* and the verse *Letter from Italy* make clear, Addison continues to adjudicate the respective contributions of art and nature in any given scene, whether in a garden or in some larger landscape outside. If he seems to spend more time recording impressions of the latter, this is partly because Latin authors have provided him with more texts on those scenes; he is alert to just proportions of art and nature in gardens – the villas at Frascati being but 'the first sketch of *Versailles*' – while the element of art is nowhere neglected, as we have seen, in his attention to Italian landscape as artifacts of the human imagination, his and the Latin poets':

> For wheresoe'er I turn my ravish'd eyes,
> Gay gilded scenes and shining prospects rise,
> Poetick fields still encompass me around,
> And still I seem to tread on Classic ground.[33]

By 1700 it was generally agreed not only that Italian gardens displayed, as we have seen, an essential and valued variety but that it was also an English quality to be especially cherished in face of a different French taste. Dryden, for example, asks why 'many others should cry up the barreness of . . . French plots above the variety and copiousness of the English'.[34] His plots are, in fact, dramatic not garden ones; but the point holds. Indeed it was made by Timothy Nourse in contrasting French with Italian gardens.[35] Dryden again would argue that 'Our [English] audience will not be pleased but with variety of accidents, an underplot, and many actors' – the profusion of nature, in short, by no means restricted as by French drama and gardens. English empiricism valued the copiousness of nature, as the many communications to the Royal Society or Sir Thomas Browne's *Pseudodoxia Epidemica* testify; equally it applauded the 'copiousness of the imagination' in imitating that natural diversity.[36] This was, then, the more 'difficult beauty'[37] of English taste – 'difficult' precisely because, as this section has shown, the representation of natural variety required of art (and above all garden art) a more careful and judicious collaboration.

These aesthetic discriminations had close parallels in natural science. Indeed, Dryden considered his dialogue on drama to be 'sceptical' and in line with other inquiries lately initiated by the Royal Society.[38] Empirical explorations of the natural world did not mean that art was banished but just properly applied. Ray banished from natural history only the arts that did not belong to it – 'hieroglyphics, emblems, morals, fables . . .' – in order that the intrinsic qualities of things themselves could be studied. Pepys records in his diary for 22 July 1666 what he calls 'the present fashion of gardens to make them plain'. Yet the control exercised over nature in, say, a botanical garden was still eloquent of man's art; herbs and flowers, according to Stephen Blake in 1664, should be placed 'in uniform ranks'; plantations of trees, according to Walter Blith in 1653, should be geometrically ordered and by no means 'rudely and confusedly' set out.[39]

Such attitudes in the last third of the seventeenth century gave to Italian gardens a special place in the English imagination. As Addison himself noted, they were but 'sketches' for later French gardens by Le Nôtre; accordingly they admitted of more variety, of flexibility in the proportions of art and nature. One has only to look at the upper garden of the Villa Aldobrandini (see figure 112) with its cascades, two of them rude and rustic, the other architectural, with its shaped pattern of box surrounded by the density of natural groves, to register at once the appeal of such gardens to those like Dryden who found French uniformity uncongenial.

Garden aesthetics in the eighteenth century increasingly fell into the gap between the traditional notion of imitation (where representation of nature and human nature in history are stressed) and a rival view which proposed the affective power of art (and therefore gave prominence to the interior and autonomous imagination).[40] Yet the enduring strength of the Italian garden is that it could be many things to many people; if it failed to present itself as the model of a proper ratio of art to nature – and therefore ceased to honour the traditional notion of imitation – it could still be admired for its classical authority and colour – and thereby gave to the perceiving mind a role in the 'making' of a garden. Though far less warmly discussed, the Italian garden continues to feature in travel writings. The Duchess of Marlborough, who received directions for travel from a Mr Holloway in 1728, was told that the Duke of Parma's country seat was 'a pleasant garden for an Italian one'. Breval is more grudging about the Boboli which are 'spacious, not ill laid out, sufficiently water'd . . . But there are not wanting many Trifles, according to the Italian taste of Gardening. . . .' Some thirty years later Northall can still summon up enthusiasm for Italian garden art: 'nothing can exceed the gardens [of the Villa Lante] for fountains, grottos, canals, walks, arbors, and groves', while the gardens of the Villa Farnese at Caprarola 'are likewise of an elegant design, and finely embellished with proper ornaments'.[41] We may even be getting the beginnings of an almost historical interest in the Italian style of garden design. With the English garden movement well established in both theory and practice by the 1750s the Earl of Corke and Orrery found Pratolino, though much run down, still of some interest:

> The water-works at this place . . . are entirely in the old taste; but that old taste, by not having been visible in *England* for many years past, is now become so new, that, at least, it gave us the pleasure of novelty. . . .[42]

The Boboli, he also says, are 'laid out in what is now deemed the old-fashioned taste'. And as late as the 1780s Hester Piozzi, recalling the 'tasteful creations in my own country, *Pains Hill* and *Stour Head*', is disappointed by the Giusti Gardens in Verona, but finds the Isola Bella of 'unequalled variety . . . a kind of fairy habitation, so like something one has seen represented on theatres'.[43]

Yet it is probably Tobias Smollett's grumpy attack on Italian gardens that is best known. Writing in *Travels Through France and Italy* (1766), he seems appreciative of gardens when they are absorbed into a general panorama ('a continent of groves and villas' at Genoa; 'beautiful plantations and villas' on the 'mountain of Viterbo'); but his hostility is reserved for gardens in close-up.[44] Yet the actual rhetoric is far more interesting than the general thrust of his critique. He begins –

> In a fine extensive garden or park, an Englishman expects to see a number of groves and glades, intermixed with an agreeable negligence, which seems to be the effect of nature and accident. He looks for shady walks encrusted with gravel; for open lawns covered with verdure as smooth as velvet, but much more lively and agreeable; for ponds, canals, basins, cascades, and running streams of water; for clumps of trees, woods and wildernesses, cut into delightful alleys, perfumed with honey-suckle and sweet-briar, and resounding with the mingled melody of all the singing birds of heaven: he looks for plats of flowers in different parts to refresh the sense, and please the fancy; for arbours, grottos, hermitages, temples, and alcoves, to shelter him from the sun, and afford him means of contemplation and repose; and he expects to find the hedges, groves and walks, and lawns kept with the utmost order and propriety.

By no means is this English vision wholly natural: alleys are cut through wildernesses; the negligence of nature only 'seems', it is an 'effect'; canals, grottoes, temples and smooth lawns all declare human art. Yet Smollett continues by declaring that 'He who loves the beauties of simple nature, and the charms of neatness, will seek for them in vain amidst the groves of Italy'. That he is not simply referring to the unkempt appearance of many Renaissance gardens by the time of his visit is clear when he goes on to sketch the gardens of the Villa Borghese:

> a plantation of four hundred pines, which the Italians view with rapture and admiration: there is likewise a long walk of trees, extending from the garden-gate to the palace; and plenty of shade, with alleys and hedges in different parts of the ground: but the groves are neglected; the walks are laid with nothing but common mould or sand, black and dusty; the hedges are tall, thin and shabby; the trees stunted; the open ground, brown and parched, has scarce any appearance of verdure. The flat, regular alleys of evergreen are cut into fantastic figures; the flower gardens embellished with thin cyphers and flourished figures in box, while the flowers grow in rows of earthen-pots, and the ground appears as dusky as if it was covered with the cinders of a blacksmith's forge. The water, of which there is a great plenty, instead of being collected in large pieces, or conveyed in little rivulets and streams to refresh the thirsty soil, or managed so as to form agreeable cascades, is squirted from fountains in different parts of the garden, through tubes little bigger than common glyster-pipes. It must be owned indeed that the fountains have their merit in the way of sculpture and architecture; and that here is a great number of statues with merit attention: but they serve only to encumber the ground, and destroy that effect of rural simplicity, which our gardens are designed to produce. In a word, here we see a variety of walks and groves and fountains, a wood of four hundred pines, a paddock with a few meagre deer, a flower-garden, an aviary, a grotto, and a fish-pond; and in spite of all these particulars, it is, in my opinion, a very contemptible garden, when compared to that of Stowe in Buckinghamshire, or even to those of Kensington and Richmond. The Italians understand, because they study, the excellencies of art; but they have no idea of the beauties of nature.

Smollett brings to his judgement assumptions which his final sentence makes clear; but what is surprising about his scorn is, first, that he does not seem to object to the kind of variety which the Borghese Gardens presented and, second, that his version of an English garden – its handling of the flower beds excepted – accords well enough with the views we have of the Villa Borghese (see figures 53 & 54). But Smollett is determined to make the invidious comparison expected of him, and he finds justification in the poor upkeep and the dryness of Roman summers. It is the final declension of enthusiasm for Italian gardens discovered and explored on their own ground. What must now be done is to retrace our steps to 1600 and chart how the English imagination realized these Italian ideas and images on native soil during the same period.

Part Two

ENGLAND
THE WORLD OF THE GARDEN

9 'My Patterne for a Countrey Seat'

i: Elizabethan beginnings

During their descriptions of visits to Italian gardens English tourists would sometimes note their determination to copy what they were viewing when they got back home. At the Villa D'Este John Raymond exclaimed that 'This shall be my patterne for a Countrey seat' and accordingly went on to provide an extensive description.[1] Lassels certainly urged the tourist to 'learn of Italy how to make a fine house' and presumably – given his attention to gardens – fine grounds to go with it.[2] From some travellers we even catch glimpses of what they were able to implement upon their return to England: Sir Thomas Hoby, for example, tells us that when he had arrived back at Blissham in Berkshire he first made himself 'new lodgings', then in 1561 planted 'the garden and orchard' and two years later erected a fountain in the new garden.[3] Some of these early bits of Italianization of English grounds obviously struck chords when visitors found themselves in Italy face to face with the more extensive originals of what England was beginning to copy: thus Coryate, at the Giusti Gardens in Verona ('contrived with as admirable curiosity as ever I saw'), is put in mind of Sir Francis Carew's garden in Middlesex, 'who hath one most excellent rocke there formed all by arte, and beautified with many elegant conceits, notwithstanding, it is somewhat inferiour unto this'.[4]

It was inevitable that English gardens would suffer by comparison with Italian examples. Even by the second half of the seventeenth century there was little in their own country that would have prepared travellers for the splendours and sophistication of Italian gardens, where Roman glories, Renaissance revivals and the delights of a warm climate combined to create images of an almost paradisal beauty. Slowly throughout the century Italianate imagery and designs were introduced into England, as Renaissance fashions belatedly trickled through and as more and more visitors returned having seen for themselves the 'garden of the world'.

The enthusiasm of Raymond for the Villa D'Este and his resolve to emulate its gardens when he returned home were not, presumably, supported by his financial resources when it came to remodelling his country seat. Very few Englishmen would have

103

been able to create an Italianate garden on the scale of the Este family. And as late as the eighteenth century there was evidently even some uncertainty as to what it was apt to emulate in Italian gardens: the Frenchman Blainville visited the Papafava garden near Padua in 1707 and thought it 'indeed a handsome enough Garden for a private gentleman' because its only 'singularity' was a labyrinth. But some fifteen years later the Englishman Wright seemed much more in awe of its 'ornaments' and therefore less inclined to think of it as a model for him or anyone else to copy.[5]

In practice, the English attempt to introduce Italian design into their own gardens was, in two respects, piecemeal. Though there were some places, like Wilton House, where a whole garden was recast in the newest style, many estates realized such transformations on a more modest scale, sometimes by simply introducing items of Italian imagery into otherwise unrevised terrain. But the models for such change were themselves somewhat randomly selected. Though, once again, items from specific Italian gardens were copied, it was much more a general impression of Italian garden arts that was attempted; to give some Italian or Roman colour to their estates, those English who had experienced a whole variety of different styles, forms and designs during their Italian travels chose eclectically – terraces, grottoes, fountains, other waterworks, statuary – and without much wish to re-create any one particular garden. So that as we trace the history of English gardening between 1600 and 1750 it will be partly a question of noticing now one theme (the theatrical disposition of a garden) now another (perhaps the antique tonality) among the various claims that Italian gardens generally made upon the English imagination.

That the Italian impact on English gardens did proceed in a somewhat piecemeal fashion is evident from the group of Oxford dons who wrote on 20 January 1659, the last year of the interregnum, to urge on the completion of John Evelyn's vast compendium, the *Elysium Britannicum*, his unfinished account of English gardens and their place in gardening history. As one of their arguments to hasten its completion they wrote of their hope that

> other . . . Italian glories and pompous beauties may be one day brought (as farre as ye tempere of ye Climate will give leave) into English gardens. Tis true wee have neither Materials nor Mechanicians like those in Italy but we suppose [that if] this Gentlemen yet writes this piece [he will find] wayes to helpe ye Nation in this particular.[6]

Clearly, Italian garden art was and had been a priority for those hortulan academics as it remained for Evelyn.

The beginnings of Italian influence can be charted in several Elizabethan gardens.[7] At Kenilworth, for instance, by 1575 the old Tudor palace garden of the 1530s and 1540s had been transformed by that most Italianate of forms, terracing, as well as by fountains and obelisks. It struck a contemporary, Robert Laneham, as just such a mythical place as similar Italian gardens seemed to be:

> Beautified with many delectable, fresh, and umbragious bowerz, arberz, seatz, and walks, that with great art, cost, and diligens wear very pleasantlie appointed; which also the natural grace by the tall and fresh fragrant treez and soil did so far foorth coomend, az Diana herself myght have deyned Thear well enough too raunge for her pastyme.[8]

Significantly, the occasion of that description was the use of the new gardens as a theatre in which the Earl of Leicester represented his sovereign, the Virgin Queen, Diana the huntress, to herself in 1575.

At Theobalds during the years between about 1575 and 1585 Lord Burghley, a self-confessed garden enthusiast, introduced descending stairways, loggias painted with genealogies, a summer house decorated with 'twelve Roman emperors in white marble' and an equally classical motif of a fishpond.[9] The compilers of the Parliamentary Survey in 1650 seem particularly insistent upon the movement up and down between various sections of the garden: 'with two stepps discendinge into ye middle of ye garden . . . . 8 stepps discendinge . . . 3 ascents . . . 3 paire of staires discendinge downe in to ye Levell from ye gravell walke . . .' So, although its arrangement in separate courtyards is still rather old-fashioned the particularly Italianate experience of exploring Theobalds was evidently striking. And other visitors remarked upon 'a little wood nearby', at the end of which 'you come to a small round hill built of earth with a labyrinth around. [It] is called the Venusberg'.[10] Exactly what the relationship of this grove and mount was to the squared gardens cannot easily be determined; it has the air, however, of the contrast between garden and grove which was remarked upon at Italian villas – compare it with the disposition of the Villa Medici in Rome (see figure 9) where the grove beyond the regular garden also has a mount. And for another continental visitor of 1600 Theobalds was full of exactly the same range of interests that we have traced in Italian gardens:

> There is a fountain in the centre of the garden: the water spouts out from a number of concealed pipes and sprays unwary passers-by . . . .
>
> In the first room there is an overhanging rock or crag (here they call it a 'grotto') made of different kinds of semi-transparent stone, and roofed over with pieces of coral, crystal, and all kinds of metallic ore. It is thatched with green grass, and inside can be seen a man and a woman dressed like wild men of the woods, and a number of animals creeping through the bushes. A bronze centaur stands at the base of it . . . .
>
> An outstanding feature is a delightful and most beautifully made ornamental pool . . . . In the two corners of this pool you can see two wooden watermills built on a rock, just as if they were on the shores of a river.[11]

Allusions to *giocchi d'acqua*, to grottoes (so-called), to representations of menageries as at the 'Palas of Negros' in Genoa, to imitations of river scenes with windmills very similar to the grotto of the mill at Pratolino, and much play with the joint possibilities of art and nature make Theobalds in this account a veritable anthology of Italianate elements.

Whether they were intended as allusions, specific or general, to Italian gardens, cannot be judged. But the work that Lord Lumley did at Nonsuch Palace after 1579 almost certainly was, since he had visited Italy in 1566 and seen for himself some of the gardens at least around Florence. Again, Baron Waldstein's visit in 1600 will serve to survey its marvels. In the palace itself he found 'so many miracles of perfected art and of works which rival those of ancient Rome', specifically in the hall 'a collection of sculptures representing stories from Ovid'. Once outside in the 'gardens, the groves', Waldstein found that there were '3 distinct parts [presumably in addition to the Privy Gardens]: the Grove, the Woodland, and the Wilderness'. This variety was further augmented with a great deal of fine statuary and fountains, records of which happily survive in the Lumley Inventory of 1590. (When the gardens were in ruin in the seventeenth century John Evelyn proposed that the statues should be preserved and displayed after the Italian fashion in a special gallery.) Among these statues Waldstein singles out 'the Labours of Hercules and a number of other subjects from the poets'; but his greatest enthusiasm is reserved for the Grove of Diana:

> by going along various paths between the growing shrubs, with trees shading us from the summer heat, we entered the famous Grove of Diana, where Nature is imitated with so much skill that you would dare to swear that the original Grove of the real Diana herself was hardly more delightful or of greater beauty. This Grove is approached by a gentle slope leading down from the garden by a path half hidden in the shade of the trees. Before you approach the actual Fountain of Diana you will pass a small stone building . . .[12]

He reads the inscriptions on the walls of this small temple and eventually arrives at the Fountain of Diana itself (the Diana of the Privy Garden had prepared the visitor for the narrative of this woodland grove). The fountain, to judge from other German visitors, seems to have taken the form of a 'grotto or cavern' – surely in the manner of those at Pratolino – in which 'was portrayed with great art and life-like execution the story of how the three goddesses took their bath naked and sprayed Actaeon with water, causing antlers to grow upon his head, and of how his own hounds tore him to pieces'.[13] The story derives, of course, from Ovid's *Metamorphoses*, Book III, and despite the lack of hydraulic equipment to start the figures into motion as happened at Pratolino, the visitors all seem to have responded to the groups of statues and their theatrical setting as if they actually saw the scene enacted before their eyes. To underline the narrative, lines of verse were attached to the group, and Waldstein transcribes them in his diary.

Waldstein's account of his visit to England in 1600 leaves no doubt that at the very start of the period with which this book deals Italianate gardening had begun to make its mark. Nor was it always manifested in the great houses of Elizabeth's nobility: Waldstein actually makes a detour to visit the gardens of Sir Francis Carew at Beddington – the same gardens that came to Coryate's mind when he was in Verona; Waldstein reports that

> A little river runs through the middle of this garden, so crystal-clear that you can see the water-plants beneath the surface. A thing of interest is the oval fish-pond enclosed by trim hedges. The garden contains a beautiful square-shaped rock, sheltered on all sides and very cleverly contrived: the stream flows right through it and washes it all around. In the stream one can see a number of different representations: the best of these is Polypheme playing on his pipe, surrounded by all kinds of animals. There is also a Hydra out of whose many heads the water gushes.[14]

The parallels with both the Villa Mattei (where Mortoft saw Hercules slaying the Hydra in a watery arbour) and Pratolino (where Galatea, the nymph loved by Polyphemus, moved whenever another figure sounded his pipe) are striking; the Polyphemus and Galatea motif may already have had a wider currency in engravings before Salomon de Caus illustrated a version of the Pratolino grotto in his book, *Les Raisons des forces mouvantes*, in 1615. And Pratolino seems to have influenced another garden, not visited by Waldstein, belonging to Lord Cobham in Kent; it was listed with Hampton Court, Theobalds and Nonsuch as one of the great gardens to see in 1586, and as late as 1629 one of its features was still worth John Parkinson's while to describe in his *Paradisi in sole*:

> a tall or great bodied Line [i.e. Linden] tree, bare without boughes for eight foote high, and then the branches were spread round about so orderly, as if it were done by art, and brought to compasse that middle Arbour: And from those boughes the body was bare againe for eight or nine foote (wherein might bee placed halfe an hundred men at the least, as there might be likewise in that underneath this) & then another rowe of branches to encompasse a third Arbour, with stayres made for the purpose to this and that underneath it; upon the boughes were laid boards to tread upon . . . .

This 'goodliest spectacle mine eyes ever beheld for one tree to carry' had, in fact, its counterpart at Pratolino where Giovanni Guerra drew a tree encircled with stairs leading to a balustraded platform.[15]

Waldstein does not mention the orangery at Beddington, but Carew had learnt, not only to hold back his fruit trees so that the Queen could be given cherries in August, but to cultivate oranges which had been given him by Sir Walter Raleigh. Carew may not have been the first to succeed in emulating the Italian Hesperides, since Lord Burghley also seems to have grown them; and they were soon joined by a few other gardeners who strove to cultivate oranges – in a special building at Somerset House in the 1610s, and at Oatlands and Wimbledon in the 1630s and 1640s.[16]

Two other Elizabethan garden layouts had clear Italian antecedents in that they introduced terraces or what Evelyn at Genoa had called a 'hilly Garden'. Wollaton was built by Robert Smythson for Sir Francis Willoughby and was unique at the time in being planned symmetrically, with the gardens taking their axis from the centre of the house. A painting of 1697 by Jan Siberechts shows the descent from the house into the first garden and another, with divided staircase, leading from the first into the lower grove (figure 57); another descent seems to have led visitors down to a grotto or orangery (the building with its back towards us), while by the time Siberechts painted the view another, exedral-shaped descent of terraces together with a fine banqueting hall had been established on the same side of the house as the grotto or orangery. It is perhaps one of these two buildings visible in the Siberechts' panorama that was noted by William Stukeley, the antiquarian with a keen interest in earlier garden forms: in *Itinerarium curiosum* he writes of Wollaton's 'pretty summer-house panell'd and ciel'd with looking-glass', which had beneath it 'a water house with grotesque work of shell, &c'. Whatever may be the architectural debts to France and in particular to Androuet du Cerceau's *Les Plus Excellents Bastiments de France*, these small moments – when garden space is organized into terrace descents and grottoes *all'antico* without the great elaboration of mannerist designs over large areas as in many of Du Cerceau's engravings – are much more reminiscent of Italian examples unmediated by France.[17]

Wimbledon, another Cecil property like Theobalds, also had some more dramatic terracing. It had a fine approach of two divided staircases (figure 58), with grottoes beneath them, which Sir John Summerson believes to have been inspired by the Villa Farnese at Caprarola;[18] but surely this striking feature, as we have seen, was widely available on Italian terraces as well as copied extensively in France. And although around the house the gardens were still the old-fashioned 'separate visual experiences bounded by walls and hedges',[19] there were loggias between the house and the Privy Garden, clearly visible on Winstanley's view of 1678 (figure 59). By 1609, as we know from a plan by Robert Smythson inscribed 'A greate Orcharde with walkes now In Plantinge', the hillside behind (at the south of) the house was laid out in groves and vineyards on long terraces which are linked by simple stairs, a feature which can also be seen at the bottom left of Winstanley's view.[20]

Figure 57 Jan Siberechts, *Wollaton Hall, Nottinghamshire*, oil painting of 1697.

Figure 58 Wimbledon House, drawing probably copied from an engraving of 1678, undated.

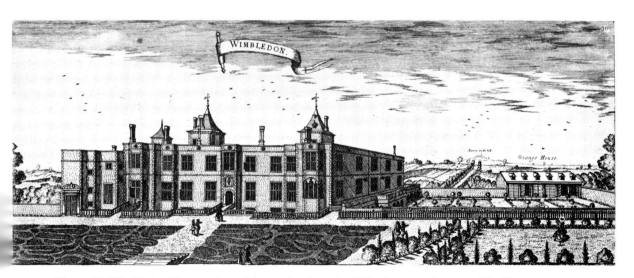

Figure 59 Wimbledon House, view of the garden front in 1678, drawn and engraved by Henry Winstanley.

ii: Gardens in the masque

Under James I the scope and quality of Italian gardening features increased, in large measure owing to more numerous contacts between England and Italy. More travellers returned with first-hand experience, and the pervasion of Italian imagery made its variety and richness better known. The King urged his nobles and gentry to reside more on their country estates; he even wrote some verses to support his royal proclamation; though his emphasis is thoroughly agricultural –

> The cuntrey is your Orbe and proper Spheare
> Thence your Revenues rise bestowe them there
> . . . .
> Take knowledge of your sheepe, your corn, your cave . . .[21]

– it cannot be doubted that if their 'Revenues' permitted landowners would also start to embellish their grounds in the latest style. The extent and the speed of such Italianization of gardens are very hazy, but what fragmentary evidence we have suggests that such improvements were by no means confined to the great houses.

Sir John Harington, translator of Ariosto, created a terrace garden at his house in Somerset, St Catherine's Court.[22] At Copthall, Essex, the Earl of Middlesex remodelled an early loggia and planned considerable extensions to the terraces on three levels – a walk accessible from the long gallery on the leads of the terrace roof, the loggia or 'stone terrace' at the next level, and the 'terrace walk' below that.[23] The Jacobean garden mania, an early example of *furor hortensis*, was commented upon in 1618 by the Venetian ambassador, who specifically singled out the fashion for terracing in the new English 'mode of *varying* the plan of the gardens and even of the orchards'.[24] Terraces were introduced by the Earl of Worcester at Raglan Castle, with busts of the Roman emperors lining the walls; by Sir Thomas Vavasour at Ham House, where the gardens were varied into three sections and juxtaposed to a grove planted with oval or circular rings of trees; by the Earl of Northampton, who is supposed to have travelled in Italy in the 1580s, at his house in the Strand where there was a terrace before the house and another at the end of the garden beside the Thames.[25] And what is also clear is that at the same time as gardens were thrown into more regular shapes, above all a regularity axially related to that of a house, they were diversified within that more organized space: the Countess of Bedford's elaborate garden, designed (so Sir Roy Strong suggests) as a model of the pre-Copernican universe in concentric circles – the garden as *theatrum mundi*, incorporated some kind of summer house in each of its corners to which one ascended by a set of stairs, the whole surrounded by terracing. In plan it may look neat and compact, but the experience of exploring it must have been far more intricate and varied.[26] Another garden, similarly cast into the form of a military fortress ('ramparts, bulwarkes, counterscarpes'), was Ware Park, owned by Henry Fanshawe. What is, however, most interesting here is that this very conceitful garden was wholly reorganized, apparently on the advice of Sir Henry Wotton, and made into something very like an Italian water garden, a less intricate Villa D'Este: the work in progress was described in 1613 –

> we are busied about new workes, and bringing of waters into the gardens, which
> have succeeded so well that we have a fine fountain with a pool in the lower

garden where the fort was . . . and a running streame (from the river) in the upper garden, between the knotts and the rancks of trees in the brode walke or alley. . . .[27]

And the writer concludes by saying that 'there is no end of new inventions' since Wotton has just arrived to 'propound many new devices'; it cannot be supposed that Wotton would not draw upon those memories of incomparable Italian gardens about which he wrote so eloquently in *The Elements of Architecture* some years later.

To end this sketch of Jacobean garden enthusiasm it is worth considering Francis Bacon's plans for Gorhambury, recorded in a manuscript in the British Library. It obviously mixed regular and irregular designs; islands in the lake were decorated with a grotto, a rock or what amounts to a terraced flower garden ('flowres in ascents') and each was presided over by its appropriate nymph or seagod represented in sculpture. When John Aubrey saw the place in 1656, that indefatigable searcher after Italianate gardens in England reported 'a curious banquetting-house of Roman architecture'; evidently a classical design struck him immediately with its antique air.[28]

Such piecemeal adaptation of English grounds to either strictly Italian or more vaguely and allusively Italianate imagery and design depended upon an owner's resources of time and money as well as upon the extent of his knowledge of new styles. The range of possibilities for anyone who contemplated improvements is clear from Robert Burton's listing of those garden scenes that he would recommend to sufferers of melancholy:

> to walk amongst orchards, gardens, bowers, mounts, and arbours, artificial wildernesses, green thickets, arches, groves, lawns, rivulets, fountains, and such-like pleasant places, like that Antiochian Daphne, brooks, pools, fishponds, between wood and water, in a fair meadow, by a river-side . . . . to disport in some pleasant plain, park, run up a steep hill sometimes, or sit in a shady seat, must needs be a delectable recreation. *Hortus principis et domus ad delectationem facta, cum sylva, monte, et piscina, vulgo La Montagna*: the prince's garden at Ferrara Schottus highly magnifies, with the groves, mountains, ponds, for a delectable prospect, he was much affected with it. . . .[29]

The language of Burton's list was certainly adaptable to any style of garden design that England might have accommodated in the previous 150 years: they were words that served to describe a wide range of constructions. But the classical colour of his list – its allusions to myth, to such Roman items as arches – as well as the quotation from Schott's *Itinerarii Italiae rerumque*, which Warcupp would translate for publication in 1660, and the specific praise of an Este garden at Ferrara give Burton's catalogue a significantly voguish emphasis and bring it into line with the advanced and Italianate gardening of his contemporaries.

Burton's list of garden features also reads like a synopsis of settings for various court entertainments, entries or progresses, in all of which gardens figured prominently. This prominence both derived from and in extra measure gave back to gardens their strongly symbolic meanings – places of man's original as well as ultimate perfection. Their creation from a successful collaboration of art and nature also authorized their use as a metaphor for all sorts of political shaping of human society into harmonious and beneficient order. Thus *Luminalia*, a court masque devised in 1638 by Inigo Jones and William Davenant, followed the imagery of chaos and disruption in the anti-masque with a metamorphosis of the scene into a garden:

> the scene was changed into a delicious prospect, wherein were rows of trees,
> fountains, statues, arbours, grottos, walks, and all such things of delight as might
> express the beautiful garden of the Britanides.

As a 'further part of the garden opened' the Queen herself was discovered, and the
association of the royal presence and will with the arts of government and social harmony
was explicitly claimed:

> the Britanides and their Prophetic Priests were to be re-established in this garden
> by the unanimous and magnificent virtues of the King and Queen Majesties'
> making this island a pattern to all nations as Greece was amongst the
> ancients . . .[30]

Luminalia was the culmination of a long association of royal power with garden art
that must be traced back to the progresses of both Elizabeth and James I around the
countryside, where their entertainment often involved adaptation or wholesale creation of
gardens as temporary stages. We have already seen the Earl of Leicester entertaining the
Queen in his new garden at Kenilworth in 1575; in 1591 at Elvetham Lord Hertford also
received the Queen and on the second day an elaborate presentation was given on a
specially excavated lake, shaped as a crescent moon to represent the Queen as Cynthia.[31]
These progresses, in which gardens became a privileged location for dramas of political
allegory, continued under James I, and the association of the garden with political
authority and will was therefore constantly made throughout the English countryside long
before it became *de rigueur* in court masques. Indeed, the state entry of James I into
London in 1603 presented him with two gardens figured on triumphal arches along his
route. Stephen Harrison described them in *The Arches of Triumph*, the first representing
the 'new Arabia':

> in a wide hollow square, were exalted five greene Mounts, the one swelling above
> the other; upon which the five Senses . . . . sate heavily drooping: before which
> Mounts, an artificial Laver was created, called the Fount of Vertue; out of which
> . . . upon his Majestie's approach, rann wine very plenteously.
>
> At the foot of this Fount lay Detraction and Oblivion, Sleeping till his
> Majesties approach; but being arrived at the place, and the Trompe of Fame,
> starting up the Senses, they two likewise, doing their best, with clubs to beat
> downe the Fount, but were hindered by the Senses . . .[32]

The following arch represented the 'Garden of Plentie' and was formed of arbours,
trellis-work and statues of Pomona and Ceres among others. The conjunction of political
theatre and new garden imagery could not be more striking.

These and other ephemeral garden settings must have been fairly elaborate in order to
have moved in ways that the printed texts described; but they were, equally, far less costly
to create than actual gardens. The same is also true of Inigo Jones's masque scenery.
Expensive, no doubt, and a drain upon the royal exchequer, they nevertheless deployed
more of the new garden ideas and made them visible to a larger number of people than in
the same number of years would have been possible in reality and, so to speak, upon the
ground. We should not underestimate the influence of court entertainments, either
presented at Whitehall or on the King's progresses, in diffusing knowledge and appreciation of Italian gardening in the years before the Civil Wars.

Inigo Jones would have been somewhat more restricted in his use of machinery when he designed for *al fresco* events, but the imagery would have been the same, like the cave and mount that he devised for some chivalric entertainment.[33] And others who arranged receptions for the King and Queen may not have had Jones's skill and imagination, but clearly they aimed for the same effects. One of the first progresses undertaken by James and his Queen, Anne of Denmark, was to the house and garden of Sir William Cornwallis at Highgate in 1604. The manner in which they were greeted testifies to the virtually indistinguishable media of garden and theatre. Their majesties were met by the figure of Mercury, like some garden statue, and directed by him first towards the southern view over the City of London and then to an arbour where the goddess of May, Flora, Zephyrus and Aurora were ensconced, equally like any grotto group. Later, after dinner, Pan and a group of satyrs danced around a fountain running with wine. The mobility of the spectators, the Ovidean *dramatis personae*, the furniture of bower and fountain ('decorated and laid out for the occasion') and the apparent transformation of the fountain's water into wine may not have any direct Italian inspiration, but it is of a piece with those things to which English visitors responded while they were in Italy.[34]

Nine years later the Queen was welcomed at Caversham with an entertainment devised by Thomas Campion. From the moment she approached the park limits and a strange figure emerged from a bower to argue with one of her retinue, the resources of its modest garden were thoroughly used. It was apparently built down a hillside, with two levels of garden (all swept away by 'Capability' Brown in the next century); after crossing the park, 'her Majestie with her Traine were all entred into the Lower Garden', where an elaborately dressed Gardener and his Boy greeted her and were seconded by singers in another arbour; from here 'the Queene ascends by a few steps into the Upper Garden', where further music awaited her; later all these gardenesque figures reappeared in the Hall after supper.[35]

Under James's successor, Charles I, both court entertainment and gardens displayed more elaborate designs and imagery. When Charles I and Henrietta Maria were welcomed at Bolsover Castle by the Earl of Newcastle in July 1634, Ben Jonson devised a neo-platonic celebration of the nature of mutual love: the characters who discoursed upon these learned themes appeared in a specially created garden, into which the King and Queen were led and which was presided over by a Venus Fountain. Despite the aspersions which his text cast upon his former colleague, Inigo Jones, Jonson was still loyal to a basic Renaissance commitment whereby ideas were realized in palpable form: gardens continued to be the most eloquent of such visible language.[36]

These garden theatres of the royal progress, however, did not realize the full potential of the Italian garden. It is to Inigo Jones's masque designs that we must look for the most complete presentation in England of the rich and exciting variety of those gardens, presented moreover by somebody who had once, maybe twice, seen them for himself. Jones was a member of the Earl of Arundel's party which visited Italy in 1613–14, and there is a document which implies that he was included because he already knew the country.[37] His own words, recorded by John Webb, in *Stone-Heng . . . Restored*, also seem to imply a visit sometime perhaps in the 1590s: 'Being naturally inclined in my younger years to study the *Arts of Designe*, I passed into forrain parts to converse with great masters thereof in Italy.'[38] And one particular set of designs, for *Oberon* in January 1611, suggest

113

that he was fully aware of the possibilities of Italian garden imagery and garden experience before the trip with Arundel. In *Oberon* the audience was first shown 'a dark rock with trees beyond it and all wildness that could be presented'; later this 'whole scene opened, and within was discovered the frontispiece of a bright and glorious palace'; later still, the interior rooms of the palace were disclosed 'in perspective' (i.e. painted illusionistically on a backdrop). This sequence exploits the general experience of movement through an Italian garden and of the transformations represented in grottoes; but in particular it seems to borrow, but reverse, the experience of a visitor's approach to Buontalenti's Grotto in the Boboli Gardens in Florence. There one is first struck by an architectural façade or frontispiece, decorated at the top with natural-looking rocks; but as one approaches, the rockwork seems to usurp the architecture until, inside, the whole world has been taken over by the 'wildness' (see figure 32).[39] Even in *Lord Hay's Masque*, three years earlier, if Jones can be assumed to have participated along with Thomas Campion, the strong emphasis upon movement has a distinctly Italian air, comparable with Wotton's description of 'mountings' and 'valings' in his preferred Italian garden. Among the 'opportunities and properties' of the scene – 'whether they be natural or artificial' – the text tells of an imaginary view from the stage into

> a green valley with green trees round about it, and in the midst of them nine golden trees of 15 feet high . . . From the which grove toward the state [i.e. in the direction of the King seated in the audience] was made a broad descent to the dancing place . . . on either hand were two ascents, like the sides of two hills, dressed with shrubs and trees; that on the right leading to the bower of Flora, the other to the house of Night. . . .

And once a song had ended another 'grove and trees of gold and the hill with Diana's tree are at once discovered'.[40]

The excitements and pleasures of sequence, as visitors moved through Italian gardens, often negotiating stairs and terraces, and the transformations of scenery as they walked or as they stood before some automaton become even more marked in his work after Jones's visit to Italy with Arundel. Such movement cannot, of course, be achieved in actual designs or in performance, when spectators are generally seated and the scenery occupies fixed locations in the stage area. What the printed texts of these masques make clear, however, is that Jones and his various literary collaborators expected an imaginative participation from the audience which would translate into this theatrical format their experience of movement and metamorphosis in real gardens at home and abroad. Inigo Jones's fondness for archways both in his masques and in his architectural work is surely not simply his tribute to Serlio's book devoted to that topic, but his recognition of their scope for signalling entry into further spaces.[41] Jones's patron in Italy, Arundel, devised a fine example of this spatial invitation in his sculpture garden (see below, p. 120).

An invitation to explore is evident in two of Jones's best-known designs for garden backdrops. That they are backcloths is important, for they cannot be removed to show further areas of the garden and must suggest this all by themselves. They do so by implying that we survey the garden from what Sir Henry Wotton called 'a high walk like a *Tarrace*, from whence might be taken a generall view of the whole *Plot* below'. From there the spectator is imagined to explore the garden, again just as Wotton described the 'incomparable' Italian garden he had seen – 'conveyed again by several *mountings* and *valings*, to various entertainments of his *sent* and *sight* . . . as if he had bin Magically transported into a new Garden'.[42] Stage directions for the masque associated with both designs make quite clear that this imaginary movement and participation in the garden's variety is what is expected:

> the scene again is varied into a new and pleasant prospect clean differing from all the other, the nearest part showing a delicious garden with several walks and parterras set around with low trees, and on the sides against these walks were fountains and grots, and in the furthest part a palace from whence went high walks upon arches, and above them open terraces planted with cypress trees, and all this was composed of such ornaments as might express a princely villa.[43]

Furthermore, it seems clear that Jones expected a fairly sophisticated response to these garden images – relying upon a ready identification of the infinite variety of fountains, grottoes, statues and other 'entertainments' which might be concealed in the arbours, walks and terraces depicted. There is some dispute, in fact, about which of Jones's two drawings matches the stage direction: Jonson's editors identified figure 60 as the setting for *Coelum Britannicum*, the stage direction for which has just been quoted; but Jones's editors say that the texts calls for 'grottoes and fountains' in the plural and therefore opt for another design (figure 61). They may well be correct; but any experienced garden visitor would not fail to see that there are several fountains in niches below the far terrace in the first drawing and would expect grottoes to be concealed beneath the terrace and stairs, as they are for example at the Villa Torrigiani near Lucca. The usual comparison of figure 60 with Callot's *Le Grand Parterre de Nancy* also perhaps fails to do justice to Jones's sensitivity to garden space – Jones's design shows a modest, though still variously exciting garden rather than a vast and spacious parterre; furthermore, the invocation of Callot's image rather ignores the frequency of such garden *ensembles* through Italy.[44]

We know that Jones borrowed extensively for his design from other available engravings, notably those by Giulio Parigi for Medici entertainments.[45] Many of these, of course, also represented gardens, and it is difficult sometimes to judge whether real or theatrical gardens have been the source for either Jones or Parigi. But since much real garden imagery and experience were so directly relevant to a masque's usual themes and presentation, it is worth stressing the extent of Jones's affinities with – if not even debts to – Italian garden design. Throughout his career parallels with gardens in Italy, apparent allusions to their special effects, at the very least a shared interest in motifs and modes of representation frequently present themselves.

Grottoes and grotto-like scenery provided opportunities for transformations, as we have already seen in *Oberon*, and for what Ben Jonson called 'that orderly disorder which is common in nature'.[46] In *Tethys's Festival*, created by Samuel Daniel and Inigo Jones in 1610, the eponymous Queen of the Ocean was suited to her changeful element at her very first appearance. The elaborate tableau is described, so the text says, in 'the language of the architector who contrived it':

> in a moment the whole face [of the first scene] was changed, the port vanished, and Tethys with her nymphs appeared in their several caverns gloriously adorned. This scene was comparted into five niches . . . [decorated with dolphins and whales and sea-horses; above Tethys' head was] a round bowl of silver, in manner of a fountain, with mask-heads of gold, out of which ran an artificial

Figure 60 Inigo Jones, Garden backdrop for a masque, drawing of 1630s.

water. On the midst of this was a triangular basement formed of scrolls and leaves, and then a rich veil adorned with flutings and enchased work with a frieze of fishes and a battle of tritons, out of whose mouths sprang water into the bowl underneath. On the top of this was a round globe full of holes, out of which issued abundance of water, some falling into the receipt below, some into the oval vase borne up by the dolphins; and indeed there was no place in this great aquatic throne that was not filled with the sprinkling of these two natural-seeming waters. The niches wherein the ladies sat were four, with pilasters of gold mingled with rustic stones showing like a mineral to make it more rock- and cavern-like . . .[47]

The description continues, elaborating upon the 'festoons of maritime weeds, great shells' and two figures 'turned half into fishes': in short, it reads like a description of any elaborate grotto at Pratolino, Tivoli (where Tethys also features), Aldobrandini or those northern imitations through which much Italian experience was increasingly filtered: for example, Jacques de Gheyn drew a remarkable grotto which was maybe an original device, an imitation or simply the representation of the experience of some Italianate grotto.[48] That Jones associated these extraordinary designs for *Tethys' Festival* with garden experiences in Italy even at this early date seems to be confirmed by the ending of the masque. Here Mercury invites the Duke of York to go in search of Tethys and her nymphs, who have vanished after marching 'with winding meanders like a river', and return with her in the

Figure 61 Inigo Jones, Garden backdrop for a masque, drawing of 1630s.

changed shape of the Queen; the Duke is told that he will find the ladies 'hard by within a grove / And garden of the spring addressed to Jove', whereupon 'suddenly appears the Queen's majesty in a most pleasant and artificial grove', just as if the audience had themselves wandered in some garden and come unexpectedly upon that grove.

The ambiguities of *boschetti*, woody groves which appear natural despite their creation by garden or masque designer, are exploited by Jones in *The Shepherd's Paradise*. The audience is shown either villas and their regular gardens at a distance from neighbouring groves – thus re-creating the Italian experience of regular gardens around the house and groves further away – or a strange cabinet composed of a mixture of architectural and sculptural forms with natural detailing that echoes their woody surroundings: a building intriguingly indeterminate, half artificial, half natural.[49] In *The Temple of Love*, performed in 1635 at Whitehall, Jones designed 'a spacious grove of shady trees, and afar off on a mount with a winding stair to the top was seated a pleasant bower'. Its winding stair apart, this feature of a mount with an arbour or temple on its summit echoes Pratolino's Grotta di Cupido or the mount of the Villa Medici at Rome, of which Moryson had published a description eighteen years before:

> The outside of the Grove was all of Firre trees, which are greene in winter, but the
> inside had most pleasant walkes among rowes of many other kindes of trees. In
> this Grove was a most sweete Arbour, having foure roofes, and as it were

117

> chambers, one above the other, the first whereof is twentie staires from the
> ground, whence lay a most large and most faire Gallery of stone. . . .[50]

A similar feature, hastily sketched for *The Triumph of Peace* in 1634, is described in James Shirley's text as 'an hill cut out like the depress of a theatre, and over them a delicious arbour with terms of young men'.[51]

The extent of this garden imagery in Inigo Jones's masque designs is not, given the political and aesthetic possibilities of garden art, very surprising. Its importance in the history of gardens as opposed to stage design or political pageantry, however, does need stressing; not least because most of these designs were available to William Kent and other members of Lord Burlington's circle in the formative years of the so-called English landscape garden. Jones's invocation of Italian imagery and his identification of it with England would be of particular importance at that later date. Then it would be the implementation of the third Earl of Shaftesbury's call for a national taste in design, a Glorious Revolution in the arts, rather than a celebration of political absolutism that would be at stake; but the role of Italy, classical and modern, would still be decisive.[52] Jones's example to these later gardenists would have been particularly striking because of the variety of his garden effects and their allusions (intended or not mattered little by then) to Italy.

Terraces were a feature that the masques frequently noticed. In *Florimène* (1635) there was a 'spacious garden, with walks, parterras, close arbours and cypress trees, and in the largest part stands a delicious villa, all which figureth the spring'.[53] Three years earlier in *Tempe Restored* terraces were involved in a whole repertoire of Italian effects:

> the lightsome scene appeared, showing a delicious place by nature and art, where in a valley environed with hills afar off was seated a prospect of curious arbours of various forms. The first order, of marble pilasters, between which were niches of rock-work and statues, some spurting water received into vases beneath them . . . . .
>
> Then the further part of the scene opening, there appears seated on the side of a fruitful hill a sumptuous palace with an open terrace before it and a great stair of return descending into the lower grounds, the upper part environed with walls of marble alongst which were planted cypress trees . . . . .[54]

It is a setting borrowed directly from Parigi's design for 'Calypso's Garden', used for the entertainment of Cosimo dei Medici and his bride in 1608. What is worth noticing about this well-known source for Jones is that the Italian design, though presented in the theatre *inside* the Uffizi, nevertheless draws for its motifs upon a whole range of Italian garden elements and themes. If gardens were nature brought to perfection upon one particular spot of ground, theatre designers were by no means so constrained and could invent stage gardens which far surpass real ones. Fame blows her trumpet from the highest terrace of the Villa Garzoni at Collodi near Lucca, while elsewhere at Pratolino or the Villa Aldobrandini the Muses have been gathered on the slopes of a Mount Parnassus; but in *Chloridia* (1631) Jonson and Jones can present them all together and with greater effect –

> Here out of the earth ariseth a hill, and on top of it, a globe, on which Fame is seen standing with her trumpet in her Hand; and on the hill are seated four persons, presenting Poesy, History, Architecture & Sculpture, who together with the nymphs, floods and fountains make a full choir. . . .[55]

The inside/outside ambiguities of Jones's 'Cupid's Palace' can rival those of the loggias at the Villa Giulia.[56] Thunder and lightning were presented in both *Artenice* and *Chloridia* ('a horrid storm, out of which enters the nymph Tempest, with four winds'), and the verbal account of them matches visitors' narratives of the same spectacle of thunder, lightning and bad weather on the terrace of the Villa Aldobrandini at Frascati.[57] And all of this imagery is offered in the service of the British state: as *Albion's Triumph* (1631) makes clear, a view of a Roman atrium, with statues between the columns, is metamorphosed eventually into 'a pleasant grove of straight trees, which rising by degrees to a high place, openeth itself to discover the aspect of a stately temple . . . sacred to Jove' and eventually this view gives way to a prospect of the palace at Whitehall.[58] The garden of the world becomes the garden of England.

iii: Jacobean garden mania

Parallel with these masques that Jones and various collaborators presented to the English court during the first thirty years of the seventeenth century, some equally grand and ambitious projects were attempted on the country estates of nobles and gentry who might well have assisted at or performed in those royal entertainments. Indeed, there were very close parallels between stage and garden: the description of the 'walks upon arches' in *Coelum Britannicum*, quoted above, is echoed in both the Earl of Middlesex's Copthall and the fabled gardens which Lucy, Countess of Bedford, created at Moor Park.[59] While the House of Oceanus in Jonson and Jones's *Neptune's Triumph* (1624) is related to the erection at about the same time of a series of famous grottoes: in the basement of the Whitehall banqueting house in the same year, by Isaac de Caus; and others, which we shall explore shortly at Moor Park, Woburn and Wilton.[60]

The art of perspective, too, played a crucial role in both masques and the new gardens. The organization of sight-lines at a royal entertainment, as Stephen Orgel has shown,[61] meant that the stage and its scenery were best viewed from the central seat occupied by the King. Gardens which were laid out along an axis also brought the fascinating skills of perspective into play; they, too, gave a privileged position to the visitor or the owner who stood on his highest terrace and gazed down the central vista. But as Sir Henry Wotton noticed, although perspective could be called 'the *Royaltie* of *Sight*', at least in gardens and landscapes this power was in fact less autocratically invoked. Gardens may, in Jonson and Jones's term, be 'princely', but they were for more than princes to explore; sight and feet are then tempted along other lines of vision (sub-perspectives, so to speak). Wotton sets out this experience with his usual concision:

> Some [considerations for choosing a site for building] againe may bee said to bee *Optical*. Such I meane as concerne the *Properties* of a well chosen *Prospect*: which I will call the *Royaltie* of *Sight*. For as there is a *Lordship* (as it were) of the *Feete*, wherein the Master doth much joy when he walketh about the *Line* of his owne *Possessions*: So there is a *Lordship* likewise of the *Eye* which being raunging, and Imperious, and (I might say) an *usurping Sence*, can indure no narrow *circumscription*; but must be fedde, both with extent and varietie. Yet on the other side, I finde vaste and indefinite views which drowne all apprehension of the

uttermost *Objects*, condemned, by good Authors, as if thereby some part of the pleasure (whereof we speake) did perish.[62]

Obviously in real as opposed to theatrical gardens this lordship of sight and feet has more ample opportunities (as well as a less restricted use, since many may enjoy what at a masque is technically permitted only to the King himself).

The Earl of Arundel returned in 1615 from Italy, where he had travelled with Inigo Jones and he set about creating a sculpture garden at his house beside the Thames. And we know that at least one vista in it was controlled in precisely the ways which Wotton discusses: Sir Dudley Carleton had presented the Earl with a fine 'head of Jupiter' and this prize item was positioned, according to a contemporary account, 'in his utmost garden, so opposite the Gallery dores, as being open so soon as you enter into the front Garden you have the head in your eie all the way'.[63] Moreover, the garden's organization of its visitors' responses was obviously contrived by a series of archways which initiated the passage from one part to another and dramatized the exploration. John Smythson, visiting London in 1618–19, noted 'The new Italyan gate . . . in the garden there'; an Inigo Jones drawing for a gateway survives; and various portraits of the Earl and his Countess give us glimpses of arches, loggias and beckoning termination points by which the visitor was manoeuvred through the galleries and gardens (figure 62).[64]

Unfortunately we know little about the exact layout of Arundel's sculpture garden. Yet it was clearly a deliberate attempt to emulate the ones which were so famous in Rome, above all the Vatican Belvedere. As we have seen,[65] gardens often had the aspect of museums and were, as was Arundel's, linked to galleries which displayed the most precious objects. Arundel House was the first English example among the 'Gardens and Galleries of great men', as Henry Peacham recognized when he included a chapter on collecting classical antiquities in a new edition of *The Compleat Gentleman* in 1634: in this he traces the Italian inspiration, notably in Florence and Rome, for Arundel's achievement which he describes as 'to transplant old Greece into *England*' in such a fashion as 'to perswade a man, that he now seeth two thousand yeeres agoe'; exactly the same point about the garden as a kind of memory theatre of classical civilization was made by Christopher Arnold when he saw Arundel's gardens in 1651.[66] Arundel had an instinct for collecting which obviously went far beyond what his garden and its loggias could accommodate – he acquired pictures, *objets de vertu*, costly stones from Daniel Nys and was eager to find out what rival *virtuosi* like Sir Thomas Roe 'hath bought, of Antiquities, Goddes, vases, inscriptions, Medalles, or such like'.[67] On his Italian travels, when he managed to visit almost all of the places where gardens were particularly admired from the Bay of Naples to Genoa and Turin, he bought statues and was allowed to excavate among the ruins in Rome; like Inigo Jones, he must have compared Palladio's designs 'with the Ruines themsealves'.[68] Upon his return to England, therefore, his determination to create a garden and cabinet to house and display his antiquities, whatever their precise forms, was necessarily executed with a full sense of classical and Renaissance precedents. The response of visitors was certainly of a piece with reactions to similar sculpture gardens in Italy:

> Foremost amongst the objects worthy to be seen stood the beautiful garden of
> that most famous lover of art, the Earl of Arundel; resplendent with the finest

Figure 63 Anonymous, detail from a portrait of the Earl of Arundel, about 1627.

gure 62 Daniel Mytens, portrait of the Countess of rundel, 1618.

ancient statues in marble, of Greek and Roman workmanship. Here were to be seen, firstly, the portrait of a Roman Consul, in long and graceful drapery, through which the form and proportion of that body could be readily perceived. Then there was a statue of Paris; and many others, some full-length, some busts only; with an almost innumerable quantity of heads and reliefs, all in marble and very rare.[69]

A glimpse of the gardens in a painting (figure 63) shows the statues prominently displayed along the edges of a terrace above the river, with steps ascending to it. And long after this famous garden was left derelict and eventually destroyed, its sculpture cast a reflected glory upon other gardens where pieces were acquired: Stukeley admired some at Lord Lemster's seat at Easton in the early eighteenth century, while Aubrey found other fragments decorating 'Cupid's' pleasure garden across the Thames.[70] There will be other important chapters in the history of the English garden that will concern sculpture's place in gardens, and the authority and example of Arundel's, despite its neglect and disappearance ('these precious Monuments . . miserably neglected, & scattered up & downe . . .'[71]), were decisive.

Arundel's gardens were what we would recognize readily as a scholarly virtuoso's garden. We find it harder to see the seriousness in some of the other garden exploits that were happening during the same years, especially those fabulous creations of which Salomon de Caus writes in his book, *Les Raisons des Forces Mouvantes*. But his love of ingenuity and his skill with hydraulic engineering were just another aspect of the age's *curiosity*. De Caus, a Frenchman with first-hand experience of Italy, was responsible for transforming several royal gardens for Queen Anne and later for the Prince of Wales between 1607–8 and 1613. They have long since disappeared, but from de Caus's own publications which were designed to record his inventions for royal patrons and from various verbal descriptions we can piece together some account of what was achieved. They are characterized above all by a bold use of Italianate elements, some modelled directly on de Caus's memory of his Italian trip (between 1595 and 1598), some on French versions of Italian items.

At Somerset House, for instance, he raised a 'new Terras', its retaining wall punctuated with pilasters and niches,[72] and a huge fountain-grotto which one German visitor recognized as being copied from the Mount Parnassus at Pratolino (see figure 46). What the young Duke of Saxony saw in 1613 was

> a Mount Parnassus: the mountain or rock is made of sea-stones, all sorts of mussels, snails, and other curious plants put together: all kinds of herbs and flowers grow out of the rock . . . On the side facing the palace it is made like a cavern. Inside it sit the Muses, and have all sorts of instruments in [their] hands. Uppermost on the top stands Pegasus, a golden horse with wings. On the mountain are built four small arches, in each rests a naked statue of marble. They have cornucopiae in hands and under their arms jugs from which water flows into the basin about four good paces wide, and is all around the mountain. They are supposed to represent four rivers. . . . It is thus a beautiful work and far surpasses the Mount Parnassus in the Pratolino near Florence.[73]

De Caus has added river gods, a familiar piece of classical and garden imagery, to the Medici Parnassus, as well as surrounding the mountain with water which also flowed down its sides. It all declares, as Sir Roy Strong has shown, the same emphasis upon royal ordering as did such masques as *Tethys' Festival*, which even had similar scenery. But the Parnassus – at least as we see it through the young German's account – is also a clear enactment of the happy rivalry and co-operation of art and nature: a statue of the Thames is placed on the mountain beside the real Thames, which flows past the garden; the materials of the hill are natural but also 'put together'. This same interest in the artist's skill which uses natural materials to fashion some artificial representation of nature is shown variously in de Caus's book, published after he had left England.

His volume also announces another important aspect of de Caus's work: its debt to antiquity, directly as well as indirectly via Renaissance imitations of classical devices. Its dedication and the preliminary address to the reader invoke Vitruvius through whose writings we know of the automata created by Ctesibius, a third-century Greek, while the main text invokes both Hero of Alexandria, the major exponent in antiquity of mechanics, hydraulics and theatrical automata, whose works were edited and copied in the Renaissance, and Renaissance figures like Michelangelo and Raphael. And just as his text honours traditions of treatises from the ancient to the modern world, so his designs present images for contemporary gardens derived from Italian attempts to realize classical inventions. And it is worth noticing at this point that these traditions, which feature centrally a link between gardens, theatres and engineering, continued well into the English eighteenth century. Stephen Switzer, seedsman, gardener and designer, published his *Introduction to a general system of Hydrostaticks and Hydraulicks* in 1729; he obviously considered that not only did its proposals for 'watering Noblemens and Gentlemens Seats, Buildings, Gardens' connect with his other writings on garden design but that its presentation of ancient texts and modern Italian and French examples of fountains and grotto mechanisms would still be of consequence.[74]

Hero of Alexander had described in his theorems such items as Hercules killing the Hydra, a tableau which was activated by the spectator lifting a representation of the golden apple of the Hesperides. This was in its turn copied by John Bate for *The Mysteryes of Nature and Art* (figure 64), a book which popularized mechanical inventions. The perpetuating of classical devices, in this particular case closely connected with gardens, was thus evidently carried on at both princely and more lowly levels of society. De Caus dedicated the second part of his *Forces Mouvantes* to the sister of Prince Henry; his untimely death in 1612 cut short the elaborate fountains which de Caus and an Italian engineer, Constantino dei Servi, were constructing for the Prince's gardens at Richmond. Some of the illustrations, de Caus tells the Princess, are of items planned for those gardens. They include (figure 65) de Caus's reclining version of the Pratolino statue of the Apennines (see figure 38), complete with a grotto inside; another of his plates represents the giant sitting upright on a mountain, the whole claimed to be three times the size of the Medici figure.[75] De Caus was evidently thinking on a huge scale for the work at Richmond.

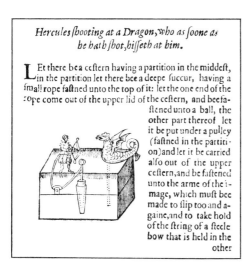

Figure 64 Hydraulic device of Hercules slaying the dragon, from John Bate, *The Mysteries of Art and Nature* (1634).

123

Figure 65 Design for reclining giant in Richmond Gardens, from Salomon de Caus, *Les Raisons des Forces Mouvantes* (1624).

Other projections for these gardens included fountains, grottoes, of which de Caus's book illustrates several examples, aviaries, and specially designated 'natural' areas. De Caus had already created a grotto-aviary for Queen Anne at Greenwich: Neumayr, the Duke of Saxony, also described it at length –

> Farther on one comes to a grotto. [It] is a small house from the front and on both sides mostly open, with great iron railings there. On the wall are three different arches, thus all along the whole wall embellished with snails, mussels, mother-of-pearl and all kinds of curious sea plants; in some places flowers, grass and all sorts of lovely herbs grow out. In the middle arch stands a figure, half a woman and half a horse in the right size, also made from shells and mussels; it gave water from itself unto the ground. In the other two arches were other figures from which water also sprang: on the ground sea stones were put together like rock. In some places there grew also flowers and small shrubs out of wood. There was also something of grass therein: on the wall sat on a branch a cuckoo, such [a cry] the gardener makes calling across the water. This house was also in the roof open in several places, although protected by wire grating, so that the birds, of which a great number were flying around inside, could not get out.[76]

The grotto elements are by now familiar, as is their play with artificial and natural components; but what is perhaps unusual is the combination of them with something that seems to have been a reconstruction of the aviary which Varro describes in *Rerum rusticarum*. We do not know whether Prince Henry, noted for his devotion to 'Building & Gardening',[77] would have been offered an even more complex version. But the combination of a classical *ornithon* with an elaborate grotto at Greenwich constituted a clear Roman gesture, which finds answering examples in the plates for the second part of *Forces Mouvantes*, where (de Caus writes) are illustrated designs intended for Richmond.[78] The inclusion of natural areas also has, as we have seen, clear classical authority in Pliny's *imitatio ruris*; so that a glimpse of a seat beside some water, with an island beyond, in the background of a portrait of Prince Henry (figure 66), which it has been suggested might be a view in the Richmond gardens, would not be out of keeping with this strange parkland of antique and Italian marvels. That such a piece of 'natural' imagery should be taken as a reference to *classical* gardening is all the more probable in that it is included in a portrait of the Prince of Wales: in the few years before his death he worked hard to establish and present himself both as virtuoso and as militant Protestant prince (unlike his pacifist father who favoured the Catholics). Henry would hardly have employed an Italian (dei Servi) to

Figure 66 Robert Peake, detail from a portrait of Henry, Prince of Wales, about 1610.

help create an Italian (and therefore perhaps Catholic) garden at Richmond; even if that is conceivable, it seems quite unlikely that he would parade a glimpse of it in one of his portraits, which were designed to create his public image; yet since one such portrait represented Henry as a Roman emperor, if the garden had associations they were likely to be antique.

De Caus also worked at Hatfield for the Earl of Salisbury; there natural elements were also introduced, both by areas within the gardens and by 'Diversified Prospects of this Charming Country' outside. These prospects were organized by establishing terraces down the hillside: a French visitor saw them in 1663 and suggests by his rather muddled prose that the experience of ascending and descending the terraces, observing the views outward and admiring the various manipulations of water (de Caus's hallmark), was a rich and enthralling one.[79] The visitor actually begins his description by noting Hatfield's range of imagery ('Objects that present themselves to us at all Sorts of Distances'); it is this versatility in the use of garden space, combined with the distinctly Italianate features of terraces, waterworks and views outward into the landscape, that marks Hatfield as a major example of Jacobean gardening. That it survived, unlike many others, into the Restoration period marks it further as a vital link in the traditions of Italian gardening: in an age when other styles of garden design became available to rival those supposedly derived from ancient and modern Rome one like Hatfield, and others we shall visit shortly, may have stood out as alternatives to the French forms by then in vogue.

iv: *The Danvers brothers, and Lucy Harington*

John Aubrey considered that it was Sir John Danvers 'who first taught us the way of Italian gardens'.[80] This claim undoubtedly signals Aubrey's sense that only piecemeal additions to or refurbishments of English gardens had been made before Danvers began to establish a wholly Italian garden at Chelsea in 1622 and another at Lavington in Wiltshire from 1628. The Danvers brothers were indeed highly qualified to have been the pioneers of the full-scale Italian garden in England: according to Aubrey, Sir John had a 'very fine fancy, which lay (chiefly) for gardens and architecture'. He had 'well travelled in France and Italy, and made good observations . . .' His brother Henry, later Earl of Danby, founded the Botanical Gardens at Oxford in 1621: with its three fine gateways, built by Nicholas Stone in the 1630s, it had the appropriate imagery (another tribute to Serlio's book of archways) to put England on the botanical map with Padua, Pisa and Florence.

John Danvers's Chelsea garden was considered so important by Aubrey that he made a special study of it; that manuscript of 1691 is an invaluable guide not only to one long-since lost Italian garden of the Jacobean period, but to habits of looking at gardens in the late seventeenth century. That second theme will be taken up more fully in due course, but what is useful to isolate now is that Aubrey's determination to trace the introduction of Italian garden design into England led him to make a particular study of the Chelsea garden even after it had been absorbed into larger grounds in the Dutch-French style. This absorption can be gauged by comparing Aubrey's rather disappointing plan (figure 67) with an engraved view from *Britannia Illustrata* of 1707, which shows the Duke of Beaufort's larger garden (figure 68): the Danvers oval and the terrace with its small pavilions at each end can be registered on the right-hand side of the Kip and Knyff panorama. To our eyes the original, Italianate garden looks perfectly at home in the large geometry; but to Aubrey's curious gaze it seemed distinctive, different. This should perhaps alert us to the extreme difficulty of identifying Italian designs surviving into a later period and being assimilated, even largely unchanged, into gardens styled in different ways.

In his discussion of the garden Sir Roy Strong emphasizes that its novelty was that it seems to have been the 'earliest instance in which house and garden were conceived *ab initio* as a single unit'.[81] Now Aubrey's sketch certainly seems to acknowledge this unified design; but his lengthy and more eloquent text adds further considerations – notably the garden's variety which was achieved despite the awkwardly flat terrain, the garden's manipulation of its spectator, and its theatrical quality.

From the house itself there were already two views: 'As you sitt at Dinner in the Hall, you are entertained with two delightful Visto's: one southward over the Thames & to Surrey: the other, northward into that curious Garden.' The rhetorical echo of Pliny describing the views from his two villas is strong even if fairly general.[82] In our gratitude to Aubrey's antiquarian instinct for careful details we should never forget the pressure upon his verbal accounts of earlier, famous literary descriptions of Roman villa life. For if the English terrain could not always match the Italian, the antique could live again in a mind which framed its own descriptions in terms of the classical literature.

The eye thus tempted by the curious garden from Sir John's dining hall was, however, cleverly frustrated from getting into it: 'You did not enter directly out of the Hall into the Garden.' Instead, the visitor first encounters 'a low semicircular wall', which Aubrey sketches and which serves to 'hinder the imediate pleasure and totall view primo introitu'.[83] At that point the visitor, confronted with a 'paire of staires', was forced to choose 'the right or the left hand', a familiar experience to anyone with direct experience of Italian terraces. The visitor had now reached a 'kind of Boscage': clearly Aubrey had difficulty with this, for above it he wrote the word 'Wildernesse'. What is shown in the two rectangular areas at the bottom of his drawing (figure 67) is a regular plantation of trees (marked by circles) with two statues (marked by squares) of the Gardener and his wife ('both accoutred according to their *Callings*'). There were apple and pear trees here as well as lilacs, sweet-briars, holly and juniper. Walks at the edge of this grove (for that is surely what Aubrey could also have called it) led the visitor towards statues of Cain and Abel on the right and of Hercules and Antaeus on the left. Both groups were from Nicholas Stone's workshop, and Aubrey records that Antonio Verrio, the Italian painter, much admired them and thought there was 'not such another piece of workmanship in England': the Cain and Abel may have been copied after the group by Giambologna at the Duke of Buckingham's York House, while the Hercules and Antaeus could have been imitated from the similar group which once stood in the middle of the Castello garden near Florence.[84]

The visitor was now in the oval part of the garden. His four entries to this were flanked on each side by further statues: sphinxes nearest the house – of the sort that John Raymond had admired at the Villa Borghese[85] – and shepherds and shepherdesses on the other three sides. The oval space was surrounded by a wall of cypress trees. In one respect it was 'an essentially English feature' – a bowling green.[86] But in another it was an amphitheatre, which the dramatic expressions of the six pastoral statues clearly

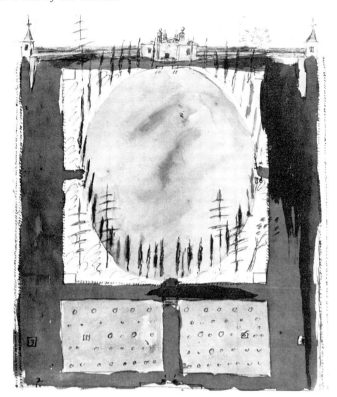

Figure 67 John Aubrey, drawing of Sir John Danvers's garden at Chelsea, 1691.

announced: Aubrey was pleased with their expressive carving – one couple leaning towards each other, their eyes almost closed; the sculptor had captured 'Love-passions in the very freestone'. Shepherds and shepherdesses were familiar *dramatis personae* in court masques and that, too, aided the theatrical aspect of this part of Danvers's garden. But the figures had other associations for Aubrey. He was struck by the statues' 'antique innocent simplicitie'; their presence on this level section of the gardens, what elsewhere Evelyn called 'that goodly plaine or rather Sea of Carpet', aptly recalled 'the pleasant lives of the Shepherds we reade of in *Romances* & truer stories'. Aubrey commented on the lifelikeness of these Danvers statues as well as on the sphinxes by citing passages from Pliny's *Natural History*.[87]

The main disadvantage of the Chelsea garden site, Aubrey notes, was its flatness. But the split descent from the house into the grove had given a preliminary illusion of varying levels which was repeated at the opposite side of the oval. A trench had been dug and the earth used to create a terrace walk beyond; bridges passed over the gap on to the terrace which was graced with a banqueting hall in the middle and two little pavilions at either end (the latter only seem to have survived by the time of figure 68). Below the brick banqueting house was a grotto (a modest version of Isaac de Caus's grotto beneath the Whitehall Banqueting House), and Aubrey was especially struck by the way that the visitor's mood was changed as he went from one to the other: 'Now, as you goe / descend, downe / from this gay Paradise into the darksome, deep Vault / Grotto where the Well is, it affects one

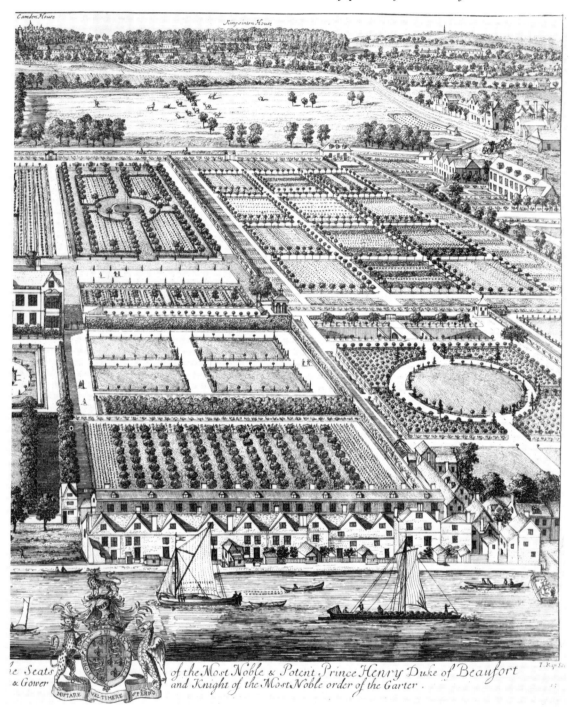

Figure 68 The Duke of Beaufort's garden, detail of engraving from *Britannia Illustrata* (1707). Danvers's garden, drawn by Aubrey in Figure 67, can be seen incorporated into the right of this detail.

129

with a kind of Religious horrour'. From simply observing the emotions of the statues as he would those of actors in a theatre ('the passion' of Hercules), Aubrey has become a participant in the garden's little dramas.

We have seen that Italian grottoes were often small theatres, where automata enacted scenes for the curious visitor. Hydraulic machinery may have been less available and less advanced in England (a clear implication of the Oxford dons who wrote in 1659 about Evelyn's *magnum opus* on garden history); but even without it grottoes could clearly work upon receptive visitors and produce comparable effects, as witness Aubrey's sublime *frisson* as he descended into the Chelsea garden grotto. Grottoes were certainly fashionable. Danvers's other garden at Lavington either had one or was intended to, for Aubrey reports an arch set in the stream that ran through the gardens, 'an admirable place for a Grotto'.[88] Wilton, Woburn and Moor Park, as we shall see, all had fine grottoes.

Lavington was a site much more conducive to a varied garden. Aubrey compares them in his manuscript account of the Chelsea garden: 'Now, as at Lavington the ground lay uneven, & irregular; the skill was, there, to reduce it into form & regularity & evennesse; *à contra* here, the Ground lay plain / flatt, and the businesse was to make elevations & depressions . . .' If the ups and downs at Chelsea were somewhat contrived, Lavington was altogether more pleasing, being 'full of irregularities, both naturall & artificiall, *sc.* elevations & depressions'. In particular, Aubrey noticed

> a very pleasant elevation on the southside of the garden, which steales, arising almost insensibly, that is, before one is aware, and give[s] you a view over the spatious corn-fields there, and so to East Lavington: where, being landed on a fine levell, letteth you descend again with the like easiness . . . . .

The gentle slope, the views over richly agricultural land from a natural terrace and the statues which Aubrey notices all about the garden but particularly those set in the stream[89] – these suggest an English version of Pratolino, as that Italian garden might have been seen by such an English visitor as Robert Bargrave. This younger son of the Dean of Canterbury, whom we have already encountered, admired Pratolino for its statues and waterworks, but his manuscript also contains a description of an unnamed garden which comes close to the experience of Lavington:

> the great garden itself; wherein are all varietie desirable of rare and numerous waterworks, stately walks of diverse sorts, Gallant Statues in great abundance, Strange Creatures, faire Ponds raild round about, curious Sommerhouses & Arbours, privat Grotta's, spacious walkes close and Open, & diversitie of rare trees, flowers, fruits and plants.[90]

Unhappily for us all that Aubrey manages at Lavington by way of a description trails off into 'It is impossible to describe this garden, it is so full of variety and unevenesse . . .' However, the mere fact that those are the qualities he applauds underlines the very close parallels between new English gardens and those most admired on the Grand Tour in Italy.

Before we move from Lavington to nearby Wilton House, where the Earl of Pembroke created gardens which were – in Aubrey's judgement – 'the third after [Danvers's] two, of the Italian mode', one other garden deserves consideration at this point. A fine Italianate garden was established at Moor Park, Hertfordshire, between 1617 and 1627 for

Lucy Harington, Countess of Bedford. Sir William Temple was to remember it years later in his meditation 'Upon the Gardens of Epicurus', written in 1685, so it is again with the aid of verbal description that we are forced to recover the experience of what Temple called a 'most beautiful and perfect' garden.

It was made, Temple recalls, 'on the sides of a hill . . . but not very steep'. His description then conducts us from the house and down through the gardens:

> The length of the house, where the best rooms and of most use or pleasure are, lies upon the breadth of the garden, the great parlour opens into the middle of a terras gravel walk that lies even with it, and which may be, as I remember, about three hundred paces long, and broad in proportion; the border set with standard laurels, and at large distances, which have the beauty of orange-trees, out of flower and fruit: from this walk are three descents by many stone steps, in the middle and at each end, into a very large parterre. This is divided into quarters by gravel walks, and adorned with two fountains and eight statues in the several quarters; at the end of the terras-walk are two summer-houses, and the sides of the parterre are ranged with two large cloisters, open to the garden, upon arches of stone, and ending with two other summer-houses even with the cloisters, which are paved with stone, and designed for walks of shade, there being none other in the whole parterre. Over these two cloisters are two terrasses covered with lead, and fenced with balusters; and the passage into these airy walks is out of the two summer-houses, at the end of the first terras-walk. The cloister facing the south is covered with vines, and would have been proper for an orange-house, and the other for myrtles, or other more common greens. . . .
>
> From the middle of the parterre is a descent by many steps flying on each side of a grotto that lies between them (covered with lead, and flat) into the lower garden, which is all fruit-trees, ranged about the several quarters of a wilderness, which is very shady; the walks here are all green, the grotto embellished with figures of shell rock-work, fountains, and water-works. If the hill had not ended with the lower garden, and the wall were not bounded by a common way that goes through the park, they might have added a third quarter of all greens; but this want is supplied by a garden on the other side of the house, which is all of that sort, very wild, shady, and adorned with rock-work and fountains.
>
> This was Moor-Park when I was acquainted with it, and the sweetest place, I think that I have ever seen in my life, either before or since, at home or abroad.[91]

The description has great precision, the sharpness of happy recollection, and the experience of exploring Moor Park is clearly conveyed.

Something of what it looked like may be derived from a rather naive painting of 1662 which shows another superb garden at Llanerch in Denbighshire (figure 69). This was created by Mutton Davies after his travels in Italy, and to 'the old gardens . . . made . . . in the foreign taste, with images and water tricks'[92] a descendant added a cabinet of curiosities. Moor Park may have been grander than Llanerch, and it was obviously more up-to-date in having house and gardens aligned on one axis. But the descents, the summer houses, the grotto set into the space beneath a divided stairway are the same in both. Llanerch also has a fine round water theatre, presided over by the figure of Neptune; this is perhaps a miniaturized version of the Isolotta in the lower western portion of the Boboli Gardens. Llanerch is also represented with a bridge leading off at the bottom right – perhaps into a grove like that which Temple describes at Moor Park ('very wild, shady, and adorned with rock-work and fountains'). But the conjunction of garden and grove –

Figure 69 Anonymous, *Massey's Court, Llanerch*, oil painting of 1662.

frustrated by the public road at Moor Park – was apparently so crucial that it was achieved elsewhere and equally commented upon by Temple. Just as much as the grottoes this juxtaposition of regular and irregular styles makes Moor Park eloquently Italian. So also does its elaborate and ambiguous cluster of 'airy walks' and cloisters down the sides of the first level: as nice a confusion of inside/outside and above/below as that at the Villa Giulia in Rome. The layout of this first level between the arcades may be visualized like the handsome parterre at Little Hadham laid out in the 1630s and seen in the portrait of Sir Arthur Capel and his family (figure 70). The spaciousness of Little Hadham perhaps better conveys what Lucy Harington achieved at Moor Park than does the slightly cramped garden at Llanerch. The latter, however, reaps a fine advantage from the naturally sloping site, whereas at Little Hadham ascents and descents are created artificially via the elaborate stairways between terrace and parterre.

Figure 70 Cornelius Johnson, detail of portrait of Baron Capel and his family, about 1639.

v: Grottoes

The grotto at Moor Park, together with its gardens and grove, succumbed to the rival ideas of garden design of 'Capability' Brown. But another of Lucy Harington's grottoes does miraculously survive at Woburn Abbey (figure 71). It allows us to appreciate far more directly than do verbal accounts or even original designs this particular aspect of garden taste. The Woburn grotto was completed sometime before 1627, and it presumably represents an enthusiasm for grottoes in the wake of King James's creation of one below Inigo Jones's Whitehall Banqueting Hall. In accounts books for 1623–4 are entries for 'making a Rocke in the vault under the banquetting house' with 'rocke stuff' and 'shells'; the name of Isaac de Caus, Salomon's younger brother, also appears in connection with this royal grotto, and his involvement with several others throughout England has been suggested.[93] Maybe he created those for Moor Park and Woburn as well as one for Lucy Harington's town house on the north side of the Strand. Perhaps figure 72 is one of his

Figure 71 Anonymous, drawing of the grotto at Woburn Abbey, perhaps nineteenth century.

Figure 72 Attributed to Isaac de Caus, drawing of grotto with Mercury and Europa.

134

designs: at any rate, in conjunction with the surviving example at Woburn, it tells us much about the extraordinary world which a grotto represented.

First and foremost, a grotto represented the natural world at *its* most artful and curious: shells, strange rock formations (porous stone was particularly favoured). But then the grotto-maker added his contribution by simulating – as at Woburn – rocks and coral. And then, using his collaboration of nature's art and the artist's imitation of nature, grottoes were supplied with imagery from classical myth. At Woburn these are *putti* astride dolphins, sea-gods riding upon shell-chariots; in the design at the Victoria and Albert Museum, Mercury playing upon his pipe, and Europa borne away on the bull (presumably when the machinery was activated, she moved off through the right-hand archway). This little drama is framed by an imitated natural arch either side of which are metamorphic figures, Daphnes caught in the midst of transformation into laurel trees. These Ovidian characters, as we have seen in section 4, lent themselves to grottoes where all the emphasis was upon change, invention, art and nature. They provided imagery which visitors could fill out with their own recollections of the *Metamorphoses*, and possibly with many other ideas and associations: the prevalence of dolphins in these underground caverns where the elements of water and earth compete may well allude to the notion of Hermes Trismegistus that the just are transformed into dolphins which represent the symbolic ascent of the soul above the waters of materialism.[94] Woburn grotto does not have and does not appear to have had any of the hydraulic machinery which we know was installed at Wilton and is clearly necessary in figure 72 to mobilize Europa and the Bull; however it seems possible that the mere presence of other imagery of change – the sea creatures riding the waves, the shells and rocks made into pictures or architectural forms as Ovid had celebrated – promoted in visitors a readiness to see movement where it was not technically possible.

The grotto's mineral and geological collections also allowed a quasi-scientific interest to exist (albeit somewhat submerged) with the delight in art and nature's curiosity. The grotto was at the exotic and magical end of a spectrum that included at its other the study of both antiquities and botanical and zoological aspects of the natural world. Some time after the Woburn grotto was completed Queen Henrietta Maria authorized alterations in the gardens of Somerset House: they included the addition of fountains with 'syrens . . . seated astride dolphins'. And at St James's she apparently installed 'a long covered gallery, where one may see the rarest wonders of Italy in a great number of stone and bronze statues'.[95] The point is that we should register both as part of larger concerns which embrace all the workings of nature and art (including the 'arts' of engineering and building). The grotto was a hugely privileged location for such concerns because it accommodated so many of them. So it is no wonder that the taste for them spread. We have encountered examples at Wollaton, beneath the terrace at Sir John Danvers's in Chelsea, within the arms of descending stairways at Moor Park and Llanerch; audiences were surely to have imagined them under the terraces which Inigo Jones's backdrops depicted (see figures 60 & 61). And there were others at Temple Newsam,[96] perhaps under the terrace and almost certainly in the central fountain on the terrace at Rycote in Oxfordshire (figure 73), from which there was also a large prospect over the adjoining parkland. We shall continue to find grottoes within terraces throughout the seventeenth century, for the creation of the latter invariably provided opportunities for the former. Both were judged by a whole series of tourists, as we have seen, to be Italian features – the terrace

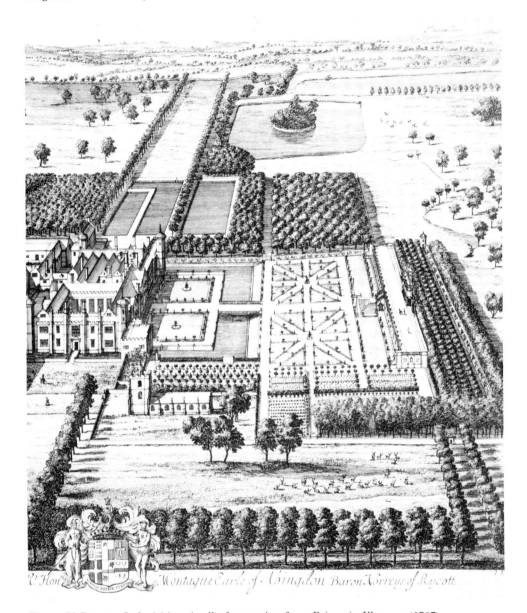

Figure 73 Rycote, Oxfordshire, detail of engraving from *Britannia Illustrata* (1707).

overlooking the sunken flower garden at the Villa Torrigiani, near Lucca, still retains its little dramas and some of its hydraulic machinery, and it is the scale of Torrigiani rather than the baroque size of similar effects at the Villa Aldobrandini, Frascati, that would have been practicable on many English country estates. It is this fairly modest scale in conjunction with fantastical shows and conceits that marks the English grottoes' debt to Italy rather than to France. It is true that terraces and waterworks set into their walls were executed in French gardens during the seventeenth century; but they were either clearly

136

inspired by Italian examples and even executed by Italian workmen, as as St Germain-en-Laye; indeed, under Le Nôtre they lost that essentially magical quality which had attracted English gardeners to the Italian grotto.

This encouragement and localization of 'curiosity' in the English-Italianate grotto, however, was annexed to the rather unsteady beginnings of experimental science. A magical Italian grotto would become a kind of laboratory. Especially for those English antiquarians who looked back to English gardening of the 1620s and 1630s from the years after the foundation of the Royal Society grottoes were clearly to be esteemed for their contributions to science. Thus in Plot's *Natural History of Oxfordshire*, first published in 1677, several grottoes are singled out for their experimental interest: at Sir Anthony Cope's there was a clock that worked by water and 'in a House of *Diversion* built in a small *Island* in one of the *Fish-ponds*' a '*Ball* . . tost by a *Column* of *Water*, and artificial *Showers* descend at pleasure'.[97] But Plot considered that the best of this kind were those contrived by Thomas Bushell in his grounds at Enstone during the late 1620s (figure 74).

Figure 74 Grotto created by Thomas Bushell at Enstone, engraving from Robert Plot, *The Natural History of Oxfordshire* (1677).

According to Plot, Bushell was clearing ground for a cistern when he discovered 'a *Rock* so wonderfully contrived by *Nature* her self, that he thought it worthy all imaginable Advancement by *Art*'.[98] He thereupon constructed various small buildings and a garden around what he himself called 'another desolate Cell of Natures rarities at the head of a Spring'. Bushell had been a secretary to Francis Bacon and was clearly inspired by Bacon's fascination with both occult and scientific mysteries; it is these interests that he maintained in what was the central feature of Enstone, a grotto built over the originally discovered rock. His hydraulic works produced rain, rainbows, a silver ball held up on a spout of water, birdsong and 'many strange forms of Beasts, Fishes and Fowls'; optical effects were added by means of mirrors; there were *giocchi d'acqua* ('a hedge of water made streaming up, about a mans height'); there was a wooden statue of Neptune aiming his trident at a duck which swam perpetually around him, a spaniel in pursuit – a device which Aubrey planned to copy at his own house. All of these were set in a small terraced garden, full of flowers and with 'a curious Walke, with neatly contriu'd Arbors', what Bushell called the 'Ornaments of contemplative Groves and Walks'.

Bushell's hydraulic machinery was Italian in origin – the ball supported on a column of water was an admired item at the Villa Aldobrandini, organs and bird-song pleased visitors to the Villa D'Este – but it was equally an imagery given wide circulation in books such as Salomon de Caus's *Les Raisons des Forces Mouvantes*. The boundaries between childish conceits, magical rites and experimental science are hard to draw in such enterprises: de Caus himself built what was certainly a cabinet of curiosities and probably a laboratory at the end of the Hortus Palatinus in Heidelberg.[99] Both in Italy and on his travels through France and England John Evelyn was constantly alert to gardens given over to scientific purposes, however quaint those may now seem. In the manuscript of *Elysium Britannicum* he records an 'Artificiall Echo' in the Tuileries gardens, exedra-shaped, and plans a section on both 'Artificiall' and natural music. He used his own garden at Sayes Court partly as a laboratory and it was there that he kept the transparent beehive given him by Dr Wilkins of Wadham whose garden was another cabinet of both botanical and hydraulic curiosities.[100]

Bushell's grotto at Enstone, born from its creator's fascination with experimentation, has a place in both the history of science and the history of the garden. In connection with its garden interest it also functioned on one occasion as a theatre: in August 1636 King Charles and Henrietta Maria visited Bushell, who presented them with an entertainment of 'speeches and songs'. The grotto was the stage and the occasion or subject-matter, for the small booklet produced to commemorate the royal visit announces the sequence of events: 'The *Hermits* speech ascending out of the ground as the King entred the Rock'; 'Mr Bushell his contemplation upon the Rock'; 'A Sonnet within the pillar of the Table at the Banquet'; 'Mr Bushell presenting the Rock by an Eccho sung to the King and Queenes *Majesty*' – a happy alliance of Ovidian fable and mechanical ingenuity; and finally, a song was sung to their Majesties 'at Mr Bushell's Rock'.[101]

Waterworks continued, certainly, to entertain and delight: Edward Wright visiting Italy as late as the 1720s was admiring the hydraulic displays at the Villa Aldobrandini.[102] But increasingly they seemed merely extravagant, frivolous, unless invoked in the name of experimental science. Something of both attitudes may be seen in Bate's *The Mysteries of Nature and Art*, published in 1634 followed by a second edition, 'with many additions unto every part', the next year. Though it popularized, it nevertheless offered itself as a serious handbook on such devices in the tradition of Salomon de Caus's book or that by his brother, Isaac, *Nouvelle Invention de lever l'eau* (1644), which received an English translation (appropriately by John Leak) in 1659 entitled *New and Rare Inventions of Waterworks*. Bate agreed with Bushell's claim that nature's contrivances may be 'advanced' by human art and skill: the dedicatory poem of the first edition argues that art helps the mind descry 'Natures obscure and hidden rarities'. But he is just as capable of treating all his devices as amusing toys, so he can suggest placing 'divers Images in sundry and severall parts of the Garden, the more antique and ridiculous, the more pleasant and delightfull'.[103] Doubtless waterworks can always appeal to the child in man, and such an appeal may co-exist readily with more serious concerns. The work of Sir Samuel Moreland later in the century suggests how this is so: his own grounds at Vauxhall contained a room of mirrors with fountains that entertained Aubrey and Evelyn, but in work for Lord Arlington at Euston and his very practical irrigation plans at Windsor he lent himself to scientific and pragmatic schemes which Evelyn also approved. Similarly, Henry Winstanley, builder of the Eddystone Lighthouse, had a mansion at Littlebury 'with abundance of fine Curiosityes all performed by Clockwork': these included both whimsical devices, such as a chair that ran backwards into the garden on rails, and more 'practical' machines that served tea and coffee in cups to the company.[104] Even Enstone achieved a new lease of life under its subsequent owner, the Earl of Lichfield, whose additions and hydraulic engineering works are carefully reported by Robert Plot.

vi: *Wilton House gardens*

John Worlidge's *Systema Horti-Culturae, or the Art of Gardening* (1677) also praised waterworks 'for your Own or your Friends divertisements'. He went on to note that historically the 'most famous of this kind that this Kingdom affords, is that *Wiltonian Grotto* near unto *Salisbury*, on which no cost was spared to make it compleat, and wherein you may view, or might have lately so done, the best of Water-works'.[105] Like Aubrey, Worlidge's instinct in face of the huge spread of gardening enthusiasm is to pin down some essential moments of its history. Aubrey and other antiquarians, however, went further and compiled notes on the Wilton grotto and its surrounding gardens. Though virtually nothing of its splendours survives, Wilton was so much the epitome of Italian gardening in the first half of the seventeenth century that it must be considered in some detail.

Both Aubrey and an entry in the Pembroke archives for 1635/6 attribute the garden to de Caus.[106] Isaac de Caus is presumably the author of the book on Wilton gardens published about 1645 which provides detailed plans and elevations including the panorama of the garden (figure 75). The brief page of text describes it as divided into three sections: the first is composed of four 'Platts, embroidered', in the middle of each of which are four 'Fountaines with Statues of Marble'; at either side of this first section are flower beds and 'beyond them is the little Terrass raised for the more advantage of beholding these Platts'. This feature, answered by the much larger terrace after the third section of the garden, is clearly an attempt to devise some variation in levels in an otherwise rather flat garden. But we must be cautious in assuming that a visitor's experience of these

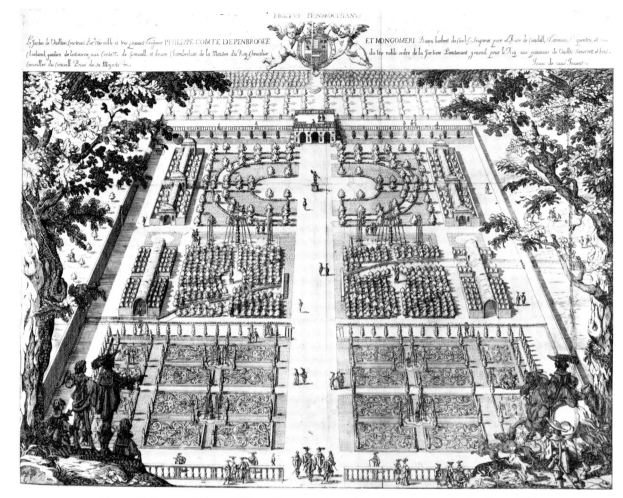

Figure 75 Engraved view of Wilton House gardens, from Isaac de Caus, *Le Jardin de Wilton* (about 1645).

gardens would have been solely of a level, Venetian type.[107] We have the testimony of the future Bishop Burnet as late as the 1680s (when we would expect admiration for level sites) that the gardens along the Brenta Canal were laid out with much 'diversity'.[108] It is precisely that diversity that Aubrey considers so important and so Italianate: at Wilton it was achieved first by the 'little terrace' and then by the strikingly different character given to each of the garden's partitions.

After the elaborate, flowery first section, the visitor passed to one composed of 'two Groves, or woods cutt with divers Walks' – a thoroughly Italian experience not confined at all to the Veneto. Like the groves of the Villa Lante or the section of the Villa Ludovisi shaped as an outdoor museum, these Wilton groves had statues of Bacchus and Flora in each part. The natural effect of this section was further emphasized by tunnels of vegetation down either side and by the very casual fashion in which the River Nadder was allowed to meander through these 'aforesayd groves', an impression that would have been far more insistent than it is from the artificial elevation of the engraved view.

The third section, lying beneath the large terrace, was an interesting compromise between the excessive art of the first and the studied naturalness of the second. It had the form of a Roman circus and appropriately was decorated by a 'Gladiator of brass the most famous Statue of all that Antiquitie hath left'.[109] The circus was ringed with fruit trees and at each side were more 'covered Arbours'.

At the end of the central walk the visitor was faced with a 'Portico of stone cutt and adorned with Pillasters and Nyches within which are figures of white Marble'. At each side of this portico were stairs, 'an ascent leading up to the Terrasse upon the steps whereof instead of Ballastres are Sea-monsters casting water from one to the other from the top to the bottome . .', a feature of gardens at Frascati and Tivoli (see the water balustrades, without sea-monsters, in figure 44). From the terrace visitors could look back over the garden they had traversed, but they could also look out upon a hillside shaped into more extensive groves and full of Italian reminiscence. There was first an amphitheatre like that in the Boboli Gardens, though here it is augmented by another piece of theatre imagery, the double staircase from the Vatican Belvedere (figure 76). A painting at Wilton House shows that the alley through the woods terminated in what looks very much like a triumphal arch and an equestrian statue of Marcus Aurelius cast from the famous original at the Capitol in Rome. There was also a cascade decorated with a statue of Pegasus, which William Stukeley engraved for his *Itinerarium curiosum*.[110] This image, apt enough for any garden whose owner wished to suggest the affinities of his waters with the springs of Helicon, released by the touch of Pegasus's hoof, was a familiar one in many Italian gardens: he greeted the visitor entering the groves of the Villa Lante and presided over the Muses at both Pratolino and the Villa Aldobrandini; he had been introduced by Salomon de Caus into Anne of Denmark's Somerset House gardens.

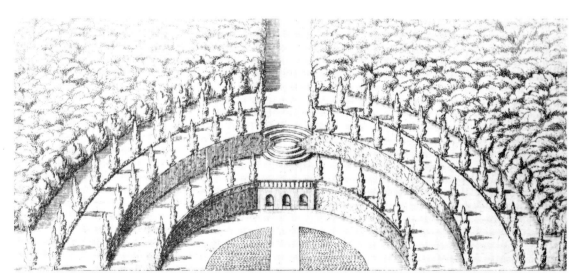

Figure 76 Detail of amphitheatre in the hillside at Wilton, engraving from de Caus, *Le Jardin de Wilton*.

But for many it was the grotto that made Wilton famous.[111] Situated under the terrace between the main garden and the hillside, it was, says Aubrey, 'paved with black and white Marble; the Roofe is vaulted'. But like the rest of the gardens that artifice was dedicated to the production of 'natural' contrivances. Tritons, 'excellently well wrought', seemed alive, and other figures wept water. Hydraulic machinery produced various bird-songs. And, besides *giocchi d'acqua* to wet the unwary, there was a device for producing three rainbows. The secret of this last device, Aubrey recounts, de Caus kept to himself and 'would not let the Gardiner (who shows it to Strangers) know how to do it and so upon his death it is lost'. In a marginal note Aubrey notes that 'The Grott & pipes did cost ten thousand pounds': whether this was a tourist's gullibility or not, Wilton's grotto must have been costly.

In all, the ambitious scope of the Wilton gardens and almost all of their details marked them as finely Italian. William Stukeley sketched many of its 'Antiquities' in June 1724 and promised himself to write 'an account of my Lord Pembroke's Antiquities about this time, with good designs of them. This [note] book was the ground plot. . . .'[112] For Stukeley, Wilton was primarily a memory theatre, a collection of 'great illustrations of history':

> That the curious spectator may be reminded at least of the character of so many illustrious personages famous in ancient times . . . a double pleasure in improving the mind & fixing in the memory a stronger impression of the qualitys & endowments, of the virtues & vices each was distinguished for; whilst the eye is surveying the lively portraits.

This visual directory of classical people ('bringing as it were all *Athens* to *Wilton*' – Stukeley included all classical antiquity in that gesture) was the more essential because, like Joseph Spence in *Polymetis* later, the modern mind could get too confused. Such a collection as that at Wilton was 'especially necessary', according to Stukeley's manuscript, 'from the great number & variety of them, to prevent the confusion of *ideas* in the mind even of the greatest scholars, if we could suppose any one acquainted with all their storys at first sight'.

Clearly by Stukeley's time Wilton offered most as a learned collection, and the waterworks had lost their attraction – presumably in no small part because the secret of their workings had not been passed down. Earlier visitors – and there were many, for the gardens were famous – responded more variously to its range of details, a conspectus of the best modern European gardening but with a strong, distinctive Italian accent. Evelyn was there in July 1654 and in his usual terse fashion summed up its achievements:

> The Garden (heretofore esteem'd the noblest in all *England*) is a large handsome plaine, with a *Grotto* & Waterworks, which might be made more pleasant were the *River* that passes through, clensed & rais'd, for all is effected by mere force: It has a flower Garden not inelegant: But after all, that which to me renders the Seate delightfull, is its being so neere the downes & noble plaines about the Country & contiguous to it . . . .[113]

His taste is for less mechanical effects and for prospects and, so his first parenthesis suggests, for more recent developments in garden design. It is to these and to Evelyn's own substantial part of them that we must now turn.

10 'The Way of Italian Gardens'

i: 'Great Changes in Gardens'

That Italian gardens provided the imagery, the structures and the ideas for all northern gardens, whether French, Dutch or English, is scarcely surprising; there was, indeed, nowhere else whence such inspiration could derive. During the first forty years of the seventeenth century England's initiatives in garden design were inspired directly or indirectly (via France) by Italian examples. But where the fact of an Italian inspiration does become significant is precisely when alternative styles were available. The choice of looking to Italy (and behind it to classical Rome) instead of to the France of Louis XIV in the latter half of the seventeenth century is, if not surprising, at least remarkable. If after 1660 an Englishman rejected the opportunity to design *à la française* or praised Italian at the expense of French gardens, then his decision becomes of some consequence, and its motives are worth examining.

So much gardening in Jacobean and Caroline England was royalist or bore unmistakably royalist implications that it cannot be a matter for surprise that the Parliamentarians destroyed some particularly fine examples of it. Accordingly, Sir Roy Strong brings his study of Renaissance gardens in England to a close on the eve of the Civil Wars; he notes, sadly, the Parliamentarian reaction to several royal desmenes: 'In one gesture of stupendous barbarism the statuary and fountains were dismantled and auctioned off, the avenues of trees felled and disposed of as timber and the gardens abandoned. Nothing could have brought the curtain down with more appalling finality . . . When Charles II returned in 1660, royal gardening had to begin again.'[1] And, of course, it resumed with new imagery derived from France and the gardens laid out there by André le Nôtre for Louis XIV, Charles II's host during his exile. But what Strong's account somehow leaves out is that by the eve of the Civil Wars Italianate Renaissance gardens were a familiar style and were even created by landowners outside the royal circles and that they continued to be designed during the Interregnum. Perhaps the antique Roman associations of Italian gardens even authorized this style for England's republican interlude: Pembroke, whose hillside at Wilton was decorated with a statue of Marcus Aurelius, was to side with Parliament when

143

civil war broke out in 1642. So what we must now attend to is the spread of Italianate garden imagery into much more modest estates throughout England and Wales; whatever the political affiliations of these landowners eager to beautify their grounds in ways that were still for them strikingly new, the 'great Changes in Gardens as well as Houses'[2] ensured that Italianate gardens were not associated exclusively with absolutist royal power nor, more importantly, with aristocracy.

The difficulty with adjudicating the spread of the Italian Renaissance garden to the properties of both gentry and lesser nobility before and after the Restoration is that its style and imagery could be confused with recent developments in French gardens. This seems, however, rather more a modern than a contemporary problem. Wilton House garden, as represented in figure 75, may seem to us today rather more an example of pan-European mannerism than anything specifically Italianate. Yet the analyses of its effects by seventeenth-century visitors which were considered in the previous chapter underline the Italian quality which could be found in them. John Aubrey's discovery and examination of the Italian character and ambience of Danvers's Chelsea garden even after it had been absorbed and exapanded into the French-inspired layout of the Duke of Beaufort's (see above p. 127) clearly suggest that Italian features revealed themselves to the experienced eye of an antiquarian and virtuoso.

Many of these same Italian features were absorbed into French gardens; but what distinguish the French version, especially in the hands of André Le Nôtre, are questions of scale and tone. Imagery may be similar; but its treatment and effects were not. Inigo Jones's parterre in the masque design for *Coelum Britannicum* (see figure 60) is much more intimate than that at Nancy to which it is sometimes compared. French gardens tended to be more 'formal' in the sense of providing forms for ceremonial, public life, such as larger open spaces, wide platforms, processional avenues: it is perhaps the manner in which the engraving of Wilton adopts those visual emphases which misleads us, since it converts the gardens there into a stage for figures playing social roles. By contrast, what the English admiration for Italian Renaissance gardens constantly emphasized in addition to their potential for that kind of public and political theatre, is the opportunities for individual entertainment, surprise and discovery; visitors seemed to participate more imaginatively than they were required to in French gardens where simple admiration was in order. That this is a false distinction will be clear to anyone who has studied the iconography of Versailles; but the demands upon the English imagination of sites upon the classical ground of Italy evidently enforced such invidious discriminations about French gardens. Furthermore, as has already been discussed (p. 97), the whole idea of variety was deemed to be a quality which did *not* characterize the French arts, but did (at least in gardens) declare itself eloquently in Italy. And we have Evelyn's testimony (see below, p. 153) that 'luxury' had spoilt too many late-seventeenth-century English garden designs: presumably he points to conspicuous expense, excess and showiness, above all a lack of appropriateness for English country gentry and lesser aristocracy. In all those respects the Italian sense of scale and tone was preferable to the French. What will concern us, then, will be the potential of Italian garden design which was discovered, just as the French did for their own different situation, by many gentry and lesser nobility after the death of Charles I.

ii: Evelyn at Wotton and Albury

Typical in many ways of such new garden owners was John Evelyn. His alert responses to gardens while travelling in Italy during the 1640s, written up in his diary years later, testify to his fascination with the subject. His own garden designs, his attention to gardens during his English travels, his writings and scholarship in garden history during the remainder of a long life – all make him the leading gardenist of England from the civil wars until the turn of the century. Furthermore, at least two of the gardens he created have survived in ways that allow us (at last) to explore gardens *on the ground*, so experiencing their spaces in ways far closer to their original creators and visitors than we can ever recover just from looking at plans and pictures.

On his way to Italy in 1644 Evelyn stopped to see the gardens which Henri IV had created in the Italian manner at St Germain-en-Laye. It had already attracted some attention, since there survives among John Thorpe's papers a plan of the palace and part of the gardens: Thorpe noted the terraces descending the hillside, linked by flights of steps, while beneath these 'is an Ile vawlted very faire with 3 rocks made very arteficially with byrds, stones & organs going with water. &c'[3] (figure 77). The obvious inspiration is the Villa Lante (see figure 6), especially for the final water parterre; more generally the descending staircases (cf. figure 43), the terraces and grottoes beneath them, together with the hydraulic effects, are all Italian. What is less conspicuous to our eyes in the engravings is any attempt to juxtapose the ordered parterres of the garden with any 'natural' groves, as happened at the Villa Lante; though Evelyn clearly found something at St Germain that matched the notion of a grove which he held in 1644. It must have been an exciting intimation for him of gardens he was expecting to see in Italy: 'I had never seene anything exceeding it'.[4]

It is therefore worth pausing to look at Evelyn's long and original description and consider what struck him as so distinctive about the gardens. He first notices that they were established 'upon an Eminence'; next he lists 'fountains, statues, & groves'. Of the statues he noted specifically a Laocoon fountain as being 'a most glorious & surprising object' and 'the figure of Cleopatra [i.e. the so-called Sleeping Ariadne] taken from the Belveders original'. In other words he already sees allusions to the Italian gardens towards which he was travelling. There was a 'Mons Parnassus' at St Germain, a grotto with a 'fayre Cupola, the Walls paynted with the Muses, statues placed thick about', these, too, being imagery he would see frequently in Italian gardens. Indeed, throughout his French journey he was observing gardens with one eye upon their Italian – including classical – inspiration. At Richelieu's estate at Rueil he appreciated not only the fine anthology of imagery which made him exclaim that 'I much doubt whither [*sic*] Italy have any exceeding it for all varietyes of Pleasure' but also a painted image of the 'Arco of Constantine . . . as big as is the real one at Rome'. Clearly, he recognized that gardens outside Italy should represent antiquity as part of their repertoire.[5]

The gardens which he designed after his return to England are, not surprisingly, full of Italian allusion and reminiscence. They reveal a confidence about new garden space and imagery which did not characterize the occasional bits of design that he undertook before his departure. He had worked first at the family home, Wotton, in Surrey, either on his brother's behalf or with his brother's approval (Evelyn himself did not inherit Wotton

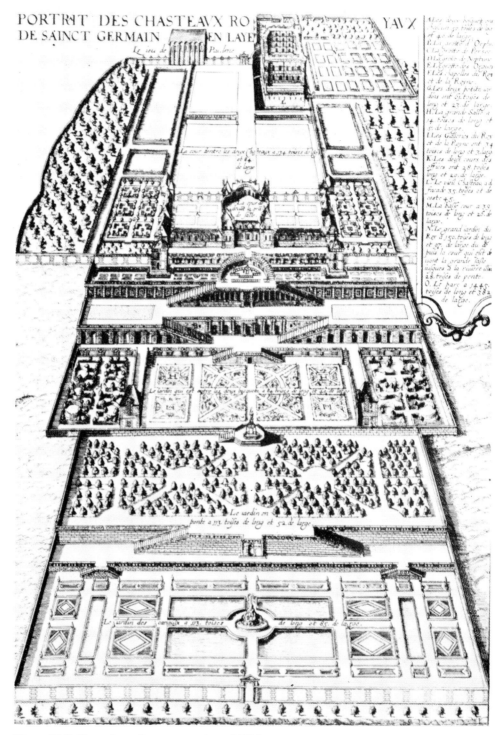

Figure 77 St Germain-en-Laye, engraving of 1614.

until 1691). As a young man he had created 'a little study over a cascade', probably in the valley to the left of figure 78; he also made a 'fishpond, an island, and some other solitudes and retirements'.[6] A sketch by Evelyn, dated 1646, purports to show the grounds of Wotton as 'altered by my Bro', but what is most interesting is its representation of a tree-house like the one at Cobham Hall and at Pratolino.[7] According to one entry in his diary he attributed to these early works which he attempted in the gardens – did they include the tree-house as one of the 'retirements'? – the inspiration of the more extensive improvements undertaken later by his brother: 'he Inlarged the Gardens, built the Portico, & Cutt the Mount into the present shape it now is of, with the fountaines in the Parterr, which were amenitys not frequent in the best Noble mens Gardens in England.'[8] His brother's changes – clearly with guidance from John – may be seen in various drawings as well as a later picture (figures 78 & 79). George Lambert's painting shows the house with the space of the parterre and a fountain just visible to its left, then the terraced mount faced with a temple front, inside of which was the grotto, and at either end of the terrace are archways through which stairs ascended. Water was brought down the valley to the left of the picture and along the contour line (the leat is still there) to drop into the grotto and so to the fountain in the parterre. The grotto front, according to Aubrey, was painted with images of Venus and dolphins by Edward Pierce who had worked at Wilton.

It was – and still is – a fine, arresting creation and Evelyn seems to have been particularly proud of the terraced mount: he drew the view from it in 1653 in a rather crude

Figure 78 George Lambert, *Wotton in Surrey*, oil painting of 1739.

Figure 79 John Evelyn, drawing of Wotton from the top of the terraces, 1653.

attempt to capture visually a visitor's experience of looking back towards the house from where he had come and seeing both the parterre with its central basin and the wide panorama of fields beyond. It was an experience on which he commented so often while in Italy (the Isola Bella on Lake Maggiore was 'a Mount, ascended by severall *Terraces* & walks . . .'[10]) that it is clearly part of the general Italian ambience which he wanted to achieve at Wotton. There appears to be no specific allusion to any particular Italian gardens: but that, as I have noted, seems more customary than is acknowledged. A terraced hillside, ascents through archways, a temple-front and a grotto were all resonant but unparticularized Italian items: as Evelyn himself told Aubrey, 'inviron'd as it is with Wood and Water, and that from different sources, capable of furnishing all the Amoenities of a villa and Garden, after the Italian manner . . .'[11] And for its creation one specifically old-fashioned English feature, a moat around the house on the garden side, had been removed by filling it with materials from the shaping of the terraced hillside: an effective translation of an English country mansion into Italianate *villa*.

Somewhat more ambitious was the reorganization of the hillside which Evelyn undertook at Albury for Henry Howard, the grandson of the famous Earl of Arundel whose sculpture garden beside the Thames was one of the first attempts to create a classical sculpture garden in England after the Italian fashion. The first Earl had been especially fond of Albury, writing to Evelyn in 1646 that he would 'have sold any Estate he had in *England*, (*Arundel* excepted) before he would have parted with this Darling *Villa*'.[12] In his self-imposed exile in Italy he commissioned Wenceslaus Hollar to do a set of twelve engravings of the place, and in one of these[13] we can see that the hillside was terraced in vineyards and adorned with a classical portico. What Evelyn designed for his grandson in 1666 was a 'Canale & Garden, with a *Crypta* thro the hill &c': the hillside was extensively transformed, long terraces established and at least one specific Italianate reference included.[14]

Evelyn explains his ideas more fully in another diary entry, where he tells of going to Albury to see how the 'Garden proceeded, which I found exactly don according to the Designe & plot I had made, with the Crypta through the mountaine in the parke, which is 30 pearches in length, such a *Pausilippe* is no where in England besides . . .'[15] The reference is to the Grotta di Posilippo near Naples, which Evelyn had visited in February 1645. It was a favourite tourist attraction and much written about and illustrated (figure 80). The Italian original cuts through the promontory between Naples and Poz-zuoli; Evelyn's goes through the Surrey hillside. By itself it seems a rather odd representa-tion of an Italian feature, however famous. But the *grotta* at Naples was associated with Virgil, whose magical powers are supposed to have cut the tunnel through the hill and who is equally supposed to have been buried in a tomb immediately above his *grotta*; it was a tomb which John Raymond had visited and found to be in a garden (see figure 10).[16] It had a square base, but the higher part of the structure was circular; and it is this circular shape which Evelyn echoes in the exedra from which the Albury *pausilippe* leads.

Figure 80 The tunnel at Posilippo, Naples, engraving from P. A. Paoli, *Antiquità di Pozzuoli . . .* (1768).

149

This specific allusion to Italy – gardenist as much in its association with Virgil as in the small garden surrounding Virgil's tomb – is confirmed by three much more general ones. The exedra is a hemicircle, with niches and a sunken pool: its prototype could have been seen in various Italian gardens, but it has clear affinities with the water theatre at the Villa Mondragone, Frascati, which we have seen that Evelyn admired.[17] Immediately underneath the exedra on the lower terrace are some *thermae* or baths; though their present façade is of a later date, their inclusion in the original project seems likely (indeed, they may have incorporated the earlier portico from the first Earl's time). But baths, as we have noticed (see figure 12), were associated with gardens in Rome, their ruins providing a loggia effect in front of modern gardens: later in the century William Bromley was at Castel Gandolfo and wrote that 'on one side of the Garden, are Ruines of ancient Baths'.[18] It is a similar conjunction, perhaps, that Evelyn wished to contrive at Albury.

His final gesture towards Italy was the terrace itself, at the centre of which the exedra and grotto were situated. This cluster of shapes and spaces could have any number of classical and modern sources: it echoes reconstructions of Sallust's garden, with the curved exedral shape and the lateral walks (see figure 8) or the same figure repeated both in the Horti Bellaiani (see figure 13) and in Ligorio's reconstruction of ancient Rome. Here on what is now the Pincian Hill, the classical hill of gardens, he showed both an exedral clearing and then wide terraces and split stairs leading to lower levels (figure 81).

Figure 81 Pirro Ligorio, detail of reconstructed plan of ancient Rome, sixteenth-century engraving.

Figure 82 Aerial view of the terraces at Albury, Surrey.

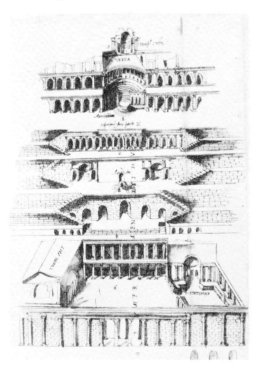

Figure 83 Pirro Ligorio, drawing of reconstruction of the Temple of Fortune at Praeneste (the modern Palestrina), sixteenth century.

But as can be seen from a modern aerial view of the Albury terraces (figure 82) they are extremely long grass walks, and their length is emphasized by the fact that the only access from one level to another is by the split stair in the centre (where the *thermae* were placed) and by gentle ramps at the extremities. As terraces, they are certainly Italianate, but their length and the method of joining them suggests a more precise reference to the remains of the Temple of Fortune at Palestrina, the classical Praeneste (figure 83), which played such a significant part in determining the form of Italian Renaissance gardens. In the context of Evelyn's other allusions, a reference to Praeneste and the ruined terraces of the temple there would not be out of place; a similar use of the classical site would be made by William Kent at Rousham in the 1730s.[19]

Albury is a vital chapter in the history of English gardening, for its deliberate representation of classical and modern Italy in the Surrey countryside would itself be much emulated. But this 'translation' of Italian into English, this metamorphosis of classical into modern culture, was not without its elegaic tones: the very fact that such translation was necessary at all is, so goes the implication, a sadness. Albury with its Mondragone-like exedra (see figure 47) may have been a small memory theatre for Arundel and (when augmented) for Evelyn, designed to recall sites of their Italian journeys – after all, it was Arundel who had advised Evelyn what to visit in Italy, including the Giusti Gardens in Verona where the walks were 'cutt out of the maine rock'. But such memories were tinged with melancholy. The allusion to Virgil himself was to his (supposed) tomb, from which in 1645 Evelyn had transcribed the inscription which, alluding to some famous lines by the Roman poet, announced that the sepulchre contained the ashes of him who, long ago, sang of fields, the countryside and princes.[20] Inasmuch as the Neapolitan building was ruined, it would have contributed much to the contemporary fashion for melancholy – James Howell remarked how the ruins of Rome 'did fill me with symptoms of Mortification, and made me sensible of the frailty of all sublunary things'.[21] Furthermore *pausilippe* was a Greek work which Henri Etienne's *Thesaurus Graecae Linguae* of 1572 had actually defined as 'appeasing, or driving away grief' and he tells us that, according to Pliny, a villa in Campania was so-called for that reason. And if *pausilippe* signalled the banishment of grief, then the re-creation of ruins in the English countryside, completing their vacancies with bricks as well as thoughts, was also an assuaging of sorrow for lost civilizations.

It was perfectly proper that Evelyn's gardens created for Henry Howard at Albury should be such a memory theatre in which the classical past, classical architecture and legends, even classical etymology were recalled. For the *crypta* or grotto was precisely the place where such philosophical thoughts were permitted and promoted. Lord Arundel previously had a grotto on the same site 'wherein he delighted to sit and discourse', and Evelyn himself told Sir Thomas Browne 'How caves, grotts, mounts, and irregular ornaments of gardens do contribute to contemplative and philosophicall enthusiasme'.[22] And the water basin set in the exedra was a spring, according to William Cobbett who admired the gardens in the early nineteenth century; such a source would also have added its resonance to this grotto or 'Home of the Muses' which Pliny and Varro tell us was a type of building often situated in gardens.[23] Sitting on Albury's terrace beside the bubbling spring, with one's back to the grotto or *pausilippe* and gazing down to the canal which Evelyn designed for the valley below the terraces and to the vineyards, a feature on which

Virgil's *Georgics* discoursed, must have been as close as anyone could get without actually being there to an Italian experience.

iii: Aubrey, and 'variety'

Wotton and Albury were John Evelyn's own contributions to a county which he considered was justly famous for its gardens: 'I should speake much of the Gardens, Fountaines and Groves that adorne it were they not as generally known to be [amongst] the most natural & [most] magnificent that England afforded – till this later & universal luxury of the whole nation since abounding in such expenses.'[24] The final phrase is a marginal note to a narrative written earlier, a retrospective gloss which hints at much in the development of English gardens that Evelyn witnessed between the Restoration and his death in 1706. As a royalist his specific invocation of Italian styles and forms for Wotton and Albury may represent his continuing loyalty to imagery from before the Interregnum. But it was imagery at once 'natural' and 'magnificent', a happy balance between nature and art, especially those arts which had brought ancient Rome to its perfection and would continue to sustain modern attempts to emulate its magnificence. But Rome's decline, it was generally agreed, could be attributed to luxury, and it is luxurious gardens which Evelyn thought had taken over England by the time of his death. These luxurious and costly works are not exclusively French in inspiration – Evelyn admired French garden art; but the taste for French gardens in imitation of Le Nôtre's did encourage and endorse a luxury which the smaller-scale Italian garden did not involve; furthermore, Italian garden imagery could be and had been applied piecemeal – a grotto here, some terraces there, a scattering of sculpture, a fountain – and it needed neither the extent of ground nor the wholesale exploitation of ground which an ambition to achieve a Le Nôtrean garden inevitably involved. Thus it was that the Italian garden – or, at least, what contemporaries thought of as an Italian style – came to have implications of proper decorum – social, political and aesthetic.

What is therefore necessary now is to sample some of the specifically Italianate gardens established or projected in the years between 1660 and 1700; to do so is not to deny the influence of the French taste, but to trace an alternative style with imagery, forms and associations peculiarly its own.

John Aubrey planned but never succeeded in taking a trip to Italy; presumably there were many like him in the late seventeenth century. But, all the more potent for being vicarious, his understanding of Italian garden style, which he could readily have acquired by a study of travel writings, engravings and sketches and by talking with those lucky enough to have travelled abroad, was sharp and alert. He registered its significance in English gardens and his antiquarian instincts were quick to seek out, as we have seen, examples of that style worth recording. But he also entertained hopes of throwing his own garden into Italian forms; when he was threatened with removal from his family home at Easton-Piercy in Wiltshire he drew up plans and a description for those alterations. The literary part of this manuscript has been lost, but what do survive are Aubrey's drawings and plans of the projected gardens, dated 1669.[25]

The title-page of this manuscript (figure 84) gives prominence to the word VILLA, surrounding it with quotations from Ovid's *Metamorphosis* and Horace's celebration of the countryside. Facing this title-page are further references to grottoes in the *Metamorphosis*, and on its verso two mottoes taken from *The Georgics*. Aubrey establishes from the start the classical orientation of his thinking about Easton-Piercy: the plans and designs that follow are all attempts to realize, to find English visual equivalents for, the Latin words and for the idea of a villa. Then comes a drawing (figure 85), a sketch of the house and its proposed garden terraces which is rendered in a more finished form a few pages later.[26] There are three terraces, linked by stairs both inside and outside the terrace walls, fountains, a grotto to the left on the third terrace (there might presumably have been another in the archway that provides access from the first terrace); in the bottom right Aubrey has noted 'the grove where the jetto is', and the sketch shows a thick grove of trees to the right of the house and in that he may have planned a *jet d'eau*. On the facing page a quotation from *The Aeneid* alerts one to the grotto or the whole villa complex as 'Nympharum domus', home of the muses. That the terraces were a crucial feature of the whole design is evident from another page which provides a cross-section of the site (figure 86): it is by no means clear whether such levels already existed or whether Aubrey planned to scoop out the declivity in order to achieve the essential element of terraced descents and ascents. The elevation shows the location of a stream, a fountain and a 'Volant Mercury', a statue of the gods' winged messenger to preside over these classical-Italianate spaces.

Figure 84 Titlepage cartouche of John Aubrey's manuscript, 'Designatio de Easton-Piers in Com: Wilts', 1669.

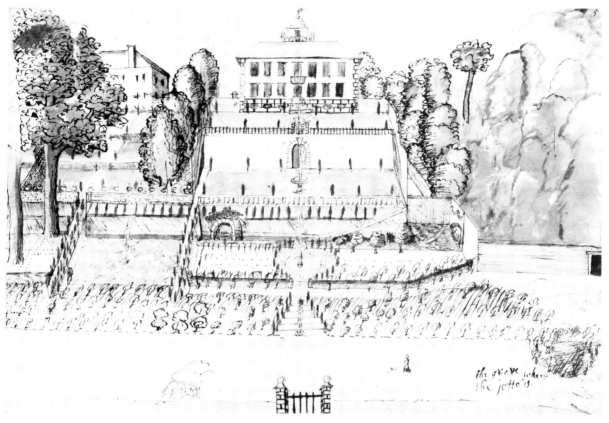

Figure 85 Aubrey, drawing of house and gardens at Easton-Piercy, 1669.

Other pages of the manuscript concern the projected grottoes and the prospects of adjacent countryside that would be available. Aubrey sketches some of the hydraulic effects he planned (or merely wistfully projected): one is a grotto with a dolphin's head spouting water (figure 87), another of a Neptune spearing a duck with the machinery that would move it around, chased by a water spaniel – this second feature presumably having been borrowed from Bushell's grotto at Enstone. Two drawings are of views out through open doorways or windows, two others of landscape lunettes showing an Italian tower and pyramids; these sketches of prospects, essentially glimpses outwards from the gardens into a larger landscape either real or imagined, are complemented by other sketches Aubrey has made in the vicinity of the house; one is inscribed 'from the fountaine-pond in the upper Sheep-souse-meade'. Since some of these are dated and presumably actual views on his property, Aubrey's 'Designatio de Easton-Piers in Com: Wilts' obviously includes memoranda both on what already existed and what was projected. It is Aubrey's attempt to realize in concrete imagery his idea (or dream) of a villa that was both classical and modern Italian: one of the quotations on the mock title-page, from Horace's *Epistles* I.10, speaks of praising the lovely country's brooks, its grove and moss-grown rocks – exactly what the whole design proposed to establish in garden terms.

155

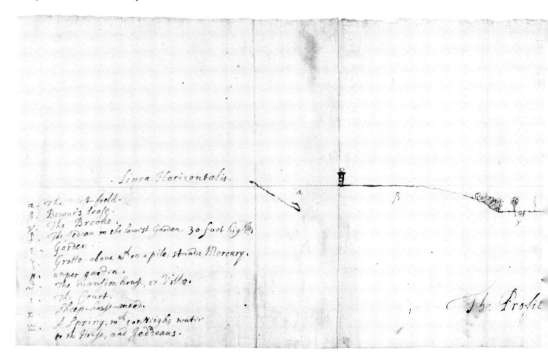

Figure 86 Aubrey, elevation of the site of house and gardens at Easton-Piercy, 1669.

Figure 87 Aubrey, drawing of figures and machinery for grotto at Easton-Piercy, 1669.

156

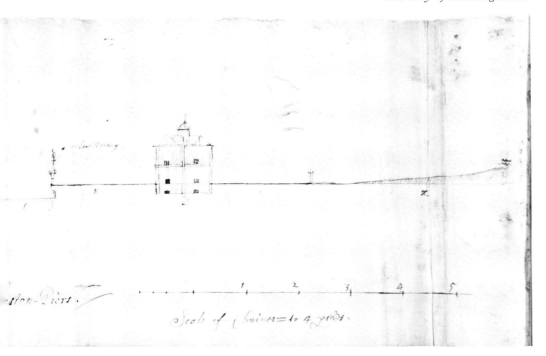

Aubrey, like Evelyn, was an enthusiast for Italian gardens. Both men travelled extensively throughout England and had opportunities to see many garden works in progress. But they were not exceptional in their concern for English achievements in this mode. They were early examples of a rapidly increasing breed of men, antiquarians who saw their researches as part of the larger scientific endeavour being mounted by the newly-formed Royal Society. Their enquiries into the visible facts of British history – monuments, churches, tombs, old buildings, inscriptions – as well as into the more fugitive remains of the past – barrows, burial sites, traces of old gardens – are one of the invaluable sources for establishing the text of this particular chapter of garden history. Empirical explorations conducted by such men as Aubrey in his manuscript memoranda and Evelyn in his journal were essentially random, notes for a history not only unwritten but unsystematically projected (witness the state of the latter's *Elysium Britannicum* or of Aubrey's *Monumenta Britannica*[27]). Then there were the published volumes, especially those devoted to the 'Natural History' of an English county, which tended to be more organized simply because they had got themselves into print – Aubrey's Surrey and Wiltshire certainly needed the assistance of subsequent editors after Aubrey's death before they could be published. By 1718 when the Society of Antiquaries was constituted the efforts of such *amateurs* were given some corporate meaning and their work, though still linked to scientific enquiries in empirical spirit, acquired an identity and meaning of its own. This antiquarian regard, when it was cast upon old and new gardens up and down the countryside, pinpointed a variety of imagery and concerns ranging from scientific interest in gardens as cabinets or horticultural laboratories to their layout and spatial excitements and often including some wish to understand a particular garden in historical terms.

Evelyn, who called in *Sculptura* for more topographical records,[28] illustrates all of these perspectives in varying degrees; so it will be useful to structure this survey around his own observations.

Evelyn's travels were often undertaken to advise friends and acquaintances on garden layout and planting.[29] And in the course of this he obviously took the opportunity to view other sites. He notes in his diary – and one supposes that these are only a small proportion of many observations not recorded – English parallels with Italy. Peter Plott's house in Chatham had a 'prety Garden & banqueting house, potts, status, Cypresses, resembling some villa about Rome', while the porticoes of Lord Berkeley's London mansion 'are in imitation of an house described by *Paladio*'; here, too, were 'incomparable' gardens 'by reasons of the inequalitie of the ground, & prity Piscina' as well as terraces which Evelyn advised him to plant with holly.[30] At Cliveden he was struck with a similarity to Frascati, but the language of his whole description equally suggests a general Italian ambience:

> The Grotts in the Chalky rock are pretty, 'tis a romantic object, & the place alltogether answers the most poetical description that can be made of a solitude, precipice, prospects & whatever can contribute to a thing so very like their imaginations: the house stands somewhat like *Frascati* as to its front, & on the platforme is a circular View to the uttmost verge of the Horizon, which with the serpenting of the *Thames* is admirably surprising . . . The *Cloisters* [i.e. loggias], Descents, Gardens, & avenue through the wood august & stately . . .[31]

Even for those who had not been to Italy like Aubrey himself a certain Italian tonality was often visible in gardens. Celia Fiennes, who travelled widely throughout England and Wales and who manifested a true curiosity – true, above all, in the quality of her careful attention to buildings and gardens – visited the garden belonging to the parson of Banstead: he 'diverted himself' with a modest but fussy attempt to ape grander achievements – there were 'stones of divers formes and sizes, which he names Gods and Goddesses', other classical figures specifically named, an 'Apolo with 9 stones round less, the Muses, this is Parnassus', and the twin pillars of Hercules; not surprisingly she also reports 'many curiosetyes' inside the house.[32]

The *color romanus* could derive most easily, as that parson realized, from arrangements of classical statuary in an English garden. An interest in specific pieces for their own sakes frequently succumbed to a simple appreciation of their general decorative value: thus the gardens at Easton are described as 'richly adorn'd with antique statues, and with other valuable pieces of ancient Sculpture: a Collection of vast Value, being all the more ornamental part of the *Marmora Arundeliana* . . .'; Evelyn at Euston found the conservatory decorated with 'the heads of *Caesars*', though 'ill cut in alabaster'.[33] Yet it is equally clear that contemporaries who chose to see English gardens in classical terms did not need any particular prompting from items in them. Evelyn's frequent invocation of the word *villa*[34] is not always in response to anything specific he has seen. Rhetorical and poetical traditions also ensured that English estates could acquire an antique patina: Marvell addresses Nunappleton House as if the Yorkshire garden and woods were some classical site; J. Howell, enthusing 'Of the most curious Gardens, Groves, Mounts, Arbours, &c contriv'd, and lately made by the Lord Vi[s]count Killmorry At Dutton-Hall in Cheshire', says that he sees

> A *Mount*, which all the *Muses* might invite,
> And make *Parnasse*-Hill abandon quite;
> A *Grove*, which chaste *Diana* with her train,
> And all the nymphs of Greece might entertain . . . ;

prospects of fields yield themselves to readers of verse 'guilded with Ceres gold'.[35]

But such tropes also throw light upon garden reminiscences of the classical world. Poets and poetasters were, at best, adapting the classical world to English scenes and themes; as Marvell wittily plays with such a literary strategy – making Yorkshire speak with Roman accent – he is also inviting our delight in the very act of translation. I have suggested that Evelyn's work at Albury, which in this respect anticipates William Kent's work at Stowe and Rousham and Alexander Pope's at Twickenham, was also designed to draw attention to the very act of recovering, re-presenting, the Roman world on English soil. For simply to confront visitors with classical items like sculpture or terrace architecture, though they might provoke thoughts of Greece and Rome, was not in itself of much consequence: what was the relevance of such allusions if they were not somehow localized, made indigenous to England? We can see this theme of the adequate translation of classical-Italian imagery beneath the surface of Plot's *Oxfordshire*: in his manuscript notes on Sir Timothy Tyrrel's seat he notes that 'the bella vista of Italy is here pretty well imitated', going on to use a reference to the *Georgics* in describing its waters; but in his published text this has become simply 'the pleasant Vista' towards the Chilterns.[36] The direct allusion to an Italian imitation has gone – the process of translation now less crucial than its outcome – and a specific landscape in the Chilterns completes the Englishing.

There were some who went further and expressed their conviction that England had every bit as resonant a scenery as Italy. Joshua Childrey's *Britannia Baconica* – a discussion of the country's natural rarities 'according to the Precepts of the Lord Bacon' – claims that 'As Italy hath Virgils Grott, and the Sybils Cave by Puteoli; so England hath Okeyhole by Wells. We have Baiae at Bath . . .'[37] When Inigo Jones, eager to see his country's origins as much Roman as possible, annexed Stonehenge to that vision, his friend Edmund Bolton affirmed that on the contrary it was a native work: 'The dumbness of it . . . speakes; that it was not any worke of the ROMANS. For they were wont to make stones vocall by inscriptions . . .'[38] If English people wanted to register local and national history in their gardens, just as the Italians had, it was fully possible.

When Evelyn finds gardens which invoke moments of the English past, he seems particularly satisfied. Althorp had

> severall ample Gardens furnish'd with the Choicest fruite in England, & exquis-
> itely kept: Great plenty of *Oranges*, and other Curiosities: The Parke full of Fowle
> & especially Hernes, & from it a prospect to *Holmby* house, which being
> demolished in the late Civil Warre, shews like a Roman ruine shaded by trees
> about it, one of the most pleasing sights that ever I saw, of state & solemne . . .[39]

Althorp's prospect has a specifically English ruin, its livestock is indigenous, it has domesticated the Hesperidean apple. In a similar spirit Aubrey sketched the ruined abbey of Newark seen down a long avenue of trees in his 'Perambulation of Surrey'; he thus may be seen as fulfilling the notion that history was a telescope, which turned upon the English countryside, 'view[s] *Chronology*, By *Optick Skill* pulling farre *History* Neerer'.[40] We may not yet have the specific commentary upon the Englishing of Italian and classical garden

159

art that Pope, for instance, would give to the art of translating Homer and Horace in Hanoverian England, but the need to accommodate the past and present of Italy into an English scenery could readily begin with ruins. Even the barest indications of British antiquity would prompt the mind as well as any Italian ones: 'a round mountaine artificially raised, either for some Castle or Monument, which makes a pretty *Land-scape*'.[41] And a prospect from a garden over English fields or 'thro the meadows towards Lond[on]' was exactly the way to adapt Italy to England.

The travel diaries of an eighteenth-century antiquarian, John Loveday, show that these preferences for an English tonality in gardens increased considerably after Evelyn's death. Loveday is frequently noting some vista which declares its history every bit as did Arundel's marbles or the statues of the villas in Rome which according to Raymond 'speak *Roman* history more palpably than any Author'. Some of what he records are seventeenth-century gardens: Sonning House, for example, was built using materials from the old palace of the Bishops of Salisbury, and when Loveday visited it he was told of old 'Foundations and Pavement-Tiles' found under the garden. The Earl of Pomfret's seat, though it had antique statues profusely scattered throughout, had one 'Vista . . . termi-nated by a Church'. In the gardens of an old house at Nether Kiddington instead of a classical fountain he discovered 'on a Pedestal . . . the Font in which King Edward the Confessor was baptised'. The Gwyns' mansion had 'one long walk' in the gardens down which, if the light had been better, Loveday would have been able to see Glastonbury Tor. And he notes new gardens, too, where the taste for an English prospect has determined the erection, say, of a 'Ruin of Flints . . . [which] represents the Eastern or Western Windows of a Chappel'.[42]

The seventeenth-century concern to transplant, so to speak, Italian garden art into English estates gave a particularly important place to classical agriculture, which we have already seen in chapter 3 was intimately related to an Englishman's notion of classical villa design. Put simply, to imitate Varro or Pliny on an English estate profited your land at the same time as it allowed you to think of yourself as maintaining a Roman stance. English landowners relied, as had Italian Renaissance ones, on the classical literature of farming as one would upon a textbook: Aubrey notes how Evelyn told him that 'out of Varro, Cato and Columnella, are to be extracted all good Rules of Husbandry: and that he wishes that a good Collection, or Extraction were made out of them'.[43] And the same manuscript, in discussing the burning of fields, notes with a quotation from Virgil that 'it is a [?piece] of the Old Roman Agriculture revived'.[44] To revive classical husbandry and to see its fruits in your gardens were not only to 'represent' the antique but to show that there were practical uses to the cult of old Rome.

An insistence upon husbandry and agriculture during the Interregnum allied puritan and royalist alike. Evelyn may have been a royalist and an anglican, but his vision of 'a society of *Paradisi Cultores*, persons of antient simplicity, Paradisean and Hortulan saints' invokes the language of puritan commitment, just as it also insists upon the antiquity of their calling.[45] During the Interregnum these terraculturalists were loosely united in a wide community of endeavour: 'what concerns Naturall Philosophy in generall must not be thought Irrelevant to Husbandry, which is but an application of it to rural subjects'.[46] Thus mechanics (including hydraulics), botany, pomology, vineyards, medicinal gardens, husbandry and horticulture were all seen as contributing to both the millenarian visions of the radical puritan *saints* and the less politically committed enquiries of gentlemen *virtuosi*. The former's publications are practical treatises – Hartlib's *Legacy* (1651), Austen's *Treatise on Fruit Trees* (1653), Sharrock's *History of the Propagation and Improvement of Vegetables* (1660), to name but three – but all envisage a better England, closer to Paradise, as a result of their labours. Ralph Austen who added an essay on 'The Spirituall Use of an Orchard or Garden of Fruit-Trees' to his *Treatise* was an energetic nurseryman who greatly increased the range and productivity of gardens in the Oxford area; yet he also dedicated himself to bringing Christ's second coming nearer by cultivation of the English land.[47]

Behind the scattered endeavours of the Commonwealth and Protectorate as behind the more concentrated enquiries of the Royal Society, into which the projections of the years before 1660 like the Invisible College or the Office of Address were more or less subsumed, lurked the authority of classical Rome. Ralph Austen had seen 'the best Workes of Ancient and of late Writers upon *this Subject*' of fruit trees, so that classical literature seemed to share an equal esteem as the Bible. The strain of classical republicanism which has been shown to colour the Puritan Revolution[48] also included a classicism of the land, just as it declared itself in literary terms. Milton urged his countrymen to look abroad for ideas, and his terminology was strikingly agricultural: 'for the sun, which we want, ripens wits as well as fruits; and as wine and oil are imported to us from abroad, so must ripe understanding and many civil virtues be imported to us from foreign writings and examples of best ages; we shall else miscarry'. Eleven years later James Harrington reminded his readers of their long-standing debts to antiquity: 'if we have given over running up and down naked and with dappled hides, learned to write and read, for all these we are beholding to the Romans'. In the rhetoric of classical republicanism it is difficult to establish anything of a coherent programme: but the advantage of a classically inspired horticulture was that it was practical and, as Austen must have realized as he lived on into the years of the restored monarchy, it flourished independently of the effectiveness of its political counterpart. The storehouse of lessons in Roman history and literature which many of all persuasions ransacked – Roman republican writers being no more the exclusive reading of the puritans than the classical horticulturalists – included, therefore, some substantial teaching for those whose prime concern was with gardens and groves.

Evelyn, though never possessed of a puritan fervour, recognized the classical dimension to what he called the 'husbandry part' of gardens.[49] A neighbour of his brother at Wotton was praised

> for curious ordering his Domestic & field Accomodations, & what pertaines to husbandry, that in my life I have ever seene, as to his severall Graneries, Tackling, Tooles & Utensils, Ploughs, Carts, Stables, Woodpiles, Woork house, even to the hen rosts & hog troughs: so as mithought I saw old *Cato or Varro* in him: all substantial, all in exact order, which exceedingly delighted me.

Not everything is as overt as that judgement of Mr Hussey by Roman standards, but much in even casual notations on English estates hints at those standards. A frequent insistence upon fishponds is not just the observation of a ubiquitous and necessary facility at a country house,[50] but the recognition of an English continuation of a distinctive Roman practice. Similarly, groves were a practical need in an England depleted of woodland; but their name carried strong classical resonance. Groves were commodity and symbol, as

Evelyn knew when he made an agreement with his brother to fell 6500 pounds worth of timber but 'Also to leave standing the woods about the seate' or when he lamented the effects of a huge tempest in November 1703 – 'the subversion of Woods & Timber both left for Ornament, and Valuable Material thro my whole Estate, & about the house, the Woods crowning the Garden Mount, & growing along the Park Meadow . . .'[51] Evelyn's practical publication on forestry was *Sylva* of 1664: its title acknowledged a debt to Bacon's *Sylva Sylvarum*. But to the next edition of *Sylva* in 1670 Evelyn added 'An Historical Account of the Sacredness and Use of Standing Groves', in which he seeks authority, both classical and biblical, for the solemnity and veneration of groves. The essay suggests the meanings with which this element of garden design could be invested, something of the mental set that was brought to bear upon even the most commonplace of features on an English estate. For what he wrote of poets involving groves was true of Evelyn himself and of many contemporaries, 'immediately some consecration follows, as believing that out of those shady profundities some Deity must needs emerge'. Groves had the authority of Latin poetry, *and* they were theatres which (as John Parkinson was told of his 'Botanicke Theater') yielded 'such excellent skill and advantage to the Spectator':

> Innumerable are the testimonies [wrote Evelyn] I might produce in behalf of Groves and Woods out of the Poets, Virgil, Gratius, Ovid, Horace, Claudian, Statius, Silius, and others of later times, especially the divine Petrarch, . . . were I minded to swell this charming subject beyond the limits of a chapter. I think only to take notice, that theatrical representations, such as . . . the scenes of pastorals, and the like innocent rural entertainments, were of old adorned and trimmed up *e ramis & frondibus*, *cum racemis & corymbis*, and frequently represented in Groves, as the learned Scaliger shews. Here the most beloved and coy mistress of Apollo rooted; and, in the walks and shades of trees, the noblest raptures have been conceived, and poets have composed verses which animated men to heroic and glorious actions . . .[52]

Not all travellers through the English counties between 1660 and the turn of the century saw groves so sharply in terms of their numinous and poetical associations. Celia Fiennes, with a shrewd eye for property, notices the groves of houses she visits without any such commentary.[53] But the classical potential of key features of country gardens – groves, vineyards, fruit trees, fishponds, aviaries – was there to be realized by individual visitors: Evelyn is doing so to his private satisfaction when his diary recorded how he went 'contentedly home to my poore, but quiet *Villa*' from the fruitless and demanding city.[54]

Groves were an admired feature of Italian gardens by virtue, not only of their poetic resonance, but because they contrasted with the more ordered sections of an estate and thus established some variety. The variety that the English came to expect of an Italian garden and, conversely, did not expect to find in French garden plots is a theme that is taken up frequently by travellers through England. Like groves themselves or the prospect of fecund fields, variety was Italian without calling attention to itself or its Italianness; it emphasized not borrowings or debts, but continuities by which classical and modern traits passed from Italian into English modes almost without notice. Variety, in all its aspects, was certainly one criterion by which gardenists like Evelyn judged the success of contemporary gardening: Cliveden may have reminded him of Frascati, but it also lacked sufficiently various prospects ('but one onely opening, & that but narrow'[55]). And it is this seventeenth-century emphasis upon variety in a fine garden that passes into the early landscape movement; the forms which landscape garden variety took were not always the same as in earlier gardens – fewer terraces, fewer distinctions between different parts of an estate; but the idea of variety itself was of prime importance and its traditional emphasis crucial. So it is necessary to look at the kinds of garden variety that were apparent to contemporaries before 1700. What will be of significance, too, is that these earlier forms of English garden variety were precisely what eighteenth-century antiquarians like Stukeley sought out in the years when the French garden style was under attack; they saw them as essential to the evolution of national gardening.

Just as Aubrey had found variety in the flat sites of Wilton and Danvers's Chelsea garden, so Evelyn saw that diversity could be skilfully achieved by the Clarendons at Swallowfield, Berkshire:

> the house is after the antient building of honourable gent: houses where they kept up the ancient hospitality: but the Gardens & Waters as elegant as 'tis possible to make a flat, with art & Industrie and no meane Expenses, my Lady being so extraordinarily skilld in the flowry part: & the diligence of my Lord in the planting: so that I have hardly seene a seate which shews more toakens of it, then what is here to be found, not onely in the delicious & rarest fruits of a Garden, but in those innumerable & plentifull furniture of the grounds about the seate of timber trees to the incredible ornament & benefit of the place: There is one Ortchard of a 1000 Golden & other cider Pepins: Walks & groves of Elms, Limes, Oake: & other trees: & the Garden so beset with all manner of sweetshrubbs, as perfumes the aire marvelously: The distribution also of the Quarters, Walks, Parterre &c is excellent: The Nursuries, Kitchin-garden, full of the most desireable plants; two very noble Orangeries well furnish'd; but above all, The Canale, & fishponds, the one fed with a white, the other with a black-running water, fed by a swift & quick river: so well & plentifully stor'd with fish, that for Pike, Carp, Breame & Tench: I had never seene any thing approching it . . .[56]

Though his superlatives strain to match his enthusiasm, Evelyn indicates that variety in a garden was achieved as much by horticultural skill as by architectural design. Here he was at one with those hortulan saints of the Interregnum who urged that 'the wit and the art of a skilfull Gardiner . . . can worke more variety for breeding of more delightsome choice and of all those things, where the owner is able and desirous to be satisfied'.[57] This could be a supremely English achievement: the *Natural History of Northamptonshire* praised Kirby for its 'Gardens enrich'd with a great Variety of Plants, particularly choice exotics. And almost the whole Variety of our *English* trees is to be met with in the pleasant Wilderness there.'[58]

That same writer wants a diversity of organization in garden spaces: 'Large walks, broad and long, close and open.' If we read verbal accounts of garden experience at this time in conjunction with bird's-eye views rather than being misled by their particular viewpoint, we should be less tempted to see English gardens as uniform and unvarious. Celia Fiennes, for example, stopped at Bretby during her tour of Derbyshire in 1698, where the gardens were in the process of being laid out by the Frenchman Grillet who also worked at Chatsworth. 'You see', she wrote, 'but one garden at a tyme', and it is clear from Knyff and Kip's engraving (figure 88) that the access through these separate gardens was arranged by a series of terraces linked via stairways. Her prose responds to these ascents and descents: 'on either side stone staires ascends it . . . enters a doore into another garden . . . severall steps up . . . which also goes out of another garden'; there is even a curious

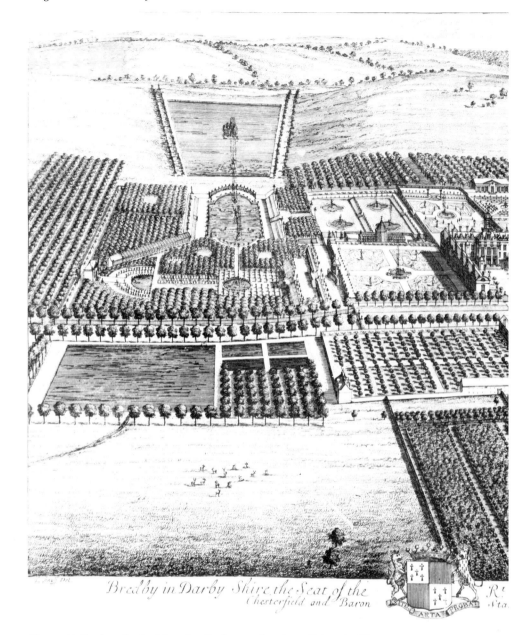

Figure 88 Bretby, Derbyshire, detail of engraving from *Britannia Illustrata* (1707).

attempt to define Bretby's invocation of the Belvedere exedral staircase, codified by Serlio (see figure 41):

> From this bowling-green in the middle you descend 18 steps in a demi-circle inwards halfe way, then the stones are set round and so the half pace is, and the other stepps are round turned outward and the lowest much the largest, as was the uppermost of the first; this leads to a place designed for ponds to keep fish in . . .[59]

A similar use of this striking staircase form in a much less elaborate garden can be seen in the view of Staunton Harold by Knyff and Kip.

Even when versions of the Belvedere exedra are installed in English gardens between 1660 and 1700, terraces of themselves clearly do not signal Italianate design. French gardens invoked terraces, too. So we must be careful not to claim too much; yet it would be claiming too little if we simply neglected both the considerable interest expressed by English travellers in Italian hillside gardens, with their terraces, ascents and descents and partitions which the site necessitated, and the inevitable imitation of those features back home in England. The evidence is there in abundance. Mutton Davies created his handsome terraced garden in the Italian mode in the 1660s (see figure 69) and as late as 1732 Loveday could still admire the 'gardens descended in "plats"' and the 'pretty waterworks in miniature'. In the summer of 1702 Lord Winchelsea was working on 'making very fine gardens which added to the beauty of the Park' at Eastwell in Kent, and one particular part of his endeavours was celebrated in his wife's poem 'Upon my Lord Winchelsea's converting the Mount in his Garden to a Terras', in which 'old Rome [which] refin'd what ere was rude' is called upon to authorize his work. Rousham, before its metamorphosis into the jewel of the English landscape movement, was 'eminent', according to Plot, for 'a Curious descent of 5 degrees to the River', a terrace recorded in estate maps at the house. Holme Hall in Derbyshire could be celebrated, too, by a versifier of 1720 for its old terraces ('Rising from height to height') worthy of a Brutus or a Cato. The engraving of Flora's garden in Richard Blome's *The Gentleman's Recreation* (1686) may suggest some fashionable French *allée*, but the scale of the terraces and divided staircases suggest a much more intimate Italian garden like the Villa Torrigiani, near Lucca, where exactly the same scaled feature decorates a Garden of Flora. Powys Castle in Montgomeryshire still retains its terracing from the late seventeenth century, with arches and niches along the walls. Others do not survive, but reveal themselves to aerial photography, like Harrington in Northamptonshire, of which Morton wrote in 1712 'For a Descent of Garden Walks there is nothing so remarkable with us as is that of the Walks of the Garden on the Northern Front of the Earl of Dysert's house' (figure 89). Archaeology, too, yields considerable evidence for terraces later swept away in the mania for subduing English estates to the lowest common denominator of 'Capability' Brownism. At Lamport, Northamptonshire, numerous changes were ordered in the gardens by Sir Thomas Isham and in 1678 his agent reported that they were making the 'Garden monstrous fine' with, among other things, a terrace walk.

Before such older features were removed at some point during the eighteenth century they were, fortunately, often recorded by various antiquarians and country house 'portrait' painters. Rycote (see figure 73) has its groves and gardens, the latter's principal feature being a terrace with the stairs leading up and down. Both Rycote and Durdans

Figure 89 Aerial photograph of Harrington, Northamptonshire.

House, Surrey, are survivals from the 1630s when such designs were new and knowingly Italian: Knyff's painting of Durdans in 1673 (figure 90) shows that little has been altered since that time, and the rising terraces at the end of the garden with their views out into the groves beyond still survive. Griffier's painting of Sudbury Hall, Derbyshire, shows an elegant but fairly simple garden, slightly contrived terraces, the final one leading via a handsome set of steps towards the fishponds; as if to show that besides being utilitarian these were valued for their Roman associations, a statue of Neptune has been set over the central pond. Both in Samuel Buck's sketches of Yorkshire gardens, drawn for a projected natural history of that county, and in Stukeley's drawings of gardens throughout the country both the incidence of terraces and the loving interest displayed by the draughtsmen in them are remarkable (figure 91). In their conjunction with groves, as at Marske Hall near Richmond or behind the rather more modest house on Blackdown drawn by an even later *amateur* (figure 92), terraces clearly signalled an important phase of English gardening to later antiquarians, what Stukeley noted in his Commonplace Book as 'the old way of building, gardening & the like in a general imitation of pure nature'. Such a

166

Figure 90 L. Knyff, *Durdans House, Surrey*, oil painting of 1673.

remark suggests that from the 1730s, for those looking back across the enormously active period of French garden designs, the earlier forms were much more acceptable representations of natural features. The Gough Collection of drawings and engravings at the Bodleian Library, although fairly eclectic, holds a large number of records of old garden structures: Buck's view of Hay Castle, Brecknock, with its descending levels beside the old building, or of the handsome garden pavilions, obviously classical and clearly giving views over adjacent countryside, at Wardour Castle, Wiltshire, and Drayton House, Northamptonshire; the orchard double-staircase at Hampstead Marshall ('built 1682'); the even more elaborate descent into the gardens at Dean House, Wiltshire; the loggia and stairways at 'Cramborn House built by Robert Cecil about 1604'; or John Drapentier's engraving of Aspeden Hall for Chauncy's *Hertfordshire* of 1700, showing the elegant loggia facing towards the groves; or Stukeley's proposal for his own gateway with urns and zig-zag stairways either side designed for Grantham and dated '15 Mar.1729'. The list could be indefinitely extended.[60]

But not all terraced gardens were by any means swept away: a portrait of Sir Roger and Lady Bradshaigh, happily ensconced beyond the terraces and criss-cross stairways at Haigh Hall, Lancashire, is as late as 1746 (figure 93). And terraces could be created, too: Kent introduced the Praeneste Terrace at Rousham in the late 1730s, while John Loveday was shown over 'the fine terrace . . . made at Farnborough' in the summer of 1742.[61] Kent's is firmly classical, alluding with its name to the famous ruined temple, set in terraces down a hillside, that many English visitors admired at Palestrina. The equally fine, though totally different Farnborough terrace was more obviously what Stukeley called 'a general imitation of pure nature'; but its command of prospect and particularly its view of Edgehill, a noted landmark of British history, made it a far more subtle localization of Italian traditions of the garden terrace.

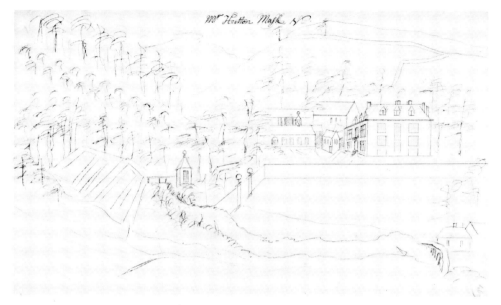

Figure 91 William Stukeley, drawing of Marske Hall, Yorkshire, eighteenth century.

Figure 92 Anonymous, drawing of 'Mr Yatsings house on black down near Fernhurst', eighteenth century.

Figure 93 Edward Haytley, *Sir Roger and Lady Bradshaigh*, on the terraces of Haigh Hall, Lancashire, oil painting of 1746.

iv: Scenes and scenery

Variety was not only a result of spatial invention and manipulation inside a garden; but as Rousham and Farnborough, Danvers's Chelsea and Evelyn's Wotton, each declare, variety was also a question of what could be seen outside the garden. The ubiquity of prospect in Italian gardens was always attested by English visitors, and this characteristic ingredient of their variousness was rarely if ever a feature of French gardens (whatever other similarities evolved from the Italian experiences of French designers up to Le Nôtre). Views out from English gardens into the surrounding countryside, with their potential for incorporating in the prospect items of local and national history, seem to have been as important an aspect of designs before the English landscape garden as after.

Whether prospect was considered as or compared to Italian garden views depended almost wholly on the experience of the particular commentator. Evelyn obviously did make comparisons between Italy and England; Celia Fiennes, who had not made the grand tour, did not. Yet even she connected the greater potential for fine views with the new architecture. At Coleshill, built between 1650 and 1662 by Sir Robert Platt with some debts to Inigo Jones, she admired gardens 'in a great descent below the house' as well as the

169

view from the top of the building – 'a great prospect of gardens, grounds, wood that appertaine to the Seate, as well as a sight of the Country'.[62] At Hillesden, the 'prospect is fine all over the gardens and parkes and the river and woods beyond them'; at Somerhill the bowling green 'discovers the Country a great circuite round'. So, fine views from houses and gardens seem to be remarkable in direct proportion to her praise of the architecture at their centre.

What we have, arguably, is a visual experience which was capable of being associated with one particular, Italian-classical mode of building and gardening, but was by no means confined to that. The same is true of both landscape painting and stage scenery during the last forty years of the seventeenth century. Both undoubtedly had strong ties with Italian traditions; both certainly contributed to a steadily growing appreciation of prospects and determined their inclusion in garden designs, and thereby lent their Italian authority to the gardenist endeavours. Yet in all three areas – garden design, landscape art and stage scenery – the Italian element was only infrequently acknowledged. A thread of Italian connections, however, exists unbroken from all kinds of garden imagery before the civil wars to the early years of the English landscape movement: it is often submerged, its distinctive colour obliterated by others in the cultural pattern, its peculiar qualities unremarked except by those like Aubrey, who set himself to trace their strain in the larger weave; but the Italian thread was there undoubtedly, ready to be taken up and augmented hugely by the early landscapists. In fact, it is a familiar story in the history of architecture, where the classicism of Inigo Jones somehow got lost during the years of English mannerism and baroque only to be restored, recovered and reaffirmed by the palladians around Lord Burlington. A difference (perhaps) with gardening is that there existed many who saw that its Italian associations and authority maintained a vital link with a true source of design and with the proper associations of gardens and even some who were able to implement this.

When Evelyn discussed the views at Roehampton House (now Putney Park) he says that 'the Gardens & perspective is pretty, the Prospect most agreable'.[63] The distinction between prospect and perspective is between actual (real) views and illusionistic (painted) ones. He had himself admired an arch of Constantine painted lifesize in oil at Rueil in France: the sky and the birds were strikingly realistic. Again, at the Count of Liancourt he discovered that a small garden was extended by means of a painted perspective of a stream.[64] It was a familiar way of making gardens larger, both spatially and associationally, and its authority went right back to Vitruvius and Pliny.[65] It united the efforts of landscape artist and scene painter, and in practice they were often the same person: Evelyn records a house in Lincoln's Inn Fields where the courtyard was 'extended' by a 'Perspective . . . painted by Streeter . . . indeede excellent, with the *Vasas* in Imitation of *Porphyrie*; & fountaine . . .'[66] Streater was a landscape painter, praised by Evelyn for his perspectives for the theatre as well as for the garden. This congruence of landscape arts, all with strong but not exclusive Italian ties, had certain repercussions for garden art.

First, the introduction of perspectives into gardens always preserved the importance to them of prospect; since prospect also meant both a real view and a stage backdrop for the seventeenth century, this in its turn maintained in a prospect the pleasures and excitements of uncertainty – was one looking at something actual or contrived, nature or art? Second, the frequent occurrence of gardens as subject matter in painted perspectives –

whether for theatres or gardens[67] – ensured their association with theatre, with play, with illusion; perspective, too, was an elastic term, meaning general views, tricks with space as well as the proper ordering of an optical scene.[68] It all confirmed the art of the gardens as the creation of a world where the spectator needed to be at least alert if not also an actor or participant if he was to derive from his experience the fullest satisfaction. The seventeenth-century connoisseur of landscape painting was prepared to be cozened by his sight into thinking a picture was an actual scene before him. The theatregoer was encouraged to see gardens as changeful worlds where intrigue (usually amorous intrigue) and social play were customary.

London theatres after the Restoration provided frequent evidence of their debts to the Renaissance (in both its antique and its modern Italian modes). Even before the Restoration and its upsurge of theatrical activity, William Davenant obtained backing for a private theatre in 1656, offering 'Entertainments . . . By Declamations of Musick: After the Manner of the Ancients.'[69] The introduction of Italian opera and the rage for changeable and perspectival scenery, both of which had strong Italian connections, must have given the impression that the Restoration English stage was indeed recovering 'the Manner of the Ancients'. Davenant had been involved with the Caroline masque before the Interregnum and he maintained its delight in the 'Representation by the Art of Perspective in Scenes' once he opened the Duke's Theatre, Lincoln's Inn Fields, in 1661. The other main theatre, the Theatre Royal, was opened by Thomas Killigrew who had spent some of the preceding years in Italy.

The considerable increase in changeable scenery after 1660 meant that audiences were entertained with some inventive and exotic settings, especially in the spectacular shows. Much of the scenery, derived from Italian traditions, was topographical; some of it was of gardens and groves. There were obviously standard garden sets, used simply to signal 'garden' during any dramatic action: others were presumably created specifically for special shows. As late as 1755 an antagonist of the theatre's love of scenic display would single out 'groves and gardens' in his indictment:

> we should not have the scenes of a play like those of an English *pantomime*, or an *Italian Opera*; because we would not have them engross that attention which is more due to the player. If, for this reason, we do not expect, or desire, to see real sheep upon the wooden plain or temples change into rocks, or deserts rise to groves and gardens . . .[70]

Gardens seemed almost *de rigueur* in the Restoration theatre, and no doubt managements liked to utilize their repertoire of sets. A production of *The Prophetess* in 1690 showed 'A long walk in the middle of a great Wood; at the farther end is a Prospect of Dioclesian's Grange in a delightful Valley'. Other classical and Italianate scenes were shown in *The Fairy Queen* (1692):

> the Scene is perfectly discovered, the Fountains enrich'd with gilding and adorn'd with Statues: The view is terminated by a Walk of Cypress Trees which lead to a delightful Bower. Before the Trees stand rows of Marble Columns, which support many Walks which rise by Stairs to the top of the House; the Stairs are adorn'd with Figures on Pedestals, and Rails; and Balusters on each side of 'em. Near the top, vast Quantities of Water break out of the Hills, and fall in mighty Cascade's to the bottom of the Scene to feed the Fountains which are on each side . . .

Further, in the middle of the stage was a fountain working with real water. The whole is a marvellous confection of earlier masque scenery, houses like Moor Park (for the 'many Walks') and Villa D'Este (for the waterworks and hillside). Settle's *World in the Moon* (1697) not only makes fun of the vogue for French stage machinery but offers this view of Cynthia's garden in Act V:

> Being a Prospect of Terras Walks on Eight several Stages mounted one above another, each Stage contains a Range of Stone-work extending from side to side, decorated with Paintings in Fresco of Heroick History; over each Piece of Painting are carved Rails and Banisters with Pedestals: On Thirty Two Pedestals are carved Sixteen Golden Flower-Pots, and Sixteen Statues of Gods and God-desses . . . Through the Center, and advancing Twenty Four Feet high, is an Ascent of Marble Steps. This Sett of Scenes is encompass'd round with Arborage-work, circled round with double Festoons of Flowers tyed up in Ribbons of Gold, terminating at Fifty Foot deep, being the Extent of the House, with a Prospect of a Garden above the highest Terras.
>
> Above Fifty Figures are seen upon the several Terras's, some of which Descend upon the Stage for the Entertainment . . . .

The general atmosphere of these scenes – busy, exotic, slightly fantastical – is Italianate, though made all the more extraordinary for the purposes of spectacle.

Evidence for stage designs is, unfortunately, patchy and not very substantial. But gardens and groves continued to function, as they had under Inigo Jones, as symbolic locations, designed to make some psychological impact on an audience, involving them (as in a real garden) in the scene's intrigues. The very fact that it was often *changing* scenery paralleled the invitations of real gardens to move through them and explore their altering scenes. Theatres presented public gardens just as much as princely gardens and villas, but the expectations of a garden world were the same: they were places of intrigue, duplicity, play, confusions and surprise. As I have discussed at length elsewhere, action set in such places as the Mulberry Garden or the New Spring Garden guaranteed excitements of play, including role-playing, and discovery, and it is evident that the audience would have been expected to bring to the single stage set their own experience of moving through a variety of real garden scenes.

In other ways we catch glimpses of the late seventeenth-century emphasis upon the theatricality of gardens, and gardens which seem generally to be classical or Italianate. The physical forms were re-used: Bretby (see figure 88) had exedras, amphitheatres, terraces like raked seats in a *cavea* or auditorium, grottoes, perhaps with entertainments. Timothy Nourse, no lover of the 'dead plains' and the lack of variety at Versailles, wished to throw the approaches to his ideal country house 'into a Figure something resembling a Theatre'.[72] Charles Howard's gardens at Deepdene, which we shall encounter again as a scientific garden, were cast into the shape of a theatre: Aubrey's delight with this place led him into maintaining the theatrical metaphor throughout his description. It was (for Evelyn) an 'Amphitheater Garden' and on its sides (wrote Aubrey) 'several narrow Walks, like the Seats of a Theatre, one above the other . . . The Pit . . . stored full of rare Flowers and choice Plants . . .' Another, later visitor considered that the gardens had been 'by nature so surprisingly contrived for . . . theatrical entertainment'.[73] It was clearly, as Aubrey's rough sketch makes evident, something like the amphitheatre of the Boboli Gardens, given over like Parkinson's *Theatrum Botanicum* to a spectacle of nature. Furth-

172

ermore, gardens could be made to seem theatrical or imply theatrical activity. This is most obvious when gardens are imaginary ones: Marvell's 'The Garden' uses its setting to dramatize and play ironically with our expectations of peace, natural creation, timeless retreat from a busy activist world. His attention to the doubleness of a garden experience in that poem allows him to present more than one side of the action; but in the Mower poems, notably 'The Mower Against Gardens', we seem to be offered single speeches from some garden entertainment – utterances that might have been made by figures springing up to welcome Elizabeth or James to a country estate only to be rebutted by subsequent interventions from other characters.

'Upon Appleton House', Marvell's long and absorbing poem on the Yorkshire estate of Lord Fairfax, whose daughter Marvell was engaged to tutor, seems to take the whole place as his theatre. It is difficult to imagine Fairfax's Yorkshire house, gardens and groves as having the layout and iconography that the poet imputes to them. Rather, it is as if Marvell 'reads' the gardens and woods as if they were a sophisticated, Italianate world.[74] He is some classical river-god ('Abandoning my lazy Side, / Stretcht as a bank unto the Tide'), Maria Fairfax some nymph of the grove or a statue which gives meaning and significance to the parts of the estate over which she presides ('Tis *She* that to these Gardens gave / That wondrous Beauty which they have . . .'). Nunappleton garden, like gardens visited on the Grand Tour, is also hailed as a miniature world ('You Heaven's Center, Nature's Lap. / And Paradice's only Map'); it is eloquent of its owner, its (very English) ruins yield a history every bit as powerful as Roman ruins did; it is divided into garden and grove and, as at the Villa Lante, the meanings continue from one part to another as the poet descends first into 'the Abbyss . . . Of that unfathomable Grass' and thence into woodland cut into walks. The poet's behaviour in the woodland, disguising himself in various shapes, brings to mind the masquing of Caroline courtiers, and the whole sequence is characterized by the masque's delight in metamorphosis. Men in the meadows seem changed to grasshoppers, grasshoppers to giants; in the woods 'arching Boughs' become 'Corintheon Porticoes'; by the riverside reflections mimic the real world to the confusion of both –

> as a *Chrystal Mirrour* slick;
> Where all things gaze themselves, and doubt
> If they be in it or without.

The painting of 'Traverse' scenes in a theatre or of landskips deceive the eye just as do the actual scenes of Nunappleton – 'They seem within the polisht Grass / A Landskip drawen in Looking-Glass'. Such transformations are simply a part of the larger theatre of the meadows where Marvell imagines a whole rural entertainment; one, indeed, that excels any actual theatre – 'No Scene that turns with Engines strange / Does oftener then these Meadowes change'. The elaborate transformation scenes of the old court masques and the revolving shutters of the Vitruvian theatre are both invoked to set the tone of the park's theatre, and 'Men the silent Scene assist, / Charm'd with the *Saphir-winged Mist*'. The 'scene' of which we are constantly reminded is both a theatrical vision and the actual Yorkshire place; in the supple and allusive flow of the poet's meditation what he sees and what he creates are one. But he responds to gardens, groves and meadows as if they were indeed some Italianate garden, full of metamorphic play and of theatrical changes – 'This *Scene* again withdrawing brings / A new and empty Face of things.'[75]

It would be tempting to see Marvell's characteristic ambivalence as happily invoking the imagery of royalist masque as well as of Italian (modern, classical and therefore republican) villas to describe the estate of his patron, the Parliamentarian general Fairfax. It is also intriguing to speculate upon the resonances which another poet, Milton, gave to his garden scenery in *Paradise Lost*. Milton was not disposed to welcome the restoration of the monarchy in 1660 and, unregenerate, lived out his days with a strong nostalgia for the republican interlude in English history. When he came to write *Paradise Lost*, with its celebration of paradise within the individual rather than realized at large throughout society, the classical republican association of Italianate gardening might have seemed a suitable imagery for the lost Eden. Addison certainly considered that Milton could not 'have laid his Paradise, had he not seen the . . . gardens of Italy'; indeed, it would be surprising if Milton did not derive his vision of paradise, not from the hated royalist style of French designs so popular at the time Milton was finishing his epic poem, but from those before the fall of the Commonwealth. To have invoked those would have been to present his readers with imagery that was familiar to them without diminishing the novelty of the Edenic landscape he needed for his poetic narrative.

This is not the occasion on which to expound in detail *Paradise Lost*'s possible debts to Italian gardening, which Milton would have seen for himself during his visit to that country in the 1640s and remembered in his blindness.[76] It is sufficient, in stressing the important connections between Milton's political opposition to a restored monarchy and his use of Italian garden imagery, to note, first, his insistence upon the variety, the 'various view' of his Eden and upon his characters' freedom to wander its 'grove or garden-plot' with full appreciation of the range of its garden imagery. The language of Milton's descriptions, too, as well as his communication of the excitements of small-scale gardenist space, where route, direction and discovery play such a crucial role, both suggest the Italian provenance of his Eden. We have been conditioned by early historians of the landscape garden to read Milton's descriptions as if they were applicable – by virtue of his prophetic gaze – to the work of Kent or Brown: thus 'murmuring waters fall / Down the slope hills' seems to honour in anticipation the gardens of Rousham or Studley Royal, when in fact it is language that could refer as aptly to the Villa Lante or gardens at Frascati. Milton's 'woody theatre', too, has seemed prophetic of the natural styles of the eighteenth century, but it just as readily echoes both Pliny's account of his Tuscan villa site and the many theatrical spaces in gardens like the Boboli. Nor should we forget Milton's original intention of casting the story of Adam and Eve into dramatic form, some fossils of which plan survive in the twelve-book epic: to have written a drama set in Eden would have been to make the stage a garden, just as the Garden had itself been the prime theatre of human history. Milton knew the modern Italian theatre well, having attended at least one opera in the Palazzo Barberini while he was in Rome; so it is also inconceivable that he would not have been prepared, however submerged the ideas may be in *Paradise Lost*, to acknowledge the connections between theatre and garden which we know to have been a vital part of the Englishman's appreciation of Italian gardens. And in *Paradise Regained*, where Milton specifically acknowledges gardens and groves among the various landscape of ancient Rome, their theatrical potential is again finely used: Christ enters a 'woody Scene', with alleys opening in perspective, and there the drama of temptation is played out.

v: *The scientific garden*

Fountains and other waterworks as well as perspectival exhibits were still clearly viewed as a proper extension of cabinets of curiosities into the garden. Evelyn at Canterbury in 1678 was shown a 'pretty melancholy Garden [where] I tooke notice of the largest *Arbor Thuyae* I had ever seene: The place is finely water'd, & there are many curiosities'. The garden is melancholy perhaps because it is a place for study and thought, and its rarities range from a thuya not much seen in England at the time through waterworks to a small museum. On other occasions, however, he felt the introspective mood too heavy: at Kew in 1683 he found Sir Henry Capel had 'roofed his Hall with a kind of Cupola, & in a niche an artificial fountaine; but the roome seemes to me over-melancholy; yet might be much improved by having the walls well painted a *fresca &c*'.[77] That he associated perspectival vistas painted on the walls with the fountain indicates Evelyn's sense that they are appropriately matched and each part of a larger scientific enterprise. Gardens in all their aspects were, as Worlidge said, 'Experimental'.[78] The Royal Society 'discoursed of Fountains' in 1675, according to Evelyn's diary, and that suggests how the former childlike wonder at the ingenuity of hydraulic display was surrendering to a more serious attention to its scientific aspect.[79] Perspectival tricks were part of optics, and Morton admired a garden precisely because of its curious lessons in the geometry of vision: 'a Walk . . . so contriv'ed that a Person standing in the middle of the Walk cannot perceive but that it is perfectly strait, whereas if he removes to either End it appears so very crooked that the Eye does not reach much above half the way'.[80] Similar auditory tricks were contrived in gardens, and Evelyn's *Elysium Britannicum* discusses an artificial echo in the Tuileries gardens, glosses it with quotations from classical authors and refers himself to Plot's *Oxfordshire* for further information on this English manifestation of the scientific garden.[81] His own garden at Sayes Court, Deptford, was as much a laboratory as a pleasant retreat: here he kept the transparent beehive given him by that other *virtuoso*, Dr Wilkins of Wadham; here, too, he built himself what he called 'my new little *Cell*, & *Cabinet*' – this last word having both gardenist and scientific connotations. In the garden's various sections ('*Gardens*, *Walkes*, *Groves*, *Enclosures* & *Plantations*') he cultivated and studied plants, shrubs and trees.[82]

Among the many occasions on which Evelyn admires others' cabinets in connection with gardens, one of the most interesting is his brief mention of Charles Howard's 'Amphitheater Garden' where he saw 'divers rare plants: Caves, an Elaboratory'.[83] Fortunately, John Aubrey recorded far more details in his 'Perambulation of Surrey' as well as making a watercolour sketch of its shape. The garden was at Deepdene, near Dorking, where (writes Aubrey)

> the Hon. Charles Howard of Norfolk hath very ingeniously contrived a long Hope (secundum Virgilium, *deductus vallis*) into the most pleasant and delightful solitude, for House, Gardens, Orchards, Boscages, &c: that I have seen in England. It deserves a Poeme, and was a Subject worthy of Mr Abraham Cowley's Muse . . .

The garden was formed from the mid-1650s and shaped like an amphitheatre, 'cast into the Form of a Theatre, on the Sides whereof he hath made several narrow Walks, like the seats of a Theatre, one above another . . . The Pit . . stored full of rare Flowers and choice Plants . . .' The combination of theatrical shape, the high terrace walks, the caves, the vineyard on top of the hill and the magnificent view over several counties all contributed to a fine English adaptation of Italian ideas suited to the site as well as to Howard's modest means, which presumably precluded any grottoes. But he established a laboratory on the eastern terrace above the amphitheatre and dedicated himself to various scientific pursuits – cultivating saffron, tanning leather, growing and pressing wild flowers – on all of which he reported to the Royal Society. Aubrey was struck by the vineyard, the collection of 'twenty-one sorts of thyme', 'many orange trees and syringas'; Howard even entertained a scheme to tunnel through the hillside at the rear of the amphitheatre and thus fashion a sort of perspective tube.

Aubrey's fascination with waterworks – he noticed that Danvers's descendants at Lavington had built a 'noble Portico, full of Water-workes': just to make sure he adds 'both Portico & grotto' – may not have sufficed the experimental temper of the Royal Society; he maintains too much of the earlier wonder at their marvels and performances, but in this he was probably closer to the average garden owner. To such a person John Worlidge's *Systema Horti-culturae* of 1688 addresses its enthusiasm for waterworks and for grottoes, singling out the one at Wilton for especial praise. Worlidge's small book was one of several publications and planned publications that were to keep Italian gardens in the public's mind during the days when the French style was much in vogue.

It was above all the scale of Italian gardens that could be recommended to the owners of modest country houses. To such readers Worlidge directed his other book, *Systema Agriculturae* of 1669: the 'Address to the Gentry & Yeomanry of England' ends with a quotation from Virgil, and the Preface, headed 'In Laudem Agriculturae', reviews the authorities – largely, if not exclusively classical – for his subject. Italy is a constant presence, both in its classical era and for its modern achievements: readers are reminded that it is the garden of the world once in *Systema Agriculturae*, twice in *Systema Horti-culturae*. The latter was written to encourage 'the honest and plain Countryman in the improvement of his Ville': the non-italicised word speaks eloquently of the domestication of word, idea and designs that Worlidge wants to achieve. Besides waterworks and grottoes, he briefly considers aviaries, terraces for hilly sites and the art of adorning them with statues: 'Herein the ancient *Romans* were excessively prodigal'; the art having been passed down to modern Italy' 'The Mode of adorning Gardens with curious Workmanship, is now become *English*'. Italian gardens having 'from Age to Age so improved', that art, says Worlidge, has come northwards with their fine architecture. It is all an interesting testimony to how in the year of the Glorious Revolution an emphasis upon Italian gardens – in both their antique and modern manifestations – could be formulated.[84]

vi: After 1688 . . .

To what extent it would be feasible to see a clear connection between Italian gardening and those who supported the Glorious Revolution of 1688 is unclear. In James Wright's *Country Conversations* of 1694 we are told that Eugenius has retired from public service to employ 'himself much after the Italian fashion in building, and imbellishing his House and Gardens'.[85] The connection between Italian gardening, rural retreat from political life and the interests of the country party is implied; it suggests that to set oneself deliberately and visibly to garden after the Italian fashion would be an ideological gesture. Clearly the strong classical emphasis which Worlidge (among many others) gave to Italian garden style would recommend it to those who looked to ancient Rome for political inspiration during the last third of the seventeenth century. The claims for a theory of limited monarchy, which was effectively what England organized for itself in 1688, had been closely affiliated with the political thought of the ancients. Machiavelli, popularized in mid-century by Harrington and later in the 1690s by Toland, had argued for a mixed government modelled upon that of the Roman republic: in English terms this meant that the monarchy was the consuls, the aristocracy, the lords, and the *comitiae*, the commons. To the extent that this Roman model ousted an authoritarian kingship in England, the claims of classical gardening over those of the French would be strong. Classical imagery, classical representations, classical architecture could have decisive political meaning in an age which devoted so much of its intellectual energies to justifying a contemporary political situation in terms derived from the classical past.[86]

We have already noticed that Evelyn came to think that 'natural and magnificent' gardening had been replaced by merely luxurious and expensive designs (above, p. 153). Those who defended Italian gardens at the expense of French ones did so because of their modest scale. Their much-praised variety had obvious parallels with the theory of mixed government, endlessly celebrated from 1688 and throughout the eighteenth century. The mixed form of gardens and groves, each holding in check the other's mode of design, seemed an appropriate version of spatial arrangement for English estates; the emphasis upon land as the basis for a freeholder's political authority and upon the agrarian values of virtue and independence could be traced from classical Rome through Renaissance examples in modern Italy to the English countryside. Substituting local references and representations in English gardens for the classical imagery – ruins, statues – visible on so many Italian sites jibed with the wish to domicile classical republicanism.

These garden perspectives become quite clear in the early eighteenth century; but their outlines are there in the final years of the seventeenth. Timothy Nourse follows Worlidge in emphasizing the classical authority for his vision of the country house and the pride which landowners should take in improving their property within decorous limits. His *Campania Foelix. Or, a Discourse of the Benefits and Improvements of Husbandry* first presents the reader with a frontispiece in which a neat and modest garden seems to become a terrace for viewing the fertile and worked countryside alongside; that this imagery is totally unlike the designs suggested in his essay 'Of a Country-House' argues for its symbolic appeal to an *idea* of a happy country life. After essays on local government, inns and alehouses, servants and labourers and the poor, Nourse prints his discussion of an ideal country house: its context is the practical social and economic matrix of rural economy.

It is a fascinating essay: he knows exactly what a *villa* in the Italian sense is:

> a *Villa*, or little House of Pleasure and Retreat, where Gentlemen and Citizens betake themselves in the Summer for their private Diversion, there to pass an Evening or two, perhaps a Week, in the Conversation of a Friend or two, in some neat house amidst a Vineyard or Garden, sequestered from the Noise of a City, and the Embarras and Distraction of Business, or perhaps the anxious and servile Attendance of a Court.[87]

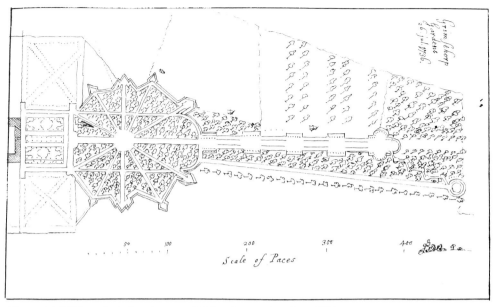

Figure 94 William Stukeley, layout of Grimsthorpe drawing, 1736.

But that is not entirely apt for the different social and climatic conditions of English estates. Its spirit, however, must somehow be translated, and as Nourse begins to detail the appearance of an ideal country mansion and its gardens and groves, it is still the model of 'The Old *Romans*' that he invokes. What follows is a lengthy description of many of the features which we have seen were those which attracted English tourists in Italian gardens and those which they tried to emulate in their own. Admittedly, much of the vocabulary of garden description fits other styles than the Italian; but the whole spirit and emphasis of Nourse's proposals are those of one who wants to naturalize classical and modern Italian gardening in modern England. He reviews the whole range of 'Curiosities of Walks, Fountains, Statues, &c'; he proposes a garden divided into three, with 'ascents' between each and a grotto ('made of Shell-work, with some little Imagery, delivering the Water through little pipes, with some wetting-Places, as also a Bathing-Place or Bason in the midst'); there would be a grove in the third section, and then views out over the wide 'Territory' around. There would be orange-trees and fishponds, and the provisions for these latter are supported by a quotation from Juvenal. In all it should be a creation where 'the unmeasurable Blessings of Nature and Fortune' co-operate with 'all the Contrivances of Art'.

Nourse was just one of several writers who were eager to guide their readers into a better taste. In 1665 John Rea was concerned that 'Gardens of the new model' would be disastrously handled by 'unskilfull persons'. Exactly which 'models' he is thinking of cannot be precisely determined; but his advice to think rather of 'a green Meadow . . . spontaneously imbroydered with many pretty Plants and pleasing Flowers' than to mismanage artificial designs suggests that he is concerned with the less luxurious end of the garden styles then available in England. Similarly, he values 'Fountains, Grottoes,

Statues, &c' as 'excellent ornaments and marks of Magnificence', but 'ill done, [they] are little better than blocks in the way to interrupt the sight, but not at all to satisfie the understanding'. Gardens on slopes should not be cast (or miscast) into levels, which 'seldom make handsom Gardens'; but they may be terraces 'with Descents, as the convenience of the place will afford . . .' It is, above all, pragmatic and sensible, trying to ensure that new ideas from the continent are aptly localized; that approach is entirely characteristic of those who wished to translate Italy into England.[88]

The Oxford dons who urged John Evelyn to complete his *Elysium Britannicum* in 1659 were also hoping that it would 'helpe ye Nation' to adopt the ways of Italian gardening. The manuscript, as it survives today, reveals that Evelyn's historical instincts led him to survey gardening ideas and practice in any location that would yield useful material: though 'a Garden was at first taken for a poore and simple Villa', 'a Garden is now a name of a large signification'.[89] But the Oxford academics who encouraged Evelyn's work clearly recognized its Italian bias, and the presence of classical and modern Italy as the fount of all current garden knowledge and practice declares itself throughout the manuscript, in the invocation of names like Palladio, Varro, Pliny and Virgil, in the identification of specific gardens in Rome, Verona and Florence. Like all garden designers, Evelyn was faced with the necessity of advising those with the funds to make wholesale improvements of a site as well as those who could only – for reasons of finance or the situation of their property – contemplate piecemeal alterations and additions. Italian garden imagery suited both ambitions, and in his detailed discussion, both historical and practical, of the various ingredients of a fine garden it is the example of that country which is constantly cited: the contribution of Italy to 'the most gracefull varieties' of gardens, 'both naturall and artificiall', is paramount.

11 'PALLADIAN' GARDENING

i: How English was the English Landscape Garden?

The English landscape garden has usually been treated as an exciting new phenomenon at the start of the eighteenth century when a reaction set in against the excessive implementation of French and Dutch garden styles. At its best this view acknowledges that the 'new' style owed some occasional debts to the past; at its worst it applauds a creation sprung fully armed from the heads of Shaftesbury, Addison and Pope. Moreover, this version of garden history argues that from the early years of the eighteenth century gardens became more and more natural until with the advent both of Kent, who 'leaped the fence, and saw that all nature was a garden', and of his successor, 'Capability' Brown, the landscape garden reached its final consummation and was indistinguishable from nature itself.[1]

The hold upon our imaginations of this Whiggish progress of natural liberties at the expense of slavish art has been strong. It clearly had its roots, as we have suggested, in the political justifications and celebrations of mixed government after 1688. We may even have an early example of its effects in Addison's failure to publish his insight that Milton's description of the Garden of Eden could not have been written without knowledge of the gardens of Italy; leaving such a claim in manuscript enabled Addison to emphasize a wholly native revolution in garden design.[2] And what Addison suggested in 1712 was taken up by mid-century and established as an authoritative narrative of the English landscape garden, a narrative which seemed fully confirmed by a trend towards far less schematic layout of grounds. But this emphasis upon the new gardening's natural progression is also a striking example of history written in the light of subsequent events. This has been called a 'mythology of prolepsis'.[3] It allows the outcome of events to explain their early and intermediate stages, for such a mythology sanctions only a teleological perspective upon the past. Garden history has been caught tenaciously in the spell of such prolepsis, which by the very terms of its analysis precludes any serious consideration of how origins determine the character of some cultural event or idea.

The most influential spokesman for that historical view of the English garden was Horace Walpole. His *History of the Modern Taste in Gardening* was written during the late

1760s, printed with his *Anecdotes of Painting in England* in 1771 but not published until 1780; the *History* was issued separately in 1785.[4] Since Walpole was writing during the years of 'Capability' Brown's ascendency, it was perhaps inevitable that he wanted to read English garden history in the light of its most advanced practitioner whom he calls the 'very able master' who has succeeded Kent. Kent is Walpole's hero in the revolutionary story of English landscape garden design. He glosses over its evolution as Kent appears, 'bold and opinionative enough to dare and dictate, and born with a genius to strike out a great system from the twilight of imperfect essays'. As Walpole puts it, his language betraying his self-confessed stance as 'the only unadulterated Whig left in England', 'more perfect perfection' of garden design was still sought; under Kent's genius such 'improvements' were realized. What such narrative neglects may be registered easily by looking at the famous analysis of Kent's 'management of water':

> Adieu to canals, circular basons, and cascades tumbling down marble steps, that last absurd magnificence of Italian and French villas. The forced elevation of cataracts was no more. The gentle stream was taught to serpentize seemingly at its pleasure, and where discontinued by different levels, its course appeared to be concealed by thickets properly interspersed, and glittered again at a distance where it might be supposed naturally to arrive.

But in Kent's own drawing of the Vale of Venus at Rousham (see figure 111) we see two forced elevations of cataracts; and if the cascades do not tumble over marble, their clear descent (so to speak) from the pools at Pratolino or the rustic fountains on the hillside at the Villa Aldobrandini by no means bid a final and decisive adieu to Italian villas.[5] *The History of the Modern Taste in Gardening* is everywhere characterized by Walpole's refusal to accept that the early exponents of the so-called English garden must have derived their ideas from somewhere in the first place. So of Milton he writes that 'One man, one great man we had, on whom nor education nor custom could impose their prejudices . . . judged that the mistaken and fantastic ornaments he had seen in gardens, were unworthy of the almighty hand that planted the delights of Paradise'. After quoting a passage of *Paradise Lost* (IV, 227–47), the language of which could be made to apply equally to Italian garden scenes of the kind Milton would have seen on his visit to Rome, Walpole asks his reader to

> recollect that the author of this sublime vision had never seen a glimpse of anything like what he has imagined, that his favourite ancients had dropped not a hint of such divine scenery, and that the conceits in Italian gardens, and Theobalds and Nonsuch, were the brightest originals that his memory could furnish.[6]

Both the specific arguments and the general historiography of Walpole's essay have proved enormously influential: B. Sprague Allen wrote in *Tides of English Taste* that 'it is impossible to discover anything that such grandly formal gardens as those of [Villa] Lante or [the Villa Farnese at] Caprarola could have contributed to Milton's conception of Eden'.[7] Other recent studies of the English landscape garden either turn their backs on 'the highly interesting period from . . 1713 to 1733' because it cannot be read as a preliminary to 'the Reign of Nature',[8] or see the contribution of a gardenist like Alexander Pope almost solely in terms of later picturesque styles which he could not have known and therefore could not have anticipated.[9]

Such garden histories beg the central question of how and from where the so-called English garden derived its basic syntax and philosophy. Sir Ernst Gombrich's *Art and Illusion* has long since made it axiomatic that an artist must create from available materials and modes of seeing. This holds equally for the designers of gardens in the early eighteenth century. One does not have to deny a steady increase in the 'natural' style of laying out grounds between 1700 and 1770 in order to argue that the sources and origins of that style are as crucial as their outcome. Nor need one dismiss 'Capability' Brown's extraordinary vision of *la belle nature*, an accomplished landscape of natural forms, in order to suggest that Lord Burlington, Kent and Pope were concerned with finding an adequate translation into English of older, Italianate modes of gardening; on the contrary, it highlights Brown's achievements. Finally, I shall have to risk being considered unpatriotic and insist that the responsibility for the 'English' style (no 'true Englishman', says a recent writer, would want to call it *Anglo-Chinois*[10]) came in large part from abroad.

One of the dangers of the proleptic view of English garden history has been that it must force itself to interpret all early statements of preference for a 'natural' style as prophetic of a future that their authors could not have known. Shaftesbury and Addison have both been invoked as early exponents of the 'natural' style of designing grounds. It is now clear that at least the first and probably the second have been misunderstood: their remarks, rather than anticipating developments as yet uninitiatcd, take up old ideas and refashion them. In Shaftesbury's case, this revision focuses upon a passage in his philosophical dialogue, *The Moralists*:

> I shall no longer resist the passion growing in me for things of a natural kind, where neither art nor the conceit or caprice of man has spoiled their genuine order by breaking in upon that primitive state. Even the rude rocks, the mossy caverns, the irregular unwrought grottoes and broken falls of waters, with all the horrid graces of the wilderness itself, as representing nature more, will be the more engaging, and appear with a magnificence far beyond the formal mockery of princely gardens . . .[11]

Rather than a simple preference for 'untamed nature', this passage has recently been shown to take its meaning from the larger context of Shaftesbury's interest in character, geometry and perspective.[12] To summarize a complicated argument briefly, Shaftesbury believed that in every natural object there was an intrinsic or inherent form which the *virtuoso* should learn to appreciate and that these nascent tendencies could be cultivated and perfected in practical gardening. He suggested modes of organizing garden spaces on perspectival lines in order that the full range of nature imagery – perfected, shaped and geometrical as well as primitive and wild – should be properly apprehended. He does not prefer one mode of imagery or design above another; both are required in order that the mind may appreciate the unfathomable forms and beauty of the whole natural creation. Hence it is that the rhapsody on 'things of a natural kind' must be read as a part of Shaftesbury's larger philosophy.

What concerns this enquiry is the coincidence of Shaftesbury's views with his political stance. He was devoted to the Whig cause, and supported Toland who was responsible for maintaining that the model for English society was that of republican Rome which, if properly followed, would make London the new Rome and enable it to grasp at empire like Rome itself.[13] The champion, too, of a new national taste in the arts,

Shaftesbury is a crucial though shadowy presence behind the English garden as it evolved from the seventeenth century into the early eighteenth. His *Letter concerning the Art or Science of Design*, written in Italy in 1712, repudiated the work of Sir Christopher Wren and all of what we would now call the baroque. Although he gave no hint of what the revised national taste should be, it is surely possible to see it as the aesthetic equivalent of his larger political position:[14] it would look to ancient Rome for its models, mediated by modern Italian examples; it would ensure a 'mixed government' of forms, a variety of structures – exactly what the philosophical views set out above argued for the proper understanding of the natural world; it would strive for the Englishing, the domiciling of older, foreign ideas. The positive side of Shaftesbury's distaste for the baroque is his wish to return to purer artistic forms which answered 'the proportionate and regular state [which] is the truly prosperous and natural in every subject'.[15] So we may, then, see parallels between Shaftesbury's Whig principles, his dismissal of the baroque, and his rejection as the sole style of design of 'the formal mockery of princely gardens'. What is common to them all is an insistence upon variety and flexibility; everything we can glimpse of Shaftesbury's own gardens at Wimborne St Giles suggests that they mirrored the larger ideas of his philosophical and political life.

The garden was divided into garden and grove, and its imagery of terraces, grotto and (especially) triumphal arch gave it an Italianate character. In 1702 he had himself painted by Closterman standing with his brother in a grove of trees where a classical temple front clearly shows: in both its classical portico and its juxtaposition of art and nature it declares its symbolic representation of Shaftesbury's ideas, just as the glimpse of grounds divided into garden, grove and distant landscape does in the frontispiece to his *Characteristics* in its second edition of 1714. Shaftesbury had travelled in Italy, and that country's kind of garden experience was ideally suited to express his philosophical viewpoint about nature. If we return to the praise of nature quoted above, which has always been a key text as well as an awkward one in garden history, we can see that its language (rude rocks, mossy caverns, irregular unwrought grottoes, broken falls of water) applies equally to wild natural scenery and to gardens like Pratolino or the upper sections of Aldobrandini. Those kinds of imagery, he says, represent nature more: that is to say, in the wild they teach the *virtuoso* the idea of things which always transcends its local embodiments; while in gardens, the creation of structures which represent those natural ideas will signal an imagination that acknowledges the beautifying process of art rather than the beautified object and thereby celebrates the forms and 'order' of all creation which a garden's variety is best suited to display.

Shaftesbury, then, ceases to be a prophet of a style of gardening nowhere available at the time he was praising it (nor for some time afterwards) and becomes instead an important spokesman for the kind of gardening which drew upon a long tradition of Italianate garden design during the seventeenth century and which strove to make it new again in England. It is therefore worth resisting the impulse to hail the English landscape garden as 'the thin edge of the wedge of Romanticism'[16] and see its early stages as the revival and reconstruction of older forms. This translation or naturalization was undertaken for many reasons, but the two most prominent were undoubtedly the impetus carried into garden design from the new political mythology which had become prominent after the Glorious Revolution; the second, linked to that, derived from new attitudes towards the natural world promulgated by the Royal Society and directed against Cartesian system. Both of these motives can be discerned in early eighteenth-century discussions of husbandry.

ii: 'Rural Gardening'

We have already noticed the authority which terraculturists of the Interregnum and the fellows of the newly established Royal Society sought for their endeavours in classical husbandry. This emphasis increased considerably in the early eighteenth century. Its connection with garden design is vital: both classical examples (largely literary) and the modern Italian experience of villa and *vigna* seemed to endorse the connections. But the topic of husbandry also highlighted two further aspects of garden design – the need to find an adequate translation of Italian modes, and its wish to avoid the luxury and the system of French gardens.

Shaftesbury was typical of an English reaction against the methods of Cartesian science when he wrote that 'the quickest way of making a fool of oneself is by a system'.[17] He criticizes any method of research or philosophy that is not conducted in the light of empirical enquiry; the Cartesians were attacked, among other reasons, for their subscription to a preconceived system rather than submitting themselves to the patient investigation of true experimentalists. English empiricism, especially in the pages of the *Philosophical Transactions* of the Royal Society, promoted 'histories' at the expense of 'systems'. Though it may appear that Shaftesbury's vision of nature implied a system, his emphasis upon seeking in every single object 'an actual figure, an ideal form, and a natural force'[18] identifies him with the experimentalists. His insistence upon the irregularity of the nature we see all around us just as much as his search for its most perfect, hidden forms, was derived from the Cambridge Platonists; one of them, Henry More, as early as 1660 voiced attitudes which would be given shape in garden design during the early years of the eighteenth century:

> that the mind of man may be worthily employ'd and taken with a kind of spiritual husbandry, God has not made the Scriptures like an artificial Garden, wherein the Walks are plain and regular, the Plants sorted and set in order, the Fruits ripe, and the Flowers blown, and all things fully exposed to our view; but rather like an uncultivated field, where indeed we have the ground and hidden seeds of all precious things but nothing can be brought to any great beauty, order, fulness or maturity without our own industry . . .[19]

The apparent lack of system in the natural world is contrasted with a wholly artificial garden; the rich variety of nature elicits our curiosity and industry in learning about it, and yet what we bring to its understanding will in its turn create both beauty and 'order'. The only way to translate such emphases upon the variety and irregularity of nature into garden art, achieving 'order' without losing its essential quality, would be to insist upon a mixed style, as Shaftesbury had done and as Italian gardenists, classical and modern, were thought to have done.

But if there were problems of translating such a philosophical view of the natural world, where the histories of each member of creation were more crucial than any overall system, into garden art, there were also fundamental problems with transferring Italian gardens to England. The topic of husbandry posed in sharp and precise terms the crux which faced architects and garden designers: namely, as Richard Bradley put it, 'the Difficulty . . . of bringing the *Italian* Management to be agreeable to an *English* climate'.[20] The very same anxiety had been voiced in 1659 by the Oxford dons who wanted Evelyn to hurry along his *Elysium Britannicum*, and indeed anyone who had tried to cultivate oranges in England and translate the mythical Hesperides to her shores would have made the same comment during the seventeenth century. But in the early years of the eighteenth century the problem seemed even more acute; I suspect that the new urgency stemmed from the recognition that what Stephen Switzer called 'Rural Gardening' could be a solution to both the problems posed by scientific empiricism and the quest for a national taste in design. Horticultural questions were susceptible of solution, and yet in their English metamorphosis retained strong associations with the classical world which was also needed for political reasons in any new national style. What we must now trace in English writings on 'Rural Gardening' was paralleled in architectural terms with the publication of *Vitruvius Britannicus* from 1715; they are intimately connected.

Addison had urged his readers to 'make a pretty Landskip of his own possessions' (*Spectator* 414).[21] Though he often seems rather muddled or uncertain in his aesthetic pronouncements, Addison's insistence upon 'the wide Fields of Nature' in almost all his discussions of garden style is clearly deliberate. It declares his Whig patriotism, his confidence that the possession of land and its cultivation give the freeholder his political base and security; it is the solid but unseen foundation of the papers which Addison published in *The Freeholder* in 1716. To view your estate 'in a Prospect which is well laid out, and diversified with Fields and Meadows; Woods and Rivers . . .' is to realize palpably the idea of your citizenship and its place in traditions which go back to the Romans. Hence Sir Roger de Coverley's abbey ruins (*Spectator* 110) 'Eccho' with more than an acoustical experiment, one suspects, since the reverberations of national history are endemic to Addison's approval, which is not always forthcoming for English gardens.

The variety, the whole surface texture of the natural world appeals to Addison's empiricism and his distrust of system. The description in *The Tatler* 161 of the land of Liberty is typical:

> The place was covered with a wonderful Profusion of Flowers, that, without being disposed into regular Borders and Parterres, grew promiscuously, and had a greater Beauty in their natural Luxuriancy and Disorder, than they could have from the Checks and Restraints of Art. There was a River that arose out of the South Side of the Mountain, that by an infinite Number of Turns and Windings, seemed to visit every Plant, and cherish the several Beauties of the Spring, with which the Fields abounded. After having run to and fro in a wonderful Variety of Meanders . . .

Again, in *Spectator* 414, Addison praises the variety of natural abundance over the checks and restraints of art: 'The Beauties of the most stately Garden or Palace lie in a narrow Compass, the Imagination immediately runs them over, and requires something else to gratifie her; but, in the wide Fields of Nature, the Sight wanders up and down without Confinement, and is fed with an infinite variety of Images . . .' Yet this is not by any means a primitivist plea for a wholly unmediated nature. It is only the checks and restraints of art that are criticized; otherwise it is the power of the mind (the Imagination) which shapes and understands, sometimes abstractly, but sometimes in actual garden designs. For the vision of the garden of Liberty, already quoted, also includes goddesses who appear exactly as some statue giving meaning to the place where it presides ('The first of them was seated upon an Hill . . . The other was seated in a little island . . .'). Leonora's country seat in *Spectator* 37 is a particularly fine example of art lent to enhance rather than constrict natural variety, and its imagery not a little recalls English praise of Italian gardens: 'The Rocks are shaped into Artificial Grottoes, covered with Woodbines and Jessamines. The Woods are cut into shady Walks, twisted into Bowers, and filled with Cages of Turtles. The Springs are made to run among Pebbles . . .' That the model which English gardens should follow is Italianate (the author of *Spectator* 477 prides himself upon 'a Fountain rising in the upper Part of my Garden') is made clear when Addison criticizes English gardens for not imitating, representing, the grand and august profusions of Nature in their gardens (*Spectator*, 414). He includes French with Italian gardens as examples of styles which present 'a large Extent of Ground covered over with an agreeable mixture of Garden and Forest'; but if we recall his strictures on Versailles in a letter to Congreve (see above p. 96), it should be clear that it is the garden art which reforms nature sufficiently to realize or at least allow the mind to register her potential that is undoubtedly the best. Italian gardens and their larger landscape of classical association come closest to that quality for many theorists and practitioners in the early eighteenth century. Above all, as Addison's various writings about Italy reveal, the play of the imagination is far greater in that country, since it is allowed more opportunities.

The role which the imagination could play in Italian gardens had always been among their strongest attractions. The fashion in which visitors were invited to consider the classical parallels and associations of modern Italian gardens, to enjoy the Ovidian marvels or the entertainments of hydraulic theatres, to consider the curiosities of cabinets and grottoes and to engage actively in understanding the various roles of art and nature in a garden's creation was part of the hugely imaginative appeal of that garden world. Addison transferred the same habits of response to the larger countryside of Italy, and in so doing he translated landscape into art (landskips). Imagination was, therefore, the means by which unmediated nature did in fact present itself as art: to see pictures or embroidery (*Tatler* 161) in the natural world, to read classical precedents into the sight of cultivated fields, these were both ways in which art reformed nature; yet its reformation was not actually *in* the scenery, but in the mind. The enormous significance to garden history of this imaginative apprehension of the natural world has been little noticed. When Addison says that 'we find the Works of Nature still more pleasant, the more they resemble those of Art' (*Spectator* 414), he is allowing a greater appeal to nature *at the same time* as investing that transaction of the senses with imaginative colour. Joseph Glanville had said much the same in 1665 when he stated that 'our *simple* apprehension of corporal objects, if *present*, we call Sense; if absent, we properly term it *Imagination*'.[22] What Addison contributes is an emphasis upon the mutual activity of sense and mind. In that way the fields of many an English estate could be, simultaneously, artificial and natural.

Such is the thrust of Stephen Switzer's arguments for what he calls 'Rural Gardening'.[23] Switzer's writings attempt to give practical form to Addison's ideas, and what sustains these efforts are his convictions of the ancient dignity and the interconnections ('inextricably wove') of gardening and agriculture: 'their *Elyzium* being no other than the happy and regular Distribution, and cheerful Aspect of pleasant Gardens, Meadows and Fields'.[24] Thus he will 'throw my Garden open to all View, to the unbounded Felicities of distant Prospect, and to the expansive Volumes of Nature herself'; but that this is no more a rude and uncorrected nature than either Shaftesbury's or Addison's is revealed by Switzer's plans, and where his physical reorganization of nature is forced to stop his imagination can take over, confident that 'The *Romans* had doubtless the same Extensive kind of Gardening'.[25]

What Switzer terms the 'honour of his subject' leads him to ground his works firmly in classical traditions: Pliny's *Natural History*, he argues, 'is of as much Value as that of all the *Germanick* Wars'. It is Pliny's authority that is cited for Epicurus' being the first to bring into cities the 'Delights of Fields and Country Mansions'; Evelyn's *Kalendarium Hortense* is said to be modelled on Palladius's *De Re Rustica*; attention is directed to various classical gardens and garden owners, and from a discussion of Diocletian he switches directly to the Villa D'Este and the Vatican Belvedere. His sense of the continuities and translations of rural gardening are quite explicit – first classical Roman, then modern Italian revivals after the devastations of the barbarians, then the 'Completion of it . . for France . . . and Great Britain'. He notices that even the French virtuoso, de la Quintinie, whose *Compleat Gard'ner* had been translated by Evelyn in 1693, had travelled in Italy and read the relevant classical texts by Columella, Varro and Virgil.[26]

Switzer's whole attitude towards French gardening is important, for he sees it basically as the first attempt to revive classical gardening outside Italy; but since 'some considerable Defects [are apparent] in that way of Gard'ning', it is the English who will have the opportunity and privilege of ensuring that the progress of gardening reaches the British Isles. Thus, Switzer may invoke French gardens, as did Addison, to correct the fussy, Dutchified taste of contemporary English gardens, but he neither approves its political associations nor settles for transplanting it unchanged. He invokes the example of classical Rome under Augustus where there was the closest harmony between politics, agriculture and the poetic imagination after a 'long Scene of Misery' and the 'Miseries of [the] Country': Virgil's contribution, above all, advanced the imagination from 'small and diminutive Scenes of Flowers, Greens, etc . . . to distant Woods and Meadows'.[27] With this political, horticultural and philosophical model, Switzer establishes his own loyalty to the Whig cause and his opposition to 'Arbitrary and Despotick Power'.[28] It is therefore England's duty to surpass '*France* our great Competitor' in garden arts as in arms: ' 'Tis then we shall hope to excel the so much boasted Gardens of *France*.'

All this, then, must be seen as the context in which Switzer explains his basic idea of extensive, rural gardening in the preface to *Ichnographia Rustica*:

> By *Ingentia Rura* (apply'd to Gard'ning) we may understand that Extensive Way of Gard'ning that I have already hinted at, and shall more fully handle; this the *French* call *La Grand Manier*, and is oppos'd to those crimping, diminutive, and wretched Performances we every-where meet with, so bad, and withal so expensive, that other Parts of a Gentleman's Care is often, by unavoidable Necessity, left undone; the Top of these Designs being in Clipt Plants, Flowers, and other trifling Decorations . . . fit only for little Town-Gardens, and not for the expansive Tracts of the Country.

> This then consists rightly in large prolated Gardens and Plantations, adorn'd with magnificent Statues and Water-works, full of long extended, shady Walks and Groves; neither does it altogether exclude the Use of private Recesses, and some little retired Cabinets. . . .
>
> It also directs, that all the adjacent Country be laid open to View, and that the Eye should not be bounded with high Walls, Woods misplac'd . . . and the Feet fetter'd in the midst of the extensive Charms of Nature, and the voluminous Tracts of a pleasant Country.[29]

When he comes in subsequent volumes to set out practical designs by which to realize his vision of the new classical gardening domiciled in England, he takes up all of the elements which generations of English visitors to Italy had noticed in gardens there; in particular he promotes terraces ('noble but expensive'[30]) and criticizes John James's translation of Dézallier d'Argenville's *The Theory and Practice of Gardening* for its neglect of them; there is even a proposal for a staircase which recalls the double form of the Belvedere exedra (see figure 41). And when he published his two volumes on hydrostatics and hydraulics it was extensively illustrated with images of Italian fountains from the Vatican gardens, the Villa Aldobrandini, Villa D'Este, Villa Ludovisi and the Villa Borghese among others, and both its preface and introductory chapter invoke the example of classical Rome.

Switzer's programme for English garden design, then, invokes classical and modern Italy to counter contemporary taste and to ensure that English country estates are the true heirs of the Roman art of gardening. He combines a shrewd, practical interest in the management of an estate – in this a true descendant of the seventeenth-century terraculturists – with a strong scientific bias, especially in the book on hydraulics where he declares his debts to early members of the Royal Society. Along with these pragmatic and experimental habits, Switzer has a clear appreciation of what has been called the '*institution of gardening*'[31] – its use and significance in cultural and political history. Thus even his more utilitarian handbooks, *Practical Kitchen Gardener* (1727) or *Practical Husbandman and Planter* (1733), are directed against the luxury, the 'vanity of expense', a cause which drew together opposition Whigs and Tories like Bathurst, to whom the first of those two works was dedicated. It was Bathurst's villa at Richings, his neighbour Bolingbroke's at Dawley or Apps Court, Walton-on-Thames, owned by George Montagu, the first Earl of Halifax, to whom *Practical Husbandman and Planter* was dedicated, that Switzer singled out for praise: they were the estates of patriotic husbandmen who had contributed to the good of their country and whose memory would be perpetuated in 'Generations yet to come' by their improvements.[32]

When Switzer writes that he has 'follow'd and *enlarg'd* on the Method laid down by Virgil',[33] he glances at the problem endemic to any attempt to realize the ideas of ancient gardeners: actual examples of their work were no longer to be seen, therefore re-creations must be extrapolated from literary texts in forms available in the present. What this produces may be seen from the projects with which Switzer was involved and which he illustrated in his books. He juxtaposed regular gardens near the house with groves, as he had done in Wray Wood, Castle Howard. The gardens were extended with bastions so that visitors could be brought to points where the whole countryside lay open before them. The groves were threaded with winding paths (these look, in plan, far too studied, but in practice would have seemed entirely natural) which also conveyed visitors to points from where further prospects could be taken. All these features are shown in William Stukeley's sketch of Switzer's work at Grimsthorpe in Lincolnshire (figure 94), where bastions have been added to the straight and rectangular garden and a long walk extended through the groves, opening and closing with alcoves in a fashion reminiscent of the sculpture area of the Villa Ludovisi (see figure 16). The projections published in his *Ichnographia Rustica* are far more ambitious than Stukeley shows Grimsthorpe to have been;[34] what these ideal plans imagine, however, is a much more extensive version of woodland walks opening into clearings in the groves or leading visitors to vantage points overlooking the countryside.

Switzer worked with both Charles Bridgeman and John Vanbrugh. Although their collaborative efforts cannot be taken up here in any detail, it is worth remarking that elements of both men's designs paralleled, confirmed or maybe were influenced by his own. Bridgeman seems to have had little interest in design theory or in annexing his work to any cultural or political cause; he seems to have been very much at the mercy of specific commissions, so it is hard to determine exactly what is truly *Bridgemanick*. Beyond his love of large scale, commented upon by various historians, he displays some fondness for a mixture of precise garden forms and more irregular groves. At Tring, Ledston, Scampston, Farley, Rousham and Stowe walks were made to wind through wooded areas;[35] at Richmond there were similar paths through groves where Sir John Clerk of Penicuik noticed that fields of corn had been incorporated.[36] Furthermore, a characteristic item on many plans drawn by or attributed to Bridgeman is some theatre or theatrical glade cut into woodland with stepped sides like *coulisses*: these occur at Sacombe, Farley, Rousham, Stowe and above all Claremont. Switzer illustrated this last in his *Introduction to a General System of Hydrostaticks and Hydraulicks*, and it was also well known through engravings of this famous garden (figure 95). But what has never been remarked is that this is an exact representation of the exedral staircase at the Vatican Belvedere as codified by Serlio (see figure 41). At Claremont this has been grassed, a happy mode of signalling its accommodation to England and the English climate. But what needs to be asked is why such a feature should have been introduced if it did not serve to signal the arrival of Italian models – in this case, classical and modern – into a country concerned to revive the principles and practices of antique gardening. The exedral stairway, as we have seen, enjoyed an extended life throughout European gardens as well as in Inigo Jones's masque designs; its function at both the Temple of Fortune, Palestrina, and then in the Vatican Belvedere where Bramante copied the classical form was both a means of descent and a calculated piece of scenography.[37] At Claremont, too, it has both functions; the theatrical element being both a stage set to be viewed from the lakeside and a platform, a *cavea*, from which to view a wide range of countryside. One suspects that it was for that reason that Switzer applauded it (as well as being himself responsible for the 'Water Spouts' below it), since it provides exactly the appropriate situation from which to appreciate extensive prospects. One can only speculate as to whether Bridgeman's other theatres were similarly designed: that at Rousham would have enjoyed exactly the same views over Oxfordshire countryside.

Switzer shared with Vanbrugh a keen sense of the need to accommodate older styles in English terrain and, above all, to use whenever possible items with historical associations, as gardens in modern Rome used classical ruins. Vanbrugh's famous recommendation to the Duchess of Marlborough to retain the remains of Woodstock Manor at Blenheim reveals a true instinct for seizing the opportunities of a site rather than simply

Figure 95 Claremont amphitheatre, engraving of 1734 by Rocque.

imposing upon it the designer's will.[38] Such appears to correspond with Switzer's practice at Leeswood, which he laid out for Sir George Wynne in Flintshire in the 1730s. A recent conjectural reconstruction of these gardens shows that, besides the characteristic Switzer signature of grounds where wood, field, water and plantations are carefully intermingled and decorated with statues, the sight was attracted outwards to 'eyecatchers' set in the landscape beyond the specific boundaries of the garden.[39]

The vogue for this extensive and rural gardening had to make its way slowly against the pomp and circumstance of French style or the fussy and intricate Dutch mode. But its costs were less than the former's and its imagery – varied as well as native English – recommended it above both. It allowed a garden and its surrounding landscape to be wholly indigenous, while recollections of how 'old Romans' were supposed to have laid out their villas gave the scenery a properly classical tonality; this in its turn could be aided by a scattering of statues and other classical effects. What Switzer had championed in the 1710s was taken up by later writers like Robert Castell, Richard Bradley and Aaron Hill just as the effects of his ideas can be traced throughout Pope's pronouncements on garden design.

Richard Bradley may be taken, briefly, as an example of the popularization and extension of Switzer's ideas: he published a greater number of works on gardening than any other writer in the first thirty years of the century.[40] Of these we are concerned with

190

one, the *Survey of the ancient husbandry and gardening . . .* of 1725 dedicated to Viscount Townsend, a noted agriculturist and member of the Royal Society (as was Bradley himself). It is the usefulness of classical authors that is stressed, and the work's full title announces that the survey is *Collected from Cato, Varro, Columella, Virgil and others the most eminent Writers among the Greeks and Romans*; just such a compilation, according to Aubrey, it had been Evelyn's wish to make. The most interesting section is chapter 20, 'Of the Gardens of the Ancients, and of Grassing', of which it is worth citing a longish passage on what Bradley calls the 'state-Gardens of the Ancients, – how they were designed for Grandeur':

> the Fashion, or Taste of the *Greeks* and *Romans*, in such Grand Gardens, was to make them free and open, to consist of as much Variety as possible; to afford Shade, and give a refreshing Coolness by variety of *Jet-d'eaux* and Water-falls. When they laid out their Gardens in any Figures (for I do find that they ever used Knots or Flourishes) those Figures were either Squares, Circle or Triangles, which they commonly encompass'd with Groves of Pines, Firrs, Cypress, Plan-Trees, Beech, or such like; in some convenient Place they also contrived their *Ornithons*, or *Aviaries* . . . add to this their fishponds . . .

> This was the Humour of the Gardens of the Ancients, which, in my Opinion, we have hardly mended by our extraordinary Regularity; which, however it may appear well on a Paper Design, is stiff and surfeiting when it comes to be put in Execution. In our Modern Designs we see all at once, and lose, the Pleasure of Expectation; fine irregular Spots of Ground, which in themselves had ten thousand Beauties, are brought to a Level at an Immense Expence, and then give us so little Amusement . . . . even in the best Performances in this Way, a good Judge cannot help discovering the *petit goust*, except in such Gardens as we find at the Earl of *Burlington*'s at *Chiswick*, where the Contrivance and Disposition of the Several Parts, sufficiently declare the grand Taste of the Master . . .[41]

Though Bradley had travelled in France and the Netherlands, he had not visited Italy; so his vision of classical gardening is all the more astonishing in its similarity to the experience of English travellers in Italian gardens – notably, his insistence on the 'Pleasure of Expectation', and the refusal to level ground. Presumably he must have read accounts or seen engravings of Italian gardens, for elsewhere he suggests items for gardens which are clearly derived from them: musical machines in summerhouses or grottoes ('first hearing the Musick faintly, and then led insensibly from it, and by turns losing and recovering it . . .'), 'Grotto's and Caves, disposed in a Rustick Manner', 'at certain Points of View, *Obelisks* might be placed, or . . . Pavilions, built after the manner of Grecian Temples'. This last suggestion is paralleled in one of William Stukeley's drawings, inscribed 'The antient manner of Temples in Groves' (figure 96), which declares how much hold on the English imagination was exercised by the wish to find forms in which to realize classical ideas.

While it would be absurd to claim that all emphases upon variety, natural appearance of ground, rural imagery, statues, grottoes and temples signalled a conscious classical meaning, it must nevertheless be apparent that during the 1710s and 1720s such equations were frequently and clearly made. They were boosted by the publication of Castell's *The Villas of the Ancients Illustrated* in 1728, to which we shall turn later, and an increasing number of theoretical statements, practical endeavours and other propaganda. The paradox of all this – an English gardening that was foreign in inspiration, a new style that was ancient – did not seem to strike its proponents. Batty Langley's *New Principles of Gardening*, published in the same year as Castell's volume, is fully committed to the style adumbrated by Switzer and Bradley; it is opposed to 'that abominable Mathematical Regularity and Stiffness' associated with French gardens, and it draws upon the full range of Italianate imagery (terraces, statuary, groves, grottoes, ruins, obelisks, amphitheatres, etc.[42]). All this is, so Langley's title claims, 'new'; yet his frontispiece (figure 97) is actually lifted from a late seventeenth-century engraving of the Villa Doria Pamphili in Rome (figure 98) – the only difference being that an 'English' ruin has been substituted for the baroque fountain. It is a striking example both of the debts of the early landscapers to Italy and of their manoeuvres to make their borrowings English.

iii: Castell, Burlington, and Pope

So far we have approached the 'new' English garden from the perspective of husbandry considered as a classical tradition remade in England. A parallel endeavour of the period was to explore and promote an Italian architecture based upon ancient models: Palladianism. Together they authorized a garden art which seemed authentically antique and at the same time truly English. The title of the volumes which Colen Campbell began issuing in 1715, *Vitruvius Britannicus*, phrased the whole ambition perfectly. Campbell's project, in

Figure 96 William Stukeley, 'The antient manner of Temples in Groves', drawing.

Figure 97 Frontispiece to Batty Langley, *New Principles of Gardening* (1728). Compare it with Figure 98.

Figure 98 View in the gardens of the Villa Doria Pamphili, engraving from D. Barrière, *Villa Pamphilia* . . . . (1660s or 1670s). Compare with Figure 97. This view is taken from the gardens into the meadows or park along the line of the watercourse which can be seen in Figure 55.

part a response to Shaftesbury's call for a national taste in the arts, was to illustrate architectural and gardening designs in England which had been classically inspired; the British Vitruvius of the title was in fact Inigo Jones who, with Andrea Palladio, is opposed to all the affectation and licentiousness of the baroque. Since the Italians, Campbell's Introduction claims, have now lost the art of building with *'Antique Simplicity'* which Palladio had displayed it may be recovered in England; Palladio's 'ingenious Labours will eclipse many, and rival most of the Ancients', and therefore as the torch is passed to England she will in her turn surpass him. A similar theme was enunciated in literature, where the progress of poetry was traced from Greece to Rome and so northwards to its final flowering in England.[43] Gardening participated in all this cultural mythology on account of its connections with husbandry, architecture and literature; it had a threefold reason for being valued as a medium of translation from the classics.

Richard Boyle, third Earl of Burlington, was the leading promoter of Palladianism in England. Spurred by Campbell's publication, by his own travels in search of Palladian buildings and drawings in Italy in 1719 and by the first English edition of Palladio's *I Quattro Libri dell'Architettura*, Burlington lent his considerable authority to reviving classical gardening. It was he who financed the publication of Robert Castell's *The Villas of the Ancients Illustrated*, which was in its turn dedicated to him, his gardens at Chiswick (as we have seen Bradley recognize) set a practical example, and his friendship with Pope and his patronage of Kent involved him directly with two of the foremost gardenists of the 1720s, '30s and '40s. So it is to this cluster of Palladian garden enthusiasts that we must finally turn: in their pronouncements and in their achievements on the ground came the final flowering of Italianate gardening in England.

The most important aspect of Castell's attempt to recreate the landscape and garden layout of Roman villas is that such a book was published at all. It underlines the need of the 1720s to orientate their own landscape work within classical traditions. The volume itself tells one much: a large and handsome folio, yet not luxurious; to be used not admired, with Pliny's letters on his two villas set out in columns with an English version *en face*, a series of glosses below; then pages of more extended commentary, plates which display the proposed reconstructions of buildings and whole landscapes as well as an aviary derived from Varro's description. It is an act of double translation: from Latin into English, from word into image.

Castell adds no really new emphases to the materials we have already surveyed, but the quality and throughness of the exercise are important. The usual parallels between ancient and modern are canvassed: Burlington is compared to Varro and Pliny as leading figures in their respective states; Castell's volume extends, as is appropriate for England, the brief accounts and hints of classical writers into more extensive commentary. And in so doing the tendentious nature of the enterprise becomes clear, for Castell unobtrusively transforms the Plinian texts into images which (necessarily) invoke the syntax of contemporary English and modern Italian designs and into language which tends to approximate (again, inevitably) an English rural scenery. The reconstruction of Laurentum (figure 99) is clearly more scholarly when it presents buildings, since ruins of classical buildings like baths, theatres and amphitheatres remained to provide some clues as to the forms of villa structures; but when Castell comes to the landscape, he is forced to rely upon memories of the Campagna for isolated temples in fields (top right of the plan) and for lines of cypress

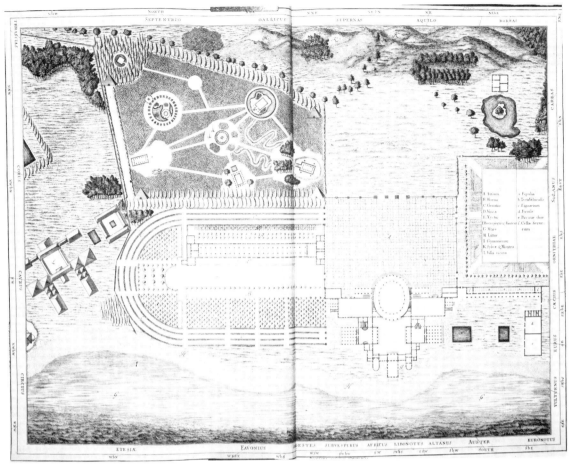

Figure 99 Reconstruction of the younger Pliny's villa estate at Laurentum, engraving from Castell, *The Villas of the Ancients Illustrated* (1728).

trees (top); from Italian gardens are taken the imagery of groves, temples set on islands (mixed memories there of the Isolotto in the Boboli Gardens and the so-called Maritime Theatre at Hadrian's Villa) and the juxtaposition of regulated nature with apparently untouched terrain (cf. figure 55); from recent English garden works comes the whole area (towards bottom left) where alleys and two serpentine paths cut through a wilderness which is opened out into half a dozen clearings decorated with buildings and statues. In the English text, too, the emphases upon being able to look out from a country house into a varied agricultural landscape, upon the practical needs of a country estate and upon the uses of different sorts of country houses are occasionally tinged with a native rather than a classical colour.

All three of Castell's reconstructed landscapes give prominence to the villa buildings.[44] That which illustrates his second part on the villa with a closely linked farm sets the buildings more uncompromisingly in fields than the other two where some more regulated gardens are introduced. The effect of an Englishman's memories of Italian countryside near Rome and Naples upon his efforts to reconstruct classical villa settings must have been considerable. We have it upon Joseph Spence's authority that Philip Southcote took 'his idea of the ferme ornée [from] Fields, going from Rome to Venice'[45], and the landscapes of Castle Howard – two temples set over or in the fields – or of Stowe and Rousham – temples scattered within the groves – are just a few examples of how classical authority attached itself to English landscapes, for they enacted a familiar sight on the Grand Tour. There is even one piece of visual evidence that suggests that any countryside of a certain topography, but without any conspicuous buildings, could have the associations of a villa: figure 100 purports to be the representation of the ruins of a famous villa in the Naples area owned by Servilius Vatia; apart from the distant buildings on the side of a hill, we see only a pastoral countryside in the style of many French and Dutch seventeenth-century landscape painters. Yet the caption gives such a vista the meaning of a ruined villa in the landscape. How easy, then, for an Englishman with the right habit of mind to look at a piece of his own native scenery and see it as classical. Where representation of ancient Rome was impossible on a country estate in England, the imagination could impose its own associations; we have seen how Addison explored this very mode of seeing.

Figure 100 The villa of Servilius Vatia, seventeenth-century engraving.

Castell narrates how Pliny repaired the temple of Ceres on one of his estates.[46] Such would be the act of any patriotic and devout husbandman if ruined temples of that sort existed in the English countryside; since they did not, the villa owner must erect new ones, which is what Burlington himself did in the gardens at Chiswick. (Neither Castell nor Burlington could presumably commit themselves, as Vanbrugh had wanted to do at Blenheim, to featuring gothic ruins; the nearest Burlington could come to such an act of historical piety was by re-erecting Inigo Jones's Beaufort House archway in his grounds. But the substitution of indigenous for classical imagery is a final stage in the Englishing of Rome[47].) It would be possible to relate Castell's plans and discussions to a whole range of contemporary gardens; those illustrated in the volumes of *Vitruvius Britannicus* would be apt comparisons, their very inclusion warranting that they be viewed in the context of the translation of classical gardening into Britain. But this translation is at its most concentrated and eloquent at Chiswick, which is both model and product of *The Villas of the Ancients Illustrated*.

The gardens at Chiswick (figure 101) were created in two phases. Burlington began work in them after his return from his first Grand Tour in 1715 and continued until 1725; a second phase that involved William Kent took place in the 1730s.[48] The building of the villa itself between 1725 and 1728, with its distinct allusion to Palladio's villas, gave the gardens their point and culmination, which later extensions and alterations to the grounds simply strengthened. The whole effect was calculated: an air of the antique, indeed almost an open-air museum of architecture; theatrical, too, in the organization of spaces where visitors were both spectators and actors in Lord Burlington's dramas of classicization. The original *patte d'oie*, echoed by two further sets of radiating walks on the other side of the river, transferred to the gardens the stage of Palladio's Teatro Olimpico in Vicenza with its illusionary streets stretching away from the spectator; a fine mixture of rural and urban – a realization of the *villa urbana* that is the subject of Castell's first section in the *Villas of the Ancients*. The translation of the streets of the Teatro Olimpico into alleys of vegetation terminated with buildings and obelisks emphasized that mix of city and country. But Chiswick was above all a miniaturization, a scaling down of classical and modern Italy to an English site.

This smallness of scale was remarked by John Macky in *A Journey through England*: he wrote that 'Every walk terminates with some *little* Building, one with a Heathen Temple, for instance the Pantheon, another a *little* villa, where my Lord often dines instead of his House, and which is capable of receiving a tolerably large Family; another walk terminates with a Portico, in imitation of Covent Garden Church.'[49] This miniaturization was an important aspect of Rousham, another exercise in accommodating Italy into England, and its significance needs underlining. The original ground at Chiswick, before Burlington acquired more land on the other side of the river in the late 1720s, was not extensive; so the small scale of Chiswick villa and gardens could easily be explained by that fact. Yet the care of the reductions seems deliberate: the villa itself measures 68 English feet, but this is a direct translation of the original 68 Vicentine *piedi* of the Villa Rotunda which thereby enforces a diminution. The other garden buildings, images of which surround Rocque's engraved plan of 1736 (see figure 101), are all small. And they are also extremely eclectic: architectural historians worry themselves considerably over the exact models Burlington and his architects used for these garden buildings,[50] but surely the

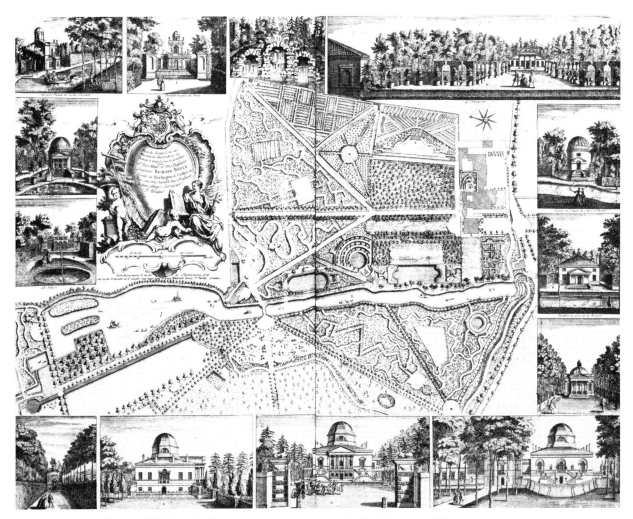

Figure 101 Chiswick House gardens, engraved plan by Rocque, 1736.

range of reference and allusion to classical buildings both antique, Renaissance and seventeenth-century English is the essence of the whole design. Both in its scale and in its concentration into a few buildings of memories of many, Chiswick and its creator declare a fundamental necessity of any English Palladianism and British Vitruvianism: that it must be a diminished glory. Whether Burlington himself would have admitted the implication of his activities of translation is perhaps doubtful; but that he deliberately engaged in reducing the size of classical and Palladian models is undeniable. And an awareness of the implications of this cultural translation was everywhere available in the circles around Burlington; Pope certainly registered it in his versions of Homer and Horace, as we shall see, and Kent participated in, even if he did not himself initiate, juxtapositions of scale in the Elysian Fields at Stowe which are clearly part of the iconography.

That it is John Macky who notices the littleness at Chiswick is perhaps revealing because he was constantly alert in his English travels to echoes of Italy. Besides paying attention to terraces, variety of views, statuary, he specifically 'fancied my self' at Stoke in Berkshire 'in some antient *Villa* near *Rome*'; the prospects from Blenheim he compared to those of the Pitti Palace in Florence; the Duke of Shrewsbury built his house at Helthrop 'after a Model his Grace brought from Rome'; and inevitably he repeated the common-place that Richmond was 'the Frescaty of England'.[51] To such an eye the extremely calculated classicism of Chiswick must have been striking. Whether or not somebody like Macky would be able to recognize it, the garden offered itself as virtually a memory theatre of architectural and garden history, especially in the second phase of works. It was then that the Jones gateway arrived, the obelisk was erected and decorated with the funerary relief which had originally been in Lord Arundel's sculpture garden (figure 102), and the grove of trees replaced by an equally classical exedra near the new villa. This exedra – over the scale of which Kent evidently concerned himself[52] – also contained imagery which sent both general and fairly specific messages to alert visitors: Defoe says some of the statues placed in the exedra were from Hadrian's Villa (whether true or not, the implication counted);[53] the specific figures of Caesar and Pompey, responsible for the decline of Roman republicanism, were confronted by Cicero, its defender, and thus constituted a traditional Whiggish critique of Walpole's administration.[54] The cascade which Kent introduced at the head of the river, like those at Rousham, derives from the upper garden at the Villa Aldobrandini (Rocque, figure 101, centre top shows what must be a projected version; cf. figure 112).

Figure 102 Jacques Rigaud, the obelisk at Chiswick, drawing of about 1733.

These final touches to the Chiswick gardens brought to a completion over twenty years' work. Though others helped him with designs for specific buildings and other features, the whole was Burlington's own vision: 'his Lordship's happy Invention', as Colen Campbell said of the *Bagnio*, the first of the miniature buildings erected in the gardens.[55] Perhaps only somebody as influential, as rich and as determined a Palladian as Burlington could have pulled off such a scheme and could, too, have called upon others and infused them with his own vision of a classical elysium at Chiswick. Its great lack was variety of terrain, virtually the only aspect of the grounds that could not be matched with Pliny's various landscapes which Burlington's protégé, Castell, had set out in his book. Some attempt to remedy the flatness was made with a terrace around the head of the river in the late 1720s; but for a proper representation of Italian 'hilly gardens' Burlington would have had to go to his Yorkshire seat at Londesborough. Today it is derelict and overgrown; but there is evidence of terraces down the hillside, confronting a fine view of the wolds, even some urns and what may well have been arcades or grottoes under the final terrace walls.[56] That Burlington may have had to go, as he frequently did, to Yorkshire to experience one essential feature of Italian garden design must have been yet another reminder of the difficulties of translating into English conditions the highlights of classical and Renaissance villa gardens. Yet his achievement at Chiswick was undoubtedly the most magnificent and accomplished of such translations; that it managed to allude through its various imagery to so many predecessors was a measure of its comprehensiveness and its confidence. Few other gardenists were able to come near it.

Alexander Pope is a good example of those who, without Lord Burlington's means, seems to have made a virtue of necessity and incorporated into his grotto and garden at Twickenham this very awareness of what could not be achieved, except in the mind's eye. He is on record as enjoying dreams and visions in his grotto,[57] and so those aspects of classical gardening which he could not or did not represent, he imagined.

His garden and grotto are well known;[58] all that will be necessary here is to explore the extent to which Pope dedicated his gardening to the recovery on English soil of classical gardens and how modern Italian styles mediated that antique experience for him. Pope's earliest garden utterance, in *The Guardian* 173 of 1713, declares that it is 'the Taste of the Ancients in their Gardens' which guides his own thinking. Virgil, Homer and Martial ('Sed *rure vero*, barbaroque laetatur': it rejoices in the true rustic, the untrimmed farm) provide him with his authority on this occasion, and having translated Homer's description of the gardens of Alcinous Pope reminds his readers that Sir William Temple had thought that 'this Description contains all the justest Rules and Provisions which can go towards composing the best Gardens'.[59] The problem is that Homer's passage yields little in the way of design hints; what it does, however, is endorse antique gardening as practical horticulture. Throughout his life Pope subscribed to the traditions of classical husbandry, admiring on his friends' estates what was not fully possible in his own, a georgic self-sufficiency, what his *Guardian* essay called 'the useful Part of Horticulture'. Switzer's 1718 *Ichnographia Rustica*, one of the prime statements of the antiquity of 'rural gardening', was dedicated to Pope's friend, Lord Bathurst.

Homer's passage, and other parts of the *Odyssey* which he came to translate later in his career, suggested garden features in only the vaguest terms: fountains and waterworks throughout, orchards, vineyards, groves 'sequester'd to the nymphs', a 'mossie altar'. But

Palladian architecture, which the Burlington circle was promoting from before the time Pope moved to Twickenham, would have suggested a model; the classical past – in the case of gardens, all but extinct – was translated to the present via Italian designs. Pope's own library at Twickenham contained busts of both Palladio and his first English disciple, Inigo Jones, and that he was aware of the architectural analogy for his gardening is evident from his compliment to Lady Howard in 1727 on the room in Marble Hill House which was modelled on Palladio's interpretation of a Roman atrium. On another occasion he told Robert Digby that he existed on a diet of 'Water-gruel and *Palladio*'.[60] His other studies included Johann Georg Graevius's six-volume *Theasaurus Antiquarium et Historiarum Italiae* (1704); modern buildings he knew from Pieter Schenk's *Romae Novae Delineatio* (?1700), his own copy of which at the Beinecke Library is bound with engraved *Veduti di Giardini e fontani di Roma e di Tivoli*.[61] Clearly, he was well enough informed to bring to his wide reading in the classical literature of gardens a visual knowledge of how modern Italy had attempted to recover those lost glories. He praised Leo X in his *Essay on Criticism* for reviving Rome, and tells how his own imagination 'brings the vanish'd piles to view, / And builds imaginary *Rome* a-new'.[62]

Pope's commitment to the word *villa* has rightly been seen as indicating his commitment to Palladian ideas; but it also signals his recognition of classical traditions. His own place in these is the theme of his gardening as it is of his writing; so it will be worth looking at the latter in order to assess the former accurately. His major work of literary translation was Homer's two epics, and he was encouraged in the task by friends who valued his skills at rendering the Greek in 'good Engish':

> I must say (and I do it with an old-fashion'd sincerity) that I entirely approve of your Translation of those Pieces of *Homer*, both as to the versification and the true sense that shines thro' the whole; nay I am confirmed in my former application to you, and give me leave to renew it upon this occasion, that you wou'd proceed in translating that incomparable Poet, to make him speak good *English*, to dress his admirable characters in your proper, significant, and expressive conceptions, and to make his works as useful and instructive to this degenerate age, as he was to our friend *Horace*, when he read him at *Praeneste* . . . .[63]

What Sir William Trumbull there urges upon Pope is to make Homer 'speak good English'. It is, of course, an essential aim of any translator: an earlier poet, Oldham, had argued that his job was to put 'Horace into a more modern dress than hitherto he has appear'd in, that is, by making him speak, as if here living and writing now. I therefore resolv'd to alter the Scene from *Rome* to *London* . . .'[64] But it is not, as Pope came to realize, as simple as it sounds. Would Homer's warriors really talk like junior officers in Queen Anne's army? Would Horace have been able to express the same convictions, the same values, so confidently in Hanoverian England? Pope had already raised this issue obliquely when he incorporated a version of Sarpedon's rousing battle cry from *The Iliad* into *The Rape of the Lock*, giving the speech to Clarissa. For those who noticed, this device wittily alluded to the differences, the declensions even, between two societies thereby compared and contrasted. In his later *Horatian Imitations* Pope carries this ironic mode to far more sophisticated and explicit lengths. In particular, among other personal, public and political contrasts enshrined within the parallel between Horace's Rome and his London, Pope dwells upon the differences between the Latin poet's Sabine Farm and his own

Twickenham, which as a Roman Catholic he can only rent, which he has financed from his own literary endeavours (principally the Homer translations) and which he is in no position to pass on to his heirs.

The whole thrust of making Horace speak good English was to make readers aware of what could not be said any more or of what had to be said as a result of different social and political and cultural circumstances. I want to suggest that something of the same habit of mind coloured Pope's gardening, his translation of what he thought of as classical designs into his own English practice. Editions of Horace published in England during the eighteenth century continued to use as little illustrations the reconstructions of Roman gardens which we considered in Part One (see figures 7 & 8).[65] If Pope saw those texts he must have been struck by his inability, for a variety of reasons, to come anywhere near such antiquity.

The verse epistle *To Burlington* sanctions the full range of traditional garden motifs: columns, arches, terraces, grottoes, fountains, theatres and amphitheatres, mounts, all set in a larger georgic landscape. In his own gardens Pope managed an approximation to them all. But they are *precisely* an approximation, and he is sometimes amused by the modesty of the whole process of imitation in his 'little' garden. Consider his profession of horticultural self-sufficiency:

> Content with little, I can piddle here
> On Broccoli and mutton, round the year;
> . . . .
> 'Tis true, no Turbots dignify my boards,
> But gudgeons, flounders, what my Thames affords:
> To Hounslow Heath I point and Bansted-down,
> Thence comes your mutton, and these chicks my own;
> From yon old walnut-tree a show'r shall fall;
> And grapes, long ling'ring on my only wall.[66]

Having no extensive and rural gardens, Pope's poetic persona enjoys the modesty which contrasts with his classical predecessor's or at least a general Roman abundance. Other discrepancies may have resulted from lack of funds, but the capital to be made from this in rhetorical terms was some compensation.

Pope's grotto was in the long line of classical and Italianate grottoes. It invoked the legends of Numa and Egeria, which Pope planned to formalize or 'complete' by incorporating a statue of the nymph with an inscription – 'like that beautiful antique one which you know I am so fond of'.[67] The whole contrivance amalgamated literary sources (classical, in the legends of Egeria and nymphs presiding over springs of water; modern, in the Latin inscription), classical sculpture (the so-called Cleopatra or Ariadne from the Belvedere sculpture garden in the Vatican, well known through engravings, much visited by tourists and celebrated in a poem of Pope's[68]), classical remains (the Egerian grotto, shown to tourists off the Appian Way and frequently engraved with a sleeping nymph in its niche [figure 103]), and the many Renaissance imitations of such grotto-nymphaeums (at the Villa Giulia, for example [see figure 34]). Whether we should read anything into the fact that Pope supposedly never installed the statue of the nymph, his failure to do so as well as his failure to install river gods on his lawn beside the Thames are interesting awkwardnesses in the translation of the classics into 'good English'. The projected nymph and her allusion to the inspiratory powers of such a spring as Pope discovered in his grotto

Figure 103 H. van Swanevelt, Grotto of the Nymph Egeria, seventeenth-century engraving.

allowed him to claim that it was a home of the muses, a 'Musaeum'.[69] But it was a striking case of association rather than representation.

Musaeum also alerts us to the fashion in which Pope's garden imitated the role of cabinet of curiosity. Its elaborate collection of mineral specimens and rocky souvenirs, celebrated after the poet's death by his gardener Serle's 'Account of the MATERIALS which compose the Grotto', was like many Italian collections and seventeenth-century English successors (see figures 51 & 71).[70] The difference consisted in a far more natural arrangement; nothing was represented, no mythological imagery, as Isaac de Caus proposed (if it was he) at Wilton House; what mattered, as Serle's account shows, was an intimate and highly personal association of some place or friend with every prime specimen on the walls. Another significant aspect of Pope's grotto was the absence of elaborate waterworks; it had no hydraulic machinery, yet by 1740 Pope had contrived 'three falls of water' which a visitor in 1748 described with enthusiasm:

> Here it gurgles into a gushing Rill thro' fractur'd Ores and Flints; there it drips from depending Moss and Shells; here again, washing Beds of Sand and Pebbles, it rolls in Silver Streamlets; and there it rushes out in Jets and Fountains; while the Caverns of the Grot incessantly echo with a soothing Murmur of aquatick sounds.[71]

The marvels of Pope's waterworks were of a piece with (if less ambitious than) Italianate predecessors and in conjunction with the mineral specimens and exhibits of his grotto go far to make us understand his claim for Twickenham as a 'study for Virtuosi'.[72] In addition, Pope's contrivance both of what he called a 'Perspective Glass', by which as through 'a sort of continued Tube' he could see the river through his temple and under an arcade of trees, and of some camera obscura, which projected moving images of the outside world upon a darkened wall inside the grotto, allowed him to maintain in a rather old-fashioned way the identity of a garden grotto with a laboratory.[73]

There were other Italianate items which he failed to establish in his gardens like the piece of fountain statuary with an inscription.[74] But perhaps nowhere do Pope's ambitions for his villa as well as his due sense of their wishful potential reveal themselves as clearly as in the scheme for his Thames riverside communicated to Spence in 1743.[75] It involved statues of river gods, terms, temples, busts and two inscriptions. The whole project has been interpreted by Maynard Mack as an elaborate testimony to Pope's sense of his place in a tradition of accommodating classical poetry to new, local situations, or, in Mack's words, 'of enlarging and enriching the natural culture by causing to be poured into it the great works of classical antiquity'. The Latin inscriptions from Politian's *Ambra* and Virgil's *Georgics* alluded to river gods, which, once installed beside Pope's own Thames, would testify to the place of his own poetic career in the continuities of antique and Italian poetry. But besides Politian's Latin poem which is devoted to praise of Homer, there was a poem in Italian with the same title by Lorenzo the Magnificent himself: this *Ambra* refers to the little river which runs near Lorenzo's villa at Poggio a Caiano and is to be seen in the upper left-hand corner of Utens's lunette (see figure 23); the villa had been visited by Spence on his first Italian tour of the early 1730s.[76] It seems inconceivable that Pope's invocation of *Ambra* in one of his riverside inscriptions was not intended to signal how his own villa beside the Thames maintained in an English setting, however modified, the potent traditions of villa life which the Renaissance had revived on the basis of their knowledge of classical literature.

We can only speculate about Pope's inability to implement that iconography. But other aspects of his attention to landscape support a theory that he was, as in his *Horatian Imitations*, sceptical about the complete relevance of a 'truer, more "primitive" classicism'[77] and its imagery to England. He showed throughout his life a fondness for old monuments of English history; especially at Sherborne Castle, in Dorset, owned by his friend Digby, he relished the associations of a Norman castle acquired by Sir Walter Raleigh before it had passed to the Digbys. He hoped that his friend would embellish it and give it prominence in his old-fashioned, Italianate, terraced gardens. For Digby, who confessed that 'I want the publick Spirit so much admired in old Rome',[78] to emphasize on his estate the memorials of an English past and its continuities within one family was equivalent to teaching Horace to speak good English. It was the English a Georgian Horace would have to speak. Bathurst's conversion of a house in his woods into Alfred's Hall or King Arthur's Castle was a similar gesture. And Pope who knew his Pliny would scarcely have missed the translation of the Roman's amphitheatre in Tusculum into Bathurst's plan for a vista to commemorate 'the meeting of the *Thames* and the *Severn*': the rivers were to be 'led into each other's Embraces thro' secret Caverns of not above twelve or fifteen Miles, till they rise and openly celebrate their Marriage in the midst of an immense Amphitheatre, which is to be the Admiration of Posterity a hundred Years hence'.[79] Perhaps it was also part of the vision of naturalizing classical ideas in England that Pope wanted to create 'an old Gothic cathedral, or rather some old Roman temple, in trees'.[80] These British scenes extended the limited ones of his little garden and gave him a larger theatre for his imagination than Twickenham permitted. We know how much he prized its theatrical potential, how much he self-dramatized his life there in the satires and Horatian poems; but in the wider reaches of his own country's history and geography were themes which also called for celebration in garden and landscape designs. Tory though he was, Pope's vision of ancient liberties and simplicities transmitted from the Roman world to contemporary England allied him with the true Whigs whose cause had so largely been betrayed by Walpole and the other Whig grandees.

iv: Kent

William Kent's work as a garden and landscape designer is both culmination and turning point in the history I have been pursuing. He brought to his work on country estates considerable experience of Italy and Italian gardens (unusually, he reached Italy by ship and thus avoided on his outward journey any sight of French or Dutch gardens which he came to despise); his enthusiasm for things Italian locates him in the long tradition of Italianate Englishmen who have given that country a place in their affections, not to say affectations. Yet his versatility with styles, his readiness to accommodate himself to different sites and different patrons and his quick eye for visual possibilities ensured that he adapted Italianate ideas to English landscapes; he began to do this so well, in fact, that his imagery could seem purely indigenous – with the result that this later mode of design came to be the only one for which he was credited. Kent, then, plays a crucial role in English gardening history. His full story is in many respects far too complicated to take up here without unduly disrupting the balance of this enquiry, and it must be reserved for another occasion.[81] But what is relevant here, his Italian experience and its impact on his English work, can be set out more economically.

Kent spent nearly ten years in Italy (1709–19); he travelled widely while he was there, visiting almost all of the cities which had featured on other Englishmen's garden tours. He was based in Rome, as was usual then for an aspiring painter, and he clearly got to know well the neighbouring hill towns of Tivoli, Frascati and Palestrina. We are forced to piece together his time and travels from patchy and somewhat random sources; he himself left only a disappointingly meagre diary of a tour he took in 1714, but this does make evident his fondness for the Medici gardens of Pratolino (see figure 36); even though by the early eighteenth century they were ill-kempt and potentially wild and *romantick*, it is still an odd taste for a garden designer who is supposed to have been dedicated to the 'natural' style. Yet he was to recall many of its features in his later career: the setting of statues, temples or grottoes in wooded groves; its descending pools; its mythological dramas enacted in the grottoes. Of course, Kent's garden visits were a very incidental part of his professional life in Italy, which was dedicated to painting (including perhaps some work as a scene designer) and by the end of his stay to architecture, and it is extremely doubtful that he ever thought that he would seriously involve himself in garden design once he returned to England. But he was taken under Burlington's wing from 1719, so that, from being required to exercise his (rather inadequate) talents as a history painter, he progressed to working on architectural projects and any other commissions that came his way: George Vertue talks of 'Mr Kent at Court and amongst people of quality, call'd on for drafts &c on all occasions'.[82] He obviously sidled into garden designing, but he did so in the context of Burlington's Palladian schemes for a new taste in the arts. To that large and ambitious enterprise Kent brought both his Italian experiences and enthusiasm, which were entirely apt for the task, and a lively, even facetious temperament, the sceptical turn of which gave to his landscape work the same sort of edge which we have encountered in that of his friend, Pope.

Perhaps the most important fact about Kent's career as a gardenist is that, for someone with his Italian tastes and an intimate of the Burlington circle, his early work was so much with *gothick*. Perhaps in the late 1720s he was involved in planning the south garden at Holkham and erecting an obelisk among the equally classical ilex groves; but he was also probably contemplating gothick modes. In the 1730s when his garden work really begins, he can provide vaguely 'British' designs for Queen Caroline in Richmond Park and classical-palladian for the Temple of Venus at Stowe or the temple in the woods at Holkham. In the mid- and late-1730s he designed the purely classical temple of Ancient Virtue and the gothick hermitage (with a turret missing, ruined) at Stowe. This eclecticism can be explained, perhaps, by Kent's visual delight with the formal properties of different styles; but I do not believe that this is the only or the more plausible explanation.

For even a failed history painter, Kent must have recognized the meaningfulness of classical or gothick forms; belonging to Lord Burlington's circle, he would have known both the Whiggish overtones of a classical (republican) architecture and been alert to any deviation from its visual message. Rather, we should see Kent's invocation of gothick as a deliberate move to accommodate English associations in his designs, to make Palladio speak good English. Furthermore, Kent's training as a history painter and his theatrical work (which we may guess was more extensive than the few references to it which survive[83]) gave him privileged perspectives upon gardens: Italian gardens had been theatres in which visiting Englishmen were entertained and instructed with stories from classical mythology and history, and Kent seems to have been eager to draw out the theatricality of gardens and landscapes; but one of the main dramas that he chose to present to their visitors and spectators, who often appear in that role in Kent's more finished sketches, was the arrival of Italy in England. We can see this in one of his designs for the hillside at Chatsworth (figure 104): it is an anthology of Italian reminiscences – the temple at the top right of the slope recalls the so-called Sybil's Temple at Tivoli (see figure 106), the cascades allude to these in the upper gardens of the Villa Aldobrandini (see figure 112), the flanking pavilions with their pyramid roofs are an eclectic concoction of famous Roman remains. It is possible to see this design in quite a precise fashion both as history painting and as theatre: the traditions of antique gardening, mediated by Italian Renaissance versions of them, are seen to arrive and settle upon English soil. Yet such an event is nothing unless that significance is perceived, as some central heroic action is watched in either painting or drama; so Kent shows us figures who gesture at this transformation of the Chatsworth hillside.

But as Pope's literary Augustanism has reminded us, the translation of classical culture into Georgian England was by no means uncomplicated. A satiric alertness to

Figure 104 William Kent, design for the hillside at Chatsworth, drawing, (?) 1730s.

discrepancies between the classical world of Homer and Horace and the characters in *The Rape of the Lock* or Grub Street is perhaps a lesson that Kent learnt of Pope; he displays it on many occasions, in one drawing of Pope's own garden by showing Pope, Pope's dog Bounce and himself happily oblivious of a cluster of Roman deities who have descended upon a rainbow into the Twickenham groves. But the two gardens where Kent displays this sense of the contrasts as well as the similarities between classical and modern, between Italy and England, are Stowe and Rousham. Though it seems generally agreed now that Kent's contribution to the Elysian Fields at Stowe was simply to design two buildings and that the overall responsibility for the programme of this valley lay with Cobham and his friends, all we know of Kent's sense of humour and his quickness to adapt suggests that he would have been a willing participant in the whole enterprise.

The Elysian Fields at Stowe are by now well known and thoroughly discussed; they bear re-examination in ways that will illuminate our particular concerns with Kent.[84] A group of buildings are set on different sides of a valley down which runs a stream which was later called the River Styx. Both the name and the classical architecture, sculpture and inscriptions on either side of this river of death are a conspectus (a 'theatre') of Italian imagery. Kent's Temple of Ancient Virtue is a modern, English, completed version of the ruined temple at Tivoli which attracted so many artists (figures 105 and 106); inside it were full-length statues of four exemplary classical figures. Juxtaposed to this handsome, perfectly circular building were the gothic of Stowe's parish church and the deliberately created rubble of a vaguely classical temple of Modern Virtue, decorated with a headless statue which visitors were meant to take for Walpole. Facing it across the River Styx was an entirely different edifice, the Temple of British Worthies (figure 107). Its architecture is a strange amalgam of Italian Renaissance exedras, but the somewhat flattened roofline recalls an earlier English classicism. Kenneth Woodbridge has suggested that the exedra derived from one at the Villa Mattei in Rome (see figure 17), which since its gardens were a Renaissance recreation of a classical funerary garden would be an aptly elegaic echo in the Elysian Fields. But the exedral shape, as we have seen, was a familiar one in many other Italian gardens, and it is perhaps the general invocation of such shapes and memories that was intended. One of the many Italian structures that Kent's building echoes is the circle of niches at the Villa Brenzone on Lake Garda, which it is entirely possible that Kent may have visited.[85] Those niches contain busts of Roman emperors: here at Stowe, as George Clarke has demonstrated, are displayed a cluster of Whig patriots. Perhaps we are meant to register not only that while four ancient worthies were needed to signal classical values in the Temple of Ancient Virtue opposite, here it takes sixteen to make up an adequate English team; they are in bust rather than full-length, too. But they are nonetheless notable British worthies, and a head of Mercury that used to be in the hollowed-out niche in the Roman pyramid in the centre signalled that the messenger of the gods would conduct them across the River Styx to join their ancient predecessors. The final joke, as is now well known, is that behind the Temple of British Worthies is an inscription commemorating what appears to be an exemplary Italian gentleman, one Signior Fido, who turns out to be a hound. Even this cheeky gloss upon the eminent British worthies may have an Italian inspiration; those niches with the Roman emperors at the Villa Brenzone have each a hollowed-out cavity behind, nowadays empty, but which has the rather disconcerting effect of undermining the firmness and grace of the circular theatre.

All of this programme depends upon two particular conditions in the spectator. He must always see any one building in some perspective with another in order to compare and contrast them; from British Worthies he has to look back towards Ancient Virtue, the ruined Modern Virtue and Stowe parish church. Such perspectival organization of space is both painterly and theatrical, and argues for Kent's hand in the arrangement. Further, the spectator must participate in reading and understanding these various devices; they are a script which, as actor now, he must learn and perform. This theatrical dimension to the Elysian Fields and its presentation of itself as some historical event may help us to understand Southcote's remark that this was the 'painting part of Cobham's gardens':[86] the whole arrangement, despite the fine use and enhancement of the natural valley, cannot entirely be seen in terms of a latter-day picturesque taste, so perhaps Spence's remark should be interpreted as his recognition that here Cobham and his designer created a history painting, albeit a history painting somewhat sceptical of the high dignity of that genre.

The personages whose busts occupy the Temple of British Worthies are ineluctably native; even the structure that houses them moderates its Renaissance classicism with a somewhat gothick squatness. In other of his designs of the 1730s Kent was able to deploy the gothick style more deliberately, but not unambiguously. Besides the temples for the Elysian Fields, he also designed the Temple of Venus at Stowe; this spoke in mixed tongues, for besides echoing various Renaissance buildings (Woodbridge has suggested Ligorio's Casino Pio in the Vatican Gardens or certain of Palladio's villas like Badoer, and other items like the garden pavilion shown in figure 13 suggest themselves), it was decorated inside with scenes from *The Faerie Queene*, Spenser's British-gothick, epic-romance, which was one of Pope's earliest favourites and which Kent himself would illustrate at the end of his career.

For Queen Caroline Kent provided even more strikingly British imagery. In 1731 he had designed for her a Hermitage in Richmond Park and four years later Merlin's Cave.[87] Doubtless Caroline dictated much of the style and imagery, but it is impossible not to think of Kent enjoying himself in these exercises in cultural history and learning much from their lessons in architectural association. Both buildings had political messages: inside the Hermitage busts of Newton, Locke and Boyle among others proclaimed the contributions of the new science to natural religion; by her use of sculpture in this way Caroline played the role of an ancient in modern times. Kent's design answered this double perspective, for on the one hand it was classical – the plan of a Greek cross, Roman altars, sofas as well as the busts inside, triangular pediment and inscription over the door – and on the other native and natural – a 'ruin' (with one turret missing), sunk into the ground, its stone work roughly hewed and laid. Contemporaries thought its appearance 'grotesque', which nicely captures both the antique and the native implications. Merlin's Cave had even more obvious British imagery in its Druidical roofs and the use of natural materials, trunks and branches, for the interior decoration. In both Kent seemed to be identifying the gothick with nature, natural materials and natural setting (the sunken effect). In this his architectural emphases endorsed the iconographical programme: British worthies require suitably local styles of both building and situation; further, the association of British empirical scientists was with 'histories' not 'system', with the careful, detailed and local exploration of all aspects of the natural world; it was this common determination that

Figure 105 The Temple of Ancient Virtue, Stowe.

linked empirical science with antiquarian research. From 1718 under its president, William Stukeley, the newly founded Society of Antiquaries did much to promote an interest in the tangible remains of British history which in its turn focused attention upon native parallels with the classical precedents for the Glorious Revolution of 1688: there was Magna Carta, or King Alfred, the founding father of a system of civil liberty lost at the Norman invasion. So that, far from being a rival imagery to the antique, the gothic of English ruins could deliver the same message: hence Cobham's erection of the triangular gothick Temple of Liberty at Stowe or Bathurst's restoration of the so-called Alfred's Hall in his park at Cirencester which paralleled Pliny's restoration of the temple to Ceres on one of his estates.[88] Seen in this light, Kent's manipulation of both classical and gothick takes on added significance; his attempts to merge them, moreover, suggest a recognition on his part that England needed to find its own accommodation of the two styles. And if, for Kent, natural settings and materials signified gothic or old English, then surely Kent's increasing tendency to set classical buildings in woodland or in other supremely English contexts must be interpreted as one way in which he wanted to register some of their shared meanings.

Of all of Kent's attempts to create some 'history painting' in English landscapes using the resources of both classical and gothick imagery the most accomplished and pleasing is Rousham, in Oxfordshire, what Christopher Hussey called 'the locus classicus for the

Figure 106 Gaspar van Wittel (Vanvitelli), *View of Tivoli*, oil painting, late seventeenth or early eighteenth century.

study of Kent'.[89] Walpole thought it both 'antique' and 'miniature': though he was emphatically right to spot the miniaturization which contained the same message as it had done at Chiswick, he seems to have missed its efforts with British imagery. At the entrance into the gardens from the road, a visitor who has entered through a palladian gateway is faced with a gothick seat. Or, if he approaches the gardens from the house, its battlements, ogee arches and niches and mullioned windows outside coexist with an interior decor that also includes *grotteschi all'antica* and ceiling paintings of classical subjects, all Kent's work.

He was called to Rousham in 1737 to redesign the house and the gardens which Bridgeman had laid out in the 1720s. Kent retained the basic plan of the grounds that he inherited, devoting himself to new structures and imagery of striking eloquence. Across the bowling green from the house, perched on the edge of a slope down to the River Cherwell and with a fine prospect over the Oxfordshire countryside, he placed a copy of Scheemaker's sculpture of a Lion Attacking a Horse (figure 108). This is one of the many pieces which General Dormer had collected, and it was part of Kent's task to provide for them a garden setting that was in a direct line of descent from Arundel's in the previous century and the famous Roman sculpture gardens which Kent would have seen for himself. Here, too, the classical – herms on the edge of the lawn flanking the Scheemakers – mingles with the northern – items by van Nost in the theatre below and to the left.

211

Figure 107 The Temple of British Worthies, Stowe.

But the Lion and Horse are not simply decoration. They recall exactly the same group in the Fountain of Rome at the Villa D'Este[90] (figure 109). That may be sheer coincidence, a casual recollection of no consequence; but in the context of the whole garden this first encounter with classical imagery as one approaches the gardens from the house takes on an altogether more calculated air. At Tivoli there is a model of classical Rome, and the sculpture placed before it was supposed to signal the domination of Tivoli (horse) by Rome (lion); but classical Rome exists only in model, and away on the horizon is the modern city, which would be visible from the platform to the right of figure 109; visitors to the Villa D'Este were thereby invited to compare old and new, especially the new prestige of Tivoli which the Cardinal's gardens proclaimed. At Rousham, a similar exercise is necessarily frustrated: there is only England on the horizon, a fine spread of Oxfordshire countryside; so that classical and modern Rome are there by omission.

A very similar but perhaps more eloquent statement is made at Kent's main structural addition to the gardens. There had been terraces on the slope below where the

Figure 108 Copy of Scheemakers's statue of a Lion Attacking a Horse, at Rousham, Oxfordshire.

Figure 109 The Fountain of Rome, Villa D'Este, Tivoli, engraving from Falda, *Le Fontane di Roma*, Part IV. The Lion and Horse may be seen on the 'stage' of the Fountain to the left of the central statue.

213

Scheemakers now stood as late as 1721.[91] Bridgeman presumably removed them; but in the late 1730s Kent reintroduces this quintessentially Italian feature a hundred yards downstream. His Praeneste Terrace, so named in a description of the gardens by a former gardener, is modelled upon the Temple of Fortune at Praeneste (figure 110; cf. figure 83). This was a famous Roman ruin, much studied by Renaissance architects like Ligorio and Palladio, and generally visited as a prime site on the Grand Tour; Addison remarked on 'fragments of this ancient temple', which 'stands high for the Advantage of the cool Breezes, for which reason Virgil calls it *Altum* and Horace *Frigidum Praeneste*'.[92] Kent mimics that elevation at Rousham and the single arcade, with its urns, statues and benches, would have been a vantage point to take in an English view; equally, just as the Roman temple could be glimpsed from across the Campagna as the tourist approached, so Rousham's Praeneste is probably first seen from afar down the Elm Walk once the visitor has circled the outside of the garden. Yet Kent's terrace is but one row of arches; he has taken the famed succession of levels at Palestrina and reduced it to this elegant single line. Despite its name, it echoes many such loggias and arcades in Italian gardens or associated with them (see figure 12); but its title calls attention to one precise model which has not been followed, perhaps which cannot be followed. Such are the difficulties of translation into modern English.

Kent's other famous contribution to the gardens was to reshape the Vale of Venus (figure 111). Softening the geometry of Bridgeman's pools, he has introduced his favourite rustic cascades from the Villa Aldobrandini (figure 112), though the sequence of descending pools also bears some relationship to those which he would have seen on his visit to

Figure 110 The Praeneste Terrace, Rousham.

Figure 111 William Kent, The Vale of Venus at Rousham, drawing of the late 1730s or early 1740s.

Pratolino (see figure 36). Unlike the sculpture of the Lion and the Horse or the classical allusion at Praeneste, this is a direct association with modern Italian gardens. For they revived the lost gardens of antiquity, and their role in passing on those Roman traditions to modern England is what is acknowledged in this valley, if only unconsciously; aptly, the presiding genius of the place is Venus, the Roman goddess of gardens.

But this attention to classical and Italian declensions is not the full story either at Rousham or in the larger arena of Kent's career. The Oxfordshire countryside, as we have seen, is a vital element in the total experience of Rousham; the visitor catches glimpses or is confronted with broad vistas beyond the gardens. To mark this Kent established his eyecatcher on a distant ridge, and his Temple of the Mill (a cottage decorated with a frontispiece) in full view from the end of the gardens. The former is gothick, but was also seen by contemporaries as a triumphal arch, and accordingly Roman.[93] The Temple of the Mill is part of a similar blend of classical and English, for its acknowledgement of classical husbandry was matched by equal attention to English agricultural activity beyond the gardens – Heyford Bridge was brought into view, with its country traffic; the fields across the river were always alive with herds or flocks, a spectacle that was to be viewed from (among other sites) the 'theatre', a relic of Bridgeman's design which was made more natural by Kent (three statues in a hemispherical glade). So besides the gestures towards Italy, Rousham also honoured its locality and its native soil into which the foreign imagery was transplanted.

215

Figure 112 Rustic fountain in the upper gardens of the Villa Aldobrandini, Frascati, from Falda, *Le Fontane . . .*, Part III.

Rousham is the culmination of what I have called 'Palladian' gardening. Its antique aspect was witnessed by many besides Walpole. The antiquarian Loveday was there in the late 1740s: in the 'celebrated' gardens he admired the *jetteaus*, the antiques, and the Roman inscription upon the pyramid; but he also thought it 'all rural and unornamented'. The same year *The Museum Or the Literary and Historical Register* published some Latin verses on 'Rowshamius Hortus': they celebrated by their very language as well as much of their allusions the *color romanus* of the gardens; but they acknowledged, as Loveday had, the beauties of locality.[94] Kent's success in localizing his Italian inspiration resulted in visitors admiring the naturalness of his scenes. When he was working, after Rousham, in larger estates like Holkham and Euston, where the density of classical images would inevitably be less, it was even more likely that he would be admired for his natural style.

v: The progress of gardening

After his death Kent was revered by Walpole and Spence for his dedication to a style in gardening that Thomas Whately would call the modern in his *Observations on Modern*

Gardening of 1770. With hindsight it was easy to see Kent's work as modern rather than antique, a prophetic anticipation of the even more English style of 'Capability' Brown. It was Brown's achievement to remove almost all traces of foreign accent from English gardens: he tended to eliminate terraces, temples, sculpture, and he taught his contemporaries to realize the most beautiful potential of nature itself. The two are related: Brown is credited with saying that one does not go up and down steps in nature, so the ideal garden will shun such evident interferences by art in her processes.[95] But, as Robert Williams has argued, Brown was architect as well as landscapist and we must not neglect his determination to organize grounds so that mansions and other buildings, like summer houses, dairies, chapels, gateways, even ruins (at Lowther Hall), would find their proper place in the total picture of *la belle nature*.[96] Brown sought to realize the Englishness of places that he made or re-made: the appraisal of their 'capabilities', which gave him his famous nickname, was his native way of recognizing the *genius loci*. The whole problem was that those who tried to imitate his style did not possess his fine eye and sense of forms: the poor, sad nudity of Llanerch (figure 113) after its exquisite Italianate gardens (see figure 69) were swept away in some Brownian fervour in the late eighteenth century only testifies to the failure of Brown's disciples to do his work credit. The solitary statue, presiding for no apparent reason over a stretch of featureless water, is an ironic reminder of the glories that were eliminated in the name of a national style in gardening; we should, however, be careful not to attribute this all to Brown himself. Yet it is to his presence on the scene of English gardening by the second half of the century that we can in part attribute certain habits of garden historiography. Walpole, Whately and Spence all saw how gardens were developing and accordingly chose to explain the history of gardening throughout the eighteenth century as progress to that end.

Whately called it 'modern' gardening; Spence thought that he could detect 'beginnings of national taste' in the gardens at Chiswick;[97] Walpole could only value Kent for his leap of the fence and his sudden descent, like some *deus ex machina*, into the fields of nature. Yet the truth of the matter was that, as with the hymnbook, ancient and modern were bound together in the early English landscape garden. Kent's significance for historians, as one suspects it must also have been for his patrons, was that he was alert to both old and new. Janus-like, he looked both ways: he knew and respected classical and modern Italian gardening, and he moved in circles where such traditions were highly respected; but also, with a shrewd eye for the formal delights of natural materials, he responded to the Englishness of the places where he was obliged to locate Italianate imagery, and among his friends were those like Pope who had troubled themselves over the translation of the classics into English. This same doubleness of response which Kent seems to exemplify to a high degree is available throughout garden history during the 1730s, '40s and '50s. Some gardens and some gardenists would insist upon ancient *or* modern at the expense of the other; some, like Kent, tried to maintain a double allegiance (like Pope's *Horatian Imitations*, the Latin words *en face* to the English, but the ultimate 'text' being both together).

The traditions of antique gardening continued to be strong; the potent myth or idea of Rome as model for England was not likely to wither away quickly. Robert Morris's *Defence of Ancient Architecture* (published in 1728, the same year as Castell's *Villas of the Ancients* and Langley's *New Principles of Gardening*) hailed Marble Hill as an example of the true

Figure 113 Eighteenth-century view of Llanerch, engraving. Compare with Figure 69: the solitary figure amid the wastes of the 'new' landscaping is the only survivor of the earlier, Italianate garden, presumably the Neptune figure without his trident.

ancient manner, and he made much of opposing the gothic; his *Lectures on Architecture* (1734–6) applied the same principles to landscaping – 'The ancient *Romans* planted their Plots in this *rural* manner', he said, 'and their *Temples*, dedicated to their peculiar GODS, were dispersed among the *Groves* and Woods, which Art or Nature had made, with *Vistas* to them'.[98] On the other hand, the English antiquarians wanted to enrol woodland, as Kent had implicitly done, in English history: Thomas Hearne in 1714 thought that the woods around Silchester were a particularly British taste and pleasure.[99] In practice, both perspectives could co-exist.

Viewing England as if it were Rome but also as itself was simply the transference and adaptation to their native land of the habits of most English tourists in Italy. Warcupp's account of the Villa D'Este reminded his compatriots that it was worthy 'the greatness and magnificence of the Ancients'.[100] Morris was saying the same of Marble Hill, Pope had claimed the same for Twickenham (though with some satiric reservations). Matthew Prior declared that he 'loved his estate more than Tully did his Tusculum or Horace his Sabine Field'.[101] Sir John Clerk of Penicuik, who had visited Italy ('a country so replenished with Antiquities of all kinds . . .'), sent an account of his Scottish mansion to the famous Boerhaave in Leiden: this, written in Latin for practical purposes of communication with

218

the Dutchman, compared his 'villa' and his rural life at almost every stage of a long description with some Roman precedents.[102]

Such parallels could be modified both by a sense of disparities between ancient Italy and Hanoverian England and by a patriotic conviction that England had much of her own to offer; both the sense of discrepancy and the native resonance had to be accommodated in English gardens. Italy had been and continued to be what William Robinson called the 'promised land'; but when he was there in 1761–2 he was reminded at the falls of Tivoli (see figure 106) of Aislabie's estate at Hackfall, Yorkshire; the Yorkshire cascades were less grand, but that, too, was only apt.[103] John Dyer had admired the ruins of Rome while he was in Italy, and indeed wrote a poem about them after his return; he also planned a book which would have included a chapter on 'the laying out of Gardens'; but this aspiring history painter's main claim to fame is that he celebrated Grongar Hill, near his native Aberglasney, first in classical pindarics and finally in the version we know which opted for octosyllabics, the metre of English Milton's academic exercises, 'L'Allegro' and 'Il Penseroso'.[104] In far more important instances we can trace a similar surrender of classical to English associations and achievements. Gardens like Stourhead, The Leasowes and Hagley, all created in the middle years of the century, testify to a continuing attention on the part of their creators to a classical and Italian heritage at the same time as they reveal, in varying degrees, an instinct to honour their purely English context.

Stourhead, with its classical temples, statues and inscriptions, has been thought of as a fine, if somewhat belated culmination of the 'Palladian' gardening discussed in this chapter. Its *color romanus* is conspicuous; but as Malcolm Kelsall has recently argued this is by no means the whole story.[105] Just as Stowe and Rousham, I suggest, have to be read as sceptical of any easy parallels between ancient and modern, so Stourhead invokes both classical and gothic architecture to present its visitors with an object lesson in the differences between 'Ancient and Modern Augustanism'. The classical imagery will probably alert them to Henry Hoare's 'claim to preserve the finest traditions of Roman antiquity': Stourhead's Pantheon re-creates 'within the green world of the English countryside' a temple believed to have been built by Augustus's marshal, Agrippa. But from the Pantheon those same visitors would have stared across the water at the gothic parish church and the medieval Bristol cross, 'representative of the piety of the mercantile class of free British burgesses'. And having climbed to the Temple of Apollo, what would have struck them 'behind the Pantheon and upon an eminence' in the distance was Alfred's Tower; should the visitor have chosen to visit this monument, its inscription would have told him, what was commonly known, that Alfred was 'The Giver of the most excellent Laws, Jurys, the Bulwark of the English Liberty'. Professor Kelsall suggests that these two traditions were contrasted at Stourhead; if Augustus is held to be the preserver of at least some semblance of republican values after the civil wars, he could equally be seen as a classical parallel to Alfred, and (as we have seen) the gothic and classical architecture would then be voicing the same message though in different accents, one Latin, the other Anglo-Saxon.

Two other gardens, also created like Stourhead during the middle years of the century, testify to this same bi-focal vision. William Shenstone at The Leasowes took his inspiration from earlier *fermes ornées*, a type of 'rural gardening' which was held to be derived from classical prototypes.[106] Its most renowned feature was called 'Virgil's

Grove', which was engraved and published as the epitome of Shenstone's seat. But though there were other classical devices – a Latin inscription to the goddess of health, urns, a Temple of Pan, a lead statue of a peeping Faunus – Shenstone also commemorated British poets like James Thomson and William Somerville; he contrived 'old English' inscriptions (in the event these turned out to be pseudo-Spenserian), the ruins of a gothic Priory ('not yet built two Years') and a gothic alcove. All this set in a landscape which Shenstone himself considered 'natural', in other words English. This is what Shenstone's friend and publisher, Dodsley, who had given him the statue of the faun, claimed of The Leasowes in one of his effusions upon it:

> No Naiad's leading step conducts the rill;
> Nor sylvan god presiding skirts the lawn
> In beauteous wildness with fair-spreading trees,
> Nor magic wand has circumscribed the scene,
> 'Tis thine own taste, thy genius that presides.

Nearby at Hagley, where Shenstone, along with Pope and Thomson, was himself commemorated, there were inscriptions from Horace, Catullus and Virgil; but also from Milton. They were all dedicated to alerting their readers to the larger landscape about them: one, from Horace, began with the words 'Inter cuncta leges . . .' (Amid all this read . . .'). It gestures to the surrounding valleys, streams, hills and trees which are the true scene of the visitor's experience; he may appreciate the rotunda and the Temple of Theseus as well as architecture in the rival gothic mode, such as Sanderson Miller's ruined castle, but ultimately he is thrown back on his own resources within the landscape.[107] It was here in 1758 that Joseph Spence planned his volume of letters on 'making the grounds around [the] house in such a method as to look pleasing and natural, according to the fashion so much in vogue among us of late years . . .'[108] Though he is attentive to the annals of English garden history, recalling Evelyn's *Sylva* at the end of his memorandum, it is modern gardening, 'pleasing and natural', that Hagley tempts Spence to annotate.

Joseph Spence is an important figure in the annals of English gardening; above all, his writings help to explain the gradual switch of emphasis in mid-century from ancient to modern gardening.[109] In 1747 he published his *Polymetis*, a study of Roman verbal and visual imagery: two aspects of this are relevant here. The eponymous character explains that his age has lost virtually all understanding of the classical gods, like those English visitors to Rome, considered in Part One, who found the array of sculpture bewildering: the person who thought the Palazzo Giustiniani gardens were simply a 'Ware-house' of statues, or Veryard who remarked that 'If antient *Rome* had Thirty Thousand Gods, as *Varro* assures us it had, . . . one might find a limb of each in some part or other of this Palace'.[110] But Spence, who was Professor of Poetry at Oxford and, later, of Modern History at Oxford, obviously wanted to ensure that this lost language of Roman mythology was salvaged; his readers obviously thought so too, since the book went into further editions in 1755 and 1774 as well as a school version of 1764 which went into six editions. Evidently there was a need as well as a wish to fill that cultural vacuum. The way in which Polymetis has chosen to set out the materials is in a garden which is 'rather wild than regular'; it is, in fact, a piece of extensive and rural gardening in which classical features are situated to make it some vast and exhaustive memory theatre. A long quotation is necessary:

220

The deities of the Romans (says Polymetis) were so numerous, that they might well complain of wanting a Nomenclatour to help them to remember all their names. Their vulgar religion, as indeed that of the heathens in general, was a sort of Manicheism. Whatever was able to do good or to do harm to man, was immediately looked on as a superior power; which, in their language, was the same as a diety. It was hence that they had such a multitude of gods, that their temples were better peopled with statues, than their cities with men. It is a perfect mob of deities, if you look upon them all together: but they are reducible enough to order; and fall into fewer classes, than one would at first imagine. I have reduced them to six; and considering their vast number, it was no little trouble to bring them into that compass.

You see that Rotonda, with a Colonnade running round it, on the brow of the hill? Within that, are the great celestial deities; as the milder ones relating to the human mind and civil life, (Fidelity, Clemency; Peace, Concord; Plenty, Health; all the Mental or Moral Deities, of the better sort;) are placed in the Colonnade about it; one in each opening between the pillars. That temple, lower down the hill to the right, contains the beings which preside over the element of fire: which, according to the antients, had its place next to the supream mansion of the gods. You may call this, if you please, the temple of the Sun and Stars. There I have lodged all my antiques that relate to the Sun, to the Planets, to the Constellations; and to the Times and Seasons, as measured by the former. That Octogon, opposite to it on the left, is the temple of the Winds, and of the imaginary beings of the air. Those two temples on either hand below them contain, one the deities of the Waters, and the other the deities of the Earth: and if I had a temple for the Infernal beings, with the Vices of men round it, in the same manner as their Virtues are placed round the celestial one, I question whether you could name any one imaginary being in all the theology of the ancients, that might not properly enough be placed in one or other of these six repositories. . . .

The statues are placed in niches made for them; and ornamented with copies of such antient relievo's or pictures as relate to them. In their pedestals, I have contrived drawers, to put in the medals, gems, prints and drawings, I have been so long getting together: such under each, as have any reference to the deity they are placed under: much in the manner as the books of the Sibyls were kept by Augustus in the base of the Palatine Apollo. And thus I have disposed of all my collection, with somewhat more of regularity and order, than is observed generally in much better collections than I am master of.[111]

Polymetis's landscape garden, seen and read as a compendium of Roman myth, is evidently ancient; as a piece of natural terrain dotted with temples, it is equally, if not modern, an attempt to translate the classical into some eighteenth-century, English mode: he tells his guests that he has

> followed the taste in fashion . . . of making my gardens rather wild than regular. Their general air, I hope, has nothing stiff and unnatural in it; and the lower part, in particular, joins in with the view of the country, as if it made a part of it. Indeed the mode has allowed me to have as many temples as I could wish, in such a space of ground; but I would not have you imagine that they are temples only for shew; I have found out a use for them, which you might not think of.

He makes exactly the same point that Pope made about Lord Burlington: 'You show us, Rome was glorious, not profuse, / And pompous Buildings once were things of use.' But what is most interesting about Spence is that the kind of gardens on which he advised his friends did not much admit of such classical imagery, useful or not. Partly owing to the exigencies of his commissions, notably the modest means and smallish grounds where he was called to design, Spence's work was in practice 'modern'.

For there was another side to his antiquarian interest in classical mythology. *Polymetis* expresses its scepticism of the understandability of iconology, singling out the garden statues at Versailles, the 'collections in Rome itself', and Ripa's emblems as examples of inventions which 'we are frequently at a loss to know what they mean'.[112] There are many different Apollos learnedly distinguished in *Polymetis*, but in the description of a garden in his *Essay on Pope's Odyssey* Spence describes a 'Dome of Apollo' with no further discriminations. He seems, in short, to bother little with precise mythology in his gardens; in *Polymetis* he even argues – in exactly the same way that we have seen at The Leasowes and Hagley, – that 'the figures of the things themselves speak . . . the clearest language'.

It was the language of things themselves that would prevail with 'Capability' Brown. Imagery that announced some antique message surrendered to a scenery where the sensibility was freed to range at will. Gardens and parks became 'Republics devoted to the cult of sentiment, they dispensed with the ideology of the Augustan garden, and allusion was now replaced by effusion and mythography by empathy'.[113] If the Villa D'Este could represent Ancient Rome in its gardens (see figure 109), if Burlington at Chiswick or Dormer at Rousham could represent in miniature the same imagery (see figures 101 & 110), the modern garden admitted it largely, if at all, by association; this was what Pope already recognized in his grounds at Twickenham. What was represented in modern gardens was *la belle nature* – the perfect forms of natural things were the material of Brown's parks in the same way that the classical past might have been at the Villa D'Este or metamorphic marvels at Pratolino. The problem was that representation was ceasing to be so revered an aesthetic activity; too many who looked at Brown's representations simply saw what they took to be the real thing.

Italian gardens continued to delight English travellers well into the mid-eighteenth century. But, as was set out in Part One, they also struck visitors as curious examples of a historical mode of gardening. When the reactions against Brown's kind of garden gathered momentum in the nineteenth century, and when in particular the social usefulness of terraces and the practical advantages of gravel paths among shrubberies near a house urged a return to more organized designs, it was in part to Italy that those revivalists looked. Even public parks sought to decorate their carefully laid-out spaces with classical imagery: one of Manchester's public parks established an English maypole on a mount and surrounded it with busts of a Roman matron, a titan, Apollo and the head of Laocoon.[114] But what is especially ironic about this later chapter in garden history is that when the nineteenth century looked again to Italy for some of its vocabulary and syntax, the *giardino inglese* had settled like a blight in the land, so ill-suited in climate to receive it. But all that is another story.

Notes

The place of publication in all references is London unless otherwise stated.

The following is a list of abbreviations used in the notes to refer to the most frequently cited of the Italian travel writings which provide the bulk of the material for Part One of this book.

Acton	William Acton, *A New Journal of Italy* (1691)
Addison, 'Remarks'	Joseph Addison, 'Remarks on Several Parts of Italy . . .', *The Works*, vol. 2 (1721).
Blainville	De Blainville, *Travels through Holland, Germany, Switzerland, and other parts of Europe; but especially Italy . . .*, transl. George Turnbull & Wm. Guthrie, 2 vols. (1743).
Breval 1726	J. Breval, *Remarks on Several Parts of Europe*, 2 vols. (1726).
Breval 1738	J. Breval, *Remarks on Several Parts of Europe . . . in several Tours since the Year 1723*, 2 vols. (1738).
Browne	Edward Browne, *A Brief Account of some Travels in diverse parts of Europe*, 2nd edition (1685).
Burnet	G. Burnet, *Some Letters containing an account of what seemed Remarkable in Travelling through . . . Italy . . . in the years 1685 and 1686*, second ed. corrected (Rotterdam, 1687).
Cogan	Henry Cogan, *A Direction For Such As Shall Travell unto Rome* (1654).
Coryate	*Coryats Crudities Hastily gobled vp in five Moneths trauells in France, Sauoy, Italy, . . .* [1611], 2 vols. (Glasgow, 1905).
Cust	*Records of the Cust Family*, compiled by Lady Eliz Cust (1898).
Evelyn, *Diary*	*The Diary of John Evelyn*, ed. E. S. de Beer, 5 vols. (Oxford, 1955). Volume II deals with travels in Italy.
Horae Subsecivae	Grey Brydges, *Horae Subsecivae. Observations and Discourses* (1620).
Kent	William Kent, Italian journal, Bodleian MS Rawl. D.1162
Lassels	Richard Lassels, *The Voyage of Italy or a Complete Journey t[h]rough Italy in Two Parts* (printed at Paris, sold in London, 1670).
Misson	Maximilian Misson, *A New Voyage to Italy*, 2 vols. (1699).
Mortoft	*Francis Mortoft: His Book*, ed. Malcolm Letts, Hakluyt Society, Second series, LVII (1925).
Moryson	Fynes Moryson, *An Itinerary . . .*, [1617], 4 vols. (Glasgow 1907). Volume I only cited.

Northall	John Northall, *Travels Through Italy* (1766).
Piozzi	Hester Lynch Piozzi, *Observations and Reflections made in the Course of a Journey Through France, Italy, and Germany*, ed. Herbert Barrows (Ann Arbor, Michigan, 1967).
Ray	John Ray, *Observations, Topographical, Moral & Physiological Made in a Journey Through part of the Low Countries, Germany, Italy and France* (1673).
Raymond	John Raymond, *Il Mercurio Italico. An Itinerary contayning a Voyage made through Italy in the yeare 1646, and 1647* (1648).
Remarks	[? William Bromley], *Remarks in the Grand Tour of France and Italy performed by a person of Quality in the year 1691* (1705).
Reresby	*Memoirs of Sir John Reresby* (1904).
Sandys	George Sandys, *A Relation of A Journey begun An. Dom. 1610*, [1615], third ed. (1632).
Skippon	Philip Skippon, *An Account of a Journey . . .* in Churchill, *A Collection of Voyages and Travels*, vol. 6 (1732).
Spence, *Letters*	Joseph Spence, *Letters from the Grand Tour*, ed. Slava Klima (Montreal and London, 1975).
***Tour* 1675**	Anon., *A Tour in France and Italy, made by an English Gentleman 1675* (1676).
'True Description'	Anon., 'A True Description and Direction of what is most Worthy to be seen in all Italy', *The Harleian Miscellany*, 12 (1811).
Veryard	E. Veryard, *An Account of Divers Choice Remarks . . . Taken in a Journey . . .* (1701).
Warcupp	Edmund Warcupp, *Italy in Its Originall Glory, Ruine and Revivall* (1660).
Wright	Edward Wright, *Some Observations made in Travelling Through France, Italy, Etc. In the Years 1720, 1721, and 1722*, 2 vols. (1730).
Yeames 1914	A. H. S. Yeames, 'The Grand Tour of an Elizabethan' [Richard Smith], *Papers of the British School at Rome*, VII (1914), pp. 92–113.

Introduction

1　Recent examples of this failure to change the map of English garden history that might be cited are the popular and much-circulated book by Christopher Thacker, *A History of Gardens* (1979) – see especially chapter 12 – and David Jacques, *Georgian Gardens* (1983).

2　There is considerable literature on the grand tour which will be cited in appropriate notes to the first section. Here it is worth noting that only very brief mentions, if any, are made of Italian gardens: see, for instance, R. S. Pine-Coffin, *Bibliography of British and American Travel in Italy to 1860* (Florence, 1974), p. 40, where one paragraph of the 60-page introduction touches upon what is called 'Italian enterprise in formal gardening'.

3　To judge by the postcard entitled 'The Italian Garden' produced for the 1984 Liverpool Garden Festival we have a dreadfully shaky notion of what the traditional Italian garden might be: it represented an olive green fibre glass pineapple dwarfing its fountain basin, set amid paths of bright white crunchy stones and box hedging municipal flowers, all backed by a rather two-dimensional temple with three arches in which cut-out statues (one of them Michelangelo's David) had been installed. I must thank Dr and Mrs John Partridge for sending me this item.

4　See below, p. 180.

5　The passage (Book IV, lines 31–8 are those quoted in the headpiece) is given to Satan, tempting Christ with all the pagan world that the English puritan poet seems to have despised so strongly by the time he wrote *Paradise Regained* in the late 1660s.

1   The garden on the Grand Tour

1   Quoted by Yeames 1914, p. 93n. See also, Thomas Frank, 'Elizabethan Travellers in Rome', *English Miscellany*, 4 (1953), pp. 95–132. For parallels and comparisons with largely French travellers in the sixteenth century, including some notes on garden sights, see G. Dickinson, *Du Bellay in Rome* (Leiden, 1960).

2   See, for example, the large *Age of the Grand Tour*, with essays by Anthony Burgess and Francis Haskell (1967), but also the printed broadsheet issued by the British Museum (1980) to accompany the exhibition on *Guidebooks and Tourism. The British in Italy*. See also J. W. Stoye, *English Travellers Abroad, 1604–1667* (1952); W. E. Mead, *The Grand Tour in the Eighteenth Century* (Boston and New York, 1914). For some comparative studies of the Dutch on the Grand Tour see A. Frank-van Westrienen, *De Groote Tour. Tekening van de educatiereis der Nederlanders in de zeventiende eeuw* (Amsterdam, 1983), and *Herinneringen aan Italië. Kunst en toerisme in de 18de eeuw*, exhibition catalogue edited by Ronald de Leeuw (Zwolle, 1984).

3   Lassels, sig. A6r. There was a second edition, 'with large additions', in 1698. On Lassels see Edward P. de G. Chaney, 'Richard Lassels and the Establishment of the Grand Tour', London University Ph.D. (Warburg Institute), 1982. Further discussions of Italian travel specifically are F. Kirby, *The Grand Tour in Italy 1700–1800* (New York, 1952); Clare Howard, *English Travellers of the Renaissance* (New York, 1914); A. Lytton Sells, cited in note 11 below; and J. R. Hale, *England and the Italian Renaissance* (1954), pp. 24 ff.

4   For the period covered by this book see R. S. Pine-Coffin, *Bibliography of British and American Travel in Italy to 1860* (Florence, 1974).

5   Lassels's book is praised and cited, for instance, by Ray, p. 153 and *passim*, and by *Remarks*, pp. 106, 224 and *passim*. Peacham, likewise, in *The Compleat Gentleman* of 1634 refers the reader to Sandys on Italy (Oxford, 1906 edition), p. 245.

6   Chaney, 'Richard Lassels . . . .', p. 557.

7   *Clarissa* (1757), letter II. Such personal directions for travel were (and despite the glut of travel books today still are) frequent: Brit. Lib. Add. MS 61479, ff. 172–7, contains directions for what to see in Italy, written for the Duchess of Marlborough in 1728 by 'Mr Holloway'.

8   Bodleian MS Rawl. D.84, f.2r.

9   Raymond, p. 69. On Schott see E. S. de Beer, 'François Schott's Itinerario d'Italia', *The Library*, fourth series, XXIII/3 (1942), pp. 57–83. For guides to Rome, see Ludwig Schudt, *Le Guide di Roma* (Vienna, 1930). For guides to Florence, the MS cited in note 7 above recommends *Ritratto delle cose piu notabili della Città di Firenze* (f. 174 verso).

10   W. E. Mead, *The Grand Tour . . .*, p. 261.

11   On Coryate, see Piero Rebora, 'Un Eccentrico Viaggiatore Inglese del Primo Seicento', *English Miscellany*, II (1951), pp. 85–93, and A. Lytton Sells, *The Paradise of Travellers. The Italian Influence on Englishmen in the seventeenth century* (1964), pp. 163 ff.

12   Pp. 161r & 6r respectively. The Doria gardens are discussed in more detail below, pp. 7–9.

13   Ibid., pp. 26v & 40v–41r.

14   *The travels and life of Sir Thomas Hoby . . . written by himself*, ed. Edgar Powell, Camden Miscellany, 10 (1902), pp. 13, 25, 28, 35, 58, 118 & 129.

15   For Coryate see above note 11 and below *passim*; Moryson's interest in gardens is also explored below.

16   *An Essay of the Meanes how to make our Travailes, into forraine Countries, the more profitable & honourable* (1606), p. 42.

17 Howell, *Instructions and Directions for Forren Travell* (1650), p. 58; Cogan, preface [p. 2], and again two pages later 'Gardens' come third after 'Temples, Palaces' among the kinds of sights to see.

18 See Pine-Coffin, op. cit., p. 30 and George B. Parks, 'Travel as Education', *The Seventeenth Century*, ed. Richard Foster Jones et al. (Stanford, California, 1951), pp. 264–90.

19 Lassels, op. cit., Preface, sig. bi verso.

20 The relations of gardens to cabinets of curiosities is discussed in detail below, chapter 7.

21 Raymond, pp. 167 et seq. Raymond is one of many travellers particularly fascinated by 'curiosities'.

22 Mortoft, p. 114.

23 On these wide themes in gardens see Terry Comito, *The Idea of the Garden in the Renaissance* (New Brunswick, N.J., 1978), and Eugenio Battisti, '*Natura Artificiosa* to *Natura Artificialis*', *The Italian Garden*, ed. David R. Coffin (Washington, D.C., 1972), pp. 3–8. On the theme of the *locus amoenus* see E. R. Curtis, *European Literature and the Latin Middle Ages* (New York, 1953), chapter ten, section 6.

24 'True Description', p. 108. See below, chapter 2, note 32.

25 Evelyn, *Diary*, II, 173–5. On Genoese villas and gardens see Emmina De Negri et al., *Catalogo delle Ville Genovesi* (Genoa, 1967); George L. Gorse, 'Genoese Renaissance Villas', *Journal of Garden History*, III (1983), pp. 225–80, and Lauro Magnani on grottoes in Genoese villas, *Journal of Garden History*, V, (1985), pp. 135–53.

26 The gentleman who advised the Duchess of Marlborough (see above, note 7) wrote that 'There is nothing worth seeing in or about Turin but the King's Palaces & Gardens' (f. 172). For views of these see *Theatrum Statuum Sabaudiae Ducis*, 2 vols. (Amsterdam, 1682).

27 See Pine-Coffin, op. cit., pp. 22 ff. The Earl of Arundel, for instance, took a more or less clandestine trip to Rome in 1614: see M. F. S. Hervey, *The Life, Correspondence & Collections of Thomas Howard, Earl of Arundel* (Cambridge, 1921), p. 83.

28 In *The Works of Sir Thomas Browne*, ed. Geoffrey Keynes, 4 vols. (new edition 1964), IV, 275. Evelyn was writing to Browne about his *Elysium Britannicum*; it remains unpublished, a huge and much inter-leaved folio in MS, in the Library of Christ Church, Oxford.

29 Lassels, p. 362 (writing of the Brenta).

30 *Tour* 1675, p. 122. This *Tour* was republished in *A Collection of Voyages and Travels* (1745), I.

31 *Miscellanies in Verse and Prose*, *The Critical Works of John Dennis* (Baltimore, 1939), ii. 381.

32 The cliché is repeated by many travellers. It occurs also in *The Taming of the Shrew*, I.i.4 ('the pleasant garden of great Italy') and in Walter Harris, *A Description of the King's Royal Palace and Gardens at Loo together with a short account of Holland* (1699), p. 4. The anonymous writer of 'A direction for a Travailer' (Bodley MS Perrott.5) writes 'Italy ye gardin of ye world' as a marginal gloss to his section on that country (f. 22 v).

33 Some of the regional differences can be seen readily from Harold Acton, *Tuscan Villas* (1973). For more detailed analyses of the regional types see Isa Belli Barsali, *Baldassarre Peruzzi e le ville senesi del Cinquecento* (S Quirico D'Orcia: Archivio Italiano dell'Arte dei Giardini, 1977); *Introduzione ai giardini del senese* (S Quirico D'Orcia: Archivio Italiano dell'Arte dei Giardini, 1976); Isa Belli Barsali's three books on Lucchese gardens – *La villa a Lucca dal XV al XIX secolo* (Rome, 1964), *Le ville lucchesi* (Rome, 1964), and *Ville e committenti dello Stato di Lucca* (Lucca, 1980).

34 *Elements of Architecture*, pp. 109–10. It has been suggested that Wotton is in fact describing the Medici villa and gardens at Pratolino.

2 Classical ground and classical gardens

1 Addison, 'Remarks', preface.

2 This is not the occasion to detail what is known about classical gardens. There is a brief survey with some quotations in Christopher Thacker's *The History of Gardens* (1979), pp. 18–25. More specialized modern studies are Pierre Grimal, *Les Jardins Romains* (Paris, 1969) and *Ancient Roman Gardens*, ed. Elisabeth B. MacDougall and Wilhelmina F. Jashemski (Washington, D.C., 1981), upon both of which I have relied extensively. Some of our most detailed knowledge of Roman gardens comes from the excavation of those destroyed by Vesuvius, on which see Wilhelmina F. Jashemski, *The Gardens of Pompeii, Herculaneum and the Villas Destroyed by Vesuvius* (New Rochelle, N.Y., 1979). These gardens were not, of course, known during the period in which this book is concerned; but Professor Jashemski is invaluable because she sets out with much illustration what we now know of those gardens and because her work often prompts the thought that Renaissance emulation of antique gardens bore an uncanny resemblance in letter and spirit to those lost examples.

3 Castell's book is discussed below (pp. 194–6). Pliny's letters are in Books II.17 and V.6 of his correspondence: all references to these and other classical texts are drawn from the Loeb Classical Library of Roman writers. In the case of these essential texts it is also useful to read them in the translation of Betty Radice, *Letters of the Younger Pliny* (Penguin Classics, 1963). On reconstructions of Pliny's villas from his literary descriptions see H. Tanzer, *The Villas of Pliny the Younger* (New York, 1924), and *Ut Architectura Poesis: La Laurentine et la Villa Romaine* (Paris, 1982).

4 P. Foster, 'Raphael on the Villa Madama: The Text of a Lost Letter', *Römisches Jahrbuch für Kunstgeschichte*, XI (1967–8), 307–12, and *Raffaelo Architetto*, ed. C. L. Frommel and others (Milan, 1984), pp. 311–57.

5 Varro, *De re rustica*, III, iv et seq. A Renaissance reconstruction is illustrated by Thacker, op. cit., pp. 20–1, and an eighteenth-century version in Castell, *The Villas of the Ancients*, between pp. 70 & 71.

6 *Observations, Anecdotes and Characters of Books and Men*, ed. James M. Osborn, 2 vols. (Oxford, 1966), II, 672–77. Most of Horace's lines on his villa and garden are set out, with references, as notes to Spence's commentary.

7 *Epigrams*, XII, 31 & 50.

8 *Natural History*, XXXVI, xlii, 154.

9 *Satires*, III, lines 17–20.

10 *Natural History*, XXXIV, xix, 84 for Domus Aurea and XXXVI, iv, 23, 25 and 26 for sculptural subjects.

11 *Epithalamium de Nuptiis Honori Augusti*, lines 50 et seq. See also Lucretius, *De Rerum Natura*, V, 74–5, on statues sanctifying pools and groves.

12 *Letters*, VIII, 8.

13 See John Pinto, 'The Landscape of Allusion: Literary Themes in the Gardens of Classical Rome and Augustan England', *Smith College Studies in History*, XLVIII (*The Survival of Antiquity*) (1980).

14 *De re rustica*, III, xiii.

15 *Carmina*, I.17.1 and I.38.6; IV.2.30 et seq.

16 For instance, Scipio's garden in *De Re Publica*, I, 9 or in *Ad Atticum*, I, 7 and IV, 10. For Horace see previous note.

17 *Scriptores Historiae Augustae*, Hadrian, XVI, 5.

18 *Ad Atticum*, I, 16 and II, 1. Pliny named two of his villas Tragedy and Comedy – which suggests the deliberate creation of idea and mood, in this instance in two villas as opposed to different parts of one: *Letters*, IX, 7.

19 Statius, *Silvae* I and II; Columella, *De re rustica*, Book X; Ovid, *Tristia*, IV.viii.27 and *Ex Ponto*, I.viii.43; Seneca, *Epistles*, LV, 6 (on garden of Servatius Vatia).

20 *The travels and life of Sir Thomas Hoby . . . written by himself*, ed. Edgar Powell, *Camden Miscellany*, 10 (London, 1902), p. 58; Raymond, p. 134.

21 On Hadrian's Villa see the bibliography in Grimal, cited in Note 1, (p. 473), and Salvatore Aurigemma, *Villa Adriana* (Rome, 1961); Veryard (p. 207) recorded that it was 'one of the most magnificent Structures of that Age. The people call it *Tivoli Vecchio*; old *Tivoli* imagining it to have been a Town, by reason of the vastness of the Ruins, amongst which we observ'd the Rests of three ancient Temples, one of them seeming almost entire . . .' Pirro Ligorio, the creator of the Villa D'Este gardens, was one Renaissance architect who explored the nearby remains of Hadrian's complex, though he noted that its scale and complexity could not correspond to the neccesities of usual country living (cited C. Lamb, *Die Villa d'Este in Tivoli* (Munich, 1966), p. 97). For Ligorio's two treatises on Hadrian's Villa see L. Canina, *Gli Edifizi di Roma antica* (Rome, 1848), V, 183, and J. G. Graevius, *Thesaurus antiquitatum Italiae* (Leiden, 1723), XI. De Blainville (II, 386–7) draws upon and mentions Ligorio's excavations in his discussion of Hadrian's Villa. For another Renaissance architect's interest in Hadrian's Villa see R. Bonfiglietti, 'Raffaello a Villa Adriana e a Tivoli', *Bollettino di studi storici ed archeologici di Tivoli*, XX (1920).

22 Lassels, Pt. II, p. 244; Coryate, I, 281 et seq. For the Domus Aurea see Seutonius, *Life of Nero*, section XXXI and above, note 3, for the elder Pliny. Breval 1726 cites both those sources in his account (II, 246 & 268).

23 Addison, loc. cit.

24 Sandys, pp. 243 & 297; Moryson, pp. 220–1.

25 Veryard, p. 160.

26 Lassels, Pt. II, p. 307.

27 Veryard, p. 208; Raymond, p. 116; *Tour 1675*, p. 92.

28 Burnet, p. 215.

29 (Naples, 1670), pp. 154 & 197; these woodcuts were derived from Mazzella's *Sito & antichità di Pozzuolo* of 1594, which perhaps explains this confusing duplication of imagery.

30 Sarnelli's bilingual (French and Italian) edition of 1709 lists villas and gardens on pp. 50–1 and 84–6. For a modern account of these see John H. D'Arms, *Romans on the Bay of Naples* (Cambridge, Mass., 1970).

31 Bartolomeo Marliani, *Urbis Romae Topographia* (Rome, 1534) lists the classical *horti*; Lucio Fauno, *Della antichità della città di Roma*, a popular guide reprinted many times, identifies ruins with classical literary descriptions. Giacomo Lauro's *Antiquae Urbis Splendor* (Rome, 1612, et seq.) contains reconstructions of classical sites; while Basil Kennett, *Romae Antiquae Notitia* (London, 1696; 5th ed. revised and corrected, 1713) discusses the location in modern Rome of such gardens as Sallust's with references to relevant Latin texts in his notes (see pp. 32–3 of fifth edition).

32 See G. M. Andres, *The Villa Medici in Rome*, 2 vols. (New York, 1976), especially the first section. The Bufalini map of Rome (1551) gives both the old and the new name to this hill – 'Collis Hortulorum Quinunc Pincius Dicitur'. The 'True Description' (p. 108) admired the Cardinal of Florence's gardens and noted 'mighty great vaults under ground, wherein they used to dine and sup in summer-time, by reason of the extraordinary heat, which are adorned with rare pictures, statues, and histories . . .'. Established about 1550, this garden stood behind the

Basilica of Maxentius (Temple of Peace) and even had gardens on the vault of the basilica; it was acquired by Cardinal Alessandro Medici (later Leo X) in 1567; the gardens no longer exist. See I. Belli Barsali, *Le Ville di Roma: Lazio I* (Milan, 1970), pp. 375–6.

33 Raymond, p. 73; Skippon, pp. 66–9; *Horae Subsecivae*, pp. 380–1; Breval 1738, pp. 257 ff. On the author of *Horae Subsecivae*, see Douglas Bush, 'Hobbs, William Cavendish and "Essayes" ', *Notes and Queries*, 218 (1973), pp. 162–3.

34 Warcupp, p. 291 (printed as 281).

35 Lassels, p. 285.

36 Reported by Sandys, p. 263, who refused to believe it. On Virgil's tomb, see J. B. Trapp, 'The Grave of Vergil', *J.W.C.I.*, XLVII (1984), pp. 1–31.

37 Raymond, p. 145.

38 Ibid., introduction sign. a¹ verso.

39 Veryard, p. 159.

40 *Remarks*, p. 183; Wright, p. 371.

41 David R. Coffin, *The Villa in the Life of Renaissance Rome* (Princeton, N.J., 1979), p. 182. See also *passim* in Coffin for further examples of this overlaying of modern upon classical gardens.

42 Moryson, p. 291; on this see Coffin, op. cit., pp. 215, 223 & 230.

43 Ibid., pp. 257–8. A fresco of this Villa Lante, now in the Bibliotheca Hertziana, shows the *Discovery of the Tomb of Numa Pompilius and the Sibylline Books* taking place in the villa grounds (Coffin, fig. 159), thus identifying it with legendary Roman events.

44 *The Works of Sir Thomas Browne*, IV, 275.

45 The elder Pliny, for example, discusses which sculptures suit various garden locations: *Natural History*, XXXVI, 23, 25, 36.

46 Raymond, pp. 91–2. There is a considerable literature on the Belvedere, but for the present purpose see especially J. S. Ackerman, 'The Belvedere As A Classical Villa', *J.W.C.I.*, 14 (1951), pp. 70–91 and Hans Henrik Brummer, *The Statue Court in the Vatican Belvedere* (Stockholm, 1970).

47 Marjon van der Meulen, 'Cardinal Cesi's Antique Sculpture Garden: Notes on a painting by Hendrick van Cleef III', *Burlington Magazine*, 116 (1974), pp. 14 ff. This Cesi garden, famous for its *Antiquario*, is discussed by D. Gnoli, 'Il Giardino e l'Antiquario del Cardinal Cesi', *Mitteilungen Deutsches Archael. Instit. Röm.*, XX (1905), pp. 267–76. For Heemskerck's drawing of Casa Galli and other Roman sites see Christian Hülsen & Hermann Egger, *Die römischen Skizzenbücher von Marten van Heemskerck . . .* (Berlin, 1913–16). When the Earl of Arundel was in Rome he obtained permission to excavate among the ruins of certain houses and discovered statues which were dispatched to Arundel House: see M. F. S. Hervey, *The Life, Correspondence & Collections of Thomas Howard, Earl of Arundel*, p. 84.

48 Anon 1610, p. 114. On the Carpi garden see Coffin, *The Villa etc.*, pp. 195–200.

49 See Elisabeth MacDougall, 'Ars Hortulorum: sixteenth-century garden iconography . . .', *The Italian Garden*, ed. David R. Coffin (Washington, D.C., 1972), pp. 53 ff.

50 Sandys, p. 272, writing of the 'duke of Toledos orchard' at Naples; Raymond, p. 78.

51 Warcupp, II, 210. Since the Carpi gardens had disappeared, Warcupp's translation of Scottus must have been from an out of date edition. See J. B. Bury, 'Some Early Literary References to Italian Gardens', *Journal of Garden History*, II (1982), pp. 17–24.

52 *Remarks*, p. 188; Evelyn, *Diary*, II, 234.

53 Mortoft, pp. 124–8.

54 Skippon, pp. 270–1.

55 Evelyn, *Diary*, II, 252; Raymond, pp. 94–5.

56 Mortoft, pp. 119–21; Moryson, p. 291. For the Medici Villa, see Coffin, *The Villa etc.*, pp. 219–33.

57 *Tour* 1675, p. 76.

58 Evelyn, *Diary*, II, 382–3; *Tour* 1675, p. 74.

59 Veryard, p. 193.

60 *Systema Horti-Culturae: or The Art of Gardening* (1677), pp. 65–6.

61 See pp. 151, 164, 132 and *passim*.

62 Skippon, p. 670.

63 Veryard, p. 160.

64 Mortoft, p. 96.

65 See H. Giess, 'Studien zur Farnese-Villa am Palatin', *Römisches Jahrbuch für Kunstgeschichte*, XIII (1971), pp. 179–320. The following quotation from Misson, I, 385. The catalogue of rare plants was *Exactissima descriptio rariorum . . . plantarum que continentur in Horto Farnesiano . . .* (1625) by either Tobia Aldini or Pietro Castelli.

66 Lassels, p. 131.

67 Wright, p. 336.

68 Turnbull's book was published in London and is largely devoted to classical paintings and decorations in the collection of Dr Richard Mead. The two examples cited are on pp. 14 & 11 respectively. Sir Alexander Dick, travelling in Italy in 1736 with Allan Ramsay, recorded his notice of 'all the Grotto's and old paintings &c in the Mount Palatine' (Pierpont Morgan Library MS 3159, folio 71).

69 On Palladio's reconstruction of the Temple of the Sun (RIBA, X/17) he wrote 'I believe these were gardens in ancient times'.

3 *Villa* and *vigna*

1 *Characteristics of Men, Morals, Opinions and Times*, ed. J. M. Robertson (Indianapolis and New York, 1964), II, p. 270.

2 Quoted John Aubrey, *The Natural History of Surrey* (1718), iv, 66. For Albury see below, pp. 148–53.

3 Bodleian MS Aubrey 17, folio 2. For further discussion of Aubrey's Italian garden interests see below, pp. 153 ff.

4 *Horae Subsecivae*, p. 151.

5 Raymond, p. 205.

6 Sandys, pp. 274 & 288.

7 Lassels, I, 189.

8 Ray, p. 364.

9 Veryard, pp. 113 & 193.

10 Northall, p. 344.

11 *The Historie of Italie*, p. 137 verso.

12 Ibid., p. 113 recto.

13 Moryson, pp. 327–8. This difficulty with new terminology was pointed out by David Coffin in a review essay in the *Journal of Garden History*, I (1980), p. 279.

14 Veryard, p. 159.

15 Warcupp, II.195 and I.106 respectively.

16 Skippon pp. 652 and 660 respectively. Nothing could be more evocative than that second quotation of the mixture of elements that went into a garden experience in seventeenth-century Rome.

17 Wright, p. 195.

18 Coffin, *The Villa in the Life of Renaissance Rome*, p. 16. See also F. Lucchini and R. Pallavicini, *La Villa Poniatowski e la via Flaminia* (Rome, 1981).

19 Coffin, pp. 16–22.

20 Coffin instances Claude Lorrain's drawings of the Campagna. André Félibien's account of Nicolas Poussin's life tells how he would 'se retirer seul dans les Vignes & dans les lieux les plus écartez de Rome, oú il pouvoit avec liberté considerer quelques Statuës antiques, quelques vûës agréables, & observer les plus beaux effets de la Nature. C'étoit dans ces retraites & ces promenades solitaires, qu'il faisoit de legeres esquisses des choses qu'il rencontroit propres, soit pour le païsage, comme des terrasses, des arbres, ou quelques beaux accidens de lumieres; soit pour des compositions d'histoires, comme quelques belles dispositions de figures, quelques accommodemens d'habits, ou d'autres ornemens particuliers, dont ensuite il sçavoit faire un si beau choix & un si bon usage' (*Entretien sur les vies . . . des plus excellens peintres . . .* (Trevoux, 1725, VII, p. 14).

21 See above chapter 2, note 3.

22 For instance, Pope's imitation of Horace's Satire II.ii in Twickenham Edition of the *Poems of Pope*, ed. John Butt, IV, p. 67.

23 Addison, 'Remarks', pp. 64 & 88.

24 Blainville, pp. 285–6 & *passim*. David Coffin frequently notes the classical authority for Italian retreat: op. cit., pp. 41, 182, 187, 241.

25 These painted lunettes are reproduced in various places. A volume containing them all, with a commentary, is Daniela Mignani, *Le Ville Medicee di Giusto Utens* (Florence, 1980); they are also beautifully illustrated in the inaugural issue of the magazine, *F.M.R.* (March 1982).

26 Reresby, p. 77.

27 *Paesaggismo e paese: immagini delle forme paesistiche nel Bolognese*, ed. F. Varignana (Bologna, 1983). Wright (I, pp. 124–5) found Foligno in Umbria 'situated in the midst of a vast Garden; so even is the Plain; so well water'd, cultivated and planted: The Mountains all about it look like so many high Walls to the great Garden'. See also among the extensive studies of rural landscape and architecture, Mina Gregori et al., *Il paesaggio nella pittura fra Cinque e Seicento a Firenze* (Florence, 1980).

28 *Letters From Italy in the years 1754 and 1755 by the late Rt Hon John Earl of Corke and Orrery* (London, sec. ed., 1774), pp. 65–6; see also p. 45.

29 Mortoft, p. 175.

30 Misson, I, 239.

31 Raymond, p. 205.

32 Warcupp, I, p. 45.

33   Browne, p. 216.

34   See Georgina Masson, 'Palladian Villas as Rural Centers', *The Architectural Review*, CXVIII (1955), pp. 17–20, and *Andrea Palladio 1508–1580*, catalogue by Howards Burns et al. (London, 1975).

35   Burnet, p. 122.

36   Breval 1738, p. 141, and Addison, 'Remarks', p. 139.

37   Warcupp, I, p. 98.

38   *Tour* 1675, pp. 33–4.

39   Northall, p. 73.

40   See Elaine Evans Dee, *Views of Florence and Tuscany by Giuseppe Zocchi* (New York, 1968).

41   Some of these drawings by Ettore Romagnoli are reproduced in Harold Acton, *Tuscan Villas* (1973). Raymond explored the Sienese countryside and reported that it was hunting country (p. 56).

42   'True Description', p. 122.

43   James Leoni, *The Architecture of Leon Battista Alberti* . . ., 3 vols. (1726), I, p. 98 verso. Alberti also discusses villa farms in chapters xv–xvi (vol. I).

44   Misson, II, p. 25. Wilson's painting is reproduced in David Solkin, *Richard Wilson* (1982), p. 184, and a sketch of the same view, p. 164. At the Villa Madama in 1736 Sir Alexander Dick 'was delighted above measure with that fine Rural scene' (Pierpont Morgan Library MS 3159, folio 85).

45   *Survey of the Great Dukes State of Tuscany . . . in 1596* (1605) p. 13.

46   Coryate, I, 238.

47   Ibid., p. 7; cf. p. 36.

48   Raymond, p. A³ verso.

49   Ferrari's *Hesperides* . . . was published in Rome in 1646 and it illustrates several gardens in which oranges flourish (see especially, pp. 11, 131, 147 & 153). The orange as Hesperidian apple has a pre-Renaissance history since Alexander Neckam's 'De naturis rerum' (12th century) called oranges *mala aurea*. For a 17th-century English usage see Abraham Cowley, *Plantarum* . . . (1721), p. 396. On the cult and myth in Italy see Lionello Puppi, 'Le Esperidi in Brenta', *Arte Veneta*, XXIX (1975). On their cultivation in England see Roy Strong, *The Renaissance Garden in England* (1979), pp. 76, 90, 189 & 191 ff.

50   *The Antiquities of Italy. Being the travels of Bernard de Montfaucon*, ed. John Healey (sec. ed. rev., 1725), p. 89.

50   *Observations, etc.* I, p. 250 (item 603).

52   Spence, *Letters*, pp. 132 & 114.

53   For Inigo Jones see also S. Orgel and R. Strong, *Inigo Jones, The Theatre of the Stuart Court*, 2 vols. (Berkeley and Los Angeles, 1973), I, p. 116, II, p. 420. Jones's garden settings are discussed below (pp. 113–19). For Aubrey, Bodleian MS Aubrey 17, folios 15 & 17, show the views he anticipated from the house and garden. For Nourse's praise of Roman and Italian gardens (at the expense of French), see *Campania Foelix*, pp. 299–300.

54   *The Genius of the Place*, ed. J. D. Hunt and P. Willis (1975), p. 206.

55   Ibid., pp. 162 and 153. See also *Ichnographia Rustica* (1718), I, pp. 22–7 for a passage on Virgil.

4 Ovid in the garden

1   G. Karl Galinsky, *Ovid's Metamorphoses. An introduction to the Basic Aspects* (Oxford, 1975), pp. 97–8.

2   References to Ovid's poem will be given in the form of book and line number(s), taken from the Loeb Classics edition, followed by pages of the Penguin Classics translation by Mary M. Innes (Harmondsworth, 1981) to make it possible for readers to find the passages in an easily available text. Thus, in this case, the reference to Salmacis is IV/286: p. 101; to Aventinus, XIV/620–4: pp. 327–8.

3   V/409–12: p. 127; II/454–6: p. 62; XIV/406–15 & 447–9: pp. 322 & 323.

4   III/30: p. 75; III/156–60 ('. . . simulaverat artem/ingenio natura suo . . .'): p. 78.

5   IV/398: p. 104; III/407: p. 85 and IV/297: p. 102.

6   V/388–90: p. 126.

7   II/406–8: p. 61

8   *As You Like It*, ed. Agnes Latham (London, 1975), III.iii.16.

9   IV/357: p. 104 and XII/797 ('riguo formosior horto'): p. 306. There were many illustrated editions of the *Metamorphoses* during the period studied in this book; see, for instance, *Ovidii Nasonis Metamorphoseon* (1680s) with engravings by C. Enoelbrecht after J. J. Sandrart: nos. 20 & 22 have villa gardens with fountains. But examples could be multiplied.

10   Evelyn, *Diary*, II, 399.

11   'True Description', p. 115.

12   Raymond, p. 119. On the Domenichino series see Luigi Salerno, 'A Domenichino Series at the National Gallery: the Frescoes from the Villa Aldobrandini', *Burlington Magazine*, 105 (1963), pp. 194–204.

13   Lassels, Pt. II, pp. 307–13, has a long passage on the Villa Aldobrandini from which the quotations are taken.

14   *Tour* 1675, p. 90; Lassels, Pt. II, loc. cit., and Raymond, pp. 117–19, similarly.

15   Evelyn, *Diary*, II, 392; *Tour* 1675, p. 90. There were, of course, many descriptions of the Villa Aldobrandini, among which the most extensive are Mortoft, pp. 164–6, and *Remarks*, p. 188.

16   C. L. Franck, *The Villas of Frascati* (London, 1966), p. 125, has demonstrated that the upper reaches of this part of the garden have been designed to accept the natural curve of the hill itself, which becoming flatter towards the top allows the water to assume 'a quieter and more pensive character the further it is from the riotous displays of the water theatre'.

17   It is difficult for us now to accept the numinous in gardens, since we have lost certain habits of mind and imagination in face of them. When Lampedusa wished to convey the vanishing of an old order in his novel, *The Leopard*, as well as the family rituals and the political rumblings he often showed his hero, Don Fabrizio, in an elegiac garden world, where decaying divinities occupy a specially poignant place: at the Villa Salina the garden has the 'air of cemetary', in which 'a statue of Flora speckled with yellow-black lichen exhibited her centuries old charms with an air of resignation'; while at Donnafugata he encounters the 'anonymous busts of broken-nosed goddesses' along the laurel walks and at the fountain of Neptune and Amphitrite, modelled in stone but softened by the play of water into particularly Ovidian figures, the Duke 'gazed, remembered, regretted'. Yet to his ancestors these sculptured presences intimated vividly the world of a poet whose narratives were alive to their imaginations.

18   See Detlief Heikamp, 'La Grotta Grande del Giardino di Boboli', *Antichità viva*, 4 (1965), and Mila Mastrorocco, *Le Mutazioni di Proteo. I giardini medicei del Cinquecento* (Florence, 1981), chap. 6.

19 Francesco Gurrieri and Judith Chatfield, *Boboli Gardens* (Florence, 1972), p. 39.

20 See IV/781: p. 115 and V/209: p. 121.

21 On temples see XIV/759 & 837: pp. 331 & 333; on inscriptions see II/327–8: p. 58 and XIV/443–4: p. 323.

22 Raymond, p. 117. The notion that gods inhabited gardens in a statuesque guise is wittily challenged by Andrew Marvell's poem, 'The Mower Against Gardens', where it is argued that the 'Gods themselves' rather than just their 'Figures' dwell in the meadows beyond the garden.

23 Sandys, p. 272. Sandys's translation of Ovid was published between 1621 and 1626.

24 'The wall of the house is overcrusted with a world of Anticallie, or old marble pieces of antiquity . . . with a world of such like fables', Lassels, Pt. II, p. 172.

25 Montfaucon, *The Antiquities of Italy*, ed. John Healey (2nd rev. ed., London, 1725), p. 109. On Montfaucon and the lines of 'Ovid', see Elisabeth B. MacDougall, 'The Sleeping Nymph: origins of a humanist fountain type', *The Art Bulletin*, 57 (1975), pp. 357–65. The anonymous visitor of 1675 went in Rome to find the 'long arch't grotta under a hill and at far end a marble figure, leaning upon her hand' which he identified as Egeria, *Tour* 1675, p. 84 (see figure 103 for an engraving of this much visited spot).

26 Evelyn, *Diary*, II, 411.

27 Raymond, p. 224; Warcupp, p. 28 and Mortoft, pp. 128–9. See also note 29.

28 Raymond, introduction a¹ verso. A similar tunnel of water could be seen at Pratolino: see Reresby, p. 78. Raymond may have confused the two.

29 Moryson, p. 291. On this apprehension of inside/outside as late as the 1720s see Wright, p. 292, where he visits the Palazzo Barberini in Rome and finds that 'there is a very pretty Fountain in the middle of the *Salone*, below Stairs, looking to the garden'. Richard Symonds was delighted in Rome by a gallery, opening into one garden, decorated with the fresco of yet another garden: B. L., Egerton MS 1635, f. 82 verso.

30 Evelyn, *Diary*, II, 288 & 357. Loggias were frequently decorated in this way and by just as accomplished artists. In the early twentieth century there were still traces of colour in the garden loggia of Lo Spedaletto, near Volterra, built for Lorenzo the Magnificent by Sangallo, its hall decorated with mythic stories by Botticelli, Ghirlandaio & Fra Lippo Lippi: see J. Cartwright, *Italian Gardens of the Renaissance* (London, 1914), p. 19.

31 On the Villa Giulia see David R. Coffin, *The Villa in the Life of Renaissance Rome* (Princeton, N.J., 1979), pp. 150–74 and the bibliography of other works on this subject, pp. 178–9.

32 'True Description', p. 110.

33 Lassels, Pt. I, pp. 25–6.

34 On the birds and other 'music' at Tivoli see 'True Description', pp. 115–16, Raymond, pp. 167 ff., and Veryard, p. 206. On the artificial rain at the Villa Borghese and Villa D'Este see respectively Raymond, p. 94 and Warcupp, p. 310. Warcupp, p. 210 notices a similar conceit in the Este gardens on the Quirinal.

35 *Papers of the British School at Rome*, VI (1913), p. 483.

36 Mortoft, p. 164 (where the *giocchi d'acqua* are included generally in the water marvels), and *Remarks*, p. 165.

37 Lassels, Pt. I, p. 247; for more discussion of the Villa Lante see below p. 91. On the rails of water at Tivoli and Frascati see Raymond, p. 168 and *Tour* 1675, p. 91.

38 Lassels, Pt. II, p. 308, reports on the staircase of water at Frascati; Warcupp, Pt. II, 309–11; on water as mirror, Raymond, p. 167 and Warcupp, p. 309.

39 Mortoft, pp. 57–8, and p. 133 for the subsequent Mattei reference.

40 Further Guerra drawings of Pratolino are reproduced in Luigi Zangheri, *Pratolino. Il giardino delle meraviglie* (Florence, 1979), vol. II. See also *Libri di immagini, disegni e incisioni di Giovanni Guerra*, catalogue of exhibition at Modena (Modena, 1978). For Lassels on Pratolino, Pt. I, pp. 206–8: grammar and spellings have been normalized.

41 There were dozens of these: some of those most relevant to the purposes of this present study are John Bate, *The Mysteryes of Nature and Art* (London, 1634), Isaac de Caus, *New and Rare Inventions of Water-Works* (London, 1659), an English translation of a French text, and Stephen Switzer, *An Introduction to a General System of Hydrostaticks and Hydraulicks*, 2 vols. (London, 1792), which illustrates continental examples.

42 Moryson, p. 328; Evelyn, Diary, II, 419; Kent, f.3. On all hydraulic and illusionist effects, Ovid's own words would seem appropriate: 'Causa latet, vis est notissima' (when that cause is hidden, the effect is stronger), IV/287: p. 101.

43 Ovid, IV/657–62: p. 111 for Atlas. Eugenio Battisti first invoked and reproduced the Ovid woodcut in his essay, '*Natura Artificosa* to *Natura Artificalis*', *The Italian Garden*, ed. David R. Coffin (Washington, D.C., 1972), but he mentions Ovid only briefly.

44 Ovid, XIII/882–4: p. 308 and XIV/181–2: p. 316. Visitors who reacted to the stone throwing giant are Lassals, Pt. I, p. 208; Wright, p. 430; Northall, pp. 80–1.

45 Lassels, Pt. I, p. 208 and Pt. II, p. 68, my italics in both quotations.

46 Moryson, p. 331, admired the artistry of the group. On Castello see L. Châtelet-Lange, 'The grotto of the unicorn and the garden of the Villa di Castello', *Art Bulletin*, 50 (1968), pp. 51–8.

47 For Evelyn, *Diary*, II, 404 and 253; for other responses to the Bernini sculptures, see *Tour* 1675, pp. 67–8, Raymond, p. 95, Skippon, p. 654, Breval 1726, II, 305.

48 There is an interesting discussion of this sixteenth and, more especially, seventeenth-century obsession with visual wit in Ernest B. Gilman, *The Curious Perspective* (New Haven, Connecticut, 1978), notably chapter three, which discusses the work of Tesauro, especially his *Il cannocchiale aristotelico*. This same work has been cited to show how its author arranged statues and inscriptions at Racconigi to promote contemplation of astronomy and human philosophy: see Elisabeth MacDougall, '*Ars Hortulorum*: sixteenth century garden iconography and literary theory in Italy', *The Italian Garden*, ed. David R. Coffin (Washington, D.C., 1972), p. 39.

49 Cited by Elisabeth MacDougall, ibid., p. 54.

50 Raymond, p. 119.

51 *Tour* 1675, pp. 24, 92, 78 & 69 respectively.

52 Misson, I, p. 145; Coryate, II, pp. 6–7.

53 Respectively, Moryson at Tivoli, p. 225; Coryate outside Milan, quoted by A. Lytton Sells, *The Paradise of Travellers* (London, 1964), p. 164; Mortoft at the Villa Mondragone, Frascati, p. 166.

5   Garden and theatre

1 The relationship of garden and theatre has largely been explored by historians of the latter; but recently garden historians have become interested, though their invocations of 'theatrical' are often merely rhetorical. See Piero Marchi, 'Il Giardino come "Luogo Teatrale" ', *Il Giardino Storico Italiano*, ed. Giovanna Ragionieri (Florence, 1981), pp. 211–19; various articles in *Natura e artificio*, ed. Marcello Fagiolo (Rome, 1979) and in *La Città Effimera e l'Universo Artificiale del Giardino*, ed. Marcello Fagiolo (Rome, 1980).

2 The major studies of courtly festivals have been those written or edited by Jean Jacquot, *Le Lieu Théâtral à la Renaissance* (Paris, 1964), *Dramaturgie et Société: XVIe et XVIIe siècles*, 2 vols. (Paris, 1968), and *Les Fêtes de la Renaissance*, 2 vols. (Paris, 1956 & 1960). See also Roy Strong, *Splendour at Court. Renaissance Spectacle and Illusion* (1973), A. M. Nagler, *Theatre Festivals of the Medici 1593–1673* (New Haven, 1964), and Margaret M. McGowan, *L'Art du Ballet de Cour en France 1581–1643* (Paris, 1963).

3 Bodleian MS Rawl. D.84, folio 20 verso. On the search for theatrical space in Florence see the catalogue, *Il Luogo Teatrale a Firenze* (Milan, 1975), the complete issue of *Quaderni di Teatro*, anno ii, number 7 (March 1980), and the catalogue, *Il potere e lo spazio. La scena del principe* (Florence, 1980).

4 Mario Verdone, *Spettacolo romano* (Rome, 1970), p. 36. For other materials on Rome's theatrical activities, though with little attention to the relationship with gardens, see C. L. Frommel, 'Raffaello e il Teatro alla corte di Leone X, *Bollettino del Centro Internazionale di Studi Architettura Andrea Palladio*, XVI (1974), pp. 173–87, and for a later period, *L'Effimero Barocco*, ed. M. Fagiolo Dell'Arco and Silvia Carrandini (Rome, 1977).

5 Respectively: Hoby, *Camden Miscellany*, 10 (1902), p. 19; Raymond, p. 12.

6 Skippon, p. 640; Acton, p. 40.

7 Lassels, Pt I, p. 136; Browne, p. 199.

8 Veryard, p. 245. For an anthology of later visitors' accounts of festivities in Florence see *Quaderni di Teatro* (cited in note 3), pp. 238 ff.

9 For reproduction of two such engravings see *Il Giardino Storico Italiano* (cited in note 1), plates 19 & 20.

10 See John Arthur Hanson, *Roman Theater-Temples* (Princeton, 1959), pp. 33–6, and F. Fasolo and G. Gullini, *Il santuario della Fortuna Priagenia a Palestrina*, 2 vols. (Rome, 1953).

11 Serlio, *Tutte l'opere d'architettura*, Book III. On the interest taken by Renaissance architects in the Temple at Palestrina see P. Fancelli, *Palladio e Praeneste* (Rome, 1974, and Maurizio Calvesi, *Il sogno di Polifilo prenestino* (Rome, 1980).

12 Burnet, pp. 100–1. On this double staircase see A. Chastel, 'Palladio et l'escalier à double mouvement inversé', *Bolletino del Centro Internazionale A Palladio*, II (1960), pp. 26 ff.

13 See Norman Neuerberg, *L'Architettura della Fontane e di Ninfei nell' Italia Antica* (Naples, 1965); and the catalogue, *Teatri e anfiteatri romani d'Italia* (Milan, 1971), which illustrates examples of Renaissance reconstructions.

14 The confusion occurs in some documents on the Lante gardens: see Claudia Lazzaro-Bruno, 'The Villa Lante at Bagnaia', *Art Bulletin*, LIX (1977), p. 559 and note 36.

15 Strong, op. cit. (note 2) reproduces an engraving of the Pitti courtyard prepared for a *naumachia*.

16 Palladio, *I Quatri Libri* (1570), II, pp. 18–19.

17 Warcupp, pp. 309–11.

18 Misson, p. 234. Such strictures were repeated by Hester Piozzi (p. 283) a hundred years or so later: she thought the Villa Doria Pamphili was 'a lovely place' despite the Italian lack of skill in 'laying out pleasure grounds'; nobody in Italy has 'higher notions of a garden than what an opera affords' (she instances one Genoese garden). On the Ovidian and theatrical dimensions of these Genovese grottoes see the catalogue, *Tra Magia, Scienza e 'Meraviglia'* (Genoa, 1984) and the article by Lauro Magnani in the *Journal of Garden History*, V (1985), pp. 135–53.

19 Wright, p. 316.

20 Warcupp, pp. 309–11.

21 Moryson, p. 329. William Kent a hundred years later responds to Pratolino with what seems like the same language '. . . Galatea coming out of her Grotto drawn by Delfini . . .' (Bodleian MS Rawl.D.1162, folio 3).

22 See Klaus Schwager, 'Kardinal Pietro Aldobrandinis Villa Di Belvedere in Frascati', *Römisches Jahrbuch für Kunstgeschichte*, 9–10 (1961–2), pp. 379–82; also Martin Steinberg, 'The Iconography of the Teatro dell'Acqua at the Villa Aldobrandini', *Art Bulletin*, 47 (1965), pp. 453–63.

23 Raymond, p. 117–19.

24 Wright, p. 341.

25 Evelyn, *Diary*, II, 393. Cf. Mortoft (p. 166) at the same villa – 'wee passed through A great grove, and so through A grott and other pleasant places, that if any thing in the world may be counted a Heaven on Earth, this place may be it' and more, praising the fullness of the experience.

26 Quoted C. L. Franck, *The Villas of Frascati* (London, 1966), p. 65, where the villa is discussed and well illustrated.

27 *Minerva Britanna* (1612), title page.

28 *Elements of Architecture* (1624), pp. 82 & 65. It is clear that some connection exists between the idea of a theatre as a complete conspectus and the early representations and imagery of anatomy theatres, where the little world of man is dissected amid images of the greater macrocosm. See W. S. Heckscher, *Rembrandt's Anatomy of Dr Nicolaas Tulp* (New York, 1958), pp. 135 & 167–8 in particular.

29 Herbert Weisinger, 'Theatrum Mundi: Illusion as Reality', *The Agony and the Triumph* (East Lancing, Michigan, 1964), p. 59. On this important theme see also R. Bernheimer, 'Theatrum Mundi', *Art Bulletin*, 38 (1956), pp. 225–47.

30 Frances A. Yates, *The Art of Memory* (1966), pp. 32 ff. I am much indebted to her book in this section. Some recent Italian criticism has related the arts of memory and specifically the memory theatre to garden design: see Marcello Fagiolo, 'Il giardino come teatro del mondo e della memoria', *La Città Effimera, etc* (see note 1), pp. 125–41.

31 As Douglas Chambers has pointed out to me, the emphasis upon learning would be Ramist, that on remembering, Brunist. Both involve responses to objects. On Colonna's *Hypnerotomachia* see the modern edition by Giovanni Pozzi and Lucia A. Ciapponi, 2 vols. (Padua, 1964) which reproduces the original woodcuts from the Venetian edition of 1499.

32 On Giulio Camillo and his *L'Idea del Theatro* (Florence, 1550) see Yates, op. cit., *passim*, the catalogue *Architettura e Utopia nella Venezia del Cinquecento* (Venice, 1980), pp. 209 ff., and Mario Costanzo, *Il 'Gran Theatro del Mondo'* (Milan, 1964).

33 Yates, op. cit., chapter 6.

34 Wright, pp. 183 (my italics) and 343 ff.

35 Warcupp, pp. 309–11. On the Castello iconography see the article cited in note 46 of the previous chapter, and on that of the Villa D'Este see David R. Coffin, *The Villa D'Este at Tivoli* (Princeton, 1960), pp. 78 ff.

36 See index under 'theatre'.

37 Raymond, introduction a¹ verso and p. 174.

38 Skippon, p. 507, together with some diagrams; Lassels, pt II, p. 251.

39 Serlio, op. cit., Book II. The Renaissance familiarity with these types of scene is suggested by Richard Krautheimer's discussion of the other two: see 'The Tragic and Comic Scene of the Renaissance', *Gazette des Beaux-Arts*, 33 (6e periode, 1948), pp. 327–46.

40 Torelli is the best documented scene designer of this period: see Per Bjurström, *Giacomo Torelli and Baroque Stage Design* (Stockholm, 1961), where many of his garden sets are illustrated.

41 Per Bjurström, *Feast and Theatre in Queen Christiana's Rome* (Stockholm, 1966), p. 23 and plate 22.

42 For full details and for some suggestions on how this Spanish garden-theatre may have influenced Andrew Marvell see my 'Marvell, Nun Appleton and the Buen Retiro', *Philology Quarterly*, 59 (1980), pp. 374–8.

43 For some festivals at the Savoy court during the mid-seventeenth century, festivals which obviously used and enhanced the theatrical layout of its palaces and gardens, see Mercedes Viale Ferrero, *Feste delle Madame Reali di Savoia* (Turin, 1965), which reproduces Tommaso Borgionio's drawings for these events.

44 These matters are taken up in Part Two.

6 Cabinets of curiosity

1 Respectively: Coryate, II, 36; Raymond, p. 6 and preface generally; Ray, p. 365. For other examples see above, p. 4.

2 On this aspect of cabinets of curiosities see *The Origins of Museums: the Cabinet of Curiosities in Sixteenth and Seventeenth-century Europe*, eds. O. R. Impey and A. G. MacGregor (Clarendon Press, 1985). An older study of the topic is David Murray, *Museums. Their history and their use*, 3 vols. (Glasgow, 1904).

3 *O.E.D.*, citing Spenser's *The Faerie Queene* (II.xii.83) among other sources. John Rea also describes a flower garden as a 'cabinet with several boxes fit to receive and securely keep Nature's choicest jewels', *Flora* (1665), p. 6.

4 Evelyn, *Diary*, III, 594.

5 A. H. S. Yeames, 'Rome in 1622', *Papers of the British School at Rome*, VI (1913), quoting British Museum MS Harl. 6867, folio 32.

6 Terry Comito, 'Renaissance Gardens and the Discovery of Paradise', *Journal of the History of Ideas*, XXXII (1971), p. 486 note.

7 See J. M. Fletcher, 'Isabella d'Este, Patron and Collector', *Splendours of the Gonzaga*, catalogue ed. David Chambers and Jane Martineau (London, 1982), pp. 51–63, and C. M. Brown, 'The Grotta of Isabella D'Este', *Gazette des Beaux-Arts*, VIe: LXXXIX (1977), p. 155–71.

8 Evelyn, *Diary*, II, 181.

9 See the section on 'Il Giardino dei Semplici' in the catalogue, *Liverno e Pisa: due citte e un territorio nella politica dei Medici* (Pisa, 1908), especially for the reproduction of the drawings; Aldrovandi is quoted on p. 523. Similar conjunctions of botany and natural history musuem were made, of course, throughout Europe: at Leiden, another famous early botanical garden, the *Ambulacrum*, built in 1599, contained a museum of *naturalia*, curious examples of which decorate the well known print of 1610; a drawing sixty years later shows the addition of an orangery for the display and winter care of plants and a small house where chemistry experiments were conducted: see W. K. H. Karstens and Herman Kleibrink, *De Leidse Hortus, een botanische erfenis* (Zwolle, 1982).

10 Raymond, pp. 21–2; Acton, p. 13.

11 See Lucia Tongiorgi Tomasi, 'Projects for Botanical and Other Gardens', *Journal of Garden History*, III (1983), 1–34. Tomasi illustrates various layouts for gardens, including the simple one at the Florentine Botanical Garden and the more intricate one at Mantua which was

(significantly for our present purposes) designed by the man who was both antiquarian and herbalist to the Gonzaga, Fra Zanobi Bocchi.

12 Ferrari, *Flora overo la Cultura di fiori* (Rome, 1638), p. 16; del Riccio, 'Agricoltura teorica', MS, Biblioteca Nazionale, Florence, folio 50r. Both passages are quoted in Peter Armour's translations; for further discussion and quotation see Tomasi's article cited in the preceding note.

13 Evelyn, *Diary*, II, 173–5. The Palace of Negros is now the Villa Rolla-Rasazza. On Furttenbach and the Genoese gardens' cabinet-like play with natural materials see the works mentioned in note 18 to Chapter 5 above as well as Lauro Magnani, 'Uno "Spazio Privato" nella Cultura Genovese tra XVI e XVII secolo', *Studi di Storia delle Arti*, II (1978–9), 113–29.

14 Evelyn, *Diary*, II, 405.

15 Ibid., 236, 297 and 391 respectively.

16 Ibid., 302–5.

17 Ibid., 392–3.

18 Ibid., 234–6.

19 See note 47 to Chapter 2 above.

20 There were examples of loggias at various Elizabethan and Jacobean houses, but nonetheless see, for example, the surprise of Fynes Moryson at the Villa Medici in Rome (I, 291) or of Evelyn at the Farnesina (*Diary*, II, 288). The special status of loggias received the attention of Scamozzi in *L'Idea dell' Architettura* (Venice, 1615), Part I, Book III, chapter xvii.

21 Evelyn, *Diary*, II, 231 (Medici) and 251 (Borghese).

22 See below, chapter 8, for a fuller discussion of this topic.

23 Evelyn, *Diary*, II, 240, 285 and 251 respectively. Collections of animals, zoos, were often part of collections housed in gardens: in 1752 John Northall (p. 74) visited the menagerie in the Boboli gardens ('several uncommon wild beasts . . . different sorts of exotic birds, particularly ostriches, Chinese geese, pheasants, parrots, and Arabian ducks').

24 An anonymous painting of the Borghese gardens is reproduced in *Mostra del Giardino Italiano*, catalogue (Florence, 1931), plate 43.

25 Georgina Masson, 'Italian Flower Collectors' Gardens in Seventeenth Century Italy', *The Italian Garden*, ed. David Coffin (Washington, D.C., 1972), 61–80. The planting ms., mentioned by Masson (p. 74, note 24), is being edited together with others related to it by Elisabeth MacDougall and will be appearing in a future issue of the *Journal of Garden History*.

26 See above, pp. 35–6.

27 Bodleian Library MS. Rawl. D. 84, folio 7 recto.

28 Moryson, I, 239.

29 Cust, p. 342. He continues by noticing that 'By this garden is a fine Gallery adorned with many naturall curiosityes'.

30 Ray, pp. 336 (Boboli) and 364–5 (Roman villas).

31 Evelyn's copy of Ray's *Observations* is in the British Library, shelf mark Eve. a. 44.

32 Piozzi, p. 220; Acton, p. 37.

33 Ray, p. 245; Reresby, p. 76 (Reresby seems to be conflating his memories of the Boboli Gardens and the Castello villa grotto).

34 Reresby, p. 50.

35 Coryate, II, 36.

36 Evelyn, *Diary*, II, 392.

37   This is illustrated and discussed more fully below, pp. 137–8.

38   On this wider context see Charles Webster, *The Great Instauration* (London, 1975), and Keith Thomas, *Man and the Natural World* (London, 1983).

39   See Walter E. Houghton, 'The English Virtuoso in the Seventeenth Century', *Journal of the History of Ideas*, III (1942), pp. 51–73 and 190–219.

40   Moryson, p. 328–9.

41   I am grateful to David Sturdy for drawing my attention to the Bargrave materials; since I studied them at Canterbury there has appeared a small pamphlet on the collection – David Sturdy and Martin Henig, *The Gentle Traveller* (1983).

42   Skippon, p. 613: cf. the Marquis of Dorchester (1606–80) whose 2,600 plants were arranged in botanical order – see Keith Thomas, *Man and the Natural World*, p. 227.

43   *Remarks*, pp. 84–5.

44   For a somewhat fuller exploration of this aspect see my article '*Curiosities* to adorne *Cabinets* and *Gardens*' in the first volume cited in note 2 above.

45   *Museum Tradescantianum* (1656).

46   In his MS *Elysium Britannicum*, Bk I, chap. xvii; also quoted by John Prest, *The Garden of Eden. The Botanic Garden and the Re-Creation of Paradise* (New Haven and London, 1981), p. 47. Prest's short but well illustrated book argues in more detail the point being made here.

47   Cited by David Masson, *Life of Milton* (London, 1881), IV, 350. See a similar remark, this time Christianized, in Thomas Tenison, *Baconiana* (London, 1679), p. 57. It is worth stressing that not only were sculpture collections in gardens like Arundel's inspired by ancient examples (Cicero's letters record purchases of statues and relief fragments for his villa; Pliny's *Natural History* includes a book on stone with several references to garden statues), but gardens as sites of more general 'museums'. Suetonius writes of Augustus' villa that it displayed not only statues and pictures but also bones and such like rarities (see volume I of Murray. cited above in note 2). There was a further connection between ancient Roman practice and the late Renaissance enthusiasm for cabinets of rarities: the decoration known as *grotteschi* was developed in the Renaissance from examples found in Nero's Golden House and it came to include exactly the same marvellously random conspectus of curiosities as did cabinets themselves – geometrical patterns, landscapes, still-lifes, bits of foliage colonized by birds, items like candelabra metamorphosed into vegetation, chained satyrs, fantastic architecture, monsters, giants, etc. For a full survey of this subject matter see Nicole Dacos, *La Découverte de la Domus Aurea et la formation des grotesque à la Renaissance* (London, 1969), pp. 52–5.

48   See the study by Prest cited in note 46.

49   *The Travels of Peter Mundy*, (London, 1907–25), III, 1–2 (my italics); see also the chapter, 'The Tradescants: Gardeners and Botanists', *Tradescant's Rarities*, ed. Arthur MacGregor (Oxford, 1983), especially p. 11. On the ever increasing profusion of species see Keith Thomas, *Man and the Natural World* (London, 1983), 226–7 *et passim*.

50   Quoted *Tradescant's Rarities*, p. 15.

51   *The History of the Royal Society* (1734 edition), p. 386.

7   Variety

1   H. V. S. Ogden, 'The Principles of Variety and Contrast in seventeenth century aesthetics, and Milton's poetry', *Journal of the History of Ideas*, 10 (1949), pp. 159–82. See also the analysis of variety in John Shearman, *Mannerism* (Harmondsworth, 1967), pp. 140–51 (together with pp. 92, 100, 109, 139 and 177). Bacon's praise of poetry's variety comes from *The Advancement*

of Learning, Pt II; Shakespeare's, from *Antony and Cleopatra*, Act II, Scene ii. Otherwise all my other examples are taken from Ogden and Shearman. See also the discussion of art and nature in the next section.

2 Veryard, p. 206.

3 See, for instance, Lassels, pp. 307 ff.; *Tour* 1675, p. 90; *Remarks*, p. 190.

4 Warcupp, p. 210; for villa Mattei see, for example, Lassels, pp. 118–19 and Skippon, p. 670.

5 Burnet, p. 126.

6 R. Throckmorton, *Several Years Travels . . .* (1702), p. 190.

7 Veryard, p. 206.

8 On Villa D'Este: Lassels, pp. 314 ff. and Raymond, p. 167; on Vatican gardens: Warcupp, p. 179 ('Gardens which are five, some in Terrace, others low'); on Genoese gardens: Evelyn, *Diary*, II, 173–5 (quoted above p. 10), and Raymond, pp. 10–12. Moryson (p. 291) saw the Villa Medici at Rome as having two gardens, and what he means can readily be seen in Figure 12.

9 The *giardini segreti*, private enclosures usually to the sides of a house, were not always available to visitors and therefore not much noticed: Warcupp (p. 309) is unusual in mentioning them.

10 Moryson, p. 331; Reresby, p. 50.

11 Skippon, respectively pp. 623 & 640. The Boboli Gardens were also frequently commended for their variety: see, for example, Raymond, p. 37, and Reresby, p. 70.

12 Lassels, pp. 206–8. The sloping site of Pratolino is crucial to its scope, and a surprise if all one has seen of it is Gustave Utens's lunette which seems rather to flatten these extensive gardens.

13 Bodleian Library MS Rawl. D 120, folio 26.

14 Wright, p. 307.

15 Georgina Masson, *Italian Gardens* (1966), p. 124; see also the works cited in note 46 to chapter 2 above, especially for illustrations.

16 *Tour* 1675, p. 94.

17 Lassels, p. 206; Warcupp, pp. 309–11.

18 See David Coffin, *The Villa D'Este at Tivoli* (Princeton, N.J., 1960), chapter 5. The same effects created by criss-cross descents can be obtained just as easily, though less extensively, in smaller gardens: see for example the little garden of Flora below the terrace at the Villa Torrigiani, near Lucca (illustrated in Masson, ed. cit. [note 15 above], plate 56).

19 Addison on the Island of Capri, 'Remarks', p. 90. For Spence, *Letters*, pp. 114 (in Rome) and 242 (Turin).

20 Elisabeth MacDougall, 'Ars Hortulorum . . .' (see note 49 to chapter 2 above), pp. 41 ff.

21 Skippon, p. 654; Lassels, Pt. II, pp. 171–2.

22 Burnet, p. 225; Mortoft, pp. 151–5.

23 Mortoft, p. 113; cf. Evelyn, *Diary*, II, 240.

24 *Tour* 1675, p. 78.

25 Lassels, Pt. I, p. 249. Others who visited Caprarola were Raymond, the tourist of 1675, and Cust; it is also mentioned by Warcupp.

26 Northall, p. 362.

27 For Pliny see above, p. 12; for Alberti on the placing of gentlemen's houses where they would enjoy fine prospects, see James Leoni, *The Architecture of Leon Battista Alberti*, 3 vols. (1726), I, 98 verso.

28 Symonds, British Library, Egerton MS 1635, folio 10.

29 *The travels and life of Sir Thomas Hoby*, in *Camden Miscellany*, 10 (1902), p. 32; Skippon, pp. 540 and 499 (where he looks out over the lagoon from the gardens of S. Giorgio Maggiore). Most travellers decided that there were no gardens at Venice (see, for example, Lassels, Pt II, p. 417); but there were in fact many gardens within the city, and I am engaged on a historical study of them and of their uses.

30 Acton, p. 68.

31 *Tour* 1675, pp. 76 ff., where the author discusses one Roman villa after another in brisk succession.

32 Lassels, Pt II, p. 307.

33 Wright, p. 41.

34 *Epistle to Burlington* (1731), line 61.

8 Art and nature

1 The term *paragone*, which means simply 'comparison', was the term used to identify Renaissance debates or rivalries between the arts; it is used in this context to highlight the contest between art and nature (and the 'arts' of nature) in a garden, a contest known at least since Roman times (see above, p. 17).

2 Kent, folio 2 r; Raymond, p. 170. Walpole's remark about Kent's leap of the fence is from *The History of the Modern Taste in Gardening*, as edited by I. W. U. Chase, *Horace Walpole: Gardenist* (Princeton, N.J., 1943), p. 25. For further discussion of garden historiography, see below pp. 216 ff.

3 Claudia Lazzaro-Bruno, 'The Villa Lante at Bagnaia: An allegory of Art and Nature', *The Art Bulletin*, LIX (1977), pp. 553–60. Iconographical studies usually consider, as does this, only meanings inscribed in artworks, rarely how such meanings were read by later visitors. But that the garden was generally considered apt territory for the *paragone* is clear from Taegio's remark on the Milanese garden of Scipione Simonetta: 'Here art and nature, at times in rivalry show their utmost in contests; at times joined, united and reconciled together, they create stupendous things', *La villa: Un Dialogo* (Milan, 1599), p. 102.

4 Raymond, introduction, a¹ verso – though it seems he may well be recalling such a feature at Pratolino; Blainville, II, 346 (criticizing Burnet).

5 Evelyn, *Diary*, II, 172–3, my italics.

6 'True Description', pp. 93 (speaking of paintings in the Villa Farnese, Caprarola), 83, 93, 108 & 114, and (Villa D'Este) 115–16.

7 Bodleian MS Rawl. D. 84, folio 7 verso.

8 Sandys, p. 272.

9 Moryson, I, pp. 293 & 328.

10 *De' Simboli transportati al morale*, quoted by Mario Praz, *Studies in Seventeenth-Century Imagery* (Rome, 1964), p. 19.

11 An example of how we can only really adjudicate these discriminations between art and nature if we know something of the speaker or writer would be the description of one of the D'Este gardens outside Ferrara as 'era senza' ordine piantata ed imboschita di varie piante' (planted without order and wooded with various plants); when it is compared to a tapestry representation of it, it becomes clear that our notions of 'without order' cannot hold, since the hill is planted with trees *in lines*! See Elisabeth Macdougall, 'Arts Hortulorum . . .', *The Italian Garden*, ed. D. R. Coffin (Washington, D.C. 1972), p. 45 and plate 9.

12 *Instructions and Directions for Forren Travell*, p. 54.

13 Moryson, I, pp. 327–30.

14 *A Survey of the Great Dukes state of Tuscany . . . in 1596* (London, 1605), p. 13.

15 Raymond, pp. 117–19.

16 Ibid., pp. 167 ff. But as Dean Tolle Mace has noted, the Italian *dramma per musica* was specially noted for its abandonment of verisimilitude in pursuit of the passions of the soul, so perhaps Raymond is making that point. See Mace, 'Dryden's Dialogue on Drama', *J.W.C.I.*, 25 (1962), p. 94.

17 Reresby, p. 50; Warcupp, II, 316; on the model of Rome, Skippon, p. 674; ibid., pp. 548 & 660; *Tour*, 1675, p. 90.

18 Warcupp, I, 67 (it is interesting to note his awkward application of literary and artistic terms to gardens); for the following, ibid., p. 28.

19 Raymond, p. 10; *Tour*, 1675, p. 27; Mortoft, p. 41.

20 Veryard, pp. 122 and 190 (referring to a garden at Mantua and the Vatican Belvedere respectively); p. 195.

21 Burnet, p. 100 (the whole passage is quoted above p. 61); Misson, I, 41.

22 Blainville reproaching Burnet, II, 346; on Villa Aldobrandini, ibid., pp. 343 ff., and Misson, II, 41; Blainville on Tivoli, II, 379, and the 'Froth of Hyperbolism', ibid., 379. It is of course well known that André Le Nôtre, while he derived a good deal of his inspiration from Italian gardens, thought their grottoes and hydraulic displays puerile.

23 Spence, *Letters*, p. 329 quoting from his notebooks.

24 Blainville, II, 285–6 & 303 ff.

25 Addison, 'Remarks', preface.

26 Ibid., p. 129; *scene* derives from theatrical terminology.

27 Abraham Cowley on 'My Self', *Essays and Plays*, ed A. R. Waller (Cambridge, 1906), p. 457; *The Garden Book of Sir Thomas Hanmer* (London, 1933), p. 48. Cf. *Paradise Lost*, VII, 323.

28 Addison, 'Remarks', p. 131.

29 On the confusions or at least indecisiveness of English aesthetics see the article by Mace, cited above in note 16.

30 *Characteristics of Men, Morals, Opinions and Times*, ed. J. M. Robertson (Indianapolis and New York, 1964), p. 125.

31 Being one of those garden historians previously in error, I am pleased to acknowledge the work that (I am sure) has put us back on the right track: David Leatherbarrow, 'Character, Geometry and Perspective: the Third Earl of Shaftesbury's Principles of Garden Design', *Journal of Garden History*, IV (1984), pp. 332–58.

32 *William Congreve: Letters and Documents*, ed. John C. Hodges (New York, 1964), p. 205.

33 *The Works*, ed. cit., I, 45; 'Remarks', p. 130 on Frascati.

34 *Of Dramatic Poesy and other critical essays*, ed. George Watson, 2 vols. (London, 1962), I, 59 and for the following quotation, II, 161.

35 Nourse, *Campania Foelix* (1700), p. 299.

36 See Dryden, op. cit., II, 32 and Hobbes's answer to Davenant's Preface to *Gondibert*, ed. David F. Gladish (Oxford, 1971), p. 53. I am grateful to Kees Schoneveld for these references.

37 The phrase is Dryden's: ed. cit., II, 162.

38 Ibid., I, 123.

39   Ray, Blake and Blith, all quoted by Keith Thomas, *Man and the Natural World*, pp. 67 and 256.

40   On these matters see the essay by Mace cited above note 16, especially pp. 88 & 110–11.

41   Respectively – British Library Add MS 61479, folio 173 verso; Breval 1738, I, p. 161; Northall, p. 122 (both references).

42   *Letters from Italy* (London, 1774), pp. 75 and (for Boboli) 149.

43   Piozzi, pp. 67 & 332.

44   *Travels Through France and Italy*, ed. Frank Felsenstein (Oxford, 1979), pp. 217 and 245 (on Genoa and Viterbo) and 263 (on Villa Borghese). For the main passage quoted, pp. 263–65.

9   'My patterne for a country seat'

1   Raymond, p. 167 and following.

2   Lassels, preface B¹ verso.

3   *The travels and life of Sir Thomas Hoby . . . written by himself* (London, 1902), p. 129. There is also the example of Evelyn: see below, pp. 145 ff.

4   Coryate, p. 36. For Carew's garden, see below, p. 107.

5   Blainville, II, 143; Wright, p. 41.

6   The letter is with the MS of *Elysium* at Christ Church College, Oxford, Evelyn MS 45.

7   I am generally indebted in this discussion of Elizabethan examples to Roy Strong, *The Renaissance Garden in England* (1979), pp. 49 ff.

8   John Nichols, *The Progresses of Queen Elizabeth I*, 5 vols. (1823), I, 427 & 472–7. Somewhat more accessible, though far less detailed in its documentation, is Ian Dunlop, *Palaces and Progresses of Elizabeth I* (1962), who summarizes the same material pp. 141 ff.

9   Alicia Amherst, *A History of Gardening in England* (1895) reprints the Parliamentary surveys which are one of the main sources of our knowledge of the gardens: that of Theobalds, pp. 319–22. On the classical motif of the fishpond English gardeners might have known Varro, *Rerum Rusticarum*, III, iii, 9–11 & III, xvii, 1–9, and Columella, *De re rustica*, VIII, 16–17.

10   Quoted Strong, p. 53. On the garden and grove contrast see above, pp. 85–6.

11   *The Diary of Baron Waldstein*, translated and annotated by G. W. Groos (1981), pp. 81–7. For the fountain of the mill at Pratolino see Luigi Zangheri, *Pratolino*, 2 vols. (Florence, 1979), II, plate 67.

12   *The Diary of Baron Waldstein*, pp. 156–63. On Nonsuch see also John Dent, *The Quest for Nonsuch* (1970), where the 1650 Parliamentary survey is reprinted; for the Lumley Inventory see *Walpole Society*, VI (1917–18). For Evelyn on Nonsuch, *Diary*, III, 427.

13   Quoted Strong, op. cit., p. 66 and *Thomas Platter's Travels in England 1599*, ed. Clare Williams (1937).

14   Waldstein, op. cit., pp. 163–5. For the Italian parallels see Mortoft, pp. 134–5 and Zangheri, op. cit., II, figure 62; Zangheri's figure 63 also illustrates Salomon de Caus' Galatea grotto.

15   *Paradisi in sole* (1629), p. 610. Cf. Pratolino, Zangheri, op. cit., II figures 228 & 229.

16   See Virginia Black, 'Beddington – "the best orangery in England" ', *Journal of Garden History*, III (1983), pp. 113–20. For mention of the other orangeries see Strong, op. cit., pp. 90. 189 & 191.

17 See Strong, op. cit., p. 57 together with the materials in his notes 27 & 28. For Stukeley, *Itinerarium curiosum* (1724), p. 50.

18 Summerson, *Architecture in Britain 1530 to 1830* (1970), p. 76.

19 Strong, op. cit., p. 60. On loggias as a new Italian experience for early English visitors, see above, p. 51.

20 *Pace* Strong, ibid., who writes that this part of the Wimbledon garden made 'no use of terracing.'. Winstanley's view, of course, shows the gardens after they were remodelled by André Mollet in 1641–2 for Queen Henrietta Maria, but since Thorpe shows stairs between terraces it is clear that Winstanley's engraving registers at least Mollet's adaptation of the older feature.

21 *The Poems of James VI of Scotland*, ed. James Craigie, 2 vols. (Edinburgh, 1958), II, 179–80. That the theme continued to be a relevant one see also Richard Fanshawe's 'Ode' on the same subject ('Plant trees you may, and see them shoote / Up with your children . . .'), *Shorter Poems and Translations*, ed. N. W. Bawcutt (Liverpool, 1964), pp. 5–9.

22 See Robert Cooke, *West Country Houses* (Bristol, 1957).

23 *The Country Seat*, ed. H. Colvin and J. Harris (1970), pp. 24–5.

24 *Calendar of State Papers Venetian, 1617–19*, p. 320. That it is a Venetian ambassador who comments upon the vogue for new garden styles is interesting: Venetian city gardens were very conservative and registered changes in fashion slowly if at all, so that the Ambassador could well have regarded any uptodate garden improvements with the same interest as the English. Another intriguing fashion in which England learnt of Italian gardens seems to have been via an exhibition of wax models of them, to which both Michael Drayton's *England's Heroicall Epistles* (1599 ed.), p. 72, and John Donne, 'Satyre IV', lines 169–70, refer.

25 See Strong, op. cit., pp. 115–17.

26 Ibid., pp. 120–22.

27 *The Letters of John Chamberlain*, ed. N. E. McClure, 2 vols. (Philadelphia, 1939), I, pp. 235 & 468.

28 Materials taken from British Library Add MS 27278, folios 24 & 25; and from *Aubrey's Brief Lives*, ed. O. L. Dick (1949), pp. 13–15.

29 *The Anatomy of Melancholy* (1621), Pt. 2, sect. 2, mem. 4, and a few pages later Burton also considers classical precedents for suitable surroundings in which to purge melancholy.

30 Stephen Orgel and Roy Strong, *Inigo Jones. The Theatre of the Stuart Court*, 2 vols (Berkeley and London, 1973), II, 708 & 706. This work will henceforward be referred to as *Inigo Jones*. On the exercise of royal power via the masque see the book cited in note 61 below.

31 See Strong, op. cit., pp. 125 ff.

32 *The Archs of Triumph* (1604), engravings 5 & 6; text sigs. F¹ recto and G¹ recto.

33 *Inigo Jones*, I, 178.

34 Ben Jonson, *Works*, ed. P. Simpson and C. H. Herford, 11 vols. (Oxford, 1941), VII, 136–44.

35 John Nichols, *The Progresses . . . of James I*, 4 vols. (1828), II, 630–39.

36 Jonson, *Works*, op. cit., VII, 807–14. On the masque itself see D. J. Gordon, *The Renaissance Imagination* (Berkeley, 1975), pp. 96–101.

37 Mary F. S. Hervey, *The Life, Correspondence & Collections of Thomas Howard, Earl of Arundel* (Cambridge, 1921), p. 74. Orgel and Strong. *Inigo Jones*, i, 20 (note 24), argue that Jones's 'theatrical machinery, like his drawing, shows no significant Italian influence until after 1614'; but that ignores the distinctly Italianate garden experience that is recreated in some of these early masques.

38 *Stone-Heng . . . Restored* (1655), B¹ recto.

39 *Inigo Jones*, I, 206 ff.

40 Ibid., I, 116.

41 On Jones's arches, see John Harris, Stephen Orgel and Roy Strong, *The King's Arcadia* (1973), *passim*.

42 Wotton, *The Elements of Architecture* (1624), pp. 109–10.

43 *Inigo Jones*, II, 579. For editorial commentary on the two designs see p. 588.

44 The Callot engraving is reproduced, ibid., II, 519.

45 See ibid., I, 41–2 for a list of some of Jones's borrowings.

46 Quoted ibid., I, 11.

47 *Inigo Jones*, I, 194 & 196 (for the final scene). There was likely to be no specific reference to the Villa Aldobrandini which was not finished till 1611.

48 Felice Stampfle, 'A Design for a Garden Grotto by Jacques de Gheyn II', *Master Drawings*, III (1965), pp. 381–3.

49 *Inigo Jones*, II, 505–21.

50 Ibid., II, 600. Cf. Zangheri, *Pratolino*, II, plates 224–53. Cupid's Mount with the grotto (invisible) below may be seen in my Figure 45 just above the point where the left-hand series of pools bends towards the lower parts of the garden. For Moryson, p. 291.

51 *Inigo Jones*, II, 562.

52 See below, pp. 182–4.

53 *Inigo Jones*, II, 633.

54 Ibid., 480 & 485–6.

55 Ibid., 422.

56 Ibid., I, 328.

57 Ibid., 385 & II, 421. The *Masque of Blackness* used grotto effects in its opening sequence of marine deities and 'one of the tritons . . . began to sing to the others loud music' (ibid., I, 90), which is also reminiscent of such hydraulic effects as Aldobrandini's.

58 Ibid., II, 456.

59 See above, p. 115 and below, pp. 130–1.

60 See *Inigo Jones*, I, 376.

61 Stephen Orgel, *The Illusion of Power. Political Theater in the English Renaissance* (Berkeley, 1975), especially pp. 9 ff.

62 Wotton, *Elements of Architecture*, pp. 4–5.

63 Quoted Hervey, op. cit. (note 37), pp. 101–2. On this collection see also D. E. L. Haynes, *The Arundel Marbles* (Oxford, 1975).

64 See John Harris, Stephen Orgel & Roy Strong, *The King's Arcadia* (1973), pp. 101–3, where these Smythson items are illustrated. Strong, *The Renaissance Garden*, pp. 169–74, discusses the sculpture garden. The portrait of the Earl by Daniel Mytens, owned by the National Portrait Gallery, shows a vista down a sculpture gallery and across the Thames where (dimly) can be seen more sculpture – I am grateful for this point to Dr David Howarth who is preparing a book on Arundel: if that is the case, then this is a fine example of 'eyecatchers' outside the gardens being used to lead the sight out beyond their boundaries.

65 See chapter 6 above.

66　Peacham, *The Compleat Gentleman* (1634), pp. 104–6. Peacham was tutor to Arundel's son.

67　Hervey, op. cit. (note 37), pp. 410 & 163.

68　Hervey, ibid., chapter VII describes Arundel's trip to Italy (his second) and also glances at Jones's reactions, from which I quote.

69　Quoted ibid., p. 255.

70　Stukeley, *Itinerarium curiosum*, p. 35; Aubrey, *Natural History and Antiquities of the County of Surrey*, 5 vols. (1718–19), V, 282 ff.

71　Evelyn, *Diary*, III, 495.

72　Strong, *Renaissance Garden*, p. 87 and pp. 87–112 on de Caus's work in England.

73　J. W. Neumayr, *Des Durchlauchtigen hochgeboren Fursten und Herrn . .* (Leipzig, 1620), pp. 184–5. The stage direction for the masque, *Tethys' Festival*, is quoted above, p. 115.

74　The frontispiece for the first of the two volumes of Switzer's *Introduction . . .*, for instance, shows a vista through an elaborate rockwork archway, guarded by seagods, towards fountains set in a canal surrounded by gardens – it is an odd design to find in Switzer if one does not take into account his obligations to much earlier garden styles.

75　*Les Raisons des Forces Mouvantes* (Frankfurt, 1615), Book II, problem xiv for the giant larger than Pratolino's, in the discussion of which de Caus cites Ovid; problem xvi is illustrated here as Figure 65, and problem xvii is the grotto *inside* its head, a group of animals listening to Orpheus playing upon the cello! The closeness of imagery in theatres and gardens at this time can be shown once again by the invocation in Jonson's masque, *Pleasure Reconciled to Virtue* (1618) of a giant figure – 'the mountain Atlas, who had his top ending in the figure of an old man, his head and beard all hoary and frost as if his shoulders were covered with snow; the rest wood and rock' (*Inigo Jones*, I, 285). The Venetian Ambassador approved its 'assai bell' artificio'.

76　Neumayr, op. cit. (note 73), pp. 211–12.

77　Cited Strong, *Renaissance Garden*, p. 97.

78　*Les Raisons des Forces Mouvantes*, dedication to Part II. The dedicatee, Elisabeth, Electress Palatine, and her husband employed de Caus after his departure from England to create the magnificent and complicated gardens at Heidelberg; some grottoes and other features for this are also illustrated in Part II. For the Heidelberg garden see Richard Patterson, 'The "Hortus Palatinus" at Heidelberg and the Reformation of the World', *Journal of Garden History*, I (1981), pp. 67–104 & 179–202.

79　S. Sorbière, *A Voyage to England* (1709), pp. 64–5. With John Tradescant's planting of Hatfield Gardens from his various expeditions (on which see Prudence Leith-Ross, *The John Tradescants: Gardeners to the Rose and Lily Queens*, 1984) they became horticulturally rich – a cabinet of nature's riches to match the architectural ones.

80　Bodleian Library, Aubrey MS 2, folio 53 recto. Further quotations are from this manuscript, folios 53 recto–59 recto.

81　Strong, *Renaissance Garden*, p. 178. The remark would be equally true of Wollaton.

82　Cf. Pliny's letter cited above, p. 12.

83　Aubrey has glossed this particular point on the facing page by transcribing some lines of Suckling:

　　　　For as in Prospects, we are there pleased most
　　　　Where something keeps the eie from being lost,
　　　　And leaves us roome to guesse.

84 Strong suggests the Giambologna source (*Renaissance Garden*, p. 179), but not the Medici one. Perhaps their 'meaning' about which Sir Roy Strong puzzles was simply that they alluded to Italy and Rome.

85 Raymond, pp. 94–5 ('In the gardens the foure Sphinxes of ancient stone').

86 Strong, *Renaissance Garden*, p. 178.

87 Strong (ibid., pp. 179–80) makes the point about the pastoral characters being masque characters; for Evelyn's remarks on their associations, made in the context of a visit to Wilton, see his *Diary*, III, 115.

88 Aubrey, *The Natural History of Wiltshire*, ed. J. Britton (London, 1847), p. 93. All other quotations about Lavington are from this source unless otherwise noted.

89 Aubrey notes 'severall Statues' placed in the stream. So important did the profusion of sculpture appear to Aubrey that the manuscript glosses the main text with a further 'severall Statues in the Garden beside' (Bodleian Library, Aubrey MS 2, folio 52 verso).

90 Bodleian Library, MS Rawl. c. 799, folio 7 verso. Bargrave may be writing about the Boboli Gardens or about a conflation of his memories of what he has just called 'ye multitude of Villa's (or Country Palaces)' around Florence. Bargrave was travelling during the late 1640s. For his father, see above, pp. 79–80.

91 Temple, *Upon the Gardens of Epicurus: or, Of Gardening, in the Year 1685*, in *Miscellanea*, Pt II (1690), pp. 53–6. Strong, *Renaissance Garden*, p. 145, has a useful reconstructed plan of Moor Park gardens.

92 See G. A. Usher, *Gwysaney and Owston* (priv. print. Denbigh, 1964), pp. 82, 107 and *passim*.

93 *Renaissance Garden*, pp. 138 ff.

94 This suggestion is made by Eugenio Battisti, *The Italian Garden*, ed. David R. Coffin (Washington, D.C., 1972), pp. 19–20 and note 40.

95 *Renaissance Garden*, pp. 188–9.

96 Ibid., p. 185.

97 Robert Plot, *The Natural History of Oxfordshire* (1677: ed. cited, 1705), pp. 240–1.

98 My discussion of Bushell's Enstone grotto is put together from various sources: Plot, op. cit., pp. 241 ff; the postscript of Bushell's own *Extract . . . of his late Abridgement of the Lord Chancellor Bacons Philosophical Theory in Mineral Prosecutions* (1660); Aubrey's *Brief Lives*; the account of a visitor called Hammond, in *Camden Miscellany*, 3rd series, III (1936), 81–3. An account of the garden and grotto based upon the same material is given by Christopher Thacker, 'An Extraordinary Solitude', *Of Oxfordshire Gardens* (Oxford, 1982), pp. 27–48.

99 See article cited above in note 78 for an argument about this building in the Heidelberg garden.

100 Plot, op. cit., p. 240, writes of Wilkins that 'he could raise a *Mist* in his *Garden*, wherein a Person placed at a due Distance between the *Sun* and the *Mist*, might see an exquisite *Rainbow* in all it [sic] proper colours'. For Evelyn's visit to Wilkins, *Diary*, III, 110.

101 *The Severall Speeches and Songs, at the presentment of Mr Bushells Rock to the Queenes Most Excellent Majesty . . .* (Oxford, 1636).

102 Wright, II, p. 366. But, interestingly, Wright is also much drawn to natural cascades and grottoes which art would not have improved (I, p. 22); while a near-contemporary French visitor, De Blainville, is simply very patronizing about Aldobrandini ('honest Pegasus . . . nobly struck the Rock') because he finds it childish not because he prefers natural effects..

103 See Bate's tenth chapter in the second edition (pp. 80 ff), 'Of waterworks for Recreation and Delight', from which the quotation about gardens is taken.

104 Vauxhall: Aubrey, Bodleian Library Aubrey MS 4, folio 32 recto; Evelyn, *Diary*, IV, 257. For other Evelyn references see III, 591, IV, 117 & 317, V, 221 & 247. For a visit by Evelyn to Bushell's grotto in 1664, see III, 382.

105 Woolridge, *Systema Horti-Culturae*, pp. 54 ff. on waterworks; on Wilton, p. 63. .

106 Aubrey's manuscript at the Bodleian Library (Aubrey MS 2, folio 31 recto and folio 30 verso) says Salomon de Caus; the Wilton document (cited Strong, *Renaissance Garden*, p. 148), 'Mr De Caux'. All further Aubrey references will be to this manuscript, which is mostly reprinted in Aubrey's *Natural History of Wiltshire* (see note 88 above).

107 Strong makes much of this flat Veneto-like terrain: see *Renaissance Garden*, p. 148 and *passim*. Nor, *pace* Strong, are the groves of the garden's second section 'rigidly balanced' (ibid., p. 152), if only because the river crosses them at an angle.

108 Burnet, p. 126.

109 This Wilton piece is now at Houghton. Strong cites an account of Hubert le Sueur being commissioned to bring back 'moulds and patterns of certain antiques' from Italy in 1631.

110 The Wilton picture, showing various views of these gardens, is illustrated in John Harris, *The Artist and the Country House* (1979), plate 129. The Marcus Aurelius statue is now to be seen over the main public entry. For Stukeley's illustration of Pegasus on the cascade, see *Itinerarium curiosum*, facing p. 35. On the ubiquity of the pegasus motif see Nikolaus Yalouris, *Pegasus: the art of the legend* (Athens, 1975), where are a few more garden images of the fabulous horse.

111 The original grotto front does survive, but has been reused as a façade for a house in the grounds which, alas, the public are not allowed to visit.

112 Stukeley's drawings are in Bodleian Library MS Top. Wilts. c.4. His notebook (Bodelian Library MS Top gen. C. 37) was, he says, sent for by Lord Pembroke who 'transposed the leaves, put out & in what he pleased, & so confounded my scheme that I left it off' (written inside front cover). My other quotations are from folio 1 recto and verso. Stukeley specifically mentions Arundel as Pembroke's precursor in respect of antiquities.

113 *Diary*, III, 114.

10 'The way of Italian Gardens'

1 *Renaissance Garden*, p. 197. The identification of gardens with absolutist royal imagery is Strong's concern in much of his book, and therefore it is apt that he should concentrate upon 'great gardens' (p. 13). However, it may be that a look at some smaller and non-royal gardens will suggest some slightly different emphases.

2 Temple, *Upon the Gardens of Epicurus . . .*, in *Miscellanea*, Pt II (1690), p. 56.

3 J. Summerson, *The Book of Architecture of John Thorpe*, *Walpole Society*, XL (1966). On St Germain-en-Laye see the forthcoming study of French gardens by Kenneth Woodbridge, to whom I am most grateful for letting me see his book in proof.

4 Evelyn, *Diary*, II, 110–12.

5 Ibid., II, 109–10. Before he left England Evelyn had acquainted himself with several of the Italianate gardens we have considered in section 9: he was at Beddington (II, 11), for example, and at Hatfield – 'built after the *Italian* Architecture . . . the Garden and Vineyard very finely Watered . . worth seeing' (II, 54).

6 Ibid., I, 55 & II, 81.

7 The drawing is in the Evelyn collection at Christ Church College, Oxford; for the other tree-houses, see index.

8 Ibid., I, 55. For Aubrey on the painted grotto front, Bodleian Library Aubrey MS 4, folio 121.

9 In addition to the two views reproduced here, another by John Aubrey from his manuscript 'Preambulation of Surrey' (Bodleian Library Aubrey MS 4) of 1673 was reproduced but misattributed in my *The Figure in the Landscape* (Baltimore, 1976), plate 14. One entry in Evelyn's diary (III, 60–1) clearly states that John directed his brother on the spot; but other versions of this incident have him sending directions from Paris (III, 24) and saying that the work was 'finished whilst I was abroad . . . conducted by a Relation of ours, George Evelyn who had been in Italy . . .' (I, 55). So the situation is not clear-cut.

10 Evelyn, *Diary*, II, 507. See also my *Figure in the Landscape*, plate 12, for another of Evelyn's drawings of a terraced garden.

11 Bodleian Library Aubrey MS 4, folios 28–9. The same remark is quoted without any reference by David Jacques, 'John Evelyn and the Idea of Paradise', *Landscape Design*, 124 (1978), p. 37. As I hope my subsequent discussion shows, it can hardly be as Mr Jacques has it that Evelyn's *pausillipe* falls short of its inspiration, for that is presumably the declension involved in translating Italy into England.

12 Aubrey, *Natural History of Surrey* (1718), IV, 66.

13 These are illustrated in Harris, *The Artist and the Country House*, plates 23 a–e: the casino or grotto is shown in 23e.

14 Evelyn, *Diary*, III, 496.

15 Ibid., 561–2. See Douglas Chambers, 'The Tomb in the Landscape: John Evelyn's Garden at Albury', *Journal of Garden History*, I (1981), pp. 37–54.

16 See above, p. 20 & Figure 10. Chambers's article cited in the previous note has more illustrations of the Neapolitan grotto.

17 See above, p. 65. Chambers draws attention to Evelyn's translation of Roland Fréart de Cambray's *Parallel of Architecture* (1664) where the use of niches or 'tribunals' to ornament plain and simple walls is urged.

18 *Remarks*, p. 183. The baths of Agrippa were discovered, for example, in the *orti* of one, Signor Stati, between 1670 and 1676: see the notes by Bartoli in *Roma Antica*, ed. F. Nardini (Rome, 1741), I, 302.

19 For a discussion of Rousham, see below, pp. 210 ff. Whatever the exact extent of Evelyn's allusions to classical prototypes, it is too extreme to claim, as does Sells (*The Paradise of Travellers* . . ., pp. 193 & 196), that Evelyn was deficient in ancient history and lacked any feeling for the ancient world.

20 *Diary*, II, 337. I am especially indebted to Douglas Chambers's article for this section of my analysis.

21 Howell, *Epistolae Ho-Elianae* (1655), I, 59.

22 Hervey, *The Life . . . of Thomas Howard*, p. 346; Browne, *Works*, VI, 301.

23 *Rural Rides* (Harmondsworth, 1967), pp. 98–100 – Cobbett especially admired the long terraces. On the grotto as a home of the muses see *Fons Sapientiae: Renaissance Garden Fountains*, ed. Elisabeth MacDougall (Washington, D.C., 1977), p. 187. And on the larger implications of Evelyn's gardening, what its author calls 'the garden of his mind', see Graham Parry, 'John Evelyn as Hortulan Saint', *Long Room* (Dublin, 1978), pp. 7–12.

24 Evelyn, *Diary*, II, 4.

25 'Designatio de Easton-Piers in Com: Wilts', Bodleian Library Aubrey MS 17.

26 The more finished drawing is reproduced in *The Figure in the Landscape*, plate 17.

27 A lovely if somewhat fussy modern facsimile edition with annotations of this unfinished work is

Monumenta Britannica or A Miscellany of British Antiquities, ed. John Fowles, 2 vols. (Sherborne, Dorset, 1980): Aubrey investigated several Roman villa remains which have a section to themselves in this work. For his *Surrey* and *Wiltshire*, see notes 12 above and 88 of the previous chapter.

28 *Sculptura* (1662), p. 101.

29 See, for instance, *Diary*, III, 380 & 381; IV, 201 & 566.

30 Respectively ibid., III, 359 and 625.

31 Ibid., IV, 177.

32 *The Journals of Celia Fiennes*, ed. Christopher Morris (1949), pp. 350–1.

33 Respectively John M. Morton, *Natural History of Northamptonshire* (1712), p. 493 and Evelyn, *Diary*, IV, 117.

34 Among others, ibid., III, 404; IV, 344, 143, 306 & 337; V, 8.

35 On Marvell see his poem, 'Upon Appleton House', and my commentary thereon in *Andrew Marvell: his Life and Writings* (1978); Howell, *Poems upon divers emergent Occasions* (1664), pp. 57–9; on Ceres, Anne Kemp's 'Contemplation on Bassets-down-Hill' quoted in James Turner, *Topographia and Topographical Poetry in English 1640–1660* (Oxford D.Phil, 1976), pp. 1–2.

36 Plot's manuscript is in Hearne's transcript, Bodleian Library MS Hearne's Diaries 158, folio 16 (I am grateful to Michael Hunter for that reference); Plot, *Oxfordshire*, p. 261.

37 Joshua Childrey, *Britannia Baconica: The Natural Rarities of England, Scotland and Wales* (1661), sig. B¹1.

38 'Philanactophil' [E. Bolton], *Nero Caesar* . . . . (1624), p. 181.

39 Evelyn, *Diary*, IV, 70.

40 Bodleian Library Aubrey MS 4, folio 184 verso; on the optics of history, see Turner (cited in Note 35), p. 67, citing *Tubus Historicus: An Historial Perspective* (1646), a key to Raleigh's *History of the World*.

41 Evelyn, *Diary*, IV, 114 and, for the following reference, IV, 93.

42 Sarah Markham, *John Loveday of Caversham 1711–1789. The Life and Tours of an Eighteenth-Century Onlooker* (Salisbury, 1984), pp. 81, 93 (this being Easton Neston), 174, 238, 139.

43 Bodleian Library Aubrey MS 2, folio 85 verso.

44 Ibid., folio 83 recto. Little would our present-day farmers, abused for their burning of stubble, either know or care to invoke the argument that it was an ancient Roman practice.

45 *The Works of Sir Thomas Browne*, ed. G. Keynes, 4 vols. (new ed., 1964), IV, 275. In what follows I am much indebted to Charles Webster, *The Great Instauration. Science, Medicine and Reform 1626–1660* (1975).

46 Webster, p. 162 (possibly Boyle writing to Hartlib). On the increase in publications on practical gardening see the invaluable volumes by Blanche Henrey, *British Botanical and Horticultural Literature before 1800*, 3 vols. (Oxford, 1975), especially volume 1.

47 See James Turner, 'Ralph Austen, an Oxford horticulturist of the seventeenth century', *Garden History*, VI (1978), pp. 39–45. The quotation in the next paragraph is from Austen's *Treatise*, 'To the Reader'.

48 For this theme, which will be taken up again below, see Blair Worden, 'Classical Republicanism and the Puritan Revolution', in *History and Imagination; essays in honour of H. R. Trevor-Roper* (1981), pp. 182–200; the quotations from Milton and Harrington are both taken from that article. See also the works cited below in note 86.

49 Evelyn, *Diary*, IV, 121 ('The Gardens are large & walled nobly, & the husbandry part made so convenient . . . .'); for the following quotation, ibid., IV, 256.

50 On fishponds see, for instance, Hearne's Diaries (cited note 36), folios 27 & 31; Evelyn, *Diary*, IV, 115.

51 Ibid., V, 89 & 550.

52 *Silva* (1670), pp. 235 & 238. For the tribute to Parkinson, see John Speed in *Theatrum Botanicum* (1640), sig. a¹ verso.

53 Ed. cit., pp. 58, 67 & 343 among others.

54 Evelyn, *Diary*, IV, 344 (cf. ibid., p. 318).

55 See above note 31.

56 Evelyn, *Diary*, IV, 481 – that was in 1685; three years later the house was largely rebuilt.

57 *The Country House-Wives Garden* (1656), pp. 70 & 53–4 and *passim*. For a later interest by a tourist/antiquarian in old garden plantings see the manuscript of 1691 read to the Society of Antiquarians in 1794 and published in *Archaeologia*, XII (1796), pp. 181–92.

58 Morton, op. cit., p. 493.

59 Fiennes, ed. cit., pp. 171–5.

60 For this long, eclectic survey of antiquarian and other interest in garden variety (specifically terraces) here is the list of sources: for Mutton Davies's Llanerch, see above chapter 9, note 92, and for Loveday's approval, op. cit., p. 128; for Lord and Lady Winchelsea, *The Poems of Anne Countess of Winchelsea*, ed. Myra Reynolds (Chicago, 1903), pp. 33–6 (for poem) and p. 419 note (for Lord Winchelsea's garden work); Plot on Rousham in both Bodleian Library MS Hearne's Diaries 158, folio 11 recto and (slightly differently) Plot, *The Natural History of Oxfordshire* (1705 ed.), p. 266; for Holme Hall, see the verses reprinted in *Journal of Garden History*, IV (1984), pp. 360–3; Blome's *Gentleman's Recreation* and Powys speak for themselves, the latter being illustrated, among other places, in C. Hussey, *English gardens and landscapes 1700–1750* (1967), pp. 53–6; the University of Cambridge Committee for Aerial Photography, whose files I have gratefully consulted, have taken a quantity of shots which reveal old garden works beneath the surface of modern fields; for the Harrington reference see *John Morton*, *The Natural History of Northamptonshire* (1712), p. 494; for some archaeological evidence, a generally untapped source of garden information, see *An Inventory of the Historical Monuments in the County of Northamptonshire* (HMSO, 1981) and page 116, for the Lamport reference; Griffier's painting of Sudbury Hall, along with other examples, is illustrated in John Harris, *The Artist and the Country House* (1979), plate 133; Buck's Yorkshire sketches are in British Library Lansdowne MS 914 – his patron's verbal account of their travels in Lansdowne MS 911 – and have been published in *Samuel Buck's Yorkshire Sketchbook* (Wakefield, 1982); Stukeley's Commonplace Book, Bodleian Library MS Eng misc. e 260, folio 74 recto; the items cited from the Gough Collection are Gough Maps 168, folio 28, Gough Drawings a. 2., item 15, Gough Maps 33, folio 43, Gough Maps 6, folio 55. For Stukeley's Grantham design and the other Buck views, British Museum, Department of Prints and Drawings.

61 For Kent's Praeneste Terrace, see below, p. 214; Loveday at Farnborough, op. cit., p. 342. Both Loveday and Fiennes make frequent references to terraces, though not by any means all of the latter's refer to stepped hillsides but rather to long(ish) gravel walks established near the house.

62 Fiennes, op. cit., p. 25 and for the two following items, pp. 29 & 137.

63 Evelyn, *Diary*, IV, 105.

64 Ibid., II.

65 Pliny, *Natural History*, XXXV, 116, and Vitruvius, *De Architectura*, VII.v.2.

66 Evelyn, *Diary*, III, 375. On Robert Streater see Harris, *The Artist and the Country House*, p. 40, and generally H. V. S. and M. S. Ogden, *English Taste in Landscape in the Seventeenth Century* (Ann Arbor, 1955).

67 For instance, Joseph Furttenbach, *Architectura Recreationis* (1640) has several painted front curtains, two of which are of gardens which he also recommends for garden use.

68 I am indebted to James Turner (op. cit., note 35), pp. 379 & 385–6 for these etymologies.

69 See James G. McManaway, 'L'Héritage de la Renaissance dans la mise en scène en Angleterre (1642–1700)', *Le Lieu Théâtral à la Renaissance*, ed. Jean Jacquot et al. (Paris, 1964), pp. 459–72, from which all my examples in this discussion are taken, unless otherwise noted. On scenery in the Restoration theatre, though with little specific attention to garden settings, see also Richard Southern, *Changeable Scenery* (1952), *British Theatre and the Other Arts*, ed. S. S. Kenny (Washington, D.C., 1984), Montague Summers, *The Playhouse of Pepys* (1935) and Eleanore Bodwell, *The Restoration Court Theatre* (Cambridge, Mass., 1932).

70 *The Actor; or, A Treatise on the Art of Playing* (1755), p. 254.

71 See my essay, 'Theatres, Gardens, and Garden-Theatres', *Essays and Studies*, ed. Inga-Stina Ewbank (1980), especially pp. 111–15.

72 Nourse, *Campania Foelix* (1700), p. 302.

73 For Aubrey and Evelyn, see below pp. 170–1 and note 83. For the later visitor cited, see John Timbs, *A Picturesque Promenade round Dorking* (second ed., 1823), p. 261.

74 See a more lengthy discussion of the poem from the same perspective in my *Andrew Marvell. His Life and Writings* (1978), pp. 90–112.

75 That it was customary to think of gardens as places of entertainment, whether theatrical or simply arising from their various imagery, there is considerable evidence: for instance, consider Mildmay Fane, at whose country house in Northamptonshire private theatricals were produced; his poem 'To Sir John Wentworth, upon his Curiosities and Courteous Entertainment at Summerly [Somerleyton] in Lovingland [Lothingland, Suffolk]' (*Otia Sacra*, 1648, pp. 153–6) likewise envisages a garden as the location, ambiguously, of both imagined and actual theatre. See also E. Withington, 'The "Fugitive Poetry" of Mildmay Fane', *Harvard Library Bulletin*, IX (1955), pp. 61–78.

76 I have discussed these matters more fully in 'Milton and the English Landscape Garden', *Milton Studies*, XI (1981), pp. 81–105.

77 Evelyn, *Diary*, IV, 142 and 347. The thuya was rare in England at that time: see Evelyn's *Sylva* (1697), p. 129.

78 *Systema Horti-culturae* (1688), p.v.

79 Evelyn, *Diary*, IV, 65.

80 Morton, . . . *Northamptonshire*, pp. 494–5.

81 Christ Church, Evelyn MS 45, folio 171 recto.

82 Evelyn, *Diary*, III, 80 and IV, 37. The plan of Sayes Court is reproduced in *The Figure in the Landscape*, plate 15. For his horticultural activities see *Directions for the gardiner at Sayscourt . .*, ed. Geoffrey Keynes (1932).

83 Evelyn, *Diary*, III, 154; Aubrey, Bodleian Library Aubrey MS 4, folios 164–7 with the plan on folios 49–50. On Deepdene see Doris Mercer, 'The Deepdene, Dorking: Rise and Decline Through Six Centuries', *Surrey Archaeological Collections*, LXXI (1977), pp. 111–38. On Evelyn's other notices of cabinets and gardens see the following references in his *Diary*: III, 96, 157, 359, 399; IV, 70, 142, 144, 162, 176, 200, 288, 337, 481 & 531–2.

84 *Systema Agriculturae*, preface D¹ verso, and *Systema Horti-culturae*, pp. vi and 4.

85 *Country Conversations* (1694), pp. 52–3.

86 On this large theme see the studies by Z. S. Fink, *The Classical Republicans* (1945), C. Robbins, *The Eighteenth-century Commonwealthsman* (1959), F. Rabb, *The English Face of Machiavelli* (1964), and J. G. A. Pocock, *The Machiavellian Moment* (1975). See also below for further discussion of these topics.

87 *Campania Foelix*, pp. 297 ff.

88 *Flora* (1665), pp. 1–3.

89 Christ Church, Evelyn MS 45, folios 1 and 2; reference is also made to folios, 3 & 52 (for application of design ideas to differently sized sites), 52 (Palladio), 95 (Verona), 127 (Pratolino), 96–7 (ancient Roman practices), and 77 (for the concluding quotations).

11 'Palladian' gardening

1 See the text of Walpole's *History* cited in note 4 below, p. 25.

2 *The Spectator*, ed. D. F. Bond, 5 vols. (Oxford, 1965), III, 564.

3 Quentin Skinner, 'Meaning and Understanding in the History of Ideas', *History and Theory*, VIII (1969), pp. 3–53.

4 See *Horace Walpole Gardenist. An edition of Walpole's 'The History of Modern Taste in Gardening' with an estimate of Walpole's contribution to Landscape Architecture*, ed. I. W. U. Chase (Princeton, N.J., 1943). On Walpole's Whiggish stance see Richard Quaintance, 'Walpole's Whig Interpretation of Landscaping History', *Studies in Eighteenth-Century Culture*, IX (1979), pp. 285–300.

5 *Horace Walpole Gardenist*, pp. 26–7. See also the discussion of the gardens at Rousham, below p. 210 ff.

6 Ibid., pp. 14 ff.

7 B. S. Allen, *Tides of English Taste*, 2 vols. (Cambridge, Mass., 1937), II, 117.

8 David Jacques, *Georgian Gardens. The Reign of Nature* (1983). One exception is his discussion of Switzer's interest in husbandry, but even here his emphasis is largely proleptic.

9 Morris Brownell, *Alexander Pope and the Arts of Georgian England* (Oxford, 1978). I have offered a rival theory of Pope's interest in picturesque gardening in my essay, 'Ut pictura poesis, ut pictura hortus, and the picturesque', *Word & Image*, I (1985), pp. 87–107.

10 Jacques, *Georgian Gardens*, p. 12.

11 *Characteristics of Men, Morals, Opinions and Times*, ed. J. M. Robertson (Indianapolis and New York, 1964), p. 125.

12 See David Leatherbarrow, 'Character, Geometry and Perspective: the Third Earl of Shaftesbury's Principles of Garden Design', *Journal of Garden History*, IV (1984), pp. 332–58.

13 John Toland, dedication 'to the Lord Mayor, Alderman and Sherifs and Common Council of London', in his edition of Harrington's *Oceana* (1700), p. iv.

14 'Letter concerning Design', in *Second Characteristics or the Language of Forms*, ed. Benjamin Rand (Cambridge, 1914): Addison writes that the English musical taste was very French under Charles II and did not improve until the nation looked to Italy; the same point is made about painting (p. 20).

15 *Characteristics*, ed. cit., II, 267. It is interesting to note that the language of this remark, while directed at aesthetical matters, is basically political ('state', 'subject').

16 A. O. Lovejoy, *The Great Chain of Being* (New York, 1960), p. 15.

17 Quoted by Michel Baridon, 'Ruins as a mental construct', *Journal of Garden History*, V (1985), p. 90. I am much indebted to this article for the discussion that follows.

18 Leatherbarrow, op. cit. (note 12), p. 351.

19 *The Exploration of the Grand Mystery of Godliness* (1660), p. 4, quoted by Charles H. Hinnant, 'A Philosophical Origin of the English Landscape Garden', *Bulletin of Research in the Humanities*, 83 (1980), pp. 292–306. This article is a very interesting attempt to explain the rise of the landscape garden as a reaction to the scientific principles of the previous century which had sustained the formal, geometric garden; but Hinnant fails to see the English empiricist reaction against Cartesian system and therefore blurs the issues.

20 R. Bradley, *A Survey of the Ancient Husbandry and Gardening*, etc. (1725), folio A¹ recto. Cf. Northall, p. 344, on differences of climate and social usage between Italian and English villas.

21 All references to *The Spectator* are taken from the edition cited in note 3; all other texts from *The Works*, 4 vols. (1721). References to Addison's periodical essays are given in the text; where a quotation appears without a reference, it is from the last cited piece. For Addison's work on *The Freeholder*, see the introduction to the edition by James Leheny (Oxford, 1979).

22 Cited by Bond, ed. cit. (note 3), III, 536 note.

23 *Ichnographia Rustica*, 3 vols. (1718), I, xv. All quotations will be from this text unless otherwise noted. The three volumes were an expansion of *The Nobleman, Gentleman, and Gardener's Recreation* (1715) in one volume. The three-volume work was issued again in 1742 with two extra essays.

24 Ibid., I, iii.

25 Ibid., I, xxxv–xxxvi & (for subsequent quotation) xxxviii.

26 Respectively, ibid., I, 2, 12, 31, 38–9 & 41.

27 Ibid., I, 20–3 and iv. On this theme see the useful essay by James Turner, 'Stephen Switzer and the Political Fallacy in Landscape Gardening History', *Eighteenth-Century Studies*, XI (1978), pp. 489–96. In practice, as Switzer does here, Augustus could be associated with the best of the republic, since his one-man rule was established behind a façade of republican appearance; in theory, there was much room for more ambiguous analyses of Augustus, but they do not seem relevant at this point.

28 *Ichnographia*, I, 55 & (for subsequent quotations) 317 & 273.

29 Ibid., I, xviii–xix.

30 Ibid., I, 181 and (for criticism of James) 151; for the exedra description, I, 124.

31 Turner, op. cit. (note 27), p. 425.

32 From dedication of *Practical Husbandsman and Planter* to Halifax. It is, of course, extremely difficult to make clear distinctions between Whig and Tory conduct in a period when party politics were in their infancy; alliances of Tories and Whigs in opposition to the extravagant expenditures of other Whigs were perfectly possible.

33 *Ichnographia*, I, xiii with my italics.

34 Ibid., II, facing p. 115 and III, facing p. 44. A 'regulated epitome' of Richings appeared in the second edition (1742).

35 These plans are all reproduced in Peter Willis, *Charles Bridgeman and the English Landscape Garden* (1977). Willis's summary of Bridgeman's design principles and practice (pp. 130–3), partly because it insists upon taking its departure from Walpole, tends to be somewhat proleptic. He does not take up the ancestry of the Claremont exedra nor analyse the significance of the theatres.

36 Quoted Jacques, op. cit. (note 8), p. 22.

37 For this exedral feature, see my index under Vatican Belvedere. Its ubiquity is striking and not always appreciated, and it can be confused with other parts of the Belvedere courtyard's elaborate stairways (see Strong, *Renaissance Garden*, p. 181). For its use in masques, see *Inigo Jones*, I, 128.

38 The text of Vanbrugh's letter is reprinted in *The Genius of the Place*, ed J. D. Hunt and Peter Willis (1975). pp. 120–1. On Vanbrugh, see Kerry Downes, *Vanbrugh* (1977), especially chap. 6 ('Castles and Landscapes').

39 Jane E. Furse and David L. Jacques, *Report on the Historical Interest of the Garden and Grounds at Leeswood Hall, Clywd* (Garden History Society, June 1981).

40 See Blanche Henrey, op. cit. (note 46, chapter 10), pp. 424 ff.

41 *A Survey*, pp. 358–60 and (for the following quotation) 361. Bradley's extrapolation of supposed classical designs into English practice may be seen in his next publication, *A General Treatise of Husbandry and Gardening*, 2 vols. (1726), II, 246–57, a passage too long to quote at length but which sets out in circumstantial detail the best kind of garden in this mode. The *General Treatise* was dedicated to Lord Burlington.

42 The whole of Langley's chapter 'Of the Disposition of Gardens in General' is reproduced in Hunt and Willis, *The Genius of the Place*, pp. 178–86.

43 On the theme of the progress of poetry see, for example, Thomas Gray's *The Progress of Poetry*, first published in 1757.

44 The two not illustrated here I have reproduced elsewhere: in *The Figure in the Landscape*, plate 44, and *The Genius of the Place*, plate 69. The Castell plate reproduced here (figure 98) has a fine balance of regulated and wild terrain.

45 Spence, *Observations, Anecdotes and Characters of Books and Men*, ed. James M. Osborne, 2 vols. (Oxford, 1966), I, 250.

46 *Villas of the Ancients* . . , pp. 76–7. Pliny's account is in the 29th epistle of the Book IX.

47 Burlington's embarrassment with the old Jacobean house at Chiswick suggests how far he was from allowing native architecture to participate in the progress of gardening from Italy to England.

48 In the absence yet of any definitive study of the Chiswick gardens, there are a group of articles to consult: H. F. Clark, 'Lord Burlington's Bijou, or Sharawaggi at Chiswick', *Architectural Review*, XCV (1944), pp. 125–9; then three articles by Jacques Carré, 'Lord Burlington's Garden at Chiswick', *Garden History*, I/3 (1973), pp. 23–30; 'Architecture et paysage: le jardin de Chiswick', *Jardins et Paysages: Le Style Anglais*, ed. A. Parreaux and M. Plaissant (Lille, 1977); 'Through French Eyes: Rigaud's drawings of Chiswick', *Journal of Garden History*, II (1982), pp. 133–42; Carré is a rare example of a historian who acknowledges the Italian debts of Burlington's gardens, as does Cinzia M. Sicca, 'Lord Burlington at Chiswick: Architecture and Landscape', *Garden History*, X (1982), pp. 36–69. In my own account of Chiswick I have emphasized those elements of the history of its creation relevant to my theme.

49 Macky, *Journey*, 3 vols. (1724), I, 87, my italics. For the following Rousham allusion, see note 89 below.

50 See, for example, Sicca, op. cit. (note 48), pp. 42–3.

51 *Journey*, respectively I, 49–50; II, 117 & 119; I, 65. On other occasions Macky approves of two different villas as being 'passable in Italy for a delicate Palace' and 'exactly after the Model of Country-Seats in Lombardy' (I, 37).

52 See *The Figure in the Landscape*, plates 41 & 42 and pp. 96–8.

53 *Tour Thro'* . . . *Great Britain*, 4 vols. (1742), III, 288–9.

54 See Sicca's discussion, op. cit. (note 48), pp. 64–6. The antiquarian, Loveday, did not

identify the figures correctly when he was at Chiswick (see Markham, *John Loveday of Caversham*, p. 365), but the message he derived was the same.

55 *Vitruvius Britannicus*, III (1725), p. 8.

56 See David Neave, 'Lord Burlington's park and gardens at Londesborough, Yorkshire', *Garden History*, 8 (1980), pp. 69–90.

57 See *The Figure in the Landscape*, p. 75.

58 See Morris Brownell, *Alexander Pope and the Arts of Georgian England* (Oxford, 1978) and Peter Martin, '*Pursuing Innocent Pleasures*'. *The Gardening World of Alexander Pope* (Hamden, Connecticut, 1984): between them they illustrate all the well-known and less well-known images of Pope's garden. Where no specific reference is given, the reader will find the relevant information set out in those two books; Martin's is much more satisfactory than Brownell's, because he is less concerned to argue a place for Pope in 'picturesque gardening'. See also Maynard Mack, *The Garden and the City. Retirement and Politics in the Later Poetry of Pope* (Toronto, 1969).

59 The *Guardian* essay is reprinted in *The Genius of the Place*, pp. 204–6.

60 *The Correspondence*, ed. George Sherburn, 5 vols. (Oxford, 1956), II, 436 and I, 45–6 respectively. In the third book of *Gulliver's Travels*, chapter iv, Lord Munodi's country house is said to be built according to Ancient rules. See Charles Beaumont, 'Pope and the Palladians', *Texas Studies in Literature and Language*, 17 (1975–6), pp. 461–79, and Howard Erskine-Hill, 'Heirs of Vitruvius: Pope and the Idea of Architecture', *The Art of Alexander Pope*, ed. H. Erskine-Hill and Anne Smith (Totowa, N.J., 1979), pp. 144–56.

61 Spence, *Observations*, I, item 557; Twickenham edition of Pope's Poems, II, 237 note. In volume one of Graevius, for example, Pope would have seen a map of Genoa with the Doria gardens marked (pp. 216 & 217); in volume three (p. 1216) a mention of Pliny's villa called Comedy.

62 *Essay on Criticism*, Pt. III, lines 140 ff.; *Epistle to Jervas*, line 32.

63 *Correspondence*, I, 45–6.

64 Advertisement to Oldham's imitation of the *Ars poetica* (1681).

65 See the edition of Horace's *Opera*, 2 vols. (London: John Pine, 1733–7), where Lucullus' gardens are shown and rudimentary sources for the illustrations given; the 'Vita' in this edition is dedicated to Pope. I am grateful to Dr Joan Friedman for alerting me to this edition in the first place.

66 Pope's imitation of the second satire of the Second Book of Horace, lines 137–46.

67 *Correspondence*, II, 296; and on Egeria, see Mack, op. cit., pp. 69–74. Although is generally assumed that Pope did not install the Statue of the sleeping nymph, at least one visitor reported seeing it ('his a Nymph sleeping in stone') in 1736 – *John Loveday*, p. 248.

68 Pope's lines 'On the Statue of Cleopatra', Twickenham edition of *Poems*, VI, 66. For an illustration of this figure see *British and American Gardens in the Eighteenth Century*, edited Peter Martin (Williamsburg, Va., 1984), plate 13.

69 *Correspondence*, IV, 262.

70 *A Plan of Mr Pope's Garden* . . . (1745), pp. 5–10. Cf. B. Seeley on the minerals in the grotto at Stowe, *Stowe* . . . (1763), p. 30.

71 Quoted Mack, op. cit., p. 42.

72 *Correspondence*, IV, 262.

73 Ibid., II, 296–7 and Mack, op. cit., pp. 44–7.

74 *Correspondence*, II, 297.

75 Spence, *Observations*, I, item 620. For Mack's commentary on this project, op. cit., pp. 37–40.

76 *Letters*, p. 125 ('one of the richest prospects of a vale that can be in the world').

77 Mack, op. cit., p. 57.

78 *Correspondence*, II, 58; for Pope's interest in Sherborne, see Martin's book cited in note 58, chapter 4.

79 *Correspondence*, II, 116; and for Pope's reading of Pliny, ibid., I, 508.

80 Spence, *Observations*, I, 619.

81 I have considered Kent's whole career as a garden designer, especially in its relationships with his painting and theatre work, in the Ferens Fine Art Lectures which I gave at the University of Hull in January 1985; these will be published later this year. Meanwhile, the only modern account of Kent's whole career is that by Michael I. Wilson, *William Kent. Architect, Designer, Painter, Gardener, 1685–1748* (1984). See, however, the articles listed in subsequent notes for attention specifically to his gardening.

82 *The Walpole Society Annual Volume*, XXII (1934), p. 73.

83 Several stage designs by Kent survive, and in my view we should consider some of his landscape sketches as designs for backdrops; Kent would have known the masque designs of Inigo Jones, which passed into Burlington's collections. There are also clear connections between the kind of work he would be required to do for the theatre and his work as a history painter; for some general considerations of this see my article, 'Ut pictura poesis, ut pictura hortus, and the picturesque', *Word & Image*, I (1985), pp. 87–107.

84 I am indebted here to essays by George Clarke, 'Grecian Taste and Gothic Virtue: Lord Cobham's Gardening Programme and its Iconography', *Apollo*, 97 (1973), pp. 566–71, and 'Moral Gardening', *The Stoic*, 24 (1970). See also Kenneth Woodbridge's pioneering article on Kent, 'William Kent as a Landscape-Gardener: A Re-Appraisal', *Apollo*, 100 (1974), pp. 126–37.

85 This part of the Villa Brenzone is illustrated in Georgina Masson, *Italian Gardens* (1961), plate 146.

86 *Observations*, etc., ed. cit. (note 44), I, 423.

87 On these buildings see Judith Colton, 'Kent's Hermitage for Queen Caroline at Richmond, *Architectura*, 2 (1974), pp. 181–9, and 'Merlin's Cave and Queen Caroline: Garden Art as Political Propaganda', *Eighteenth-century Studies*, 10 (1976), pp. 1–20.

88 See above pp. 148 ff and the article by Baridon cited in note 17 to the present chapter.

89 *Country Life*, 150 (1946), p. 900. Further important articles on Rousham to which I am indebted in what follows are Kenneth Woodbridge, 'William Kent's Gardening: The Rousham Letters', *Apollo*, 100 (1974), pp. 282–91; Simon Pugh, 'Nature as a Garden: A Conceptual Tour of Rousham', *Studio International*, 186 (1973), pp. 121–8; Mavis Batey, 'The Way to View Rousham, by Kent's Gardener [John Macclery]', *Garden History*, XI (1983), pp. 125–32. For the observation of Walpole, quoted next, see *Horace Walpole Gardenist*, pp. 29 & 210.

90 See David R. Coffin, *The Villa D'Este at Tivoli* (Princeton, N.J., 1960), p. 27.

91 An estate map of Rousham, dated 1721, is reproduced by Peter Martin, op. cit. (note 58), plate 5.

92 Addison, 'Remarks', p. 131.

93 See *Country Life*, 100 (1946), p. 448.

94 Sarah Markham, *John Loveday of Caversham*, p. 375; *The Mueseum*. etc., XXXII (1747),

pp. 204–5 – I am indebted to Robert Williams for drawing this Latin poem to my attention.

95   It is a witticism which I have occasionally heard lecturers attribute to him, but cannot find any source for it. It captures, as do all convincing but apocryphal aphorisms, something essential about his attitude. The standard study of Brown is by Dorothy Stroud (1950).

96   Williams, 'Making Places: Garden-Mastery and English Brown', *Journal of Garden History*, III (1983), pp. 382–5.

97   Spence, *Observations*, I, 405.

98   *Essay in Defence of Ancient Architecture* (1728), p. 84; *Lectures* (sec. ed., 1759), p. 183.

99   *Letters Written by Eminent Persons*, etc., 2 vols. (1813), II, letter 192.

100 Warcupp, II, 309. Cf. Wright on Ligorio's Casino Pio in the Vatican Gardens – 'a Pleasure-House, made in the manner of an antique villa' (p. 273), and Breval upon the same – 'a little villa . . . upon the Model of an antient one that stood pretty entire in his Time, on the Gabinian Way' (Breval 1738, p. 101).

101 Quoted E. Malins, *English Landscaping and Literature 1660–1840* (1966), p. 38. Cf. similar remark by Pope, *Correspondence*, II, p. 436.

102 John M. Gray, *Memoirs of the Life of Sir John Clerk of Penicuik*, Publications of the Scottish Historical Society, XIII (1892) pp. 19 (on Italy) and 236–40 (on his villa).

103 Quoted P. F. Kirby, *The Grand Tour in Italy 1700–1800* (New York, 1952), pp. 347 and 353.

104 See A. H. Collins, *The Life and Writings of John Dyer*, MA Thesis, London University, 1930, pp. 33 and 171.

105 Malcolm Kelsall, 'The Iconography of Stourhead', *J.W.C.I.*, *46 (1983), pp. 133*–43, from whom are all the otherwise unidentified quotations. Kelsall's article may be consulted for the other accounts of Stourhead, to which his own article is a convincing response. Kelsall actually quotes the draft of that inscription for Alfred's Tour, which I repeat here.

106 See John Riely, 'Shenstone's Walks: the Genesis of The Leasowes', *Apollo* 110 (1979), pp. 202–9, from whom all the quotations are drawn. Dodsley's lines are quoted by Malins, op. cit., p. 68 in the course of an interesting chapter on Stourhead, Hagley and The Leasowes.

107 Joseph Heely, *Letters on the Beauties of Hagley, Envil, and The Leasowes*, 2 vols. (1777), I, 215 for the inscription cited.

108 Spence, *Observations*, I, 420.

109 On Spence's numerous gardening activities, see the series of articles by R. W. King, 'Joseph Spence of Byfleet', *Garden History*, VI (1978), pp. 38–64; VII (1979), pp. 29–48; VIII (1980), pp. 44–65 & 77–114.

110 See above chapter 2, note 58.

111 *Polymetis* (1747), pp. 2–3 and (for the following quotation) p. 1.

112 Ibid., p. 292; for the Apollos discussed, ibid., pp. 82–8. *An Essay on Pope's Odyssey*, Pt II (1717), p. 2.

113 The remark is Robert Williams's, op. cit. (note 96), p. 384. Cf. my 'Emblem and expressionism in the Eighteenth-Century Landscape Garden', *Eighteenth-century Studies*, 4 (1971), pp. 294–317: the contrast that I drew there between emblematic and expressionistic designs seems analogous to that which I have drawn in this book between representation and association, between ancient and modern.

114 See Hazel Conway's article on Manchester public parks, *Journal of Garden History*, V (1985), pp. 231–60.

Index

(The italic numbers refer to Figures throughout the book)